THE BEDFORD
HISTORICAL RI
SOCIETY
2000

Frontispiece: Old Warden: Interior view looking east, showing the church as fitted out with carved woodwork by Lord Ongley in 1841–2. Notice the south gallery, the pulpit and desk on the north side, the encaustic tiles on the floor and the hatchments over the chancel arch.

(*Lithograph: John Sunman Austin 1854*)

THE PUBLICATIONS OF THE BEDFORDSHIRE
HISTORICAL RECORD SOCIETY
VOLUME 79

BEDFORDSHIRE CHURCHES IN THE NINETEENTH CENTURY

Part III:
Parishes Salford to Yelden

Edited by

Chris Pickford

PUBLISHED BY THE SOCIETY   2000

©
THE BEDFORDSHIRE
HISTORICAL RECORD
SOCIETY
2000

ISBN 0 85155 063 0

© Bedfordshire Historical Record Society and the editor, 2000

First published in 2000 by the Bedfordshire Historical Record Society, Bedford.

This volume has been published with the help of grants from Bedford Borough Council and South Beds. District Council.

Cover design by Justin March, Park Farm Studios Ltd.,
Riseley Road, Bletsoe, Bedford MK44 1QU

Printed and bound by Stephen Austin and Sons Ltd., Hertford

IN MEMORIAM

Joyce Godber (1906–1999)

Amy Joyce Godber was born on 24 June 1906, the only daughter of Isaac Godber of Willington, nurseryman, by Bessie Chapman, his wife. After Bedford High School and St. Hilda's College Oxford, she soon moved to the Oxford University Press, and learnt there something of the work of compositors and printers. In 1938 she went to London as Assistant Secretary at the Institute of Historical Research under Guy Parsloe (who in 1949 edited the First Minute book of the Bedford Corporation for this Society).

At the outbreak of war in 1939 most Institute activities ceased, but Joyce continued in the Library. It was there she said she first saw the row of volumes of the *Bedfordshire Historical Record Society* publications and developed her interest in the history of Bedfordshire and in local history generally. At weekends she was back at Willington, and on Saturday mornings visited the Record Office at the Shire Hall, with the idea of working on the Newnham Cartulary for a research degree. Joyce attended the Society's A.G.M. in 1939 where she met Dr. G. H. Fowler, founder and editor, and his friend and executor Mr. F. M. Manning, the Society's treasurer. She had planned to visit Dr. Fowler at Aspley Guise on the weekend he died in 1940.

Mr. Manning persuaded her to complete Dr. Fowler's work on the Bushmead Priory cartulary, which was published in 1945, and at the A.G.M. in 1946 Joyce was confirmed as general editor. To make up for the missed war years two volumes were published for each of the years 1946, 1949 and 1950. By this time Joyce was County Archivist, but she did all her editorial work in her own time. Volumes under her own name were vol. 43 parts I and II (the Newnham Priory cartulary), vol. 44 (the Oakley Hunt), and vol. 47, (the life of the Marchioness Grey of Wrest Park), and there are many contributions to other volumes. She was made F.R.Hist.Soc. in 1946, and in 1948 was elected a Fellow of the Society of Antiquaries of London.

Some thought her a ruthless editor, removing unnecessary words for the sake of economy, and she wrote or rewrote much text that appeared under the names of others because, although she liked to have local people involved in the Society, she made sure their contributions were up to her own high standards. She wanted the Society to accumulate sufficient capital to allow it to publish her county history, when this had been written. In the event, the publication was funded by the Bedfordshire County Council.

Joyce Godber retired from the editorship in 1976, and volume 57 (1978) consisted of articles written by friends and colleagues in her honour. She remained a keen supporter, attending every A.G.M. unless she was ill or out of the country. She had known many of the great figures in the Society's history including Dr. Fowler himself, F. J. Manning, Dr. F. G. Emmison, Tom Bagshawe, Charles Freeman, and H. G. Tibbutt.

In her retirement she wrote on the Society of Friends (of which she was a member), on the Harpur Trust and the Womens' Institute movement in the county, as well as many short articles and pamphlets. When in her retirement home she could no longer do any historical work, she organised the other elderly residents to knit squares for blankets for Oxfam. For Joyce Godber life when she could do nothing useful was unbearable, but her constitution was strong, and her death on 20 December 1999 was a release.

Nicholas Bagshawe (1927–1999)

Nicholas, then reading engineering at Cambridge, was first introduced to the Society in about 1950 by his father T. W. Bagshawe, founder of Luton Museum, collector/student of Bedfordshire rural industries and a long-standing member of B.H.R.S. He qualified as an accountant after leaving Cambridge and served as Auditor for B.H.R.S. from 1957, then in 1962 succeeded F. J. Manning as Treasurer, a post he held until 1967. He remained on Council until his death last year, in the latter years as a conscientious Vice-President. Despite making his home in Kent for over forty years, he maintained a close commitment to Bedfordshire and its history and hardly ever missed a Society A.G.M.

Nicholas was a whole-hearted supporter of the study of local history in all its forms and, when B.H.R.S. led the movement to form a county Local History Association as an 'umbrella' for interested societies, he was one of its most enthusiastic advocates. In 1992 he took the chair at the public meeting in Ampthill that resulted in the formation of the now flourishing B.L.H.A., and continued to take an interest in its progress.

His own research covered fields as varied as medieval guilds, his father's Antarctic exploration, the history of the family firm of Bagshawe and Company of Dunstable and the work of the Pradier family, crystal engravers of Dunstable and Luton – not to mention a survey of former and present *Curriers' Arms* public houses all over the country, stimulated by his involvement with the Worshipful Company of Curriers, of which he was Father. Nick's own published work was not extensive but he encouraged new authors, and gave carefully considered counsel to the Society's officers.

CONTENTS

Page

List of Illustrations   viii

Preface and acknowledgements   x

Foreword by the Bishop of St.Albans   xiii

Introduction   xiv
    The *Bedfordshire Churches* series
    Notes on the sources
    1. Glebe terriers (extracts) 1822
    2. Archdeacon Bonney's historical notes, c.1840
    3. Archdeacon Bonney's visitation notebooks 1823–1839
    4. Articles on churches by W.A. – John Martin, the librarian at
       Woburn Abbey – 1845–1854
    5. Church descriptions by Sir Stephen Glynne 1830–1870
    The commentary and footnotes
    Using the material

Abbreviations, references and symbols used in transcription   xvi–xvii

Supplementary bibliography   xviii

THE CHURCHES (Parishes Salford to Yelden)   615

Note: There is no index in this volume. An analytical index to the entire series will follow in the final volume.

LIST OF ILLUSTRATIONS

Plate   *Page*

Cover: Toddington: N view   Cover
Frontispiece: Old Warden: Interior looking east   Frontispiece
1. Salford: W view   616
2. Sandy: SW view   620
3. Sandy: Composite view   624
4. Sharnbrook: SW view   632
5. Sharnbrook: Interior   634
6. Shefford: N view   638
7. Shelton: S view   642
8. Shillington: N view   648
9. Silsoe: Drawing   657
10. Silsoe: Interior   658
11. Souldrop: S view   662
12. Souldrop: Interior   665
13. Southill: SE view   669
14. Stagsden: SE view   675
15. Stanbridge: W view   682
16. Stanbridge: Interior   682
17. Staughton, Little: SE view   687
18. Steppingley: E view   691
19. Stevington: E view   695
20. Stondon, Upper: SW view   701
21. Stotfold: N view   705
22. Streatley: SW view   711
23. Streatley: Interior   712
24. Studham: SE view   716
25. Sundon: S view   721
26. Sundon: Interior   723
27. Sutton: W view   727
28. Swineshead: SE view   732
29. Tempsford: SW view   736
30. Thurleigh: SW view   741
31. Thurleigh: Interior   743
32. Tilbrook: SW view   747
33. Tilsworth: SE view   753
34. Tilsworth: Interior   754
35. Tingrith: S view   759
36. Toddington: NE view   764
37. Toddington: Interior   766

38. Totternhoe: SE view   774
39. Turvey: SE view   780
40. Turvey: Interior   782
40a. Turvey: Interior looking east   786
41. Warden, Old: SE view   792
42. Warden, Old: Interior looking west   793
43. Westoning: SE view   799
44. Whipsnade: NW view   804
45. Wilden: SE view   808
46. Willington: SE view   814
47. Wilstead: S view   819
48. Woburn: NE view of old church   824
49. Woburn: Interior of old church   825
50. Woburn: SW view of new church   826
51. Wootton: NW view   833
52. Wrestlingworth: Interior   841
53. Wymington: W view   846
54. Yelden: SE view   854

Map

Fig.1 Map of Bedfordshire showing the churches (S–Y) included
in this volume   facing p.615

Sources of illustrations:

All the pictures are reproduced from originals or copies held by the Bedfordshire and Luton
Archives and Records Service apart from illustrations specially loaned for use in this volume
(nos.7 and 8). Owners who have kindly allowed the reproduction of their material include the late
Mr. D.W. Armstrong 36; Messrs. N.T. and R.W. Bagshawe (Fisher collection) 26 and 27; Bedford
Borough Council (Town Hall Collection) 2, 6, 11, 13, 14, 15, 22, 25, 29, 44 and 53; Miss D.
Bennett 49; the British Library 24; Mrs. H.J. Casebourne's collection 32, 43 and 51; Hitchin
Museum 21; John Kent 37; Mrs. Leigh Lancaster 50; Luton Museum Service 38, 41 and 48; the
late Mrs. E. Munns 52; the Shuttleworth collection 1, 18, 20, 30 and 45; the Society for the
Protection of Ancient Buildings 7; the late Mr. H.G. Tibbutt 54; Mrs. M.F. Wade-Gery 17; the
Rev. Roger Wood 23; and the Wrest Park (Lucas) archives 9 and 10. The frontispiece and items
3, 8, 16, 28, 34, 39, 40 and 42 are copied from original illustrations either in the churches to which
they relate or among the deposited parish records at BCRO. The remaining illustrations are from
published books, engravings and postcards or from originals owned by the Archives and Records
Service. The map (Fig.1) was prepared specially by the County Hall Graphics Unit.

Preface and acknowledgments

Thanks to the support of Bedfordshire County Council and my former colleagues in the Bedfordshire and Luton Archives and Records Service the bulk of the work for this volume was completed before I left Bedford in August 1998 to take up a new appointment in London. The task of completing the book for publication has been relatively simple.

Thanks are due to the authorities and owners who have allowed the publication of their material. The 1822 glebe terriers are published here by kind permission of Lincoln Diocesan Record Office. Archdeacon Bonney's church notes were among the manuscripts transferred to the County Record Office from the old Bedford Library, while Bonney's visitation notes appear by kind permission of the present Archdeacon of Bedford, the Ven. Malcolm Lesiter. Sir Stephen Glynne's Bedfordshire church notes are published by kind permission of Sir William Gladstone. Thanks are also due to Geoffrey Veysey for providing information on the notes and for allowing me to quote from his article about Sir Stephen Glynne. The sources of illustrations are acknowledged separately.

Material for this volume has been gathered from several record repositories and institutions. My first debt of gratitude is to all my friends at Bedford, but I must also thank the staff at the British Library, the British Newspaper Library, the library of the Society of Antiquaries of London, the Bedfordshire County Library Service, Lambeth Palace Library, Cambridge University Library, Lincolnshire Archives and the Hertfordshire County Record Office for their help and advice.

Although acknowledged in the first part, special thanks are due to Pauline Newbery who typed most of the text of the original sources and to Neil Alston who prepared the initial selection of illustrations. To these names must be added that of Jackie Croot who has worked carefully through the newspaper files extracting useful references to churches and chapels. Her work has added enormously to the available information, making it possible to solve many problems of interpretation for which answers would otherwise have been impossible to find.

I owe a great deal to the support and contributions of people who have accompanied me on my visits and to the many local experts who have made their knowledge of individual churches available to me and commented on the draft text. The Bishop of St.Albans has very kindly contributed a foreword. Thanks are also due to the clergy and keyholders through whose cooperation I have been able to visit all the churches covered in this volume. Gordon Vowles, the General Editor, and my colleagues on the Editorial Group have again provided constructive comments and suggestions throughout its gestation period.

Finally, I must thank my partner Heather who has supported me through the final stages of completing this book. Visiting churches and finding out about them can be fun, but the concentrated effort required for writing leaves little room for normal social and domestic activities. She has not only endured this with great patience but she has also helped in a number of ways. It is in no small measure thanks to her support that the task has been accomplished.

Sevenoaks   CHRIS PICKFORD
April 2000

Foreword by the Bishop of St. Albans

I have enormous admiration for people who with a rare mixture of tenacity, scholarship and flair are able to open up the past so that it enriches the present. Chris Pickford is one such person.

He has been researching the churches of Bedfordshire for very many years but has done so with a lightness of touch which belies the underlying hard work. We now have the result of this in front of us.

Yet again he has shown us the eccentricities, the skills, the dedication that each generation has put into the care of their church buildings and has reminded us that these buildings are treasure-houses of the spirit as well as places of prayer and service.

The rootlessness and restlessness of contemporary society is counterpointed by the stillness and centredness of many of our churches – and that is a significant part of their importance for us; but to be able to enter those churches accompanied by Chris Pickford's researches is to be even more fully enriched.

It is a great privilege to have been invited to write this Foreword and I do so in the belief that the churches of Bedfordshire will continue to be uniquely important resources for the well-being of mind and spirit for the life of our communities in the years ahead

+Christopher

INTRODUCTION TO THE VOLUME

The Bedfordshire Churches series

This is the third in a series of volumes covering Bedfordshire churches in the nineteenth century. It contains descriptions of churches "on the eve of restoration" together with contemporary illustrations. This volume contains the text for each church in the final section of the alphabet (parishes Salford to Yelden).

It was originally intended that this volume should also include three appendices together with an analytical index to the whole series. For reasons of space, these sections will now appear in a fourth and final part to be published in 2001.

The final part will therefore contain:

1. Information on new churches and churches in the present county otherwise excluded from the survey
2. A table summarising the main stages of C19th restoration for each church
3. Addenda and corrigenda for parts I–III and the index.

The sources

For each church, there are extracts from original records amplified by a commentary and explanatory footnotes. The main source material consists of:

1. Extracts from church inventories – mainly 1822
2. Antiquarian notes on churches by Archdeacon Bonney, c.1840
3. Archdeacon Bonney's visitation notebooks 1823–1839
4. Articles on churches by W.A. (John Martin, the librarian at Woburn Abbey) 1845–1854
5. Church descriptions by Sir Stephen Glynne 1830–1870

These sources are described in greater detail in the first volume in the series, BHRS Vol.73 (1994) pp.1–25

The text of the contemporary sources is presented in its original form, to convey a feeling for the times as well as to provide information. Most of the sources could have been condensed by editing but the Society's Editorial Group felt that they should nevertheless be published *in extenso*.

Commentary and footnotes

The introductory commentary for each church includes a brief history of the building, with special reference to eighteenth and nineteenth century restoration and alterations. Detailed footnotes explain and amplify features mentioned in the text.

The illustrations are drawn chiefly from the County Record Office collection. They include early watercolours and photographs of the churches as they appeared – sometimes in advanced stages of neglect and decay – before the arrival of the Victorian restorers. Where they exist, pre–restoration interior views have been used.

The background research for the commentaries and footnotes has involved investigation of a wide range of sources. These include parish records (especially churchwardens' accounts, vestry minutes and papers relating to church fabric and furnishings), Diocesan records at Lincoln, Cambridge and Hertford (including the Ely material), the Incorporated Church Building Society (ICBS) files at Lambeth Palace Library, the archives of the Society for the Protection of Ancient Buildings (SPAB) and searches in local newspapers and contemporary periodicals. Every church has also been visited.

Using the material

Some readers will be happy just to read and browse, but those who wish to use this volume as a quarry for information may find it helpful to have some guidance on how to search it thoroughly.

The aim has been to provide a simple chronological account of each church, giving the key facts and emphasising special points of interest. While the introduction provides a summary, the detail is to be found in the footnotes. The footnotes also point the way to sources of further information. For example, at St.Mary's, Luton, the text reads:

> ...This [the removal of the baptistery to the south transept] was in preparation for the reseating of the church which took place between 1823 and 1829.[32] A west gallery was erected in 1823, with a new organ by Lincoln of London.[33] At the same time, repairs to the church and steeple were being undertaken under Archdeacon Bonney's orders.[34] In 1827–9 the interior was refitted with new galleries and pews,[35] and on the north face of the north transept there is a rainwater head dated 1829.

The footnotes have three main purposes, 1) to justify statements made in the introduction, 2) to offer the reader guidance on where to find further information and 3) to link the references in the contemporary sources. The supporting notes thus provide quite a lot more detail, (e.g. on the organ) as the following examples show:

> *Notes*: **32.** The west gallery of 1823 and other work of this period is described by Davis (p.39) Cobbe (p.635) and Austin (Vol.II pp.115–7) and documented in the charity accounts (P 85/25/1/1). Costs are summarised in a letter in the ICBS correspondence (LPL ref: ICBS file 851); **33.** The organ by Lincoln was "built by subscription" at a cost of three hundred guineas in 1823 (Davis p.39). At the restoration in 1864–6 it was moved from the west gallery into the Wenlock chapel. In addition to the keyboards for manual playing, it seems to have been fitted with barrels for automatic operation. Boston and Langwill *Church and Chamber Barrel-Organs* (1967) p.73 mention two barrels from the organ "preserved in the parvise museum"; **34.** The ICBS application dated 20 July 1827 mentions that "repairs to the church and steeple within the last year cost £250" (LPL ref: ICBS 851); **35.** The sources include a faculty for new free seats 1827 (ABF 1 p.149 and ABF 3/136–7), correspondence supporting the ICBS application for a grant (£200) 1827–9 (LPL ref: ICBS 851) including plans, a plan of seats and galleries by John Williams 1829 (P 85/2/5/3) and the painted board in the tower recording the reseating in 1829.

The same footnote number may be used for several references to a particular topic and to be sure of extracting all the available information the reader should trace all occurrences of the footnote from the beginning to the end of the material for the church concerned.

ABBREVIATIONS

AASRP	Reports and papers of the Associated Archaeological Societies
b.	Born (e.g. b.1765)
BAAS	Bedfordshire Architectural and Archaeological Society (established 1847)
BAJ	*Beds. Archaeological Journal* (continued from Vol.16 (1983) as *Bedfordshire Archaeology*)
BC	*Biggleswade Chronicle* (1891–date)
BCRO	Bedfordshire County Record Office – re-named the Bedfordshire and Luton Archives and Records Service in 1997, but for consistency the abbreviation BCRO will be retained throughout this series
BE	Bedfordshire Express (linked with the Hertfordshire Express but published as a separate title in Bedford in the 1870s to 1890s)
BHRS	Bedfordshire Historical Record Society
BL	British Library
BPRS	*Bedfordshire Parish Registers Series*
BM	*Bedford Mercury* (1837–1857) or *Bedfordshire Mercury* (1857–1912)
BNQ	*Bedfordshire Notes and Queries* (3 vols. 1886–1893)
BS	*Bedfordshire Standard* (1883–1939)
BT	*Bedford Times* (1845–1859), *Bedford Times and Bedfordshire Independent* (1859–1872), or *Bedfordshire Times and Independent* (1872–1939) etc.
B.Mag.	*Bedfordshire Magazine* (1947–date)
C...th	Century (e.g. C13th for thirteenth century)
c.	circa (e.g. c.1700)
CERC	Church of England Record Centre (Bermondsey)
CT	Church Times (1863–date)
CUL	Cambridge University Library
d.	Died
DBG	*Dunstable Borough Gazette* (1865–date)
DNB	*Dictionary of National Biography*
fl.	Flourished (e.g. Fl.1810–26)
GM	*Gentleman's Magazine*
HCRO	Hertfordshire County Record Office
HE	Hertfordshire Express (1875–1962)
ICBS	Incorporated Church Building Society
Kelly	Kelly's *Directory* [date given]
LAO	Lincolnshire Archives Office
LBO	*Leighton Buzzard Observer* (1863–1954)
LPL	Lambeth Palace Library

NM	*Northampton Mercury*
PRO	Public Record Office
RC	"Round the County" articles by Arthur Ransom in *BT* 1899–1909 [date given]
RCF	Redundant Churches Fund (renamed The Churches Conservation Trust in 1994)
SPAB	Society for the Protection of Ancient Buildings (established 1877)
V&A	Victoria and Albert Museum
VCH	*Victoria County History*
W.A.	W.A. – John Martin – the writer of the articles on Bedfordshire churches

REFERENCES

All references are to documents in the Bedfordshire County Record Office (BCRO) unless otherwise stated.

Principal publications listed in the Bibliography are normally cited only by the author's surname (plus initials if applicable) e.g. Pevsner. Where more than one work by a given author is listed the date of publication is also given, e.g. Clarke (1938).

The citation of illustrations causes some difficulty, as many well-known engravings and prints were originally incorporated in printed books. The Record Office collection includes multiple copies of many such views, but full publication details are not always included in BCRO catalogues. Even where publication details are known, it cannot be guaranteed that a copy of a particular book will still contain a specific illustration. Views are therefore generally identified by their BCRO reference rather than by other means. BCRO slide numbers are also used to refer to 35mm colour transparencies of original watercolours in the collection or in private ownership. This system should ensure that people wishing to check details can be sure of identifying and locating copies of a particular view.

SYMBOLS USED IN TRANSCRIPTION

Cancellation or deletion	(^{c})
Insertion	(^{i})
Marginal note	(^{m})
Additions by the transcriber	[ ]
Omissions by the transcriber	...
Illegible or torn parts of the manuscript	– – –
Line breaks (in line-by-line transcripts)	/

SUPPLEMENTARY BIBLIOGRAPHY

This bibliography supplements those in part I (BHRS Vol.73) pp.xiv–xv and part II (BHRS Vol.77) pp.xvii–xix). It only lists additional works along with further information on some of the publications previously listed.

a) Bedfordshire
Bedfordshire Magazine (1947–1999)
Pickford, Chris *Victorian and later stained glass in Bedfordshire* (2000)

b) Architectural history etc.
Cunningham, Colin *Stones of Witness – Church Architecture and Function* (1999)
Morris, Richard *Churches in the Landscape* (1989)
Twentieth Century Society *The Twentieth Century Church* (1998)

c) General works [none]

d) Churches and Church Furnishings
Incorporated Church Building Society *New Churches Illustrated* (1936)
Incorporated Church Building Society *Fifty Modern Churches* (1947)
Incorporated Church Building Society *Sixty Post-War Churches: Churches, Church Centres, Dual-purpose Churches* (1956)
Jenkins, Simon *England's Thousand Best Churches* (1999)
National Association of Decorative & Fine Arts Societies (NADFAS) *Inside Churches: A Guide to Church Furnishings* (2nd ed) (1993)

e) Individual C19th architects and artists
AUSTIN, John Sunman (artist) – "John Sunman Austin, Artist, Architect and Surveyor c.1806–1860" by Chris Pickford in *Beds. Mag.* Vol.26 no.204 (Spring 1998) p.140–5
FOWLER, James (architect): *Fowler of Louth: The Life and Works of James Fowler, Louth architect 1828–1892* by David Kaye and Sam Scorer (Louth Naturalists', Antiquarian and Literary Society 1992)
MYERS, George (builder): *Pugin's Builder: The Life and Work of George Myers* by Patricia Spencer-Silver (Hull University Press 1993)
RICHARDSON, Sir Albert (architect) – *Sir Albert Richardson (1880–1964)* by Alan Powers, John Wilton-Ely and Simon Houfe (RIBA exhibition catalogue 1999)
STREET, George Edmund (architect) – *George Edmund Street: a Victorian architect in Berkshire* edited by John Elliott and John Pritchard (Reading University Press 1998)

f) Periodicals
Church Times (from 1863)
Ecclesiastical Gazette (from 1839)

Fig.1 Map of Bedfordshire showing the churches (S–Y) included in this volume

S

SALFORD

The list of incumbents at Salford goes back to 1229, but the present church is entirely of later date. The nave and south aisle were built in the late C13th and the chancel in the early C14th.[1] The timber-framed north porch includes a beam with C13th dogtooth ornament.[2] The nave roof dates from the C15th and there are some C15th pews. The church also has monuments to the Salford, Polein and Peddar families.[3]

In 1552 it was noted that "the said churche and steple coveryd with lede and the chancell and porch tyled".[4] The inventory also lists the mediaeval plate, ornaments, and three bells one of which still hangs in the open bellcote over the west end of the church. In 1617 the church was reported to be out of repair.[5] One of the bells was recast in 1626 and another (now lost) in 1661.[6] Dates of 1632 on a beam in the nave roof and 1633 in the porch clearly relate to repairs at that time.[7] A new chalice and paten were obtained in 1638.[8] The plate was later supplemented by the gift of a salver (hallmarked 1763) in 1771 and a flagon in 1802.

In 1750 the benefices of Hulcote and Salford were united, and from this date the churches share a similar history.[9] Salford Vicarage was demolished when the Rectory at Hulcote was repaired and enlarged in 1824.[10]

At some time around 1760, the original "steeple" over the west end of the church was taken down and replaced by a new tower of brick with corner pinnacles, pyramid roof and weathervane.[11] When William White reported on the condition of the church in 1866 he considered the tower to have been built about a hundred years earlier.[12] He also noted that it was built from the oak beams which carried the original bell turret. There was also a west gallery under the belfry. At about the same time, c.1760, the chancel was partially rebuilt and a plaster ceiling erected.[13] Visiting in 1827, Boissier described Salford as "a small poor Decorated church with low tower & N porch".[14] Some repairs were ordered by Bonney in 1823 and 1833.

In 1836 the church was re-pewed, the south doors stopped up and other improvements carried out at the expense of the parish.[15] Hulcote church was also repaired after the work at Salford had been completed. In 1848 the Rural Dean noted that the pulpit and desk had been "bought from Wavendon church".[16] No date is given, but these fittings were probably displaced from Wavendon in the 1830s when that church acquired (through the Hoare family) a fine C17th pulpit from St. Dunstan-in-the-West, London.[17]

In 1845 W.A. described the church as "in very bad condition" and observed that "when the day of restoration arrives much will be required to redeem it from the indignities it has suffered". In 1866 William White reported on the condition of the church and prepared plans for restoration which was carried out in 1867.[18] The work involved substantial improvements to the chancel, general

1. Salford: View of the west front showing the C18th brick tower which was replaced in 1867 by an open wooden bellcote and shingled spirelet   *(Watercolour: George Shepherd 1825)*

repairs to the walls and roof, and the erection of an open wooden bellcote in place of the old brick tower. The church was re-opened on 16 October 1867.

In 1889 an American organ was introduced,[19] later replaced in 1930 by an organ.[20] A new altar cloth was provided in 1890.[21] The vestry was added on the north side of the chancel in 1900 to the designs of William Poole of Woburn Sands.[22] It was erected in memory of the Rev. Boteler Charnock Smith (incumbent 1865–1898), who is also commemorated by a stained glass window by Hardman erected in 1901 by his widow.[23] In 1916 a new pulpit was presented.[17] The lych gate at the entrance to the churchyard was erected as a war memorial in 1920.[24] In 1921 a further window of stained glass was placed in the north side of the nave.[25] Later work includes repairs to the roof and bell turret in 1960 and the removal of the Victorian fittings from the chancel in 1971.[26]

1. Extract from glebe terrier, 28 June 1822

SALFORD.

Church yard. The Church yard is Fenced with Oak Posts and Railing at the Parish Expence and Contains three Roods of Ground.[27]

Church. The Church is in Length including the Chancell twenty four yards, in Breadth Ten yards, and Ten yard and half in height the Steeple.[11]

Furniture and ornaments. There is a Communion Table and Covering for the same. Also one Linen Cloth for the same with two Napkins. Communion Plate and Chalice of Silver.[8] One Chest with three Locks. One one (*sic*) Pulpit and Reading Desk[17] cover'd with Cloth. Bible, Prayer Book &c. and the King's Arms with the Ten Commandments. Three Bells,[6] the First Bell two feet one inch in Diameter date 1626, second is two feet four Inches with this Inscription "Christopher Gray made me 1661", the third Bell is two feet seven in diameter.

2. Archdeacon Bonney's historical notices of churches, c.1820–1840

SALFORD. This church consists of a Nave and south Aisle, Chancel & low Tower at the West End,[11] 3 Bells.[6] In the Nave is a brass Plate bearing the Effigies of a Male and Female,[3] with this Inscription "Pray for the Sowls of John Peddar and Alys his wife, which John decessed the XXVI day of November the Yere of our Lord MCCCCCV on whose Sowls Jhu' have mercy, Amen".

In the upper part of the South Side of the Nave and Aisle are three Tombs.[3] On one of these are these Bearings [*Sketch of two coats of arms*]. On another a Cross [*Sketch of cross with coat of arms*] and on the third under a Monumental arch with Cusps & croketted, the Effigy of a Man; his head reclining on a cushion supported by two Angels & his feet on two Lions. He is in Armour Cross legged. There is a North Porch.[2] The East Window is decorated.

On the Flagon "The Gift of M[rs] Eliz. Harvey to Salford Church, Bedfordshire".[8]

On the Patin "The Gift of Henry Odell to Salford Church 1771."

On the Chalice "Salford Parish Bedfordshire 1638". All of these are of Silver.[8]

3. Archdeacon Bonney's visitation notebook, 1823–1839

SALFORD. This Church consists of a Nave and South Aisle, a Tower[11] at the West End of the Nave and Chancel at the East End thereof, a Porch on the North side.[2]

At the Visitation of 1823 the following Order was given that the Communion Table and Rails be oiled; a new surplice and linen Cloth for the Table be purchased, a Casement be placed in the South Window of the chancel, and others in the North & South Windows of the Church; the Seats be neatly repaired, cleansed and oiled; the Pulpit & Reading Desk be also refreshed;[17] the bible be rebound; the Clerk's Prayer Book be repaired; the Earth be moved from the Walls & proper Drainage be made; the Munions & Tracery of the Windows be restored; and glass inserted in the blank places thereof; the Floors in the North Porch,[2] near the Steeple, and in the Chancel be repaired.

The orders were complied with before the Visitation of 1824.

At the Visitation of 1826 – no further order was given.

At the Visitation of 1833 the following Order was given – that the green moss be brushed from the Walls of the Chancel, & the Buttresses repaired – the ceiling be repaired[13] – a small window in the South Aisle be repaired with cement – the Weeds be removed from the upper part of the Walls – and the Walls be secured with Lime or Cement – a casement be made in the South Window of the Chancel – the Top of the Pulpit be repaired – the Seats be taken up, reset, & made commodious – also cleaned and oiled.[15]

At the visitation of 1836 ordered that the Porch and tiling on the Chancel be repaired, and also the Communion Cup.[8] The Revd. B.C. Smith showed me a plan for repewing the Church – which plan he stated to have been agreed upon in Vestry – and a Rate for carrying it into Execution granted – and approved of it.[15]

At the Visitation 1839 Ordered the Churchwardens to notify my Order to the Impropriator to repair the Roof & Ceiling of the Chancel[13] – and suggested the propriety of having Double Doors at the Entrance instead of the Misshapen Porch.[2] If the Doors be not so constructed – then, to put the Porch into Substantial repair – The interior of the Church has lately been arranged and cleaned.[15]

4. Article on the Church by W.A. (no.11), NM 23 August 1845

SALFORD. This building appeared to be in very bad condition: the approach to it, through a nearly ruined porch,[2] was not calculated to give a good impression of its interior. It was dismal and dark, in a great degree to be attributed to the favourite plan of excluding the western light by a miserable gallery. To remedy this in some degree a circular light had been punched through the wall, totally out of character with any part of the edifice. The roof was ceiled; a good proportion of the open seats remained, with some enclosed of the usual ugliness.

The chancel has a great portion of its space taken up by three square pews. The roof was ceiled.[13] When the day of restoration arrives much will be required to redeem it from the indignities it has suffered.

The leaden roof remained on the nave, but that of the chancel was tiled, a matter of very frequent occurrence. It falls not into my plan to give a reason for this.

20 August 1845   W.A.

Notes **1.** Pevsner pp.138–9, *VCH* III pp.424–5, and *A History of the Parish of Hulcote cum Salford* by Maurice Rust (Typescript 1971); **2.** The porch is described and illustrated by Terence Paul Smith in "Timber framed porches to Bedfordshire churches" in *BAJ* Vol.17 (1986) p.90–2. Smith considers the porch to date from "any time up to c.1500" but does not mention the 1633 repair date. Bonney ordered repairs to the floor in 1826 and refers in 1839 to the "misshapen porch" which W.A. described as "nearly ruined". There is a sketch of the porch of 1845 in the Hartshorne collection (MIC 117); **3.** The monuments noted by Bonney are described in the *VCH* and by Rust. They were illustrated by Fisher (*Collections* pp.82–4) and George Shepherd did a watercolour of the effigy in the south aisle in 1813 (slide 853). There are drawings of an effigy in the church, C19th (BL ref: Add.Ms. 42013 f.38) and in the notes of the Rev. D.T. Powell, 1810–12 (BL ref: Add.Ms. 17456). For the Peddar brass, see Lack *et.al.* (p.82); **4.** Eeles and Brown p.7; **5.** Presentment, 1617 (ABC 5 p.94); **6.** The bells (North p.181) were by James Keene 1626, Christopher Graye 1661, and Roger Landen of Wokingham c.1450. They were rehung in the present open bellcote in 1867. The middle (1661) bell was broken in the 1950s and stolen from the roof during at the time of repairs to the bellcote in 1960 (Rust); **7.** The dates of 1632 and 1633 on timbers in the nave and porch are noted by Rust; **8.** The plate described by Bonney is listed in the 1925 schedule (ABE 5). It includes cup and paten of 1638, a plate (hallmarked 1763) given by Henry Odell in 1771, and a flagon given by Elizabeth Hervey in 1802; **9.** Faculty for union of benefices of Hulcote and Salford, 1750 (in Hulcote parish records, P 113/2/1); **10.** Faculty for parsonage, 1824 (P 77/2/2) and faculty papers (ABF 2 fol.134 and ABF 3/178–181); **11.** There is no firm date for the brick tower, but it was probably built in about 1760 as suggested by White. The architect prepared plans for an enclosed wooden belfry in 1866 (P 77/2/1) but the present open bellcote on the west gable was built instead in 1867; **12.** White's report and estimate, 1866 (P 77/2/0) and plans (P 77/2/1); **13.** As with the tower, William White suggested that the chancel had been ceiled in about 1760. In 1833–9 Bonney ordered repairs to the roof and ceiling, and White's report indicates that by 1866 the chancel was in particularly bad condition; **14.** Boissier (f.416d); **15.** The repairs to the seating in 1836 are documented in Bonney's notebook, but his orders for Hulcote for 1836 (*q.v.*) indicate that the work there was to be done "as soon as the Church at Salford is finished"; **16.** Rural Dean's notebook, 1848 (AB/RD/A O); **17.** Rust suggests that the pulpit and desk (replacing those listed in the 1822 terrier and mentioned in Bonney's orders) were acquired when Wavendon church was restored in 1848, but the story seems to be less straightforward. St.Dunstan's was rebuilt in 1830–3, partly with the assistance of the Hoare family who also had a seat at Wavendon. The C17th pulpit, probably acquired for Wavendon in the early 1830s, was retained when Butterfield restored Wavendon church in 1848. The present pulpit at Salford is of 1916 (Rust); **18.** The sources for White's restoration in 1866–7 include the report and plans (P 77/2/0–1), register entries for baptisms at Hulcote while Salford church was closed for repair 1867 (P 77/1/6), and report in *BT* 22 Oct.1867; **19.** American organ reported in *BS* 16 Feb.1889; **20.** The organ by Jennings (*ex.inf.* National Pipe Organs Register) was bought for £250 in 1930 and restored and electrified in 1965 (Rust); **21.** Altar cloth noted in Bathurst's notebook (ABE 3); **22.** Vestry documented in vestry minutes and accounts (P 77/8/1) and letter from Poole (the architect) to Mann (the contractor) 1900 (X 320/13–14); **23.** The window is recorded in the Hardman daybooks (Birmingham City Archives, ref: Ms.175/36/21 p.24); **24.** Accounts for lych gate, 1920 (P 77/8/1); **25.** Vestry minute regarding the window, 18 March 1920 (P 77/8/1); **26.** The repairs to the roof and belfry and clearance of Victorian fittings from the chancel are described by Rust; **27.** The parish register (P 77/1/1) includes an undated C17th note on responsibility for maintaining the churchyard fences.

SANDY

A church here is first mentioned in c.1214. Sandy is a large parish and by 1304 there was also a separate chapel at Beeston. The present church dates mainly from the rebuilding and enlargement of 1859–60, but it retains a C15th west tower. Although heavily restored, parts of the old fabric survive in the chancel, nave and aisles.[1] The form of the mediaeval church is known from early C19th views and from Bonncy's description.[2] The C15th font[3] and the

2. Sandy: SW view showing the south side of the church before rebuilding in 1859–60, including the clerestory windows described as "rather roughly built" by Boissier who also noted "the rather unusual buttresses" on the tower   *(Watercolour: Thomas Fisher c.1815)*

piscina and sedilia in the chancel survive, and Fisher recorded a carving from the mediaeval rood.[4] In the chancel there is a fragment from the mediaeval alabaster reredos.[5]

Documents of 1556 refer to the removal of two bells from the tower by Robert Burgoyne whose widow took the metal to pay off his debts.[6] By 1708 the number of bells had been restored or increased to five and there was also "a little Saints Bell under a cover of boards" outside the steeple.[7] One of the bells was cast in 1602.[8] An inventory of 1601 mentions "a piece of timber to drawe up a bell", a "leaded wayte for a clocke",[9] a "a payre of organs" and various books, vestments, furnishings and articles of plate.[10] A new chalice was given by the Rector in 1661 and there is a paten of 1739.[11] The 1708 terrier records that a pall with the arms of the Clothworkers' Company embroidered in silk had recently been given to the parish by Luke Cartwright.[7]

Dated pieces of lead (now in the base of the tower) record repairs to the tower roof and leaded steeple in 1692 and 1756. Bells were recast in 1723 and 1733 by Thomas Russell of Wootton and in 1769 by Joseph Eayre of St.Neots.[8] In 1755 Elizabeth Kingsley obtained a faculty for a vault in the north transept which was used until 1860 for members of the Kingsley and Pym families of Hasells Hall.[12] In 1760, Elizabeth Kingsley also erected a pew in the church adjoining the pew of the Rev. Lewis Monoux of Sandy Place.[13] These private pews are noted in the C19th accounts of the church. By

1823 there was a west gallery or singing loft, and Bonney's order book indicates that the creed, Lord's prayer and commandments were painted on a "framework under the arch leading to the chancel". Bonney had these set up elsewhere in the church in about 1826.[14]

Various repairs and improvements were carried out from 1823 in response to the Archdeacon's orders. A new organ was installed in 1830 and possibly replaced in 1853.[15] It was on the west gallery. The vestry minutes refer to repairs in 1840,[16] and in 1841 the churchyard was enlarged.[17] One of the bells was recast in 1852.[8] In 1854–5 the accounts record expenditure of £54, possibly on repairs.[18]

The arrival of a new Rector in 1858 heralded improvements to the building. The Rev. John Richardson (Rector 1858–1913) quickly set about restoring the church.[19] The plans of W.G. Habershon were adopted by the vestry in December 1858, and work began in 1859.[20] The church was rebuilt and enlarged, re-roofed, re-seated and generally improved. The flamboyant Decorated window tracery, the carved heads on the exterior and the gable crosses are Habershon's work. Some of the monuments and memorials were resited,[21] the organ was moved from the west gallery to the new chancel aisle,[15] and a new pulpit in Caen stone and a new clock were provided.[9] The re-opening took place on 26 April 1860 but the occasion was marred by the death of Francis Leslie Pym (the squire and patron) who was killed in a railway accident while on his way to Sandy for the event.

After the church had been restored, new fixtures and furnishings were provided. In 1861 a statue by William Theed was placed in the chancel in memory of Capt. Sir William Peel (1824–1858)[22] and a window in the chancel was filled with stained glass by Charles Gibbs in memory of the Rector's wife.[23] This was the first of several stained glass windows in the church, followed in 1867 and 1881 respectively by the south and north windows in the transepts.[24] Additional plate was obtained in 1869.[11] In 1872 a new organ was installed.[15] Gas heating was provided in 1874.[25] A brass eagle lectern was presented in 1889.[26]

From 1889–99 improvements to the church are recorded in the parish magazine.[27] The east window was presented by the Speaker of the House of Commons, the Rt.Hon. Arthur Wellesley Peel, in memory of his wife, in 1892.[28] In the same year the bells were rehung and a new clock set up in the tower.[8, 9] In 1893 a new window was placed in the south chapel in memory of Francis A.K. Foster.[29] There was a fire in the chancel roof in 1894, fortunately extinguished promptly. In the following year the old heating system was renewed.[25] In 1895 a wooden screen executed by Horace Richardson was placed in the tower arch in memory of Mrs. Jefferies.[30] Two new stained glass windows were installed in 1902, the west window in the tower as a memorial to Queen Victoria and a striking window of the Annunciation by Mary Lowndes in the south aisle in memory of the Rector's daughter.[31] In 1908 the vestry was enlarged to commemorate the 50th anniversary of the Rector's induction.[32]

Later work includes the war memorial chapel in the south transept, furnished in 1920 with a memorial (by Maile & Son) and a stained glass window (by Percy Bacon).[33] Bacon was also responsible for another window in the south chapel in 1922. Two windows in the north aisle were filled with stained glass in 1926.[34] A new font cover was provided in 1937.[3] There are modern windows of 1951 in the south chapel and of 1965 in the baptistery.[35] The tower was restored in 1955–7,[36] and in 1961 the south chapel was refurbished as a Lady chapel in memory of Alderman W.G. Braybrooks.[37] Screens were erected to enclose the organ chamber in 1970,[38] and in 1973 a new ringing gallery was constructed in the tower.[39]

1. Extract from glebe terrier, 4 July 1822

SANDY.

Church yard.[17] Item the Church yard containing 3 Roods 22 Perches. The Stone Wall next to the Road is kept in repair by the Churchwardens.

Church. Belonging to the said Parish Church there is first the Church containing in length 45 feet, in breadth 50 feet. There are also two Ailes each in length 18 feet in Breadth 11 feet. The Belfry is 15 feet one way and 13 feet the other. The Chancel is 45 feet in length and in Breadth 17 feet. There is also a Vestry adjoining in length 15 feet and in Breadth 8½ feet.

Furniture and ornaments. Within and Belonging to the Church are one communion Table with a covering for the same of Green Cloth. Also one linen cloth for the same, with one Napkin. One Silver Flaggon.[11] One Silver Waiter. One Iron Bound Chest with three locks standing in the Chancel, to contain the Plate. One Deal Trunk to contain the Surplice. One Pulpit & reading Desk. One Pulpit Cushion covered with red cloth. One large Bible of the last Translation. One large common Prayer Book. One church Clock.[9] Five Bells with their Frames.[8] One Bier. One Funeral Cloth.[40] Two Surplices.

Parish Registers. Five Parchment Register Books, one begining 1538 and ending 1642 Scarce Legible. The second begining 1643 and ending as near as can be ascertained between 1679 and 1690. The third begining 1690 and ending 1739 Complete. A fourth begining 1740 and ending 1803. The fifth begining 1803 & ending 1812. There is also another Register Book of Paper made on the improved plan begining 1812 and continued up to the present time. There is also a small Iron Chest with one Lock in which are contained the Register Books.

Parish Clerk. There are also Due to the Parish Clerk for the Publication of Banns one shilling and sixpence, also for every Wedding by Publication of Banns one shilling and sixpence, For every Wedding by Licence two shillings and sixpence. Also for every funeral (viz. for ringing the Bell and digging the Grave) one shilling and sixpence.

2. Archdeacon Bonney's historical notices of churches, c.1820–1840

SANDY. This church consists of a Nave and Aisles separated by octagonal Piers with ogee mouldings and acute angled Arches. There are Transepts, Chancel & a Tower embattled at the West End. The general Character of the Church is the Decorated; but there are some perpendicular insertions. The Font is circular upon a beautiful Perpendicular Pier.[3] A Reformation Pulpit. In the Tower there are five Bells.[8] There is a South Porch.

On the chalice is this Inscription,[11] "Franciscus Walsall. S.T.P. indignus Rector de Sandy in Agro Bedfordiensi hunc Calicem Benedictionis propinavit dilecto Georgii [sic. recte Gregi] Maii 23° Anno Salutis 1661 libertatis restituta Sub Auspiciis Augustissimi Principis Caroli 2°. Quid retribuam Domino!"

On the Flagon "Sandy in Bedfordshire" the same is on the Patin and Plate.[11]

3. Archdeacon Bonney's Visitation notebook, 1823–1839

SANDY This Church consists of a Nave, North and South Aisles, Transepts, a Tower at the west end of the Nave and Chancel at the East end thereof. A porch to the South Aisle.

At the Visitation of 1823 the following order was given, That the Earth be moved from the exterior of the Walls and proper Drainage made; the Open Seats to be neatly repaired according to the Old pattern; the Pulpit and Gallery painted oak colour; the Doors to be repaired, according to the ancient pattern and oak grained, the Stonework of the Windows and Doors be restored according to the ancient Architecture; a portion of the Leads of the Roof be recast and relaid every year until the whole be compleated; After the Church is thoroughly repaired, the cracked Bell be recast.[8]

To this order the following was added – That the Font be cleansed and repaired with Cement;[3] the Top be improved by a new Handle & be oiled; a proper font Bason be be (sic) purchased; the framework under the Arch leading to the Chancel be taken down;[14] the Creed, Lord's Prayer, and Ten Commandments be set up in the Church. The Bible & Prayer Book be repaired.

At the Visitation of 1826 – the above order had been complied with except as follows – which was then ordered. That the cracked Bell be recast, the seats be repaired & the wood inserted made to correspond in colour with the rest of the Seats & the whole refreshed with oil. The Ten Commandments and Table of Degrees be set up.[14] The doors including those of the Chancel and Vestry be cleansed & painted oak colour.

At the Visitation of 1833 it was ordered that the seats be cleansed & oiled. The Pulpit, Desk, & Church Doors including those in the Chancel be oak grained, before Easter 1836. The walls be cleansed by dry brushing. After 1836 the Cracked Bell be recast.[8]

3. Sandy: This composite view of the church "as restored" was contributed by the architect to help the parish to raise money for the work. The SE view shows the south chapel added in 1859–60 and the plan shows seating (since removed) in the chapel, transepts and under the tower.

(Lithograph: W.G. Habershon 1859)

At the Visitation of 1836. Ordered, that the Surplice be repaired and also the Ministers Prayer Book and that the previous orders be proceeded with.

At the Visitation of 1839 Ordered the Churchwardens to have the exterior of their Church cleansed from Moss & Weeds & pointed where necessary – also the plaster inside to be repaired, and the walls washed a light drab colour, also a Panel in the Transept to be repaired, also the Floor. The Beams & Vestry Door to be cleansed and refreshed with oil & Umbre.[16]

The Parish is negotiating with Mrs. Ongley for an exchange of Property, which will enable it to enlarge the Churchyard towards the West, a thing much wanted.[17]

4. Article on the Church by W.A. (no.110), NM 22 January 1853

SANDY, St. Swithin: Two dilapidated square pews,[13] one if not both, manufactured of wooden work, which had adorned in days gone by, some part of the fabric; perhaps reliques of the screen.[4] An ancient chest in melancholy decay.

The nave and aisles open roofs – some open sittings; those that are closed, are a motley hotch-potch of the village carpenters's skill and taste. A flying cage in the transept for the accommodation of servants,[13] who are there most ludicrously suspended over the heads of the congregation.

In the churchwardens' seat, are some reliques of carving,[4] arranged on a shelf in the manner we have seen ornaments on the mantel-piece of a private residence.

Another flying pew abuts the singing loft,[13] but a green curtain cautiously secludes its occupants from their neighbours "who sing".

The various stair-cases, necessary to reach these dovecotes will immediately suggest the utter unecclesiastical appearance the interior presents; of course the belfry arch is hidden from view.

The font appears an interesting example, but the pedestal, apparently of a different period, is so bedaubed, as to render any attempt at making out its details, hopeless.[3]

The exterior is in tolerable condition. The churchyard locked and overrun with weeds and high grass.[17] When a deeper reverence shall be entertained for the care of our last home, we may hope that the spirit of the following beautiful passage will be realised:-

> "Give us we say, whenever the appointed hour arrives, no other monument than a parterre, six feet by two; not hung about with trumpery-dyed wreaths of *eternelles* and fragile amarynths, but planted with humble, homely, low-growing favourites; the aconite and the snow-drop, to make a resurrection from the death of winter; the violet and the lily of the valley to join peacefully in the sweetness of spring; the rose to sympathise with the beauty of summer; and the Japan anemone and the

chrysanthemum to carry a smile into the failing light of autumn.
So best may the corruptible body be rendered up to nature."
O fortunate, e ciascuna era certa
Della sua sepoltura * * *

n.d.   W.A.

Notes **1.** Pevsner p.139, *VCH* II pp.244–5, and *A Guide to St.Swithun's Church, Sandy* (1985). I am also grateful to Barry Groom for providing information on the church and for commenting on the text; **2.** Pre-restoration views include a Fisher watercolour of c.1815 (slide 2265), and a sketch on John Sunman Austin's map of 1855 (Z 50/99/29) and there is a description of the church in 1827 by Boissier (f.429d–30) and by Addington (1848) no.122; **3.** The font, which stands on a C15th base, may be ancient. It now has a modern stone pedestal, dating from 1962 and replacing a mediaeval heavily carved pedestal which became unsafe (P 9/2/3/12 and P 9/2/5/8). The wooden cover of 1937 commemorates the Coronation of George VI but now lacks the silver band and other decoration stolen in 1995; **4.** The figures from the rood drawn by Fisher (*Collections* p.114a) may be the "reliques of carving" in the churchwardens' seat mentioned in 1853 by W.A. who also refers to old woodwork from the screen reused in the pews; **5.** A report in *BS* 12 April 1901 records that the fragment of the alabaster reredos (discovered in 1859) had been recently set in the south wall of the chancel. For the fragment see the guide (p.4) and *VCH* II p.245; **6.** Eeles and Brown pp.29–30; **7.** Glebe terrier 1708 (ABE 2 Vol.I p.133); **8.** Of the five bells listed in 1708 none now remain, the 1602 bell having been recast in 1892. North (pp.181–2) gives details of the C17th and C18th bells. Bonney ordered the recasting of a cracked bell several times from 1823, but it was not until 1852 that the work was done. The bells were rehung in a new frame and a sixth bell was added in 1892 (covered in Parish Magazine and local papers, especially *BM*, *BS*, and *BC* 16 Jan.1892 and 7–14 May 1892). The bells were again rehung in 1952–3 (P 9/2/6/2–6); **9.** A clock is listed in the 1708 terrier. A new clock was put up in 1859 (*BM* 5 Dec.1859) but it was replaced by the present one in 1892 (Parish Magazine 1892, and report in *BS* 14 May 1892). It was repaired in 1951 (P 9/2/6/1) and converted to automatic winding in 1976; **10.** Inventory, 1601 (in P 9/1/1 – published in BPRS Vol.6 p.A135); **11.** The plate listed in the 1925 schedule (ABE 5) includes the chalice of 1661, the 1739 paten, a silver spoon of 1867, and a set of plate of 1869; **12.** Faculty for the Hasells vault, 1755 (ABF 2 p.1 and PM 2717). The vault, described in the guide (pp.5–6) was sealed in 1860 and in 1888/9 new vaults were created in the churchyard for the Pym and Pearson families (faculties at HCRO ref: DSA 2/1/197). There are specifications and plans for the Pym vault (PM 1/120); **13.** Faculty for pew, 1760 (ABF 2 p.6, ABF 3/182 and PM 2718). Writing in 1853 W.A. describes the "motley hotch-potch" of pews and the "flying cage in the transept" for the servants. Until the south chapel was refurbished as a Lady chapel in 1960–1 it contained the manor pew (*ex.inf.* Barry Groom); **14.** Until 1823 the commandments etc. were probably painted on the screen in he chancel arch, hence Bonney's order that they be set up in the church after the screen was removed; **15.** Letters of 1830 refer to the organ supplied by J. Buchinger for Sandy church (PM 2722 and D 119). A bazaar at Hasells Hall in aid of new organ for Sandy was reported in *BT* 23 July 1853. The organ was moved from the west gallery to the new north choir aisle in 1860 (*BT* 1 May 1860 and plan of church). A new organ by Hill & Son was obtained in 1872 (*BT* 29 Oct.1872); **16.** The vestry minutes for 4 Sept.1840 (P 9/8/1) refer to work ordered by the Archdeacon but the details do not correspond with Bonney's orders of 1839; **17.** Bonney noted the churchyard extension as "a thing much wanted" in 1839. The vestry minutes of 1841 refer to the enlargement of the churchyard and the erection of an iron fence to the extension which was consecrated on 18 August 1842 (*BT* 20 Aug.1842). There is a conveyance of the extension (P 9/2/8/1). At the time of the restoration the churchyard was again enlarged, the new section being consecrated on 17 July 1863 (P 9/2/8/2–4). The churchyard was closed when the new cemetery was built in 1891; **18.** Churchwardens' account book, 1804–1867 (P 9/5/1). "Last repairs in 1854 (cost £10)" mentioned in later application form (LPL ref: ICBS 5372); **19.** An "In Memoriam" booklet of 1913 outlines Richardson's work at Sandy (P 9/28/3). Members of his family are commemorated in stained glass windows in the church (1861 and 1902), the vestry was enlarged to mark his 50th anniversary as Rector in 1908, and one of the windows in the north aisle is a memorial to Richardson; **20.** Sources for the

Habershon restoration include vestry minutes 1858–9 (P 9/8/1), churchwardens' accounts 1859–60 (P 9/5/1), ICBS correspondence and papers (including plan) 1859–60 (LPL ref: ICBS 5372), lithograph by Habershon showing the church "as restored 1859" (Z 50/99/64), reports in *BT* 1 Jan.1859, *BT* and *Builder* 16 April 1859 (tenders), *BM* 13 June and 5 Dec. 1859, *BT* 17–23 April and 1 May 1860 and *BM* 7 May 1860 (reopening), and account in the Richardson booklet (P 9/28/3); **21.** The monuments are recorded in a C18th account of the "epitaphs in Sandy church" (BL ref: Add.Ms. 5832 f.171) and in notes on the church by the Rev.W.D. Sweeting, 1880 (BL ref: Add.Ms. 37178 f.19); **22.** Report of the Peel statue in *BM* 26 Oct.1861. It was moved from the chancel to the south transept in the 1960s; **23.** Richardson window reported in *BT* 11 June 1861 and in *Builder* Vol.19 (1861) p.449; **24.** The new south transept window is mentioned in a report in *BT* 28 April 1868 and the new window in the north transept was reported in *BM* and *BT* 6 Aug.1881; **25.** The vestry minutes refer to gas heating, 1874 (P 9/8/1). In 1894 Archdeacon Bathurst advised "the underground place where the gazometer & the wood for firing is kept needs to be locked up" (ABE 3). The fire on 12 Dec. 1894 was reported in the Parish Magazine and noted in the Richardson booklet (P 9/28/3) which mentions the new heating apparatus of 1895; **26.** The lectern in memory of Charles Pope (d.1886) was given by his widow, Easter Day 1889. It was re-gilded in 1984 (guide p.5); **27.** Parish Magazines 1889–1899 (BCRO has an incomplete photocopied set only); **28.** When the church was restored it was hoped "that stained glass will be installed in the new four–light east window" (*BT* 1 May 1860). This hope was not realised until 1891–2 when the present window given by Speaker Peel (reports in *BM* and *BC* 28 Nov.1891) and made by Belham & Co. of London was installed (reports in *BS* 17 Dec.1892, *Builder* Vol.63 (1892) p.507, *BC* 24 Dec.1892, and Parish Magazine Feb 1893); **29.** The Foster window (by Frederick Drake of Exeter) was reported in *BC* 2 Dec.1893; **30.** The belfry screen was installed in 1895 (*BC* 13 Sept.1895 and Parish Magazine, Sept.1985); **31.** The west window was unveiled on 1 Dec.1902 (*BC* and *BM* 5 Dec.1902). It is by Powell of Whitefriars (V&A ref: AAD 1/64 p.68) but designs by Mary Lowndes had also been considered (reports in *BC* 26 April, 10 May and 20 Nov.1901, *BS* 6 Dec.1901 and 27 June 1902). Contemporary sources clearly indicate that the window was a memorial to the late Queen, but the marble plaque erected in 1912 states that it was a Jubilee window (faculty P 9/2/3/2). The Abernethy window in the south aisle is by Mary Lowndes of Lowndes and Drury, 1902 (*BC* 22 August 1902); **32.** Faculty for vestry enlargement, 1907 (P 9/2/3/1) and faculty papers (HCRO ref: DSA 2/1/197). The vestry enlargement was designed and executed by Samuel Foster of Kempston, and a brass plate over the vestry door commemorates the work which was completed in 1908; **33.** Faculty and papers regarding War memorial and window, 1920 (P 9/2/3/4 and P 9/2/5/2) and report in *BT* 14 Jan.1921; **34.** The 1922 (Percy Bacon) and 1926 (Jones & Willis) windows are signed and dated; **35.** The modern window in the south chapel dates from 1951 (P 9/2/3/8 and P 9/2/5/6) and the baptistery window of 1965 is by John Hayward (British Society of Master Glass Painters *Directory* (1966) p.46); **36.** Papers concerning tower repairs, 1955–7 (P 9/2/3/10 and P 9/2/4/6); **37.** Papers concerning the Lady chapel, 1960–1 (P 9/2/3/11 and P 9/2/5/7), and Guide (p.4); **38.** Organ screens, 1970 (Guide p.5); **39.** Ringing gallery, 1973 (Guide p.7); **40.** The 1708 terrier (ABE 2 Vol.I p.133) mentions "one Pall lately given to the Parish by one Mr.Luke Cartwright a cloth worker in London & have-ing on it the Arms of that Company Embroidered with Silk & edgd with white Calico".

SHARNBROOK

Sharnbrook is mentioned in the Domesday Book of 1086, but the oldest parts of the present church date from the C13th.[1] The arcades of the nave, the outer walls of the aisles, and the chancel arch are of C13th date. The Tofte chapel on the north side of the chancel,[2] the north and south porches, and the lower stages of the west tower date from the C14th. In the C15th the spire was added, the north aisle was extended westwards and the window tracery throughout the church was mostly renewed in the Perpendicular style. The building is on a sloping site and the chancel is lower than the nave. There is a fine stone font with Perpendicular decoration.[3] The screen is of c.1500 and there are fragments of carved tracery in the screen to the north chapel.[4] Bequests in wills illustrate the interior furnishing of the church on the eve of the Reformation.[5]

One of the bells was cast between 1611 and 1617 by Newcombe of Leicester, and the ring was remodelled in 1683 when three of the five bells were recast and a new frame provided.[6] The tenor bell was recast in 1699. The pulpit and reading desk in use until 1858 were dated 1636.[7] In 1659 seats in the church were exchanged between the Cobbe and Toller families.[8] The chancel windows were repaired in 1687/8.[9] The goods and ornaments in the church are described in an inventory of c.1708.[10] These include a C17th church clock,[11] and the rails to the communion table.[12] The roof of the nave was apparently renewed in the C17th. There was a fire in the west end of the south aisle in the C18th.[13]

In 1768 Richard Antonie of Colworth obtained a faculty for a pew in the north-east of the church.[14] The faculty papers also give information on other pews in the church. Further pews were erected in 1818 and 1821, one in the south aisle for John Lee of Colworth and another in the north aisle for his servants.[15] Edward Arpin, the Felmersham diarist, records that a new gallery was built in Sharnbrook church and opened in 1824.[16] The 1822 terrier indicates that at this date the Royal Arms were hung near the pulpit and the commandments, which Bonney ordered to be painted in 1823, were displayed over the north door.[17]

In 1827 Boissier noted the roof of the chancel as being in a bad state.[18] In 1844 the churchwardens reported that "the body of the Church requires some new pews".[19] W.A. records that by 1854 the chancel had been lately repaired and improved, and he expressed the hope that "the hand that has gracefully restored the chancel" would see to the removal of the ugly pews in the nave.[20] In May 1854 a local benefactor offered to pay for the reinstatement of the pinnacles on the tower if the parish would meet its share of the cost.[21] The stained glass in the east window also dates from about 1855.[22]

The body of the church was restored between 1855 and 1858 under Thomas Jobson Jackson.[23] The roof was restored in 1856-7, and then in 1858 the church was re-seated. The work also involved a new pulpit and desk,[7] moving the font[3] and the removal of the old singing gallery.[16] After the work had been completed, further improvements were undertaken, including a new dial for the clock in 1861,[11] new south doors on the south and repairs to the north doors in 1866,[24] the erection of the Magniac monument (designed by William Burges) in the Tofte chapel in 1870,[25] the removal of pews in the chancel in 1871,[26] and a new stained glass window in the south chancel wall in 1873.[27] In 1874 Archdeacon Bathurst noted "The chancel north wall and roof bad".[28]

During the incumbency of the Rev. H.B. Wilkinson (1877–1908) various improvements were carried out.[29] By 1876 there was an organ and in 1882 a new organ (apparently a second one) was obtained on loan from Messrs. Strolmeyer.[30] Shortly after Wilkinson's arrival the tower and spire were restored in 1881–2 under W. Talbot Brown of Wellingborough.[31] In 1882 the five old bells were rehung in a new oak frame, a sixth being added in 1887.[6] However, the affairs of the parish were complicated by a bitter dispute between the Vicar and the lay Rector, Leonard G. Stileman-Gibbard, who ceased to attend church at Sharnbrook in 1883 because he "disapproved of the mode in which services were conducted".[32] Matters came to a head in 1894 when Stileman-Gibbard removed the Vicar's reading desk from the chancel. In court Wilkinson lost the case when it was decided in 1896 that the Vicar had no rights over the seating in the chancel.[33] The clergy desk was placed in the nave, where it remains, and the "seats in the chancel were furnished with brass rods and padlocks at the ends by Mr.Stileman Gibbard as a token of his rights over them".[28]

In the context of this extraordinary controversy, it is not surprising that parts of the church fell into disrepair. In 1888 the Archdeacon noted that "the north aisle roof lets in water" and that an improvement was needed "in water draining for the church".[28] In 1895 the parish applied for a faculty for alterations to the chancel seating, for work on the organ, and for a new heating system.[34] This was opposed by Stileman-Gibbard, who also took legal action after a new heating system had been installed without a faculty in 1899.[35] The matter was resolved by the issue of a confirmatory faculty.

Matters gradually improved. The roofs of the north and south porches were renewed in 1897 and 1899 respectively,[36] and in 1902–3 Stileman-Gibbard was persuaded to carry out repairs to the chancel roof.[37] A new wrought iron and copper lectern was presented in 1900,[38] and in 1901 the Watson family of Colworth paid for the new reredos, altar rail and marble paving in the sanctuary.[39] These were executed by Powell of Whitefriars. In 1907 the position of the organ was moved slightly and a new organ case was provided by J. Trustam, the Bedford organ builder.[30] When the Tofte chapel was restored in 1908 Alexander Alston provided a new carved wooden screen in the arch connecting with the chancel.[2] In 1910 new plate was provided,[40] a new pulpit was obtained from Jones & Willis,[7] and a new font cover was given in memory of Miss Edith Martineau (d.1909).[3] Also in 1910 a new lych gate was erected at the south-west corner of the churchyard. It was designed by Gotch & Saunders of Kettering who were also responsible for the new Vicarage built in the same year.[41]

Later work includes the new clock and the restoration of the bells in 1924,[6, 11] the wooden screen and organ loft in the tower of c.1933,[30] the replacement of the pinnacles on the tower in 1934,[21] and the stained glass windows of 1939 in the porch.[42] The spire was repaired after lightning damage in 1951, the roof of the Tofte chapel was renewed in 1954 and extensive work on the main roof was carried out in 1953–5 and 1969–71.[43] In 1963 the fine C18th wrought iron gates from Sharnbrook House were re–erected at the edge of the church-yard by St.Peter's Close.[44]

1. Extract from glebe terrier, 23 June 1822

SHARNBROOK.

Church yard. Item the churchyard containing One Acre one rood and twenty seven poles adjoining to the public road on the south, to the grounds of John Gibbard Esquire on the West, North and East. The walls and gates thereof round about made by the parish.

Church. Belonging to the said parish are, first the parish church, an ancient building, containing in length (with the chancel) eighty four feet, in breadth forty three feet six inches. The chancel in breadth, one part nineteen feet, the other part eighteen feet. The steeple, twelve feet six inches by fourteen nine inches within the walls, in height one hundred and thirty two feet.

Furniture and ornaments. Within and belonging to which are one communion table with a covering for the same of green cloth. Also one linen cloth for the same with one napkin. One pewter flaggon, one silver chalice weighing about seven ounces.[40] Two boxes for the offertory. One chest with three locks. One pulpit and reading desk made in the year 1636 with this inscription on the back of the Pulpit (Prædica Evangelium).[7] One pulpit cushion covered with greed (*sic*) cloth. One Bible of the last translation. Two large common prayer books. The King's arms near the pulpit.[17] The ten commandments over the north door.[17] The Lord's prayer and belief over the south door. One church clock.[11] Five bells with their frames,[6] the first or least bell being two feet four inches and half in diameter with this inscription (Henry Bagley he made me 1683). The second, two feet seven inches in diameter with this inscription (Thome Mountagu de Varton Cornet Northampton Rectoris 1683). The third, two feet eight inches in diameter with this inscription (Matthew Bagley he made me 1683, John Sharp and John Merrill Churchwardens). The fourth, three feet in diameter with this inscription (A°. 161 Newcome of Leicester). The fifth or largest, three feet three inches and a half in diameter with this inscription (William Corby and Rogers C.W. Henricus Bagley me fecit 1699). One Bier, one hearse cloth, two surplices.

Parish Registers. Four parish register books, one begining in 1596 and ending 1676 and seems to have been copied into the second register which begins 1653 and ends in 1764. There seems to have been two leaves cut out from this register. The third register begins in 1766 and ends in 1812. The fourth register begins 1813 and continues to 1822. there are at this time three parish registers, one for Baptisms, one for Marriages, one for burials, duly secured in an iron chest under lock and key according to an act of parliament made the fifty second year of George the third.

Seats in the Church. The seats in the church (except the pews lately erected) have been repaired for time immemmorial at the publick expence of the parish.[20] There have been four pews erected south and south west, north and north west, by John Lee Esq[r]. Colworth in the parish of Sharnbrook, a faculty having been first duly taken out.[15]

Parish Clerk. There is also due to the parish clerk; for every wedding by publication of banns one shilling, by licence two and sixpence. For every house not included in the parish rates four pence for easter offerings. To the clerk who also acts as sexton for making a grave and ringing the bell eighteen pence.

2. Archdeacon Bonney's historical notices of churches, c.1820–1840

SHARNBROOK. This Church consists of a Tower with a coping pierced with Quarterfoils & the remains of pinnacles at the Corners from the centre rises a well formed Spire.[21] Nave and aisle, Chancel and Chapel on the North side of it. There are decorated Windows in the South Aisle & North Chapel. The rest are of the perpendicular. The Piers and arches are of the decorated. There are perpendicular Screens to Chancel & Chapel. The Font is octagonal & perpendicular with Panels Quarterfoils & Roses.[3] There are North & South Porches, & the Tower contains four (*sic*) Bells.[6] There is a Piscina in the Chancel & also in the South Aisle. There are three Sedilia under three Trefoil Arches in the Chancel. In the North Chapel is a Pew with good perpendicular panelling.[4] On a corbel at the End of a label Moulding on the North side of the nave is this head. [*Sketch of a Bishop's head*].

In the Nave under three Effigies in Brass is this Inscription.[45] "Of your Charite pray for the Soules of Will[m] Cobbe Smythe and Alys his wife and for the Soule of Thomas Cobbe theyr Son – which William decessyd the XXIII day of October Anno Domini MV°XXII and y[e] said Alys decessyd the XXIIII day of May."

Also "Here lyeth the bodies of Sibell Payne late wife of Wm Payne of Podington within this County Gent Daughter of Thomas Cobbe Gent. deceased, who died y[e] ... day of ... Anno Domini ... and of Elizabeth Cobbe one of the Daughters of Thomas Cobbe Gent. brother of the said Sibell who died y[e]... day of December Anno 1603.

On wood against the North Wall of the Chancel. "In the third Grave lyeth the Body of M[r] W[m] Cobb who died the 4th of Nov[r] 1675 leaving a Son named W[m] by Mrs Sarah Cobb his Wife, both surviving." Under this the following armorial Bearing. [*Sketch of coat of arms*].

3. Archdeacon Bonney's visitation notebook, 1823–1839

SHARNBROOK. This Church consists of a Nave, North and South Aisles, Tower surmounted by a Spire at the West end of the Nave and Chancel at the East end thereof. Porches North & South of the Aisles.

At the visitation of 1823 the following Order was given that the Earth be moved from the Exterior of the Walls; the Stonework of the Windows and

4.Sharnbrook: SW view showing the tower and spire with the stumps of the missing pinnacles. A window in the south wall of the chancel is accidentally omitted in this version of the picture. The sketch below the main view illustrates the carved head and arms of the Braybrook family of Colworth (extinct in the male line by 1429) from a label stop on the north arcade

(Engraving: Thomas Fisher 1812)

Doors be restored with Parker's Cement; the Walls pointed; the open Seats be cleansed and oiled; the Pulpit and Reading Desk be oak grained;[7] the Font be cleansed & repaired;[3] the Belfry be cleansed; the Pillars be coloured to resemble Stone; the Ten Commandments be newly painted;[17] a proper Font Bason, a Prayer Book of the Largest Volume, and a plated Flagon be purchased.[40]

At the Visitation of 1826. The only order deemed necessary was as follows that The Windows so far as the Stone Work was defective, be restored with Parker's Cement; and the Framework above the Screen at the Entrance into the Chancel be removed.

At the Visitation of 1833. Nothing was ordered or required.

At the Visitation of 1836 ordered that the Cornice on the South Side of the Church be restored with Parker's Cement.

At the Visitation 1839 – Ordered the Church Warden to remove the Elder Bushes from the battlements of the Steeple.

4. Article on the Church by W.A. (no.120), NM 30 September 1854

SHARNBROOK, St.Peter: Chancel, open roof, but is disfigured by two square boxes, one of which is amply supplied with green baize, rendering its ugliness more conspicuous.[26]

The arch has lately been displayed, and some seats, open and appropriate, have been fitted up – a striking contrast to the two above mentioned.

Some of the original wood carving of the screen has been used to make a small closet for the incumbent's robes.[4]

The nave has its open roof, and all here is in excellent order. Some of the benches are still preserved; we would indulge the hope that the hand that has gracefully restored the chancel will exert its influence in removing the ugly pews,[20] some of which are manufactured from the spoliation of the old oak benches.

This is too bad; those who require these separations from the common herd of worshippers should at least find their own materials.

Although the west window is not hidden from view, a singing gallery has been erected,[16] miserably interfering with the general view of the interior, and the congregation regularly face about when the music plays. If these instruments, with their choirs, were placed on the basement, galleries might be abolished, and this irreverent custom abandoned. A seat, said to be the property of the chief owner of the land, is fitted up in true parlour style; a suite of chairs such as would adorn an opera box, or a lady's boudoir.[14–5, 20] Wretched taste this. As Charles Lamb in one of his admirable essays said, the benchers must account for sundry alterations in his ancient Temple walks, so we think the learned and amiable antiquary of Hartwell must see to this.[15]

We omitted to mention that the remains of the chancel screen are bedaubed with paint, and amply supplied with hat pegs.[4]

The exterior is in very good order; the porch requires a little restoration.

5.Sharnbrook: A view of the interior showing the seats, pulpit and desk of 1858 in the nave, a massive cast iron stove and the screen at the entrance to the chancel. The C17th communion rails and the C18th hatchments of the Bullock family can be seen in the chancel

(Lithograph: Anonymous 1878)

The churchyard is locked, but is apparently well looked after, and did not bear the marks of cattle trampling the humble graves of the departed.
Sept 27, 1854   W.A.

5. Sir Stephen Glynne's Church notes, before 1840. (Vol.1, pp.29–30)
SHARNBROOK, St. Peter. This Church is not large, but has at the West end a lofty & handsome Tower & Spire, forming a fine object in the surrounding country. The whole of the steeple is of Curvilinear period, but plain – On the West side is a fine 3 light window lately restored, but singularly placed, being not in the centre – on one side of it is an ogee niche. The belfry windows are plain & of 2 lights – the parapet has a series of pierced quatrefoils – at the angles are the beginnings of pinnacles never completed.[21] The Spire is well proportioned & has 3 tiers of small windows. The body is somewhat low, but has some very good portions. The parapets are plain & there is no Clerestory. There are North & South porches – the Northern having fine Early English doorways with mouldings & shafts. The nave has on each side 4 pointed arches, with pillars alternately circular & octagonal. The windows are mostly Rectilinear of 3 lights in the nave, but one on the South

side is Curvilinear & very good, having internally very fine mouldings and shafts. The Chancel has some Rectilinear windows & one small early Curvilinear one of 2 lights. It has a North Aisle wider than that of the Nave, having some square headed Curvilinear windows & a wood screen.[2] There is also a screen between the nave & Chancel. The arch between the Chancel & its aisle is walled up, but the shafts from which it springs are clustered.[2] The font is octagonal, & richly panneled with quatrefoils, below which is a moulded band containing sprigs of foliage.[3]

Notes **1.** Pevsner pp.140–1, Harvey pp.470–6, *VCH* III pp.92–4, James Collett-White *St.Peter's Sharnbrook: A History and Guide* n.d. (1984). I am grateful to my colleague James Collett-White for kindly providing information on this church and for commenting on the text; **2.** The origins and history of the Tofte chapel are outlined by Collett-White (pp.40–1) and there is a short description of the house in *VCH* III p.88. Glynne mentions that the arch between the chancel and the chapel was walled up, but it was apparently opened up when the chancel was restored in about 1854. The chapel was restored by A.R.Alston in about 1908 (the date of the wooden screen between the chapel and chancel) and the archdeacon noted in 1910 that it had been restored (ABE 3). In 1910 Alston obtained a faculty for a grave–space outside the chapel (HCRO ref: DSA 2/1/198); **3.** The font, described by Bonney, was illustrated by Fisher (slide 864) and by Harvey (p.500). The cover was given in memory of Miss Edith Martineau (d.19 Feb.1909) in about 1910 (Collett-White p.34); **4.** Screens to the chancel and chapel are mentioned by Bonney, but the chapel screen must have been between the chapel and the north aisle as Glynne indicates that the connecting arch with the chancel was then blocked up. W.A. mentioned in 1854 that some of the original carving from the screen had been used to make "a closet for the incumbent's robes" and this may refer to the screen erected when the arch was reopened in about 1854. W.A. also states that the remains of the chancel screen were "bedaubed with paint and amply supplied with hat pegs". Parts of the 1636 pulpit and desk were used to repair the screen in 1858; **5.** Information from wills etc. noted by Collett-White (pp.8–9); **6.** There is a detailed account of the bells in Collett-White (pp.48–52), including information on the bells of c.1611–7, 1683, 1699 and 1887 and on the people named in the inscriptions. The restorations of 1882 and 1924 are also mentioned; **7.** The 1822 terrier mentions the 1636 pulpit and desk. The inscription means "preach the gospel". In 1823 Bonney ordered that the pulpit and desk be "oak grained". They were replaced in 1858 and the later pulpit and desk can be seen in Harvey's 1878 view of the interior. A new pulpit by Jones & Willis was provided in 1910 (faculty papers 1910, HCRO ref: DSA 2/1/198); **8.** Parish register memorandum concerning seats, 1659 (in P 112/1/2 – transcribed in BPRS Vol.24 p.B41); **9.** Bill for repairs to the chancel, 1687/8 (OR 1896 – text given in Collett-White p.39); **10.** There is a copy of the terrier of c.1708 in the parish register (P 112/1/2) but there is no terrier for Sharnbrook with Archdeacon Frank's registered copies (ABE 2); **11.** The 1708 terrier mentions a clock. The old Sharnbrook church clock is now (1998) in Felmersham church. It is of C17th date. It was saved by Capt. Stephen Helps Starey after the new clock was installed in 1924 and kept in a barn at Milton Ernest until 1984 when it was acquired and restored by Ken Shrimpton of Felmersham. The erection of a new dial was reported in *BT* 31 Dec.1861; **12.** The C17th communion rails are shown in Harvey's 1878 view of the interior, but they were replaced by new altar rails in 1901; **13.** The evidence for the C17th work on the roof and the C18th fire is discussed by Collett-White (pp.10–1); **14.** Faculty citation regarding a pew for Richard Antonie, 1768 (ABF 3/183) and related papers (ABCP 312–5). For the Antonie family see Michael Jones *Colworth in Context: A History of Colworth Estate, Bedfordshire, from 1720 to 1947* (Bedford 1997); **15.** Faculty for John Lee's pew in the south aisle, and another for his servants in the north aisle, 1818 (ABF 2 p.114, ABF 3/184–190 and BS 687), and faculty for two pews in north–west aisle for the tenants, 1821 (ABF 2 p.116, ABF 3/191–3 and BS 688). For Lee see Jones *op.cit.* and Dr. John Lee of Hartwell 1783–1866 (Buckinghamshire Record Office, n.d.) by H.A. Hanley; **16.** The diary of Edward Arpin of Felmersham records "A new Gearley [Gallery] Bulte at Sharn Brok 1824 And opned Octr the 3 1824" (AD 1714 – published in BHRS Vol.40 (1960) pp.139). W.A. mentions a singing gallery in 1854; **17.** Unusually, the 1822 terrier gives the positions of the Royal arms and commandments. When Charles Magniac bought the living in 1873 the Royal Arms were removed from the church and displayed in the entrance hall at Colworth (Jones p.161); **18.** Boissier (f.370d); **19.** Presentment, 1844 (ABCV 131); **20.** The register memorandum (note 8) shows that seats in the body of the church were already appropriated by 1659. Further faculty pews of 1768, 1818 and 1821 (notes 15 and 16) were installed for successive owners of the Colworth estate, and there were also pews in the chancel for the impropriator (note 26). W.A. alludes to the use of wood from the old open benches to make the enclosed pews, perhaps when the pews were "lately erected" as noted in the 1822 terrier and in the faculties of 1818 and 1821; **21.** Bonney noted "the remains of pinnacles" and Glynne thought the pinnacles were never completed. The letter from "F.S.A." in *BT* 27 May 1854 indicates that two of the pinnacles from the tower had been lying in the Tofte chapel for some years. The offer of help towards restoring them was not taken up, and it was not until the time of the Rev.C.E. Howlett (Vicar 1932–1949) that the present pinnacles and flying buttresses were erected in 1934 under Professor A.E. Richardson (HCRO ref: DSA 2/1/35/32); **22.** The east window commemorates John Gibbard (d.1849) and his wife Mary (d.1855). Probably by Charles Clutterbuck, it must have been put up in about 1855. Pevsner (p.141) describes the style as "still pictorial"; **23.** The sources for the restoration in 1855–8 include the vestry minutes and accounts (P 112/5/1), advertisement for tenders for the roof (*BT* 30 June 1855), faculty papers regarding seating (including plan) 1858 (HCRO ref: DSA 2/1/198 and copy of plan at BCRO ref: CRT 130 SHA 58), advertisement for tenders for seating and list of tenders (*BT* 27 March and 17 April 1858), and reports in *BT* 24 July 1858 and BAAS report 1858 (p.299). The work on the roof was completed by about March 1857, and the re–seating in 1858. Some of the source material listed here came to light since James Collett-White wrote his account of the restoration (pp.15–6); **24.** Payments to Mr. Stonebanks for new doors, 1866 (P 112/5/1); **25.** For the Magniac monument in the Tofte chapel and the mausoleum in the churchyard see J. Mordaunt Crook *William Burges and the High Victorian Dream* (1981) pp.153–4 and Collett-White (pp.16–7, 41 and 46); **26.** The enclosed pews in the chancel belonging to the Gibbard family as lay rectors were described by W.A. in 1854. One of them was "amply supplied with green baize, rendering its ugliness more conspicuous". They were removed in 1871 (noted in Collett-White (p.38) and in *BS* 25 Dec.1895) and the woodwork was taken to Sharnbrook House; **27.** The stained glass window commemorates John Gibbard (d.1871) and was erected in 1873 (Harvey p.474); **28.** Bathurst's notebook (ABE 3); **29.** For Wilkinson's incumbency generally see Collett-White (pp.17–21); **30.** The removal of the organ – apparently from the west gallery to the Tofte chapel – is mentioned in the 1858 faculty papers (HCRO ref: DSA 2/1/198). The later history of the instrument from 1879 is summarised by Collett-White (pp.17–8, 20, 24 and 32). There is additional information in a report of the installation of a new organ (*BM* 30 Sept.1893), the faculty papers of 1895 (HCRO ref: DSA 2/1/198) when it was proposed "to take out and sell the old organ at present in the side chapel on the north of the chancel" and "to remove the present organ from the west end of the church into the said side chapel". The faculty was opposed and this work was not carried out, but the documents provide evidence that there were two organs by 1895. There is also a faculty for the organ case and for other alterations by Trustam, 1907 (HCRO ref: DSA 2/1/198). This work was reported in the Deanery Magazine in 1908 (P 80/30/1); **31.** The work on the tower and spire in 1881 was reported in *BT* 4 June and in *BT* and *BM* 12 Nov.1881, and details are given in Kelly's *Directory* 1885 (p.107). The spire was again restored in 1913 (P 112/28/6) and the pinnacles were rebuilt in 1934 (note 21); **32.** For Stileman-Gibbard's activities see Collett-White (pp.18–21); **33.** The controversy of 1893–6 is documented in Archdeacon Bathurst's notebook (ABE 3), a statement of Stileman-Gibbard's right (P 112/28/3), the 1895 faculty papers (HCRO ref: DSA 2/1/198), and reports in *BM* 5–26 Aug.1893 and 5 Dec.1896 and *BS* 25 Dec.1896. Events are described by Collett-White (pp.18 and 38). Bathurst commented "the Vicar's rights were decided to be non-existent. I venture to suggest that the case was not properly argued in court"; **34.** Vestry minutes regarding faculty application (P 112/5/1) and faculty papers, 1895 (HCRO ref: DSA 2/1/198). The architect for the scheme was Henry Young; **35.** The new heating system was first used on 15 Jan.1899 (*BS* 20 Jan.1899), and the confirmatory faculty was issued on 22 June 1899 (P 112/2/2) after it had been certified by an architect "that the stability of the church had not been endangered by the construction of the heating apparatus nor had the risk of fire been increased" (HCRO ref: DSA 2/1/198); **36.** The porch repairs are noted by Collett-White (pp.18, 21); **37.** The vestry minutes of 1902–4 refer to the chancel roof repairs (P 112/5/1); **38.** The wrought iron lectern is by Starkie

Gardener & Co of London, 1900 (Collett-White p.20), and it is documented in the faculty papers (HCRO ref: DSA 2/1/198); **39.** The sanctuary paving, altar rail, and reredos were installed by faculty in 1901 (HCRO ref: DSA 2/1/198). They are also documented in the Powell archives (V&A ref: AAD 1/63 p.329) and in a report in *BS* 18 Oct.1901. Pevsner (p.141) wrongly describes the reredos as "probably of c.1855 ... a typical piece"; **40.** The old plate is described in the terriers of 1708 and 1822. Bonney ordered the purchase of a new plated flagon in 1823. A list of plate prepared in 1924 (ABE 5) indicates that the present cup and paten (date-lettered 1898 and 1892 respectively) were presented in 1910; **41.** There are plans by Gotch & Saunders for the lych gate, 1910 (RDBP 1/126). The lych gate and parsonage of 1910 are noted by Collett-White (pp.22 and 45) who states that Charles Saunders, the architect, lived in Sharnbrook at the time; **42.** Faculty for the stained glass in the porch erected as "A Thank Offering for the hospitality shown by the people of Sharnbrook to the children of London September 1939" (HCRO ref: DSA 2/1/59/71); **43.** The work of 1951 to 1971 is summarised by Collett-White (pp.25–8) and documented in the ICBS file (LPL ref: ICBS 13058); **44.** For the churchyard gates of 1963 <u>see</u> article by George Wilkinson in *B.Mag* Vol.IX no.68 (Spring 1964) pp.149–50; **45.** For the brasses, <u>see</u> Lack *et.al.* (p.84).

SHEFFORD

Although Shefford was an established market town by the C13th[1] it did not become a separate ecclesiastical parish until 1903.[2] The church was a chapel of ease in the parish of Campton, apparently used only for "divine service" until provision was made for the celebration of communion services in 1853.[3] By 1708 there was a brick font but all baptisms were recorded in the Campton registers until 1902.[4] The chapel was licensed for marriages from 1873.[5] There is no burial ground.[6]

The chapel is of mediaeval origin and its substantial rectangular tower dates from the C14th. Little else is known of the original building. Its site was hemmed in by other buildings, but after adjoining properties were acquired in 1822 and 1847 the chapel was rebuilt and enlarged.[7] Major structural work was undertaken at various dates between 1807 and 1933 but it is hard to determine exactly what was done because the entire building has been re–faced in a uniform style. Consequently there have been several different interpretations of the present building.[8] On the evidence now available it seems that the outer shell (including the south aisle)[9] is essentially of 1822–3 although the east end was rebuilt in its present position when the church was extended to the east in 1852–3.

Parish accounts of 1691 refer to minor repairs at the chapel,[10] and there are inventories of 1705 and 1708 which list its furniture and ornaments.[11] These included a green pulpit cushion, a bell, and a clock.[12] From 1791 the chapelwardens' vouchers provide information on the upkeep of the chapel and there are vestry minutes from 1809.[13]

In 1807 a faculty was obtained for enlarging the chapel which was virtually rebuilt on its existing site in 1808. It was also re-seated at a cost of £338.[14] At the same time, the old porch was taken down and a new engine house was erected on the north side of the church for the parish fire engine.[15] The seating was increased in 1814, but by the early 1820s the accommodation

6. Shefford: This view shows the church as rebuilt and enlarged in 1807–8, with simple "Y" tracery in the windows. Notice the rectangular C14th tower, the projecting clock dial and the engine house (with instructions on the doors regarding the keys)

(Watercolour: Thomas Fisher c.1815)

was inadequate for the "population growing rapidly as the navigation of the river Ivel will shortly be brought up to Shefford". In 1822 the Rector of Campton purchased an adjoining house and garden so that the chapel could be enlarged. After the addition of the south aisle and extensive remodelling, apparently to the designs of John Austin, the chapel was reopened on 26 October 1823.[16]

Further ground was acquired in 1847, money being borrowed to pay for the site.[17] In January 1852 an appeal was launched for £500 to alter and enlarge the chapel and add an extension at the east end.[18] The leaflet states that there was no chancel or communion table,[3] and the subscription list includes a promise of "communion rails & pulpit cloth" from the Rector. By November 1852 building work was in progress,[19] and the enlargement was completed in 1853 at a cost of £775.[20] Freshwater was the contractor, and the architects may have been either Wing & Jackson of Bedford who were paid for a survey or a Mr. Parker who received twelve guineas for plans.

After the church had been remodelled, various improvements were made. An organ was installed by subscription in 1862,[21] new communion plate by

Cox & Sons was provided in 1875,[22] and in about 1892 a stained glass window was placed in the south aisle in memory of Sir George Osborn of Chicksands.[23]

In 1894 Archdeacon Bathurst noted cracks and other defects in the church.[24] Fund-raising began in 1896 and although no major work was done until ten years later the gallery under the tower was removed in 1901 and alterations to the seating were carried out in 1902 when the organ and pulpit were moved.[25] Mallows and Grocock prepared a scheme for restoration in 1901, and their proposals were eventually carried out in 1906–7 when the church was re-roofed, re-floored, re-seated and provided with new sanctuary furnishings.[26] In 1910 the new Archdeacon approved of the improvements, but he considered the arrangement of the twin naves "unsatisfactory ecclesiastically" and noted that the tower was in urgent need of repair.[24] Proposals were drawn up in 1913–4 but abandoned on the outbreak of War and the tower was eventually restored in 1928.[27]

The Rev. G.H. Strange (Vicar 1920–1934) oversaw extensive repairs and improvements to the church.[28] A new organ was dedicated in 1922.[21] In 1925 additional land to the south and east of the church was acquired for possible enlargement and some repairs were undertaken, especially at the east end. Professor Richardson, who had restored the tower in 1928, was also responsible for improvements to the interior completed in 1933 when a brick arcade was built to replace the old cast iron columns between the two sides of the church.[29] Between 1931 and 1937 three stained glass windows by Warren Wilson were placed in the church.[30]

Further work was carried out in the 1970s, and in 1993–4 space on the north side of the church was converted to provide modern facilities and new parish rooms.[31]

1. Extract from glebe terrier, 5 July 1822

SHEFFORD.

Chapel yard. Chapel Yard 43 feet East and West, 32 feet North and South.[7] Pale fenced next the Street with one Gate North.

Chapel. Imprimis Shefford Chapel, 55 feet East and West, 17 feet North and South inside the Walls. The Tower 17 feet by 10 feet 8 inches.

Furniture and ornaments.[3] One Bell,[12] one Bier, three fire–hooks,[15] one Clock,[12] one Bible Folio, one Common Prayer Book, one Surplice, one Chest, purple Pulpit Cloth and Cushion.

Parish Officers. One Chapel Warden and two Overseers chosen annually by the Inhabitants in Vestry, on or about the 25th day of March.

2. Archdeacon Bonney's historical notices of churches, c.1820–1840

SHEFFORD, St. Michael. This chapel has nothing worthy of remark,[8] except its Tower, which is at the West End, and is of the Decorated Character with a plain Coping. The rest of the Fabrick which is modern except the East end, consists of Two Aisles.[9]

3. Archdeacon Bonney's visitation notebook, 1823–1839

SHEFFORD. This Chapel consists of Two Aisles, the northern of which may now be called a Nave having the Tower at the West end thereof. There is no Communion Table, the Lord's supper being solemnized only at the Mother Church at Campton.[3] There is no burial ground about the Chapel.[6]

At the Visitation of 1823 no orders were given the Archdeacon finding at that time the South Aisle not compleated.[9] And at the Visitation of 1826 – no order necessary.

At the Visitation of 1833 no order required.

At the visitation of 1836 – ordered that a crack at the South East corner be filled with good cement.

At the Visitation 1839 Recommended the Church Warden to wainscot the East End as high as the Seats, and to stucco above it, as a finish to that part of the Chapel.

Notes **1.** For the origins of Shefford and its market see *VCH* II p.268 and "Shefford" by Eric Rayner in *Beds. Mag.* Vol.8 no.62 (Autumn 1962) pp.247–53; **2.** The parish of Shefford was created from Campton, Clifton and Southill in 1903 (Youngs p.9); **3.** No plate is listed in the terriers of 1705/8 or in 1822 and Bonney's statement that "The Lord's supper is solemnized only at the Mother Church at Campton" indicates that communion was not administered at Shefford. This became possible after the alterations of 1852–3; **4.** The font is mentioned in the 1708 terrier (ABE 2 Vol.I p.382). The separate register of baptisms for Shefford begins in 1902; **5.** The Shefford registers of marriages and banns commence in 1873 and 1874 respectively; **6.** Burials took place at Campton until a new cemetery was opened at Shefford in 1903 by the Campton and Shefford Burial Board (established in 1854). The cemetery registers survive from 1903 (X 842); **7.** No deeds have been found, but the additions of 1822 and 1847 are assumed to be on the south and east sides of the church respectively. The dimensions in the 1822 terrier indicate the constricted size of the original site; **8.** Pevsner p.142, *VCH* II pp.269–70, *A History of St.Michael & All Angels, Shefford* n.d. [c.1958 – reissued 1962]. Pevsner says, unequivocally, that the church was built in 1822 while the guide suggests a restoration of the north side in 1828 and enlargement in 1850; **9.** Bonney's visitation orders for 1823 refer to the south aisle "not compleated" and his later notes describe the chapel as having "two aisles". This seems to provide conclusive evidence that the south aisle was built in 1822–3, and the iron columns must have been contemporary with the enlargement; **10.** Churchwardens' accounts for the parish of Campton and Shefford, 1691 (P 18/5/1), printed in the guide (p.4); **11.** There are two inventories, one of 1705 (in P 18/5/1 – noted in the guide p.4) and the other of 1708 (ABE 2 Vol.1 p.382); **12.** The present bell was cast in 1808 (North p.184). The clock probably dates from the C17th. In the early C19th it had a projecting dial which can be seen in contemporary illustrations of the church (slides 674 and 2267) and in Fisher's general view of the High Street (slide 283). By 1905 (Z 240/62) this had been replaced by an ordinary dial in the north side of the tower; **13.** Churchwardens' vouchers 1790–1829 (P 70/5/1a) and vestry minutes 1809–1895 (P 70/8/1–2); **14.** Faculty for alterations to the chapel, 1807 (ABF 2 p.102 and ABF 3/194–5) and statement regarding the work of 1807–8 in later ICBS papers (LPL ref: ICBS 403). There is a reference to subscriptions to church repairs in 1808 (M 10/5/595) and Fisher's view (slide 2267) shows the appearance of the chapel after these alterations had been completed with simple "Y tracery" on the north side; **15.** There are bills (P 70/5/1a) of 1807–8 for erecting the engine house which can be seen on the north side of the church in Fisher's view (slide 2267). The doors carried a note of where they keys were kept! The 1822 terrier lists three fire hooks in the church; **16.** The ICBS papers 1822–4 (LPL ref: ICBS 403) are the main source for the acquisition of the adjoining property and enlargement of the church in 1822–3, and refer to the additional seating provided in 1814. There are no plans, but Austin signed the certificate of completion as "surveyor"; **17.** Deeds for enlargement of chapel ground, 1847 (P 70/5/2) and mortgage with related papers (P 70/5/3); **18.** Appeal leaflet and subscription list, 1852 with manuscript additions (X 254/73); **19.** A report in *BT* 13 Nov.1852 refers to the enlargement of the chapel and mentions that a workman was attacked by an adder!; **20.** Accounts, 1853 (P 70/5/4). In addition to the main contract, Freshwater was paid £36 "for pulpit, reading desk and communion rails etc" and Johnson received £5 "for set of Commandments". Given the cost of the work, it seems likely that Freshwater was also responsible for the complete refacing of the building in ironstone with limestone dressings at this time; **21.** Vestry minute regarding the organ, 1862 (P 70/8/1). A new organ was proposed in 1914 and in 1915 the parish received an offer of £150 from Andrew Carnegie towards the cost (P 70/2/8). A new organ was eventually installed in 1922 (guide p.9). It was replaced in 1995 by an organ from a church in Hitchin; **22.** Schedule of plate 1925 (ABE 5) lists the plate of 1874–5; **23.** Osborn died in 1892 and Archdeacon Bathurst noted the new window when he visited in 1894 (ABE 3). The new window was reported in *BE* 2 and 9 June 1894; **24.** Bathurst's notebook (ABE 3); **25.** The work of 1901–2 was reported in *BS* 3 May and 22 Nov.1901 and 10 and 24 Oct.1902, and in *BC* 25 Oct.1901 and 9 May 1902, but it is not easy to distinguish between proposals and work done. The guide (p.8) states that the gallery was removed in 1904. In 1905 Bathurst noted "Pulpit has been put in better position & other improvements, but sadly needed" (ABE 3); **26.** The sources for the work of 1906–8 include bills (P 70/5/7), accounts (P 70/2/7 and in P 70/8/2), the ICBS papers (LPL ref: ICBS 10691), and report in *BC* 9 Nov.1906. The work included new heating (Kilpin & Billson), a new font cover (Page), and furnishings for sanctuary (Wippell, Mowbray and Jones & Willis); **27.** Minutes of tower restoration committee 1914–21 (P 70/2/8), accounts 1928 (in P 70/5/7), letter in SPAB archives complimenting Richardson on the work, and account in report of the Council for the Care of Churches for 1928–9 p.48; **28.** Work during Strange's incumbency noted in the guide (p.9); **29.** Faculty for the new brick arcade, 1933 (P 70/2/16) and the comments of the Vicar of Henlow who attended the reopening service in July 1933 (P 39/0/5); **30.** Faculties for windows, 1931–7 (P 70/2/15–7); **31.** There is a logbook of the work done in 1974–9 (P 70/2/25).

SHELTON

Shelton is mentioned in the Domesday book of 1086 and the church may be of Anglo-Saxon origin.[1] The east end of the north arcade dates from the late C12th and the south aisle may have also been first built by 1300. The chancel was rebuilt in the C13th but the fine Decorated east window dates from the C14th when the north chapel and west tower were also added to the church. The clerestory was added to the nave in the C15th.[2] The church has a delightfully unrestored interior, with a Perpendicular screen, a C14th font,[3] old benches, a C16th pulpit,[4] some fragments of mediaeval stained glass,[5] and several wall-paintings.[6]

There is an Elizabethan communion cup of 1569.[7] One of the three bells is dated 1599.[8] There is another of 1634, and the bells hang in an early C17th frame in which there are pits for four. The clock is said to have been exchanged for a bell with the neighbouring parish of Hargrave, apparently before 1700.[9] In the church there is an alms box of 1620.[10] One of the bells was recast in 1770,[8] and by 1840 a C18th plated flagon had been added to the plate.[7]

A note in the parish register records that in 1823 "the floor of the Chancel was levelled, and raised at the Altar, and a new pew erected".[11] Bonney ordered various minor repairs in 1823, and in 1826 he told the Rector to repair

7. Shelton: South view of the church before it was restored in 1931 by Professor Albert
Richardson.   *(Photograph: Unknown c.1930)*

the partition between the chancel and the north chapel which was then used
as a vestry.[12] In 1833 the Archdeacon ordered repairs to the tower which was
soon afterwards strengthened with iron bands.[13] There are mid C19th boards
for the ten commandments, Lord's prayer and creed.[14] W.A. gives an account
of the condition and appearance of the church in 1852, drawing attention to
the vestry in the north chapel,[12] the private pews,[15] a stove in the chancel and
heavy applications of whitewash and paint on the stonework including the
font.[3] In 1863 the curate carved a wooden lectern for New College, Oxford,
exercising "his art for the benefit of the restoration fund" of Shelton church.[16]
The Victorian lectern now in the church may also be the work of the same
curate, the Rev. Robert Sibley Baker.[17]

No major work was to be done to the church until 1931. Archdeacon
Bathurst's notebook chronicles the progress of decay from 1874.[18] A visitor in
1887 described the tower as "very much dilapidated".[19] In 1894 Bathurst
noted the church as "most unsatisfactory as to reverent state of inside", adding
that the churchwarden had offered £500 if the building were to be pulled
down and replaced by a smaller church "but will give nothing for restoration
of present one".[18] In 1897 the clock dial was re-done for the Jubilee.[9] In 1908
a new concrete floor was laid in the north chapel and the church was cleaned
and colour washed in 1910.[20]

Having escaped the attention of the Georgian and Victorian restorers, the
church was eventually rescued from its near derelict condition in 1931 by
Professor Albert Richardson.[21] After a thorough but conservative restoration

in accordance with the principles advocated by the SPAB the church was reopened on 31 October 1931. Robert Marriott of Rushden was the contractor and Percy Bentham carved the new figure for the rood beam. Since then it has been carefully maintained and a further programme of restoration has recently been completed.

1. Extract from glebe terrier, 1 June 1822

SHELTON.

Church yard. The Church Yard containing two Roods and ten perches, the fence of which is repaired by the parish as far as it is walled, which is next to the Street, the other fence being part quickset and part dead fence is repaired by Mr. Harris the Lord of the Manor whose Ground and buildings lies next to it.

Church. Belonging to the said parish are first the Parish Church, an ancient building containing in Length Thirty feet six Inches, in breadth Thirty eight feet. The Chancel containing in length Twenty five feet, in breadth thirteen feet. The old Vestry Twenty five feet in length, and in breadth thirteen feet.[12] The Church Porch in length Eight feet, in breadth six feet. The Tower Eight feet by six feet within the Walls, in height Forty six feet six Inches.

Furniture and ornaments. Within and belonging to which are one Communion Table with a covering for the same of Green cloth, one linen cloth for the same with one napkin, one Silver Chalice,[7] one pewter Plate, one iron Chest, one Pulpit and reading Desk,[4] one Pulpit Cushion cover'd with red stuff cloth, one large Bible, one common Prayer Book &c &c. Two Surplices. The King's Arms with the ten commandments.[14]

Bells. Three Bells with their frames;[8] The first or least Bell Two feet in diameter with this inscription ("Praise God 1592"). The second Two feet four inches in diameter with this inscription ("Joseph Eyre S^t. Neots fecit 1720").[8] The third or largest Two feet six inches in diameter with an Ancient inscription ("Jesus Hominum Salvater Nazarenus Rex Judæorum Fili Dei miserere mei 1634"). There is also a Clock in the Tower.[9]

Parish Registers. A Register Book of Baptisms and Burials beginning 1565 and ending 1705. A Register Book of Baptisms, Marriages, and Burials commencing 1706 and terminating with the Baptisms and Burials 1812. A Register Book of Marriages commencing 1754 and terminating 1812. Register Books of Baptisms, Marriages and Burials beginning 1813 and continued to the present time.

Parish Clerk. There is also due to the Parish Clerk, for every Wedding by the publication of Banns Two shillings and sixpence, by Licence five shillings, For digging a Grave and Tolling the Bell two shillings, also a payment of three pounds annually from the Parish.

Church Land. The Church Land (in the Parish of Shelton) contains Three acres two Roods and Twenty two perches, is now let at Four pounds ten shillings per Year for the repairs of the Church,[22] bounded on the East by a Close of M[r]. Harris's and on the West by a Close of M[r]. Marchant's (in Rowley field). The Minister and Churchwardens Trustees.

2. Archdeacon Bonney's historical notices of churches, c.1820–1840
SHELTON, St. Mary. This Church consists of Nave, Aisles, Tower at the West End, Chancel and North Chapel.[12] Piers and Arches Early English. Most of the Windows are decorated. The rest are perpendicular. A Piscina at the End of the North Aisle at the Entrance into the Chapel, another in the Chancel, & another in the South Aisle. There is a small Arch on the North side of the Chancel with a Square hollow on one side of the bottom of it – for what purpose is unknown.[23] There is a South Porch. Chalice Silver Elizabethan, a pewter plate & plated Flagon.[7]
[*Sketches of:* Specimen of the Pier and Arch of the Nave; *secondly a triangular device* In the East Window; Pater, Filius, Spiritus Sanctus; *to illustrate the Trinity*].[5]

3. Archdeacon Bonney's visitation notebook, 1823–1839
SHELTON. This Church consists of a Nave, a Tower at the West end & Chancel at the East end thereof – a North Aisle and Chapel on the North side of the Chancel. A Porch on the South side –
At the Visitation of 1823 the following Order was given that the Earth be moved from the exterior of the walls; Casements be made in the North Aisle & South window of the Chancel; the Chapel on the North side of the Chancel be thoroughly cleansed;[12] the floors of the Steeple be thoroughly cleansed and repaired; shutters be placed in the Windows of the Bell Chamber; the Open Seats be taken to pieces, neatly repaired, set up again, cleansed and oiled; the other Pews be repaired;[15] the Stone work in the West window of the Tower be restored with Parker's Cement, before Easter 1825.
The only order given at the Visitation of 1826 was that the Rector repair the Partition between the Chancel and Chapel on the North Side thereof.[12]
At the Visitation of 1833 It was ordered that proper drainage be made on the South Side – the Tower be braced round by some able workman so effectually as to tie the whole together[13] – the Roof of the South Aisle be thoroughly repaired – the old & decayed Timber thereof be taken out – and that blue Slate be used instead of Lead for the covering thereof, if desired by the Parishioners. A new Prayer Book be purchased for the Minister, & that these repairs be compleated by the end of three years ensuing. The East and West ends of the Nave be also repaired.
At the Visitation 1836 a new Prayer Book for the Minister and the Bible to be repaired.
At the Visitation 1839 Ordered the Doors to be repaired and Oak grained – The Commandments, Lord's Prayer and Creed to be set up over the Arch to the Chancel.[14]

4. Article on the Church by W.A. (no.103), NM 6 November 1852

SHELTON, Virgin Mary. The chancel has an open roof, besmeared with the usual application. A stove seems here utterly unnecessary, unless it is for the sole benefit of the occupants of the two pews.[15]

The decorations of a piscina, quite choked up with plaster. A frightful wooden framing vainly attempts to conceal a portion of the building set apart for the reception of all manner of filth; anything so disgraceful in a church we have never before witnessed.[12]

Portions of the rood screen remain, for the most part hidden by a miserable arrangement of pulpit, reading desk, and a very comfortably cushioned and carpeted square box.[4]

The nave and aisles preserve their open roofs; where whitewash did not abound, paint did; the latter application is used elsewhere, leading us to believe that the practice of this art divides the palm with the lime brush. The columns are painted; one appears an interesting example.

The old open benches remain, but two particular boxes have been manufactured,[15] well covered with matting to preserve the sitters from the contagion of the columns, for which, in their eyes, painting is no security.

The western arch is boarded up, forming, as usual, a receptacle for various uncleanly affairs. In this instance it would appear unnecessary, since there is ample space in the dirty corner by the chancel.[12]

Some of the open benches have been used as a foundation for miserable wainscoting, that the choristers might be more elevated.

The font is painted,[3] has its leaden lining, but no drain; this matters not – it is not used. In fact, we much wonder why churchwardens do not turn out these useless appendages. They might adorn the incumbent's or their own gardens, or be turned into a horse-trough.*

A small portion of some early frescoe painting is left exposed to view;[6] how this ancient memorial has been suffered to remain we cannot explain. The alarmed churchwardens of a county parish, when they uncovered in the process of cleaning, a representation of Purgatory, Paradise, and St. Peter, on the chancel wall, took good care it should very speedily return to that concealment whence their care had unintentionally dragged it. We are no advocates for the worship of images, but surely these decorations are more harmless than the weeping cupids, urns, and other pagan ornaments which are allowed to be introduced, without any remonstrance; these, at least, should receive the same punishment. "I am no advocate," says a writer whom we have often quoted, "for image worship; but I am very sure that the Protestantism of London would have found itself quite as secure in a cathedral decorated with the statues of good men, as in one hung round with bunches of Ripston pippins."

From the architectural remains in the dirty corner already mentioned, it was most likely the site of a chantry chapel, now so ignominiously perverted.[12]

The porch is in bad condition, and has been sadly tampered with; the only wonder is to find the windows not blocked up, and no wicket.

The churchyard is kept locked, "Because things get in it." The pedestrian can, however, with little difficulty, jump the barrier.

The external part of the church exhibits decayed and decaying remains of its former beauty.

We omitted to mention that the stump supporting an alms chest remains.[10] Admirable satire on the state of the whole fabric.

n.d.   W.A.

* See one so appropriated in the Swan Inn yard, Bedford. We would wish to see the worthy proprietor turn this to at least a better use, as a receptacle for flowers in his beautifully arranged garden. It would be a graceful ornament, and a grateful act.

Notes **1.** The possibility of early work in the fabric is discussed by Michael Hare in "Anglo-Saxon work at Carlton and other Bedfordshire churches" in *BAJ* Vol.6 (1971) pp.38; **2.** Pevsner pp.142–3, RC article in *BT* 30 Nov.1900, *VCH* III pp.163–4, and *A brief guide to the Church of St.Mary's, Shelton* (1928). The *VCH* includes a description of the church before the 1930s restoration; **3.** There is a drawing of the font, done in 1852 (BL ref: Add.Ms.39920 f.46) ; **4.** The C16th pulpit was part of an ensemble, described by W.A. in 1852, consisting of pulpit, desk and a "very comfortably cushioned and carpeted square pew"; **5.** There are C19th drawings of glass quarries in the church (BL refs: Add.Ms. 39918 f.45; 39919 ff.24, 42, 88 and 92). Bonney sketched the emblem of the Trinity in the east window; **6.** The survival of paintings was noted by W.A. but the discovery of paintings was reported in 1910 (P 94/0/1). The paintings are described in the *VCH*; **7.** The plate listed in the 1916 schedule consists of the 1569 chalice and a flagon of old Sheffield plate of c.1780. The flagon mentioned by Bonney in c.1840 is not listed in the 1822 terrier; **8.** The 1708 terrier (ABE 2 Vol.I p.336) shows that there were then only three bells at Shelton. Of these the second was recast in 1770 (and not 1720 as noted in the 1822 terrier). Having been cracked for many years, the tenor bell of 1634 was repaired by welding in 1931 by Barimar Ltd, a London firm which pioneered this method of repair. This was reported in *The Engineer* 17 July 1931 and *The English Mechanic* 18 Sept.1931; **9.** The tradition of an exchange was noted in both parishes by North (p.185) and in the same author's *Church Bells of Northamptonshire* (1878) p.292. As the 1708 terrier mentions a clock at Shelton, the exchange with Hargrave must have already taken place. It is said that Shelton got the worst of the bargain because the tower was not tall enough to give sufficient fall for the clock weights. RC notes the refurbishment of the dial in 1897; **10.** The alms box noted by W.A. is now damaged, but it was intact when seen by the Rev.W.D. Sweeting in 1877 (BL ref: Add.Ms. 37178 f.20) and by L.H. Chambers (AD 3869/6 p.204); **11.** Parish register note on the chancel, 1823 (P 94/1/4); **12.** The 1822 terrier describes the north chapel as a vestry, and Bonney's orders of 1826 refer to the partition between the chapel and chancel. It seems to have been used as a vestry throughout the C19th, as described by W.A., and the account in the *VCH* indicates that it was separated from the chancel by a wooden screen with spikes and from the north aisle with a plaster partition; **13.** According to the guide the bands were put round the tower in 1833 by the blacksmith, Tirrell of Yelden, but a report of the restoration in 1931 states that the tower was strapped in 1840 by Mr. Richardson, blacksmith, of Kimbolton. No evidence has been found for either statement; **14.** The four boards for the commandments, Lord's prayer and creed are now in the tower. They were probably re-painted in about 1840 in response to Bonney's instructions; **15.** A new pew was erected in the chancel in 1823 (P 94/1/4). The pews in the nave are described by W.A. Some of the panels from the enclosed pews survive as panelling in the base of the tower; **16.** Report on the lectern for New College in *BT* 29 Dec.1863; **17.** The Rev. Robert Sibley Baker (c.1823–d.1897) was curate of Shelton from 1847–1866 and Rector of Hargrave from 1865 until his death in 1897. The Bakers owned the living of Hargrave from the early C19th, and when he became Rector the Rev. R.S. Baker personally superintended the rebuilding of the tower and spire in 1868. Another member of the family, William Lewis Baker, designed the 1892 organ chamber at Yelden; **18.** Bathurst's notebook (ABE 3); **19.** The notes of the Rev.W.D. Sweeting, 1877 (BL ref: Add.Ms. 37178 f.20); **20.** The work of 1908 and 1910 is noted in the service register (P 94/0/1); **21.** Sources on the 1931 restoration include the SPAB archives, and reports in *BT* 6 Nov.1931, *The Builder* 1 April 1932 (p.586 and pp.597–8), SPAB report no.55 (June 1932) pp.79–82, and Report of the Council for the Care of Churches for 1930–1 (pp.54–60); **22.** According to the guide this land produced £5 per annum in 1928; **23.** The *VCH* suggests that this was "probably to hold the *loculus* used in the Easter sepulchre".

SHILLINGTON

Standing proudly on a hilltop site, Shillington church is a prominent feature of the local landscape. The present building, largely of the C14th, replaced an earlier Norman church.[1] There is a C13th crypt under the east end.[2] The nave must have been built after 1333 when the Bishop of Lincoln ordered repairs. The east end is flanked by square turrets, and the frieze above the east window carries the rebus of Matthew Assheton (d.1400)[3] who is also commemorated by a fine brass in the church.[4] It was during Assheton's incumbency (1349–1400) that the whole church was completed, probably by about 1370. In the C15th a Perpendicular east window was inserted within the original opening. Inside, the church is in the form of a great hall, the chancel being partitioned off from the nave and aisles by fine wooden screens.[5] Mediaeval wills give an indication of the pre–Reformation interior in which there were several altars and a chapel of St.Giles.[6]

The church is particularly well documented in a series of churchwardens' accounts beginning in 1571 and much of the source material has already been published elsewhere.[7] The early accounts refer to the recasting of several bells between 1573 and 1588 and the present bells (dated between 1602 and 1638) and bellframe (1632) are also documented in the accounts.[8] A clock, apparently new in 1574, is mentioned in 1575.[9] The ten commandments, creed and Lord's prayer were set up in 1588.[10] There were extensive roof repairs in 1595 after the fall of part of the church. In 1604 the King's arms on canvas were set up in the church.[11] New flagons were bought in 1607.[12] In 1611 the wardens bought a poor box, setting up a new pulpit cover in the same year.[13] The accounts reflect the religious changes of the period, with the erection of Laudian altar rails in 1635, their removal in 1640, the sale of organ pipes and boards in 1648,[14] "pulling down the crosses & other worke about the Church & Churche lofte" in 1648, a new hour glass for the pulpit in 1654 and the reinstatement of the King's arms in 1660.[11] As well as the accounts, there is also an inventory of church goods dated 1640.[15] New plate was acquired in 1677 and 1702.[12]

Disaster struck in 1701 when the upper stages of the tower collapsed, causing damage to the west end of the church.[16] In 1705 it was reported that "the steeple is fallen down & lies in ruins".[17] By 1708 the bells had been salvaged and placed in the north aisle.[18] The small bell was hung among the ruins. Although the damaged parts of the church were repaired, the tower remained

8. Shillington: View of the north side of the church before it was restored in 1881–5, showing the west tower of 1750, the new "spike" of 1846 and the clerestory windows of 1778 or c.1810 in the chancel   (Photograph: Unknown c.1870)

in a ruined state until the Rev. George Story set about finishing the repairs. Some of the money was raised by brief in 1746.[19] The work was completed in 1750, as recorded on a stone tablet on the south side of the tower. A small stone in the clock chamber also bears the date 1750 with the name of Matthew Lacy who may have been one of the workmen involved in the rebuilding.

There are no churchwardens' accounts for the period 1666 to 1775, but terriers of 1708, 1724, 1745 and 1763 provide detailed information on the church and its furniture and ornaments in the mid C18th.[20] Panels of lead from the roof record repairs in 1764 and 1774, and on the north and south sides of the chancel clerestory there are dated rainwater heads of 1778. This may have been when the chancel was restored by Samuel Whitbread, whose architect placed "churchwarden gothic" tracery in the three easternmost clerestory windows and ceiled the chancel.[21] Although not documented in the surviving accounts, other alterations to the church in the C18th or early C19th evidently included the erection of a new pulpit and desk,[13] a singing gallery,[22] and new boards for the commandments, creed and Lord's prayer.[10] Several private pews were also erected in the church.[23] There is a faculty of 1826 for Mr. Musgrave's pew.[24]

Bonney ordered extensive repairs in 1823 and 1826 and the accounts record expenditure of over £150 on the church in 1825–7.[25] The churchwardens also bought a new flagon[12] and had the font moved as required by the Archdeacon.[26] Further work was carried out in 1829 when John Stevens of Clophill plastered the inside of the church, and in 1830 repaired "the coping of the church together with the cornices and butments connected with the same".[27] The small service bell was recast in 1828,[8] and in 1829 two Windsor chairs were bought for the vestry room.[28] Also of this period were the constables' staves bearing the crest of King William IV, purchased at the time of the agricultural unrest in the County in 1830–1.[29] Dilapidations on the chancel were assessed in 1834 and repairs to the east end were carried out a few years later.[30] The vestry minutes provide information on work done to the roof and steeple by Lot Richardson in 1840 and 1846.[31] A new church clock was set up in 1839.[9]

Under the Rev. J.A. Frere (incumbent 1853–1877) several improvements were made to the church. A finger and barrel organ by J.W. Walker was obtained in 1858.[14] In 1861 Frere personally constructed a new pulpit.[13] William Watson of Henlow advised on roof repairs in 1862, and in 1875 the partition between the church and tower was removed.[32] Improvements to the belfry were undertaken at this time. The stone work of one of the north windows was restored in 1877 as a memorial to Frere.[33] A brass lectern was presented to the church in 1878.[34]

In 1874 Archdeacon Bathurst described the church as in "substantial repair but sadly needs complete restoration".[35] The parish embarked on a major restoration programme in 1881.[36] The architect was Vincent Wing.[37] In 1882 Trinity College, Cambridge, restored the chancel, removing the plaster ceiling and placing proper tracery in the clerestory windows. The first stage of repairs to the body of the church was completed by August 1882, the south side being restored first. Work on the north side began in 1883, and the dated rainwater heads of 1885 mark the end of the main restoration.

After the church had been restored, attention turned to the fittings and ornaments. The bells were rehung in 1883.[8] In 1886 the east window was filled with stained glass by Shrigley & Hunt of Lancaster.[38] A new communion cup[12] was presented in 1888 by the Rev. J.A. Bonser (d.1898) who is commemorated by the pulpit[13] of 1898 and a stained glass window[39] in the south chapel designed and made by his friend the Rev. Charles Kerry, Rector of Upper Stondon. Under the Rev.Langdale Postgate (Vicar 1898–1934) new altar rails were provided in 1907, in 1908 Charles Baker of Pirton Hall gave new candlesticks made from old oak from Winchester Cathedral, and in 1910 the church received the gift of a fine jewelled processional cross. Full details of these and other gifts to the church during Postgate's incumbency are to be found in an inventory of the time.[40]

In 1911 the tower was restored and a new belfry screen erected.[41] In 1918 a faculty was obtained to restore and open out the south chapel and for other work.[42] This involved moving the organ to the north side of the church in 1919,[14] the erection of an external pulpit (known locally as Postgate's folly!) on the north side of the church in 1920,[43] and the restoration of the south chapel as a war memorial in 1920.[44] Further improvements to the pulpit, tower screen and sanctuary were completed in 1928.[45] Access to the crypt was improved in 1932,[2] and in 1938 a stained glass window was erected in memory of Postgate.[46] More recently, in 1993, a striking new stained glass window has been placed in the north aisle as a memorial to members of the Hillyard family.

1. Extract from glebe terrier, 28 June 1822 [47]

SHITLINGTON.

Church yard. Item the Church-yard containing Two Acres Two Perches adjoining the Vicarage Garden and the Grounds of Trinity College Cambridge on the South, to the Grounds of the said Trinity College on the West, to the Grounds of the said Trinity College on the North, and to the White Horse public house belonging to John Pryor Esquire on the East. The fences on the West, North and part of the South side are Kept up by the Parish.[48]

Church. Belonging to the said Parish are first the Parish Church, an ancient building containing in length with the chancel Ninety feet, in breadth Fifty two feet. The Chancel in breadth Twenty feet. The two Aisles on each side of the Chancel in breadth Sixteen feet each. The Steeple in breadth Fourteen feet and a half by Seventeen and a half within the walls, in height Sixty feet.[16]

Furniture and ornaments. Within and belonging to the Church are One Communion table with a covering for the same of Green cloth. One Linen cloth for the same and Two Napkins. One Silver Chalice and Paten.[12] One Bason for the Offertory. One Chest with three locks (in the Keeping of the Churchwardens).[49] One Pulpit and Reading desk.[13] One Pulpit Cushion covered with Green cloth. One large Bible of the last Translation. One large Common Prayer Book.[50] The Book of Homilies. The King's Arms[11] with the Ten Commandments.[10] Five Bells with their Frames.[8] The First or least Bell being Two feet Ten inches and a half in Diameter with this Inscription (Praise the Lord 1602). The second Bell Two feet Eleven inches and a half in Diameter with the same Inscription (Praise the Lord 1638). The third Bell Three feet Two inches and a half in Diameter with this Inscription (Be yt Knowne to all that doth me see, that Newcombe of Leicester made mee 1603). The fourth Bell Three feet Seven inches in Diameter with this Inscription (Non clamor sed amor cantat in aure Dei 1624). The fifth or largest Bell Four feet in Diameter with this Inscription (Cum cano busta mori cum pulpita vivere disce, Disce mori nostro viveri disce sono 1624). Also one other little Bell. One Bier. One Hearse cloth. Two Surplices.

Parish Registers. Three Parchment Register Books, the first beginning in

1543 and ending in 1653, containing Baptisms, Marriages and Burials, The second beginning in 1653 and ending in 1812, containing Baptisms and Burials up to 1812, and Marriages up to 1754. The third containing Marriages only, beginning 1754 and ending 1812. Also Three other Parchment Register Books one containing Baptisms, one Marriages, and one Burials each beginning in 1813 and continued up to the present time.

Parish Clerk. There is also due to the Parish Clerk for every Funeral Five shillings, for every Wedding by publication of Banns Two shillings and Sixpence, by Licence Five shillings, for every Christening one shilling, and for every Churching of Women Sixpence.

2. Archdeacon Bonney's historical notices of churches, c.1820–1840

SHITLINGTON OR SHEDLINGTON, All Saints. This beautiful Church consists of a Nave, Aisles, Chancel and side Chapels reaching the whole length of the Chancel. A Tower of brick supplies the place of the original Tower, which fell at the beginning of the last Century.[16] Beneath the Chancel is a Crypt,[2] the Entrance to which is from the East End of the North Chapel. The String Course below the parapet of the East End of the Chancel is ornamented with a Rose (or Flower) with a P in the centre of it.[3] The next has an A, the next an Ox (or Bull) and the last a Tun [*Sketch of a tun*]. There is a rich decorated Rood Screen, and there are similar Screens on the Sides of the Chancel & at the West Entrance of the Chapel.[5] the general Character of the Piers, Arches and Windows is the decorated. The East End of the Chancel is flanked by two Square stair case Turrets. The position of this church is remarkable. Inscriptions on the Communion Plate are,[12] on the chalice, "Shitlington Church Plate 1702", the same on the Cover – on the Patin, "Shitlington Parish Plate Dec 1777." Instead of a Flagon there is a plated Cup with Two Handles & a Cover.

3. Archdeacon Bonney's visitation notebook, 1823–1839

SHITLINGTON. This Church consists of a Nave, North and South Aisles, a Tower at the West end of the Nave, and Chancel at the East End thereof – on the sides of the Chancel are Chapels, being continuations of the North & South Aisles.

At the Visitation of 1823 It was ordered that the Eastern part of the Roof of the Nave be repaired,[25] but the old work neither altered not painted; the Door on the South side of the South Chapel be new faced; according to the Original Pattern; and the other Doors of the Church be repaired and oak grained; The open Seats be repaired, cleansed and oiled; the Bible & Prayer Book be repaired;[50] The Old Flagon and Bason be changed for new ones;[12] The Stonework of the Doors and Windows be restored with Parker's Cement; The Font be cleansed from Wash; and repaired with Parker's Cement.

At the Visitation of 1826 the following Order was given That a Cover to the font of a proper Form be made; & the Font be moved to the End of the South Aisle;[26] the top of a pew to be removed, which has been erected without leave;[24] The Cornices be renewed with proper Cement, and the Walls pointed;[27] the wood work in a North window to be replaced with Stone as originally the Case.

There is a Charity here out of which 16[s]. per ann is paid to the repair of the Church –

The glebe House is a Cottage.

At the Visitation of 1833. It was ordered that the Communion cup be put into shape[12] – & a new Pall be purchased[51] – The Arch now blocked up by the King's Arms[11] be restored –

At the Visitation of 1836. Ordered that the North Door and also the Staircase Door leading up to the Roof be repaired. The seat at the bottom of the Nave be repaired and cleansed.[23] A new Pall be purchased[51] – the Old Surplice be mended, proper drainage made under the Spouts – The Turrits at the East End to be repaired and the Door thereunto belonging[30] – The gudgeon of one of the wheels of a Bell to be repaired – The Communion Cup to be put into Shape.[12]

At the Visitation 1839 Ordered the Church Wardens to have the Timbers of the Western Bay of the Roof of the Nave examined and substantially repaired – and such of the Leads as are decayed to have re-cast.[31] The Communion Table Cloth to be repaired – The floors of the Open Seats, of Mr. Musgrave's Servants Pew and a Pew at the West End of the Nave to be repaired[24] – The Turrets at the East End belonging to the Chancel to be repaired[30] – NB. Mr. Richard Paine, Churchwarden June 29th 1839 wrote to me that the Bursar of Trin. Coll. Camb. Impropriators had given an order to the Occupier of the Rectory Farm to have this done without delay.

4. Article on the Church by W.A. (no.56), NM 24 April 1847

SETHLINGDUNE (SHITLINGTON), All Saints. This is another of the fine churches of Bedfordshire; built on a commanding situation, rendering it a conspicuous and interesting object from various points.

The chancel has a ceiled roof;[21] an eastern window with very ordinary glazing. The children are most unjustifiably placed on forms, in this part, during Divine service. Square pews are also here – very ugly – containing tables, forming a convenient resting–place, we suppose, for the boas, parasols, or reticules of the occupants.[23] Nothing can be more out of harmony than such wretched fittings-up. When will the Clergy set their flocks the example of polishing these miserable innovations, denounced by so many of the highest dignitaries of our Church. 'The time will come, ere long,' says Archdeacon Hare, 'when the example set (in Sussex) by such true members of our aristocracy will be catching; when the pens and sties by which our churches have been so long disfigured will be swept away; when people will become ashamed of sitting imprisoned in their lonely cells, and will feel that the noblest and most blessed position for the high as well as the low is that of a member of the congregation of the Lord.' Here also we again observed a musical instrument,[22] indicating that the irreverent practice noticed at Higham Gobion obtains here. A portion of the south aisle is boarded off as a vestry, to the great disfigurement of the church, increased by the ugly chimney-shaft poked through the roof, rendered most offensively conspicuous. When the chancel was disfigured by a plaster ceiling, it became necessary to deprive the clerestory windows of their fair proportion,[21] thus adding another instance of the injury this lath-and-plaster substitute for the timber roof creates. The rood-screen is in good order, most probably oak, but it has not escaped the painter's daubing.[5]

The nave has a timber roof; a portion of it is coloured. It is to be regretted that this well-intentioned proceeding had not been directed by a better knowledge, Open seats prevail for the most part, the selfish boxes are confined to the aisles.[23] Pulpit and reading-desk modern work,[13] wrongly placed; the former is surmounted by one of the ugliest of sounding boards. The columns are whitewashed; our guide seemed very anxious for another dose of this damp-engendering composition. The western window is open to view. The poor tower that replaced the ancient one has a portion boarded off,[16] for fear the ringers should be under the eye of the Churchwarden, we suppose, and by any disorderly conduct disturb his quiet repose, that might call him from his comfortable pew. But it is the rule, with few exceptions, to exclude the ringers from observation, and it has been, more than once, our fate to hear the rattling of the heavy shoes of these men on the stairs, flying from the church the moment the minister enters the desk. It has been well observed by the same excellent and indefatigable labourer in the cause of church reform and restoration – 'Quiet and decorum amongst the ringers would be produced by the removal of all platforms and ceilings which would thus be rung by them upon the *floor* of the church, where their behaviour would be exposed to general observation. A convenient disposition of the bell-ropes might easily be managed without detriment to the appearance of the church.'* The roof, although not of its original height, is still lofty. A square box appropriated to the singers,[22] in the south aisle, is in a most dirty condition. The pavement is in a deplorable state. Two enclosed pews are partly made up of portions of the pannelling of the screen;[23] 'they break down all the carved work thereof.' In a corner, is the usual refuge for brooms other defilement, which it is so lamentable to witness in so many instances. The font has no lead or drain,[26] but contains the usual pottery crockery. In the north aisle, a flaming new square box has been erected; its rawness rendering it more than usually offensive.[24] The churchyard is a grazing-ground for sheep; an apology seemed to be offered for their being out on the day of our visit. The lead remains on the roof. There is no weekly service, and no school but one established by Dissenters. Now as the wealthy College of Trinity appears to take the lion's share of these revenues, leaving a small stipend for their Vicar, it is hardly to be expected that he should build a school for the children of his own congregation.[52] But it will be vain for these bodies to utter a syllable about lay impropriators, while they set such a flagrant example of dereliction of duty. Far better would their money be spent in assisting to raise a county in which they hold such valuable preferments from the discreditable position it holds in the statistics of education and pauperism and rendering it a byword and reproach,+ than in lavishing it on the vain and fleeting vanities of inaugurations.

> 'Their little triumphs, o'er,
> Their human passions now no more,
> Save Charity, that glows beyond the tomb.'

19 April 1847   W.A.

* On the Reverence Due to Holy Places

\+ 'The English is, therefore, better educated ...

Notes **1.** Pevsner pp.143–4, *VCH* II pp.297–9, and Paul Lanham *The Ringing Grooves of Change* n.d. [1983]. I am grateful to Paul Lanham and Margaret Rees for their help in compiling an account of this church; **2.** The crypt has been the subject of much speculative interpretation (<u>see</u> Lanham pp.6–7), but it seems to represent the first stage of the rebuilding begun in the late C13th. There is a reference to "the dungeon windoes" in the accounts 1638 (P 44/5/2). The present access was provided in 1932 (faculty P 44/2/2/2); **3.** For Assheton <u>see</u> Lanham (pp.12–3). The rebus is described by Bonney but not explained. The beast is an ass (not an ox); **4.** For the Assheton and other brasses <u>see</u> Lack *et.al.* (p.84–8); **5.** In 1827 Boissier (f.431–d) noted that "the number of screens & the length of the Chancel ... give it a peculiar interest"; **6.** The information from early wills is summarised by Lanham (p.18); **7.** There are churchwardens' accounts in two volumes 1571–1666 (P 44/5/1–2), two further volumes for 1775–1936 (P 44/5/3–4) and bills of 1827–30 (P 44/5/5). The accounts for 1571–1604 were published, with an introduction, by the Rev. J.E. Farmiloe and Rosita Nixseaman in *Elizabethan Churchwardens' accounts* (BHRS Vol.33 (1953) pp.60–109). The BCRO catalogues contain detailed abstracts of the accounts from 1605 and there is a summary 1575–1863 in Lanham (Appendix II); **8.** Bells cast between 1573 and 1588 were again recast in the early C17th, in 1602–3 (Newcombe of Leicester), 1624 (Haulsey of St.Ives) and 1638 (Oldfield of Hertford). The bellframe was renewed by John and Richard Cheese in 1632. There is a full account of the history of the bells (CRT 130 SHI 14), including information on the small bell (recast in 1828) and on the rehanging of the bells in 1883 and 1925; **9.** The clock is mentioned frequently in the earlier accounts from 1575 and may have been renewed in 1639 (P 44/5/2). After the fall of the tower the old clock was noted in the 1708 terrier as "taken in pieces and lying useless in vestry". A new clock by Thomas Bingham of Birmingham was put up in 1839 (P 44/8/1). It was restored in 1931 (P 44/28/5) and again in 1958 (P 44/2/2/7); **10.** The commandments were set up in 1588. The early C19th boards for the commandments etc. are now in the base of tower; **11.** The accounts show that the King's arms were set up in 1604 and restored after the Civil War in 1660 (P 44/5/1–2); **12.** The present plate (listed in the 1924 schedule, ref: ABE 5) includes a cup and paten of 1702 (the year after the fall of the tower), a plate inscribed "Shitlington Parish Plate Dec.24.77" (Bonney took this to be 1777 but other sources give the date as 1677), a cup given by the Rev. J.A. Bonser in 1888, and a plated cup of c.1800 (mentioned by Bonney in 1840) used as a flagon. The accounts mention "two flagons for to serve at the Communion" in 1607 (P 44/5/2). Bonney authorised the exchange of plate in 1823 and a new flagon and cover were purchased in 1826 (P 44/5/3). He ordered repairs to the cup in 1836–9; **13.** A sounding board or cover was provided for the Pulpit in 1611, and there are references to pulpit hour glasses in 1587 and 1654. A pulpit cloth and cushion were provided in 1636. In 1847 W.A. described the pulpit and desk as "modern work" (i.e. C18th or early C19th) with "the ugliest of sounding boards". This was superseded in 1861 by a pulpit made by Frere. The present pulpit of 1898 was made by Rattee & Kett (P 44/5/4 and cutting in ABE 3) and improved in 1928 with new carved panels (P 44/2/1/1); **14.** There was an organ in 1600 when the churchwardens paid an "orgin plaier". It was later dismantled, and pipes and boards from the organ mentioned in 1640 (P 44/6/1) were sold in 1644 and 1648 (P 44/5/2). The Walker finger and barrel organ was obtained by subscription (P 44/8/1) and opened in May 1858 (report in *BT* 15 May 1858). It was moved to its present position in 1919 when it was enlarged and rebuilt by F.W. Whiteley of Chislehurst, organ builder (P 44/0/2); **15.** Inventory 1640 (P 44/6/1); **16.** There are inconsistencies in the evidence regarding the collapse of the tower in 1701 (CRT 130 SHI 13 summarises the evidence). The 1708 terrier states that it fell on St.Cecilia's day (22 November) but the later brief papers (note 19) give the date as 25 December. It may have fallen through decay and antiquity or, as later claimed, "by reason of a very great tempest". The extent of the damage is also uncertain. Gordon's map of 1736 (MC 2/8) shows the church without tower or spire and the Browne Willis notes (BL ref: Add.Ms. 5836 f.111) provide a brief contemporary description of c.1740. A report in *NM* 4 June 1759 refers to the visit of five ringers from Pirton (their combined ages amounting to 383 years) who had rang at Shillington "when their ages amounted to but 80 years" – i.e. in 1699. Their first visit was just two years before the steeple collapsed in 1701 and when they revisited in 1759 the present tower had quite recently been built; **17.** Archdeaconry returns, c.1705–6 (CRT 170/2/16); **18.** Glebe terrier, 1708 (ABE 2 Vol.I p.145); **19.** Papers concerning the brief include the Quarter Sessions minutes (QSM 7 p.164 and QSM 8 pp.82–4). There is a copy of the actual brief of 1746 in the Stoke Mandeville parish records (Bucks.R.O. ref: PR 198/7/1 – copy at CRT 130 SHI 11); **20.** Terriers of 1703, 1724, 1745 and 1763 (FAC 35/17); **21.** The date of the alterations to the chancel is uncertain. The rainwater heads of 1778 clearly provide evidence of repairs, but Boissier (f.431) attributes the work to "the able manner in which the late Mr. Whitbread repaired & beautified the Church". This must refer to Samuel Whitbread I (d.1796) who held the Rectory from Trinity College, Cambridge, under separate leases of 1773 and 1778 and undertook to bear the cost of any necessary repairs to the chancel (*ex.inf.* Jonathan Smith, Trinity College). These alterations gave the chancel clerestory its simple wooden tracery and plaster ceiling, all reversed when the chancel was restored by Trinity College in 1882 (*BM* 19 Aug.1882); **22.** A singing gallery and musical instruments in the church were noted in 1847 by W.A., who draws a comparison with Higham Gobion where he observed part of the church "appears to be used as a concert–room, for we observed two musical instruments". At Shillington the accounts record payments for musical instruments from 1785 (P 44/5/3–4), including a fife for the psalm singers 1785, hautboy and reeds 1786, clarinet reeds 1815, new clarinet and music 1822, reeds 1824 and clarinet and reeds 1838; **23.** There were private pews by 1827 when Boissier (f.431) noted "the appearance of the church is much injured by some deal pews in the S aisle". Bonney refers to a pew at the west end of the nave, and W.A. describes pews in the chancel and aisles. There is an account of the church and its pews in the 1850s from Lady Robertson-Nicholl's *Bells of Memory* (c.1935) in Simon Houfe's *Through Visitors' Eyes: A Bedfordshire Anthology* (1990) pp.101–2. These pews were all removed in 1882 (*BM* 19 Aug.1882); **24.** Musgrave's pew is mentioned in 1824 (P 44/5/3) and Bonney's orders of 1826 refer to alterations to a pew (possibly Musgrave's) "without leave". Musgrave was granted a faculty for his pew in 1826 (ABF 2 p.146) and the papers include a plan. Bonney also ordered repairs to Musgrave's servants' pew in 1839; **25.** Repairs carried out by Mr. Pollard (£73), Mr. Betts (£20 and £33) and Mr.Francis (£21) in 1825–6 are recorded in the accounts (P 44/5/3); **26.** The font was moved in 1826–7 (P 44/5/3). A new font cover was provided in 1928 (P 44/2/1/1); **27.** The work of 1829–30 by Stevens is recorded in the accounts and associated bills (P 44/5/4–5) and in the vestry minutes (P 44/8/1); **28.** Bill for two Windsor chairs, 1829 (P 44/5/5 no.19); **29.** The staves or truncheons bore the crest of William IV (1830–7). There were 59 of them in 1914 (P 44/2/1/1), but most were afterwards lost (Lanham p.39) and the remainder were stolen in 1992. For the background, see "The 1830 Riots in Bedfordshire" by Alan Cirket in BHRS Vol.57 (1978) pp.75–112; **30.** Dilapidations report by Thomas Smith of Hertford, surveyor, 1834 (L 27/21). Bonney's order book suggests that the work was not done until after 1839; **31.** Work by Lot Richardson to the roof in 1840 and work on the steeple (including a new "spike") in 1846 is documented in the vestry minutes (P 44/8/1) and accounts (P 44/5/4); **32.** The vestry minutes (P 44/8/1) refer to Watson's survey of the roof in 1862 and improvements to the belfry and base of the tower (details given) in 1875; **33.** The window has an inscription recording its restoration in 1877, and the accounts include a subscription list (P 44/5/4); **34.** The lectern was given in 1878 (P 44/2/1/1) and the rostrum or lectern stand (by Rattee & Kett) was added in 1898 (P 44/0/1 and P 44/5/4); **35.** Bathurst's notebook (ABE 3); **36.** Sources for the restoration of 1881–5 include the vestry minutes (P 44/8/1), the service register (P 44/0/1), faculty papers (including plans) 1881 (HCRO ref: DSA 2/1/199), and reports in *BT* 12 Aug.1881, *BM* 19 Aug.1882 and *HE* 15 Nov.1884 and 1 Aug.1885; **37.** Vincent Wing practised in London but he may have been related to the Bedford family of architects. He trained in Leicester, and his career is summarised in the RIBA *Directory* p.1009; **38.** Report of new east window in *BT* 24 April 1886; **39.** The Bonser memorial window of 1898 (Lanham pp.44–5); **40.** The inventory of 1914 (P 44/2/1/1) contains many subsequent additions and amendments and the improvements during Postgate's incumbency are listed in a souvenir programme of 1934 (P 44/28/5); **41.** In 1910 the Archdeacon noted "external repairs to tower and battlements about to be done" (ABE 3). The completion of the work in 1911 is recorded on a tablet on the south side of the tower. Postgate erected the screen in memory of his wife and the cresting was added in 1928 (P 44/2/1/1); **42.** Faculty, 1918 (P 44/2/2/1); **43.** The external pulpit was first used on 16 July 1920 (P 44/0/3); **44.** The War memorial chapel was dedicated on 2 July 1920 (P 44/0/3); **45.** The improvements of 1928 are noted in the inventory and souvenir brochure (P 44/2/1/1 and P 44/28/5); **46.** Faculty for Postgate memorial window, 1937 (HCRO ref: DSA 2/1/50/44); **47.** The accounts include payments for making the terrier in 1822 (P 44/5/3); **48.** In 1578 "Certayne pales belonginge to Holwelberye of our Churche yarde" were "owte of reparation" (Archidiaconal Visitations (ABC 3 p.7) in BHRS Vol.69 (1990) p.177). There is a memorandum on responsibility for churchyard fences c.1658 (in P 44/1/2); **49.** The chest may date from 1626 when the churchwardens paid 7s.8d. "to Matthew Hare for the chest in the Vestry" (P 44/5/2); **50.** A "new Church Prayer book" was bought in 1807–8 and in 1826–7 the Bible and prayer book were re-bound (P 44/5/3). In the church there are prayer books and other volumes marked "Shidlington parish 1816" and "Shillington church 1845"; **51.** A new velvet pall (£2) and a new surplice (£2 15s 10d) were bought in 1837 (P 44/5/4); **52.** A new school was built in 1855–6 (*VCH* II p.184).

SILSOE

Silsoe was in the parish of Flitton until 1846,[1] but the present church of 1829–31 replaces an earlier chapel first mentioned in the early C13th.[2] The old chapel consisted of chancel, aisled nave, south porch and a wooden bell turret. There are several plans and illustrations of the old chapel, which seems to have had a Decorated west window and Perpendicular tracery in most of the other windows.[3] Boissier considered the pillars of the arcades to be of late Decorated work.[4]

The C17th altar rails,[5] originally from the private chapel at Wrest Park,[6] seem to have been in Silsoe chapel by 1828. The plate includes a chalice and paten of 1667 and a flagon of 1686, also from the chapel at Wrest.[7] There is an embroidered pulpit cloth of 1684.[8] The furniture and ornaments of Silsoe chapel are listed in a terrier of 1708.[9] There was a clock in the steeple.[10] From 1731 there are chapelwardens' accounts which give details of expenditure on the fabric and fittings.[11] Some repairs were carried out by John Rentham, bricklayer, in 1782 and in the same year John Favell was paid £18 7s 6d for "Painting the Kings Arms,[12] Printing the Lords Prayer, Ten Commandments &c,[13] & Repairing the Windows". These Royal Arms are now on the front of the west gallery of the new church. A sundial was set up in the chapelyard in 1787.[14]

In the early C19th repairs were carried out in 1801 by Johnson and Devereux.[15] In 1820 the pews were repaired and painted and a new west

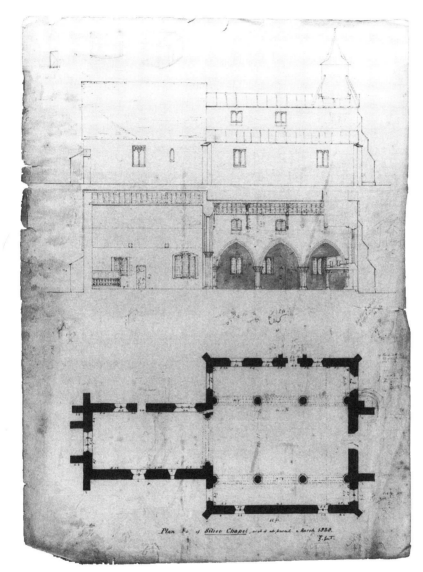

9. Silsoe: North elevation, section and plan of the old chapel, showing the C17th altar rails from the chapel at Wrest and the west gallery erected in 1820.   *(Drawing: Lord Grantham 1828)*

gallery was erected.[16] At about this time, Mrs. Lloyd presented an altar–piece of the Adoration of the Magi.[17] In 1827 Boissier described Silsoe as "a small poor Church".[4] In the following year Earl de Grey (then Lord Grantham) pre–pared a scheme for improving the building. He made detailed drawings of the chapel in March 1828 and on 25 June 1828 Thomas Smith of Hertford

10. Silsoe: Interior of the new chapel looking east, showing the box pews, raised pulpit, C17th altar rails and east end with decalogue boards and heraldic glass in the window
(Watercolour: John Buckler 1831)

reported on its condition.[18] Smith recommended the rebuilding of the old bell turret and other repairs to the roofs and west wall.

When work began in 1829 the intention was to repair the chapel and add a tower at the west end. However, the new tower collapsed in April 1829 when only half built.[19] After this it was decided that the chapel should be completely rebuilt slightly to the east of the original building. De Grey provided the designs himself, but left the detail and execution to Thomas Smith. The new church was completed in 1830 and opened on 20 February 1831.[20] Built in the Perpendicular style it is a remarkable building for its time when few architects showed concern for stylistic accuracy. The original furnishings included box pews, heraldic glass in the windows to designs provided by Lord Grantham,[21] new decalogue boards on the east wall,[13] a new velvet pulpit cloth and a new clock.[10]

The buildings materials were not entirely satisfactory and Bonney noted problems with decay in the woodwork and damp in the walls. Re-seating was considered in 1855 and some time later, probably in about 1873 when Archdeacon Bathurst advised on the internal arrangements,[22] W.G. Habershon & Pite prepared plans for new pews and seats.[23] This was never done, but in 1884 the box pews were removed and the present seating, pulpit and desk installed to the plans and specifications of Ewan Christian.[24]

Other C19th improvements included a new east window by Thomas Baillie in 1857,[25] new bells in 1857 and 1887,[26] an organ,[27] improvements to the sanctuary and east window in 1888–9,[28] and a new font in 1890.[29] The early years of the present century saw the erection of a new clock in 1909,[10] a new heating system in 1911,[30] and in 1923 new stained glass windows were placed in the sanctuary.[31] The reredos and altar are also of this period and the stained glass window in the tower dates from 1924. Further bells were added in 1926 and 1951 to complete a ring of six.[26]

1. Extract from glebe terrier (Flitton), 28 June 1822

SILSOE.

Chapel yard. Item Chapel Yard at Silsoe Containing nearly half an Acre.[32]

Silsoe Chapel. Also a Chapel at Silsoe in Length thirty Eight Feet, In Breadth thirty six feet.[3]

Furniture and ornaments.[33] Within & belonging to which are one Communion Table with a covering for the same of red cloth. Also a linen cloth for the same with two napkins. Also a silver cup and a plate.[7] A pulpit and reading Desk. A Pulpit Cushion covered with crimson.[8] A large Bible & prayer book. The King's Arms[12] and Ten Commandments.[13] Two bells with their frames.[26] One surplice.

Sunday School. There is a Sunday School at Silsoe[16]

2. Archdeacon Bonney's historical notices of churches, c.1820–1840

SILSOE, St. James. This Chapel (an appendage to Flitton)[1] has been recently rebuilt by the Countess De Grey,[20] is of the red Sandstone of the Country, & consists of Nave, Aisles, Chancel, Vestry, & a Tower with a Staircase Turret at the West End. The Windows are flat headed except the East & West; and are adorned with the Armorial Bearings of the House of De Grey with intermarriages[21] – all designed by Lord Grantham (now Earl de Grey). The Nitre contained in the Materials of which the Fabrick is composed proves very injurious to the Wood Work of the interior. The whole Character is of the Perpendicular except the West Window which is of the decorated. The Armorial Bearings are, In the East Window are De Grey Duke of Kent, the Earls of [*blank*] and Hardwick, the Marchioness De Grey, the Royal Arms, De Grey Earl of Kent, the Crest of Glenorchy, Kent, Hardwick, Polworth, Kent and Lucas, Sutton Archbishop of Canterbury, Pelham, Bishop of Lincoln, Hall Dean of Christ Church (Patron) and James M.A. Vicar of Flitton with Silsoe; also the Arms of the See of Lincoln, Lord Grantham, Christ Church Oxford (Patrons).[21] The Font is a circular & plain.[29]

3. Archdeacon Bonney's visitation notebook, 1823–1839

SILSOE. This is a Chapel to Flitton and since the visitation of 1826 has been entirely rebuilt.[30]

At the Visitation of 1833 and 1836. All in admirable order.

At the Visitation of 1839 ordered the lead work to be examined to ascertain whether the marks of dampness on the Walls proceed or not from any defect in the Roof – advised a solution of corrosive sublimate to remove the Green moss which appears on the damp parts of ye Walls in Churches.

Notes **1.** Papers concerning the creation of Silsoe parish, 1845–6 (L 27/31–68). The registers of baptisms, marriages and burials at Silsoe start in 1846; **2.** Pevsner p.144 and *VCH* II pp.332–3 (Flitton). I am grateful to John Corfield and the late Canon Bernard Nixon for information on this church; **3.** There are plans (L 33/245–8), NW views (L 33/248, slide 2268) and SW view (slide 2270). Fisher's original sketch indicates that the chapel was "plaistered & washed yellow" (Micf 66 FB 210); **4.** Boissier (f.417); **5.** The altar rails can be seen in Lord Grantham's 1828 section of the old chapel (L 33/246) and in Buckler's 1831 interior view of the new chapel (L 33/256). They were probably transferred when the chapel at Wrest was refitted in 1769 (BL ref: Add.Ms, 35693 f.135); **6.** For the chapel at Wrest Park (demolished 1833) see James Collett White's account of the old house in *Inventories of Bedfordshire Country Houses 1714–1830* (BHRS Vol.74 (1995) pp.243–73). The inventory of 1740 lists (p.259) the fittings in the chapel; **7.** The old plate is listed in the terrier of 1708 (ABE 2 Vol.II) when "the plate at Silsoe weigheth twenty & three ounces, & there are two pewter Flagons belonging to the Church of Flitton & Chappell of Silsoe". The plate from Wrest chapel is mentioned in a report in 1888 (*BT* 16 June 1888) when two chalices were given by the Misses E. and V. Blackburne-Maze. The plate is listed in a schedule of 1924 (ABE 5); **8.** The pulpit cloth or tapestry frontal dated 1684 was embroidered by Amabel Countess of Kent. It was restored in 1958 (*B.Mag* Vol.6 no.45 (Summer 1958) p.168); **9.** Terrier, 1708 (ABE 2 Vol.I); **10.** The clock is mentioned in 1708 and the C18th chapelwardens' accounts include regular payments for winding and maintenance (P 54/5/1). The clock dial is dated 1830 and the accounts show that a new clock was provided by Skerman & Son of Hertford (L 26/1454). A brass plate in the base of the tower records the erection of the present clock in 1909; **11.** Chapelwardens' accounts 1731–1821 (P 54/5/1); **12.** Pardoe (p.5) notes that the arms are of the period 1714–1801, carved on wood and painted; **13.** The commandments etc. were done in 1782, but replaced in 1830 by new ones on the east wall of the chancel by Newton & Son of Hitchin (L 26/1454); **14.** The sundial was purchased from John Troughton of Fleet Street, 1787 (P 54/5/1) and re-erected on a new post in the chapel yard in 1827 (P 54/5/2); **15.** The repairs in 1800–1 cost £38 (P 54/5/1); **16.** The gallery is shown in Lord Grantham's 1828 section of the old chapel (L 33/246) and payments to Burrows (£299) for building it are recorded in the accounts for 1820 (P 54/5/1). A letter of 1 May 1819 mentions the erection of the gallery for the Sunday School (LPL ref: ICBS 145) and the work is described in an account of the chapel in *GM* Vol.91 (1821) Pt.1 p.395 (quoted in *B.Mag* Vol.7 no.54 (Autumn 1960) p.222); **17.** The altar piece is mentioned in the *GM* article and by Boissier (f.417); **18.** An undated sketch by Lord Grantham shows the outline of a tower alongside the west elevation of the old chapel (L 33/245) and another drawing of March 1828 shows the proposed tower and alterations to the roof and parapets of the nave and aisles (L 33/247). Smith's report is dated 25 June 1828 (L 33/244). Lord Grantham, who inherited the earldom in 1834, was the first president of the Royal Institute of British Architects and he was personally involved with the work at Silsoe. For de Grey and Smith see Colvin (1995) pp.431–3 and pp.901–2; **19.** The collapse of the tower was reported in the *Herts. etc Mercury* 18 April 1829, in an undated press cutting (in AD 4000/1 p.40), and in Earl de Grey's memoir written in 1846 (CRT 190/45/2). The unfortunate contractor may have been John Stevens who is mentioned in the accounts (L 29/1454); **20.** Sources for the new church of 1830–1 include a plan and elevation signed by Thomas Smith 1830 (L 33/248), a ground plan (P 54/2/2/1), accounts (L 29/1454), ICBS correspondence (LPL ref: ICBS 145), Buckler's watercolours of 1831 (L 33/255–6) and sketches (BL ref: Add.Ms. 36356 f.52–55r) and Earl de Grey's memoir of 1846 (CRT 190/45/2); **21.** Boissier (f.417) describes the faded "modern" heraldic glass in the old chapel, evidently replaced by the present windows (described by Bonney) in 1830. Lord Grantham's working drawings for the present window survive in the Wrest Park archive (L 33/250–254); **22.** Bathurst's notebook (ABE 3); **23.** Habershon's plans (P 54/2/2/2) are not dated and no mention of the scheme has been found in the vestry minutes 1849–1881 (P 54/8/3) which refer to the 1855 proposals. Habershon & Pite were in partnership from 1863 to 1878 (RIBA *Directory* p.390); **24.** Christian's work is documented in the vestry minutes 1883–5 (P 54/8/4), papers and accounts (P 54/2/2/3–5), and reports in *BT* 30 June 1883 and *BT* and *BM* 25 Oct.1884; **25.** The window is listed in the *Catalogue of Painted and Stained Glass Windows by Thomas Baillie & Co.* (1875) p.3; **26.** There were two bells in 1708, apparently rehung in the new tower in 1830. They were replaced by two new bells in 1857 (P 54/8/3), and a further bell was added for the Jubilee in 1887 (P 54/8/4 and reports in *BT* 4 and 25 June, 16 July and 13 Aug.1887). Two more bells were added in 1926 and a sixth bell provided in 1951 when the bells were rehung; **27.** The organ is said to be dated 1870 (National Pipe Organs register). It was by Bevington, altered in 1884 by Hill (*BM* 25 Oct.1884); **28.** The improvements to the sanctuary and east window were reported in *BT* 16 June 1888 and *BS* 29 Dec.1888 and 3 Aug.1889; **29.** There is a sketch by Buckler of the old font 1823 (BL ref: Add.Ms 36356 f.55). The present font and cover were given by the Misses Delmé Radcliffe in 1890 (*BT* 6 Dec.1890); **30.** Faculty papers for heating system and boiler house, 1911 (HCRO ref: DSA 2/1/200); **31.** The 1923 windows are by Arthur Savell of Cambridge (HCRO ref: DSA 2/1/3/30). The old east window was transferred to Flitton in 1924 (P 12/2/2/6); **32.** There is a plan of the chapelyard (L 27/49) which was enlarged in 1894 (*BS* 2 March 1894); **33.** Details for Flitton and Silsoe are combined in the original terrier (e.g. two Communion Tables, seven bells, two silver cups, two Bibles etc.). The version given here represents a disentanglement of the details for Silsoe, Flitton being given separately (BHRS Vol.73 pp.297–8).

SOULDROP

There was a church here in 1270 when Roger le May was killed in an affray between the Hospitallers and Hugh Bossard of Knotting over the rights to the advowson.[1] The tower dates from c.1275 and carries a contemporary broach spire, but the body of the church has been twice rebuilt. The present building is of 1860–1.[2]

The plate includes an Elizabethan chalice and paten of 1569.[3] At least two of the mediaeval bells survived until modern times, but one was recast in the early C17th.[4] In 1708 there were three bells and a clock.[5] The livings of Knotting and Souldrop were united in 1735,[6] and the church at Souldrop went through a period of neglect in the C18th. The churchwardens were presented for failing to maintain the church in 1768–70,[7] and the church became so badly decayed that the roof collapsed in 1795.[8] From 1796 to 1800 baptisms took place at Knotting because Souldrop church was unfit for use.[9] A sketch plan shows that the building consisted of a chancel with north chapel used as a schoolroom, nave with north aisle, south porch and west tower.[10]

The story of the rebuilding by Robert Salmon in 1800 is told in detail in the 1822 terrier, but other sources indicate that this account is not wholly reliable. In 1799 the parish obtained a faculty to sell two of the bells.[11] The faculty papers mention that the church was being taken down and rebuilt, but it is stated that the proceeds from the sale were to be used on the purchase of a clock and not towards the cost of rebuilding. When the new church was opened in June 1800 it must have been furnished with seats from the old church. In 1802 Salmon prepared a plan for fitting up the church with new pews, pulpit and desk.[12] The Rev. John Whitehouse, then Vicar of Sharnbrook, painted an altar–piece, representing Jacob's Ladder, for the new church.[13] A new font was set up after 1823.[14] By 1826 the remaining mediae-

11. Souldrop: S view showing the C13th tower and spire with the nave and short chancel built by Robert Salmon in 1800 in place of the old church   (Watercolour: Thomas Fisher c.1815)

val bell had become cracked and it was replaced in 1828 by three small bells.[4]

When completed, the church was a typical "preaching box" of the period and it was just the sort of building that distressed the later C19th reformers. In 1827 Boissier described it as "a rebuilt Church with pointed windows and wooden mullions".[15] W.A.'s article of 1854, the last in the series, drew attention to the cheapness of the structure and ridiculed its furnishings.

Shortly after his arrival as Rector in 1856, the Rev. George Digby Newbolt[16] set about improving the Rectory with the support of the Duke of Bedford who was the patron and principal landowner.[17] Soon afterwards the

Duke agreed to rebuild the church if Newbolt would meet the cost of rebuilding the chancel. The old tower was retained, and in 1860–61 the present church was built to the designs of Henry Clutton.[18] The nave is plain, but the vaulted chancel has French gothic detail. The church has rich Victorian fittings.[19] They include the carved stone pulpit and font by Thomas Earp, encaustic tiles in the sanctuary by Maw & Co., and the stained glass in the east window by O'Connor. The Walker organ is also contemporary with the rebuilding in 1860. Harvey considered the new church to be "of a substantial and handsome character" and the Rev. W.D. Sweeting who visited in 1871 thought the style "very effective" and the "interior delightful".[20]

After the church had been rebuilt, further stained glass by O'Connor was set up in the rose window above the organ (1865 and 1869) and in the side windows of the chancel (1869).[21] There is an inventory of 1886.[22] In 1887 the tower was underpinned and strengthened.[23] The Archdeacon noted defects in the north wall in 1895.[24] In recent times the spire has again been restored.

1. Extract from glebe terrier, 5 July 1822 [Knotting with Souldrop] [25]

SOULDROP.

Church History etc. Belonging to the said Parish are first the Parish Church of which the following mention is made in Ecton's thesaurus. Souldrop alias Soulthrop (probably a corruption of South-hill-throp from the extensive view which it commands southwards).[26] Rectory, certified value £48 5s. 8d. dedicated to All Saints, united to Knotting in 1735.[6] Patrons The Hon[ble]. Edward Carteret & Carew Harvey Esq[r]. 1710. Hen. J. Pye 1771. The height of the spire is about 30 yards. Owing to it's own elevation & the high ground on which it stands, it is one of the stations laid down in the grand trigonometrical survey of England now making by order of Government, and communicates with Bow-brickhill Church in the County of Buckingham.[27] The body of the church is an entirely new structure. The old body and chancel having been suffered to go to ruin, the roof fell in after the severe frost in Christmas 1795 and divine service was necessarily discontinued.[8] In August 1799 the Rector J.W. Hawksley obtained a Faculty to enable him & the parishioners to dispose of the bells & the old materials for the purpose of obtaining a fund to rebuild the body & chancel of the church.[11] Two out of the three bells were accordingly sold for upwards of £60,[4] the old lead for about £80, Francis the Duke of Bedford gave £100, William Lee Antonie of Colworth Esq[r]. 30, J.W. Hawksley [the Rector] 20, William Gibbard Esq[r]. Impropriator of Sharnbrook £5, Mr. Joseph Eden of Souldrop £5, arrears of rent of church land about £32, sundry materials sold for £20 making in the whole the sum of about £350. For which sum the new body & chancel with reading desk, pulpit, pews and commodious open seats were erected & divine service recommenced on Trinity Sunday 1800.[12] The carriage of the materials was given by the parishioners & the whole was completed under the direction of J.W.H. the Rector and Mr. Richard

Radborne Churchwarden. Mr. Robert Salmon Surveyor to the Duke of Bedford furnished the plan & estimate gratuitously.

Church yard. The church-yard and orchard separated from each other by an old quickset hedge on the North of the churchyard, containing together 2 roods 31 perches bounded on all sides by lands the property of the Duke of Bedford. The south wall and all the gates made by the parish. The west fence by the Duke of Bedford, the north wall by the rector. The east side is open to the plantation walk.

Church. The Church including the Chancel within [the walls] contains in length 45 feet, in breadth 26 feet. The chancel in breadth 15 feet, in depth 9 feet. The steeple 8 feet square within the walls, its height about 90 feet.

Furniture and ornaments. Within and belonging to the said church are one communion table. A linen cloth for the same. A Pewter flaggon. A silver chalice weighing between 6 and 7 ounces, without inscription, the cover of which is used as the Paten or plate to receive offerings.[3] No plate for bread. An old oak chest for the Clerk's use with a lock & key. An iron chest according to the late Act, for the registers kept at the Rectory. One large bible. A common prayer book. D°. for the clerk. The Book of Homilies. A Register for freeholders. The King's arms with ten commandments. No font.[14] One ancient bell with frame,[4] being the second bell of the former set of three: the diameter of which is about 2 feet 10 inches from outside to outside, with the inscription "Sit nomen Domini benedictum." A bier. Two surplices.

Parish Registers. Two parchment register books. The oldest beginning October 4th 1670 ending June 1789 containing the baptisms and burials during that time and Marriages to March 1757, containing also a terrier of the Rectory of Souldrop dated 1708,[5] signed John Tiffin, Rector. The second parchment register book contains baptisms & burials only beginning October the 4 1789 ending 29 May 1813. Also one paper marriage register book beginning 3 April 1757 ending 27 May 1812. Also three new Paper register books for baptisms, burials & marriages respectively beginning in 1813.

Church Estate. By the Award of Inclosure is allotted to the Rectors and churchwardens for the time being in lieu of 3 Acres of land called the Church land and all common rights thereto belonging, one plot of land or ground parcel of the said fields, grounds & premises containing five acres two roods & twenty one perches including all roads passing through & over the same as now admeasured & set out [bounds given]. To be made and for ever thereafter maintained and kept in repair by and at the expence of the said rector and churchwardens & their successors for the time being which said last mentioned allotment in lieu of the church land is so allotted in trust that they shall from time to time apply the rents & profits thereof to & for the support & repairs of the parish church of Souldrope and for such other uses & purposes as the rents & profits of the said church lands have been heretofore usually paid & applied.

12. Souldrop: The interior of Clutton's new church of 1860–1, with the stone pulpit carved by Thomas Earp and the rich Victorian fittings in the chancel. The vaulted chancel has French gothic details. *(Lithograph: Anonymous 1878)*

Parish Clerk and Sexton. There is also due to the Parish Clerk & Sexton, who is appointed by the rector, a certain sum from every house besides 21 [altered in Parish copy to 26] shillings paid by the Churchwarden, and the customary dues for a Marriage by banns 6 pence [now 2 shillings[i]], by a licence 1 shilling now 2s. 6d. For a Burial 2 shillings including the doing up of the grave.

Sunday School. No school except a Sunday school supported by the voluntary contributions & attention of the rector & parishioners.[10]

2. Archdeacon Bonney's historical notices of churches, c.1820–1840

SOULDROPE, All Saints. This Church is comparatively modern, and consists of a Nave & semihexagon recess at the East End with an Early English Spire at the West End.

Under a Brass inserted in a panel of grey Marble, now placed against an inner Wall of the Steeple, is the Effigy of a Man in a kneeling posture, with this Inscription:[28]

Hangerus jacet hic notus pietate Johannes / et sacra æterni Religionis dei / Pertæsus lites observantissimus Æqui / Ætas maturum quem tulit albasem / obiit XIIII die Maii Anno Dni 1608 / Anno ætatis suæ Septuagesimo. / Deflevit Johannes Hangerus nepos amantissimus.

There are three Bells, recently cast.[4]

There is a Chalice and cover, Elizabethan, a plated Flagon and a pewter Plate.[3] A South Porch.

3. Archdeacon Bonney's visitation notebook, 1823–1839

SOULDROP. This Church consists of a Nave, at the East end of which is a recess for the Communion Table, and a Steeple at the West End thereof. A Porch on the South side.

At the Visitation of 1823 It was ordered that a new Font of Stone be set up in the Church,[14] and a proper Font Bason purchased; also a Prayer Book of the large size & plated Paten be bought.[3]

At the Visitation of 1826, It was Ordered that the Bell (being cracked) be sold,[4] and two sufficient Bells be placed in the Steeple in lieu thereof, before Easter 1827.

At the Visitation of 1833 It was ordered that the Book of Homilies be rebound – the walls be cleansed – the slated roof be repaired.

At the Visitation of 1836 Ordered that the Steeple be pointed and the Shafts of the Windows restored either with Stone or some material of the like colour, but not with wood – and that a blue covering be procured for the Communion Table.

4. Article on the Church by W.A. (no.122), NM 14 October 1854

SOULDROP, All Saints: On requesting to see the interior of this church – a matter we believe of right, but which, as one of courtesy, had never been refused – the venerable sexton, worthy to rank with Crabbe's "Old Dibble," and like him, we hope, "His eightieth year he reach'd still undecayed," evidently ashamed of his commission, informed us that "if we were the gemmen that had been saying things of Melchbourne and other churches, his master said we were not to be admitted." This entertained us amazingly, and on his wishing to retire to consult a superior (a farmer churchwarden, we believe) sufficient view of the interior was obtained from a window not to surprise us at the reluctance this very conservative guardian of Souldrop church evinced to its being exposed.

It abounds in high deal pews,[12] most probably after the pattern which decorate the farmer's cattle stalls; with a limited number of open sittings; abundantly covered with limewash; and plenty of hooks to save the hats of the congregation from its contamination.

The chancel window is entirely closed; how it is adorned inside we are not able to say; but if it at all rivals the painting externally, it beats the most outrageous "sham" Mr. Ruskin's wildest dreams ever contemplated. It is intended to represent a window, an essay which would dishonour the most vulgar of those coloured blinds that frequently offend the eyesight. It is no doubt judged a capital work by the worthy guardian, for it appears to have been not long since executed, and is free from damp and dirt.

This terminates the notices of the churches in the County. [various general remarks follow][29]

October 10, 1854   W.A.

Notes **1.** Details of the affray in 1270 are recorded in R.F. Hunnisett's edition of the *Bedfordshire Coroners' Records* in BHRS Vol.41 (1961) pp.42–4; **2.** Pevsner pp.144–5, Harvey pp.452–3, and *VCH* III p.95; **3.** The plate listed in 1916 (ABE 5) includes an Elizabethan cup and paten and new plate of 1860; **4.** The inscriptions of the three old bells were recorded in about 1790 by Oliver St.John Cooper (BL ref: Add.Ms. 34366), the first being "Sancta Katerina ora pro nobis", the second (as noted in 1822) "Sit nomen Domini benedictum", and the third "Soli Deo Gloria Pax Hominibus". The inscriptions of the first two were in gothic lettering, but the third had Roman capitals. The first two were evidently mediaeval, but the third was probably of early C17th date. The present bells are dated 1828 (North p.191) but letters of 1834 (R 3/3790, 3795–7) refer to financial problems regarding the work on the bells; **5.** The 1708 terrier (ABE 2 Vol.I p.266 and parish copy in P 108/1/1) mentions a clock, although nothing else is known of it. In 1799 the parish planned to put up a clock with the money received for the old bells, but this was never done; **6.** Bishop's faculty for the union of Knotting and Souldrop, 30 June 1735, entered in the Knotting register (P 107/1/1). At that time the parsonage was at Knotting and this may explain the neglect of Souldrop church in the later C18th. A new Rectory was built at Souldrop by faculty in 1793 (ABF 2 p.61 and ABF 3/122); **7.** Archdeacon's court papers 1768–70 (ABCP 317 and 326); **8.** The main source for the collapse in 1795 is the account in the 1822 terrier; **9.** The registers record that baptisms and marriages took place at Knotting between 1796 and 1800 (P 108/1/3); **10.** Sketch plan with dimensions, c.1799 (R 4/534/20/4). This shows the schoolroom on the north side of the chancel; **11.** Faculty for sale of two bells (one of them broken) 1799 (ABF 2 p.83 and ABF 3/196); **12.** Salmon's plan and estimate, 1802 (R 4/534/20/2–3). This evidence must show that the 1822 terrier is wrong in stating that the church and furnishings were completed for the opening in 1800; **13.** Boissier (f.371) states "Over the communion table is a picture of Jacob's Dream" and details of the altar piece are given by Harvey (p.452); **14.** There was no font in 1822 but in the following year Bonney ordered that one be obtained. In 1827 Boissier (f.371) noted "the font is of stone and modern"; **15.** Boissier (f.371); **16.** Newbolt's diaries for 1856–95 are preserved with the parish records (P 108/28/1–2) and Patricia Bell's edition of the text was published in *Some Bedfordshire Diaries* in BHRS Vol.40 (1960) pp.200–225. The Rectory was enlarged and improved for Newbolt by James Tacy Wing in 1856 (CUL ref: EDR/G3/40 MGA/BED/25); **17.** The Dukes of Bedford were the principal landowner in the parish, and they bore most of the cost of the rebuildings of 1800 and 1860. Work on the Rectory is documented in the Estate Reports (R 5/869/2) for 1851 (p.49) and 1858 (p.54), and that on the church in the reports for 1858 (pp.7 and 55), 1859 (p.8), and 1861 (pp.26, 128–9). The estate accounts include bills for some of the work on the church (R box 504); **18.** Sources on the new church include Newbolt's diary (P 108/28/1), the Bedford Estate reports (R 5/869/2) and vouchers (R box 504), and reports in *BM* 13 Feb. and 18 Aug.1860 and 22 Dec.1861, *BT* 14 Aug 1860 and 24 Dec.1861. Henry Clutton later designed the former village school at Souldrop, built in 1867–8; **19.** There is a good account of the furnishings and ornaments (including the east window) in Newbolt's diary (P 108/28/1), and the estate accounts include bills for some of them (R box 504); **20.** The Rev.W.D.Sweeting's notes, 1871 (BL ref: Add.Ms. 37178 f.22); **21.** The later stained glass is mentioned in Newbolt's diary (P 108/28/1) and in a report in *The Builder* Vol.27 (20 March 1869) p.232; **22.** Inventory, 1886 (P 108/2/2/1); **23.** The tower repairs in 1887 were paid for by Charles Magniac of Colworth who bought the living from the Duke of Bedford in 1884. They are noted in Newbolt's diary (P 108/28/1) and by Archdeacon Bathurst (ABE 3). Newbolt had married Hollingworth Magniac's daughter (*BM* 4 Jan.1862); **24.** Bathurst's notebook (ABE 3); **25.** This version of the text is taken from the parish copy of the terrier (P 107/1/2) used in conjunction with a photocopy of the Diocesan copy at Lincoln; **26.** Mawer & Stenton (p.43) derive the name Souldrop from "thorp by the well-marked valley"; **27.** For the making of the Ordnance Survey see Vol.IV (Central England) of *The Old Series Ordnance Survey Maps of England and Wales* (Harry Margary, Lympne, 1986); **28.** For the brass, see Lack *et.al.* (p.88); **29.** The passage omitted here has already been published in full in part I (BHRS Vol.73 pp.21–3).

SOUTHILL

This church, standing at the eastern edge of the grounds of Southill Park,[1] dates mainly from the C15th. As the list of vicars begins in 1225 the church presumably stands on the site of an older building from which the Decorated window at the north-west end of the north aisle may have come.[2] Evidence from wills indicates that the north aisle was under construction in 1522–4.[3]

In 1578 the chancel was reported to be "in decaye".[4] In 1674 the chancel was under repair.[5] Lady Elizabeth Kelyng of Southill Park gave plate consisting of "A Silver Cup, two Silver Plates for the Communion" to Southill church in 1691.[6] This plate is described in a terrier of 1707[7] which also lists the furniture and ornaments, a clock[8] and five bells.[9] Further plate was given by Sir George Byng in 1715.[6]

The Byng family acquired the Southill estate in the late C17th and owned Southill Park until it was bought by the Whitbread family in 1795.[10] Sir George Byng was created first Viscount Torrington in 1721, and the ill-fated Admiral Byng (who is commemorated on a tablet in the church) was one of his younger sons. In 1733, the Torringtons obtained a faculty to erect a family burial place or dormitory on the north side of the chancel.[11] This was built shortly afterwards. The roofline was altered in 1814 when the body of the church was remodelled. Bonney's order book refers to the upkeep of the mausoleum.

From 1751 there is a remarkably complete set of churchwardens' vouchers and the surviving accounts commence in 1785.[12] These provide information on repairs and improvements to the fabric, including regular repairs to the clock[8] and the erection of new charity boards in 1811.[13]

In 1811 George Cloake reported on the condition of the church and prepared a scheme for restoring and improving the building.[14] He died before the work was commenced, but the church was later remodelled in 1813–4 under S.W. Reynolds. Samuel Whitbread II bore the cost of refurbishing the chancel and assisted the parish with the work on the rest of the church. The work was financed by annuities.[15] In what amounted to a virtual rebuilding, a brick clerestory was added (replacing large dormer windows on the south side of the church), the buttresses and parapets were restored in brick, the exterior was finished with stucco, and the whole church re-seated (with box pews in the aisles)[16] and roofed in copper. When the church was reopened on 20 November 1814 it was complete "all but the painting" and "some other particulars".[17] The tower roof was repaired, the clock rebuilt,[8] and six new bells were put up in place of the old five.[9] A new south porch[18] was added and the Royal Arms were displayed above the south door.[19] The work was completed by 1816 as recorded on an inscription on the west gallery.[20]

The churchwardens' accounts contain information on later repairs and improvements. In 1824 a new font basin was obtained.[21] A velvet cloth for the communion table was bought from Swan & Edgar, London, for £20 18s in

13. Southill: The exterior before the remodelling of the church in 1813–4 when the rooflines and parapets were completely altered, the dormers in the roof replaced by a clerestory, the porch rebuilt and windows in the east end of the aisle and south side of the chancel blocked up. This view also shows the Torrington vault on the north side of the chancel.

(Watercolour: Thomas Fisher c.1810)

1830. In 1836 the parish undertook repairs to the roof and in 1839 a new slate dial was put up when the clock was repaired.[8] New stoves were placed in the church in about 1840.[22] In 1841 an organ by Flight and Robson was presented by Lady Elizabeth Whitbread.[23]

The church of 1814 was very much a period piece, falling between the fanciful gothick of the C18th and the archaeological correctness of the mid C19th. The use of poor quality building materials and methods is all too apparent now the stucco has been removed from the exterior, and W.A.'s article of 1846 illustrates how unfashionable the internal arrangements had become just thirty years after the work was finished. The Whitbread family pew is ridiculed as "the drawing–room brought into God's house".

W.A.'s criticism seems to have prompted the parish to carry out some improvements. In 1848 new tracery was placed in the east window by James Tacy Wing.[24] The pulpit and reading desk were moved from the east end to new positions under Wing and Jackson. In 1854 the interior was redecorated, and new tablets for the commandments, Lords Prayer and Belief were put up in the east wall.[25] In 1867 a new organ was provided,[23] the tenor bell recast,[9] and stained glass placed in the east window in memory of William Henry Whitbread. Another window in the south side of the chancel was filled with stained glass in memory of Harriett Whitbread in 1871.[26]

Roof repairs were undertaken in 1891.[27] In 1894 a memorial window by Powell to the Rev. Charles Baldock was installed in the north aisle.[28] A new pulpit by Jones & Willis was put up in 1912 and in the following year S. Howard Whitbread gave a new lectern.[29] The outside walls were repaired in 1923–7.[30] In 1936–7 a new font designed by Professor Richardson was placed in the south-west corner of the church in memory of Joscelyne Whitbread (d.1936) who is also commemorated in the adjacent stained glass window by Hugh Easton.[31]

Later work includes repairs to the tower and church exterior under Professor Richardson in 1951–4 and the removal of the enclosed pews from the aisles in 1958.[32]

1. Extract from glebe terrier, 25th June 1822

SOUTHILL.

Church yard. The Church yard is surrounded by a brick wall and bounded on every side by the land of W.H. Whitbread Esquire[1] and contains twenty nine Timber Pollard and other trees and measuring, including the Church, One acre and twenty two poles, a part of which, two poles and a half and one large timber tree, on the West Side of the yard adjoining the Steeple has been taken into the Shrubbery of W.H. Whitbread Esquire for which an acknowledgment of sixpence yearly is paid to the Vicar.

Church. Belonging to the said Parish are first the Parish Church, an ancient building repaired and new pewed, the roof covered with Copper in the year 1814 at a cost of three thousand eight hundred pounds to the parishioners and the Chancel repaired at the same time by Samuel Whitbread Esq[r]. at a cost of two thousand pounds, and covered with Copper.[14] The length of the Church with the Chancel within the walls one hundred and four feet, breadth of the Church within the walls forty eight feet, breadth of Chancel within the walls thirteen feet. Adjoining and under the same roof is a Vestry room in length fifteen feet, breadth eight feet. The height of the Steeple is Seventy two feet and thirteen feet square within the walls.

Furniture and ornaments. The Chancel contains a Tablet of the Ten commandments, the Lord's prayer and the Belief,[25] a Communion table with a covering of red cloth, also a linen cloth for the same with one napkin. The Church contains a font of stone,[21] a Pulpit, Reading and Clerk's desks, a cushion for Pulpit, the King's Arms.[19] [The Vestry contains] six chairs, an Iron chest, with the Registers of Parchment. A strong iron bound chest with three locks containing a box with the Parish papers, and a box with the Communion plate consisting of two Silver Salvers weighing twenty five ounces,[6] a Silver Cup weighing twenty five ounces, and a Silver flaggon weighing Sixty one ounces, and one large chest with one lock containing two Surplices, a large Bible of the last Translation, two large Common Prayer Books, a pall to cover the Dead. [The Steeple] contains on the bottom floor a Bier to carry the dead, second floor a peal of hand bells twelve in number, third floor a Large Clock,[8] on the fourth floor Six large Bells with oak wheeles and frames,[9] the first bell being two feet seven inches in diameter, the second two feet eight inches in diameter, the third two feet ten inches in diameter, the fourth two feet eleven inches in diameter, the fifth three feet two inches in diameter, the sixth three feet six inches in diameter with this inscription " Southill Church repaired and the Bells recast 1814: Gloria dei in excellsis. John Bryant Hertford Fecit".[9]

Parish Clerk. Clerk's fees, Marriage by Banns two Shillings and sixpence, by Licence Five Shillings, for Burials two Shillings. At Easter two of the Stanford farms pays three Shillings each, one Rowney farm two Shillings and sixpence, the other farms two Shillings each. The three Mills one Shilling each, and each remaining farm one Shilling each. Thirteen Shillings and four pence yearly as Basket Money by the Churchwardens, and every housed-weller at Easter the sum of four pence.

2. Archdeacon Bonney's historical notices of churches, c.1820–1840

SOUTHILL, All Saints. This Church consists a Nave, Aisles, Chancel, a Vestry at the End of the North Aisle & the Mausoleum of the Byng Family beyond it.[11] A Tower at the West end Embattled and a South Porch.[18] The Piers are low, clustered with plain Mouldings supporting low pointed Arches. The General Character of the Windows is perpendicular or transition Decorated. The Window here sketched is in the North Aisle.[3] [*Sketch of the upper part of window tracery*].

The Church was refitted in 1816.[20] In the Chancel are buried some of the family of Nodes of this Parish and of Shephallbury in C° Herts., – and Sir John Kelynge, Serjeant at Law, who died 29 Dec 1680. There is a Monument in the South Aisle.

On the Chalice and on the Flagon,[6] which are large, and on the Two Patins, all of Silver is the Armorial Bearing of Sir ... Byng.[10] On one of the Patins, it is impaled with his Wife's.

[*Sketch of coat of arms* 3 Griffins heads erased].

3. Archdeacon Bonney's visitation notebook, 1823–1839

SOUTHILL. This Church consists of a Nave, North and South Aisles, A Tower at the West End of the Nave and Chancel at the East End thereof. The Mausoleum of the Family of Byng is on the North Side of the Fabrick.[11]

At the Visitation of 1823 It was ordered that a Covering of Cloth for the Communion Table be purchased.

At the Visitation of 1826, No order was given, or required. This Church was refitted entirely in 1816.[20]

At the Visitation of 1833 – no order was required, but at the Churchwardens request the Archdeacon wrote to Lord Torrington & expressed a wish that the Churchwarden might keep the Family Mausoleum in order, which he offered to do for 2/6 per ann: To this Lady Torrington, in behalf of her Son, replied in the affirmative.[11]

At the Visitation of 1836. I wrote to Lord Torrington – and stated the dilapidated State of his family Mausoleum –

At the Visitation 1839 – no order required.

4. Article on the Church by W.A. (no.38), NM 19 December 1846

SOUTHILL, All Saints. The whole of this church has not long since suffered what an inscription chooses to term a repair.[20] A reward is offered by the Churchwardens for the discovery of any person defacing the fabric,[33] a privilege which we presume these functionaries desire to monopolize, and it must be confessed that the aspect of the church affords abundant proof of their fitness for the task. Numerous as are the injuries visible, we doubt not that many more would be brought to light if the thick coating of white-wash, that great concealer of the ravages of decay and restoration, was to be removed. The roof of the nave and aisles are plaster, high pews are attached to the walls,[16] and such seats as are open are in the centre. An organ obscures the western window,[23] underneath which is an enclosure which appears more like a private box at the theatre, than a place for devotion. The internal fittings up correspond: bee-hive chairs, arm chairs covered with chintz, and other inappropriate furniture. Though the unhappy pew cannot escape observation, its fitting-up might, had they not been pointed out as objects of admiration. It is impossible to see without deep regret "the splendour, the carpeting, and tapestry, the gilding and painting of the drawing-room brought into God's house". The luxurious couches in this enclosure exhibit a painful contrast to the Windsor chairs fitted for the kitchen, which are appropriated to the communion table. Nothing is considered too costly where man's pride or comfort is concerned, nor too mean where the service and honor of God are the only objects of consideration. Two stoves,[22] with their hideous chimnies, mar the view of the building. The pulpit and reading-desk are better placed than usual; but they are very poor examples – the work most probably of the village joiner.[29] The glazing of the windows is of the commonest description, without the slightest attention to a tasteful arrangement for which it is so well adapted, and examples so abundant. The chancel roof is of plaster and has been lowered; perhaps when the repair took place, as the crown of the arch is concealed. The whole is as smooth as the handywork of the plasterer could render it, and consequently all vestiges of architectural ornament either removed or covered over. One window, if no more has been blocked up. A wooden erection at the back of the altar fortunately excludes a portion of the eastern window,[24] substituted at some period for the original, which, perhaps owing to neglect, was beyond the art of the local mason to restore. The font is a poor modern affair;[21] strict search might discover the ancient one devoted to some ignoble use. We have known such searches successfully rewarded. The churchyard, as is too often the case, a pasture ground for sheep.

December 7th, 1846   W.A.

Notes **1.** The west end of the church abuts directly on the grounds of Southill Park as shown in Badeslade's engraving of c.1730 (AD 1589) and as described in the 1822 terrier. Badeslade's view shows the church with a spire; **2.** Pevsner p.145, *VCH* III pp.260–1, *The Parish Church of All Saints, Southill: A short history and guide* by Kenneth Ashworth (1969); **3.** The curious window in the north aisle was sketched by Bonney and it has attracted the interest of Pevsner and other writers. The aisle itself was built in about 1520–5 as shown by bequests in the wills of John Cotton of Broom 1515, John Maynard of Broom 1522 and William Stanton of Southill 1524; **4.** Archidiaconal Visitations, 1578 (ABC 3 pp.8 and 209) in BHRS Vol.69 (1990) pp.178 and 181; **5.** Archidiaconal visitations, 1674 (CRT 170/9/1 p.11); **6.** The plate of 1691 is not listed in later terriers. The plate listed in the 1822 terrier and in the 1927 schedule (ABE 5) is that presented by Sir George Byng. For some years it has been on permanent display in the Cecil Higgins Art Gallery at Bedford (Ashworth p.29); **7.** Glebe terrier, 1707 (ABE 2 Vol.I p.159); **8.** The clock is first mentioned in 1707 and minor repairs and maintenance are recorded in the vouchers and accounts from 1751. It was taken down and re–erected by Thomas Inskip of Shefford when the church was restored in 1814 (W 1/6060–1). Inskip again repaired it in 1839 when Thomas Cubitt supplied a new slate dial (bills in W 4054). A new clock was put up by Hampden Inskip in 1864 (P 69/5/3) but this was replaced by the present electric synchronous movement in 1968; **9.** There were five bells in 1707. At the time of the rebuilding, the agent suggested that the bells should be disposed of but this was opposed by the parish (W 1/6035). Instead six new bells were cast by John Briant of Hertford in 1814 (W 1/6052 and 6063). Their inscriptions (including that of the tenor recast in 1867) are given in the 1822 terrier; **10.** For Southill and the Byng and Whitbread families <u>see</u> Patricia Bell in *Southill and the Whitbreads 1795–1995* (1995); **11.** Faculty petition for the Torrington vault or dormitory (also referred to as the mausoleum or columbarium) 1733 (LAO ref: Fac 9/19) cited by Clarke (1963) p.150. There is a modern copy of the 1733 faculty in the parish records (P 69/2/2/4). In a letter of 26 Dec.1811 (W 1/6032) George Byng stated that he did "not want the catacombs increased or altered as the family are no longer to be buried in the vault". He agreed to "send his own surveyor in the spring" and to have "the vault ... put in compleat repair". The roofline must have been altered shortly afterwards when the church was restored. Bonney expressed concern about the state of the Mausoleum in 1833 and 1836. The vault and its tombs are illustrated by Thomas Fisher (*Collections* p.89) and described by Ashworth (pp.26–9); **12.** The churchwardens' vouchers cover the period 1751–1852. Some are with the parish records (P 69/5/1–2) and others are among the Whitbread family archives (W 4054/1–47). The accounts are for 1785–1952 (P 69/5/3); **13.** There are two charity boards at the east end of the north aisle, one probably painted in 1811 (P 69/5/3) and the other recording later benefactions to 1842; **14.** Sources for the work initiated in 1811 include the Whitbread correspondence (with letters from Cloake and Reynolds) 1811–4 (in W 1/6028–65 *passim*) and the minutes and churchwardens' accounts (P 69/5/3). The work is summarised in Ashworth (pp.8–12); **15.** There are minutes (P 69/5/3) and letters (W 1/6038–65 *passim*) regarding the annuities, and the system of raising money is explained and analysed by Ashworth (pp.8–11); **16.** The pews in the aisles and open seats in the middle of the church were completed in 1814 (W 1/6063). New pews at Stotfold in 1840 were modelled on those at Southill (LPL ref: ICBS 2742). The high pews in the aisles, much disliked by W.A., were removed in 1958–9 (faculty P 69/2/2/17 and Ashworth p.13); **17.** A letter of 13 Nov.1814 refers to the completion of work in time for the reopening (W 1/6063); **18.** Ashworth (p.17) says the south porch was built in 1816. It replaces an earlier porch; **19.** Pardoe (p.5) says that the Royal arms are those in use from 1801–16 and therefore date from the time of the rebuilding; **20.** The inscription on the gallery reads: "The alterations and repairs of / This Church / were begun A.D. 1814 and completed A.D. 1816 / at the expense of the Parishioners and / under the auspices of / SAMUEL WHITBREAD, Esquire / Frederick Hervey Neve, A.M., Vicar / James Snitch [and] John Humberstone, Churchwardens". This wording probably explains why Bonney and other writers give the date of rebuilding as 1816, although it is clear from other sources that the main work was finished in 1814; **21.** There is an illustration of the mediaeval font (slide 1465) which was removed at the time of the rebuilding. A new font basin was obtained in 1824 (P 69/5/3). In 1827 Boissier (f.432) noted "New font" and in 1846 W.A. described it as "a poor modern affair"; **22.** Ashworth deduces (p.15) that the stoves were obtained in about 1840 when the first payments for coal appear in the accounts; **23.** Report of the new organ in *BM* 11 Dec.1841. This was a finger and barrel organ, mentioned in Boston and Langwill *Church and Chamber Barrel-Organs* (Edinburgh 1967) pp.69 and 73. A new organ by

Walker was obtained in 1867 (W 3527 and report in *BM* 22 Jan.1867); **24.** The work 1848–50 by Wing and Jackson is recorded in the accounts (P 69/5/3) and in a bundle of papers which includes a sketch of the window tracery (P 69/2/2/1); **25.** The work of 1854 included new commandments etc (by Wing) and repainting the church (P 69/5/3); **26.** The Whitbread windows of 1867 and 1871 are described by Ashworth (pp.20–1); **27.** The sources for the roof repairs in 1891–2 include the accounts (P 69/5/3), minutes (P 69/8/1) and the Whitbread estate accounts (W 4040 p.171); **28.** The window commemorating the Rev. Charles Baldock (Vicar 1867–77) is described by Ashworth (p.19). It was made by Powell of Whitefriars in 1894 (V&A ref: AAD 1/62 p.92); **29.** The 1912 pulpit replaced the deal pulpit and desk of 1814 which were moved from the chancel to the nave in 1848. Faculty papers, 1912 (HCRO ref: DSA 2/1/201). The new pulpit and lectern are mentioned in a report in *BT* 25 April 1913; **30.** The repairs in 1923 and 1927 are noted by Ashworth (p.13); **31.** Faculty for font and window, with related papers 1937 (P 69/2/2/10–11); **32.** Faculties for work in 1951–8 (P 69/2/2/14–7); **33.** The reward notice, which states "NOTICE / Whoever will / give information to / the Church Wardens / of any person / wilfully defacing / this Church shall / receive a reward / of 5 Shill[s].", still hangs in the porch.

STAGSDEN

The oldest parts of the church date from the C13th when the building apparently consisted of a chancel, nave and west tower. The south door, moved to its present position in the C14th when the south aisle and porch were added, is also of the C13th. In the C15th a north chapel was added, the top of the tower added or rebuilt and the nave walls raised by the addition of a clerestory.[1] The font dates from the C14th.[2] There is a Perpendicular screen[3] and there are C15th niches in the south aisle.[4]

In 1552 the commissioners reported "The churche and the steple covered leade and the chancell covered with tyle and slate".[5] There were then four bells.[6] Three of the present bells date from the C17th, two cast in 1652 and another in 1684. In 1668–9 it was stated that "The Chancell windowes want glasseing" and in 1674 the chancel was reported to be "out of repair".[7] In 1769 a bell was recast or added.[6] Dated rainwater heads on the south clerestory relate to repairs in 1790.

The repairs ordered by Archdeacon Bonney in 1823 had been completed by 1826. In 1825 the parish bought a new communion cup.[8] In 1833 Bonney noted that the church was "under thorough repair both internally and externally" and the accounts record expenditure of some £92 in 1833–4.[9] In 1835 the church was struck by lightning. Further work is recorded in 1839 and 1842. One of the bells was recast in 1844.[6]

The main Victorian restoration seems to have taken place between 1848 and 1850 under Thomas Jobson Jackson of Bedford.[10] A sketch dated 1850 shows that the chancel roof was off when Lord Northampton visited the church with the Rev.C.H. Hartshorne in that year.[11] A new flagon was also added to the plate in 1850.[8] The bells were rehung in a new frame in 1856.[6] The leaded spire may also have been reconstructed in 1856 and in 1870 a further £200 was spent on repairs to the church.

In about 1870 a second-hand organ was obtained from St.Mary's, Bedford.[12] A clock was put up in the tower in 1872 in memory of Lord

14. Stagsden: SE view showing the downpipes on the clerestory with rainwater heads dated 1790. The east and south windows of the chancel were altered at the restoration in 1848–50 when a gable cross and buttresses were added at the east end.   *(Watercolour: Thomas Fisher c.1815)*

Dynevor.[13] The east window was filled with geometrical glass in 1874 as a memorial to Charles Bass.[14] The parish register gives details of improvements to the church during the incumbency of the Rev W.H. Jackson (Vicar 1879–1916).[15] These include painted texts on the walls in 1884 and 1887, new fittings for the sanctuary and chancel in 1887, a new brass lectern in 1895, the addition of the vestry in 1896 and internal redecoration of the church in 1908. Hailstorm damage to the west-facing windows in 1906 is also recorded.[16]

Major changes of the present century include the restoration of the bells in 1932,[6] the furnishing of the east end of the south aisle as a chapel dedicated in memory of Madeleine Bonavia Hunt (d.1937), the stained glass windows of 1949–50 in the south aisle[17] and the enlargement of the organ in 1948 and 1977.[12]

1. Extract from glebe terrier, 5 July 1822
STAGSDEN.
Church yard. Item the Churchyard containing three roods and twenty eight poles and three quarters surrounded by a wall and paling and adjoining the Road except towards the South-West and North West where it is bounded by a Close belonging to Lord Hampden in the occupation of Thomas Watford. The Gates and Boundaries are kept up by the Parish.

Church. Belonging to the said Parish are First the Parish Church, an ancient structure containing in length (with the Chancel) One hundred and two feet, and in breadth thirty six feet. The Chancel is eighteen feet wide. The Belfry is about eighteen feet square with a ring of five bells[6] and the Tower about seventy feet in height.

Furniture and ornaments. Within and belonging to which Church are One Communion Table with a covering to the same of blue cloth. Also one linen cloth to the same and two napkins. One pewter flaggon, two pewter plates, One silver cup and cover.[8] A bier, cloth pall & surplice. The old Parish Chest with three locks & another box or chest containing some few articles of little value. Also two Common Prayer Books & the Bible of the largest size. An Edition of the Book of Homilies printed in 1633 and another Copy printed in 1815.

Parish Registers. Also Eight Register Books as follows: the First beginning in 1666 and ending in 1705, the Second beginning 1705 and ending 1761, the Third containing Baptisms and Burials from 1761 to 1816, the Fourth containing Marriages & Banns beginning 1755 and ending in 1812, [no fifth] the Sixth, Seventh and Eighth are the New Registers of Baptisms, Burials and Marriages respectively provided according to the late Act of Parliament commencing in 1813 & continuing to the present time. The whole are kept in an Iron Chest and are in tolerably good preservation.

2. Archdeacon Bonney's historical notices of churches, c.1820–1840
STAGSDEN OR STACHDEN, St. Leonard. This Church consists of a Nave with a Chapel at the North East end of it, a South Aisle & Porch, Chancel & a Tower embattled with leaden roof drawn up to a point. The South Door is Early English & The window in the South of the Chancel. The East window is decorated. The font is octagonal with panels,[2] two of which only remain, with two figures, supported by a central Pier with four short Piers round it. The Tower is Perpendicular. From a small external Niche on the East Gable of the Nave, it appears that the Chancel was higher than at present and had a Chamber over it for a Priest. The Piers and Arches are Early English. The Rood Screen is perpendicular.[3] On Brass against a Pier on the South side of the Nave are the Effigies of John Cooke in Armour and his Wife, both kneeling.[18] He was a General in the Reign of James 1st. There are two decorated Windows on the North Side of the Nave, and there is a plain Tomb under a Sepulchral Arch.

There are two plated Plates, and a Chalice. On the latter is inscribed "Thomas Gregory, Richard Sleath Churchwardens of the Parish of Stagsden Beds 1825".[8]

This Church was struck by Lightning in the Harvest of 1835. There are five Bells.[6]

3. Archdeacon Bonney's visitation notebook, 1823–1839
STAGSDEN. This Church consists of a Nave, South Aisle, and part of a North Aisle, a Tower at the West End of the Nave, and Chancel at the East End thereof.

At the Visitation of 1823 It was ordered that the Earth be moved from the Walls all round the exterior of the Fabrick, the floor of the Middle Chamber in the Tower be repaired; the Stairs in the Tower be repaired; the Seats in the Church & also the Chancel be repaired and oiled; a casement be placed in one of the Chancel Windows, and two other Casements in the Church; the windows be glazed down to the Sill; the Chancel Roof be thoroughly repaired & ceiled; a new plated Flagon be purchased:[8] the Font be restored,[2] and a new Font Bason purchased; a new Communion Table & linen Cloth to cover it be bought; the blue Cloth Covering of the Communion Table be cleansed: the Door of the Chancel be repaired.

At the Visitation of 1826 – The above order had been complied with and the following order only thought necessary – that the Walls of the Church and Chancel be pointed, and the Munions & Tracery of the Windows restored with Parker's Cement; a new Door be placed in the Chancel – before Easter 1828.

At the Visitation of 1833 The following Order was given that the Screen before the Chancel be laid open – The church was then under thorough repair both internally and externally.[9]

At the Visitation of 1836 ordered that the Tower be pointed, the battlements on the South side be repaired also the Tiling on the Chancel, also the floor of a Pew – pointed out at the time – the Pavement kept clean – the Open Seats set even – and the Clerk's Prayer Book repaired.

At the Visitation 1839 Found this Church externally under repair. Ordered the floors of some of the Open Seats to be repaired – & a proper Font Bason.

4. Article on the Church by W.A. (no.71), NM 21 August 1847

STAGSDEN, St. Leonard. The difficulty in obtaining a view into this church was considerable. The church-yard is not only locked, but the gates have spikes on top lest any unhappy tourist, or it may be relative of the departed, should attempt to scale the gates to inspect the grave-stones. When, however, the janitor is found, you will perhaps have to wait whilst he makes his bargain for a fee in opening the gates of the church, which has been emphatically styled as that of the poor man. Having concluded your bargain, the first set of gates is opened, not a wicket as is usually the case, but stern, repulsive prison doors. Then you attain the church gates themselves. After all the chaffering for admission, and throwing open the various obstacles, you would naturally expect to be introduced into some very beautiful specimen of church architecture, admirably arranged, and in high preservation. Bitter will be your disappointment, for you will witness the ravages of damp and dirt most extensively, and the whole fittings-up in a very disgraceful condition. The chancel is ceiled,[11] well plastered, a common brick floor, and all in a very neglected condition.

Worn-out matting, a ruined prayer–book rotting on a bracket, the window a repository for the tattered books of a Sunday School, the children of which we presume receive their first lessons, of order and decency, and reverence of

Holy things, in this quarter. Some stall sittings are in a very dirty state. The upper part of the chancel-arch is boarded up, built on the remains of the rood screen.[3] The nave has a timber roof. The pulpit and reading-desk are wrongly placed; there are some open sittings mingled with enclosed boxes. The western window is shut out. There are festoons of hat pegs. The panelling of the rood screen is hidden by two large square pews erected close to it.[3]

We avail ourselves of every opportunity to bring forward the protest of other writers against these wretched deformities; the removal of which we are aware is chiefly opposed, not by the highest of the land, but by those of inferior rank. In a neighbouring county, where the work of restoration has proceeded, a writer of the present day observes: "More would be done but for the pride and prejudice of the parishioners, and the farmers – these tillers of the soil – these village shop-keepers, these genteel families of yesterday's growth – have their spheres and distinctions, and stone walls of separation; they must have their big, ugly, tall pews, and their doors and their locks and keys, and their hassocks; they cannot worship the God that made them upon a footing of equality with the poor, or with their neighbours, and, therefore, these vile enclosures – these pews for Christians to worship in – are all left standing, to the destruction of the harmony and effect of the ancient and holy edifice? Are men never to learn that the first sentiment on entering a church ought to be that of humility? Are we to despair of the coming of the day when the very greatest and wealthiest among us shall feel how poor a worm he is when brought to pray before the Almighty God? Is every Roman Catholic country in Europe to continue to show us examples in this respect, which put every thinking Englishman to the blush?"*

The niches in the south aisle are plastered over,[4] and destroyed without remorse to let in wood-work for suspending hats. The flooring is common brick. The remains of an alms-box are a sufficient comment on the rest of the neglect exhibited in this church.

The font has its drain and lining,[2] but is not used. The columns are all plastered. The windows of the porch are blocked up. The chancel-roof is tiled, but lead remains on the nave and aisles.

August 16th, 1847   W.A.

* Knight's Land We Live In, Part 3d, page 150

Notes **1.** Pevsner pp.147–8, Harvey pp.132–6, and *VCH* III pp.98–100; **2.** The font is illustrated by Harvey (p.135); **3.** In 1827 Boissier (f.371–2) noted "Rood loft screen retains some gilding, but is in part plastered up". W.A. states that in 1847 the upper part of the chancel arch was boarded up and part of the panelling of the screen was hidden by pews; **4.** W.A. noted that these niches were "plastered over and destroyed without remorse"; **5.** Eeles and Brown p.15; **6.** As there is no terrier of 1708 it is uncertain whether the treble bell of 1769 was added to the ring or recast from an earlier bell. The fourth was recast in 1844. The bellframe (dated 1856) was probably made by Mr.Maxey whose name appears in the accounts. The bells were again rehung and a sixth added in 1932; **7.** Visitation returns 1668–9 (ABC 7) and 1674 (CRT 170/9/1 p.5); **8.** The old plate is listed in the 1822 terrier. In 1825 the churchwardens bought the chalice noted by Bonney and by Harvey (p.136) and a flagon was purchased in 1850 (ABE 5) from Bull of Bedford for £3 3s (P 79/5/1); **9.** Churchwardens' accounts 1831–1917 (P 79/5/1). These accounts generally give only names and sums, with little information on how the money was spent. They seem to indicate major repairs in 1833–4 (£93), 1850 (£225), 1856–7 (£248) and 1870–1 (£250); **10.** The BAAS report in *GM* Vol.29 (May 1848) p.529 mentions work about to be done at Stagsden and the accounts for 1850–1 record expenditure of £225 on the fabric. The RC article in *BT* 28 July 1899 attributes the restoration to Jackson; **11.** The chancel had a plaster ceiling when W.A. visited in 1847 and so Hartshorne's sketch of 1850 (Mic 117) evidently pinpoints the date of the present chancel roof; **12.** A barrel organ made by William Allen of London in 1804 for St.Mary's, Bedford, was converted to manual and transferred to Stagsden when St.Mary's obtained a new organ in 1870 (Boston and Langwill *Church and Chamber Barrel-Organs* (Edinburgh 1967) pp.47 and 73). It was rebuilt in 1897 by Trustam and later by the Rev. Noel Bonavia Hunt, an authority on organs, who was Vicar 1937–55; **13.** The clock is by Bull of Bedford. There is a subscription list with accounts (in P 79/5/1) and a description of the clock in a report in *BM* 9 Nov.1872; **14.** The east window of 1874 is by Cox & Sons (*British Architect* Vol.2 (1874) p.249 and *CT* 16 Oct.1874 p.506); **15.** Parish register memorandum concerning the work of Jackson's time (P 79/1/8); **16.** The hailstorm was noted by Jackson (P 79/1/8) and by Archdeacon Bathurst (ABE 3); **17.** The windows of St.Michael (1949) and St.Leonard (1950) in the south aisle are by G.Maile & Son, and the Dimmock window (1950) is by Francis Spear (*ex.inf.* Muriel Bonnett); **18.** For the brass (illustrated in Harvey p.137) see Lack *et.al.* (p.88).

STANBRIDGE

Stanbridge, like Billington, Eggington and Heath and Reach, was a dependent chapelry of Leighton Buzzard. There was a chapel here by 1277 and in 1406 the inhabitants gained the right of burial in their own chapel.[1] In 1735 the chapelry became a separate benefice,[2] still within the jurisdiction of the Leighton Buzzard Peculiar. Augmentations of the perpetual curacy in the late C18th funded the purchase of land at Mursley which provided income for the minister.[3] Stanbridge eventually became a vicarage in 1866.[4] Because it was a chapelry and outside the Archdeacon's jurisdiction neither W.A. nor Bonney refer to Stanbridge.

The oldest part of the present church is the chancel which was built in the late C13th. The north and south arcades are of c.1300 and c.1330 respectively. The west tower and clerestory date from the C15th when Perpendicular tracery was inserted in other parts of the church.[5] There is a font of c.1300,[6] and the pulpit dates from around 1600.[7]

In the early C17th a charity was established to provide ropes for the bells.[8] The oldest of the existing bells is dated 1637 but the others (dated between 1709 and 1807) may have been recast from earlier ones.[9] A communion cup was given by Daniel Ellingham, who was churchwarden, in 1683.[10] Ellingham (d.1713) and his wife Elizabeth (d.1723) are commemorated on a monument in the nave.

From 1733 information on work on the church is recorded in the wardens' accounts.[11] Repairs costing almost £40 were carried out in 1752, the bells were repaired by Thomas Sharp in 1780, and in 1793–4 some major work was done on the roof and windows. At a visitation of the Peculiar in 1827 it was reported that the chancel was "in great want of repair".[12] In the same year Boissier noted "The Tower is greatly decayed, & was originally very roughly built".[13]

In 1833 the vestry had the church surveyed. Four people submitted estimates for repairing and restoring the church, that of Mr. Nixon (£290) being
accepted.[14] The vestry took out a loan on the security of the rates to pay for
the work.[15] Apart from substituting slate for the lead on the roof it is not
known what was done, but the work probably included the erection of the
west gallery, partial re-seating, and the insertion of iron ties between the north
and south clerestory walls. The vestry accepted a tender from Mr. Jones (£45)
for repairs in 1860, but the wardens could not obtain a rate and so the work
was never done.[16]

The Rev. Thomas Green became vicar of Stanbridge and Tilsworth in 1871
and during his incumbency the two churches were eventually restored. A new
Vicarage was built at Stanbridge for the combined parishes in 1874.[17] The
architect was Ewan Christian, who first prepared a scheme for restoring
Stanbridge church in 1873.[18] In 1873 Archdeacon Bathurst described the
church as "very unsound" and in 1888 he found it in a "very bad state".[19] By
1881 the organ could not be used, and so the choir was moved down from the
gallery to pine benches in the chancel where a harmonium was provided.[20]

Lack of money delayed the planned restoration, but in 1890–2 the scheme
was revived. The whole church was restored in 1892–3 under Ewan Christian
at a cost of £2229 (including the chancel which was restored by the
Ecclesiastical Commission).[21] The south aisle, porch and chancel arch were
rebuilt, the roofs restored and re-covered with lead, the floors re-laid and new
seating provided. The organ was repaired by Atterton. The Vicar gave a new
silver paten. The church was re–opened on 13 July 1893.

Later improvements include the new table made from the old pulpit sounding board,[7] stained glass by Horace Wilkinson in the east window in 1913,[22]
the clock placed in the tower in 1923 as a War memorial,[23] a new wooden font
cover in 1928,[6] and the new organ chamber and organ completed in 1932.[24] In
more recent times the bells have been rehung and augmented to six (1951 and
1988).[9] Further restoration work has been carried out on the roofs and fabric
(1952–9),[25] and a vestry and ringing loft in the tower were created in 1965.[26]

1. Glebe terrier, 24 June 1822 [27]

STANDBRIDGE.

Chapel Yard. Imprimis, the Chapel Yard containing three roods or there-
abouts, bounded on all sides by the Common Green and Highway, with the
pale fence thereto belonging and repaired by the said hamlet.

Endowments of the Cure, and Fees. Item, to the said Curacy belongeth
the Tithes as expressed in the endowment of the Mother Church to which
Chapel they were ceded by the Vicar to procure the augmentation of Queen
Ann's Bounty and are compounded for as heretofore, The sum of Eight hundred pounds was allotted by the Governors of the said Bounty to the Chapel
of Standbridge, Four hundred pounds of which was laid out in the Purchase

of Land in the parish of Mursley in the County of Buckingham which produced the Yearly Rent of Sixteen pounds per annum, and consists of a Close of Pasture Land, containing by estimation fourteen acres, and eight pounds per annum is paid by the Treasurer of the Bounty for the remaining four hundred pounds.[3] Which said Curacy is worth at the present time about Thirty pounds a Year. Item, for every funeral one shilling and sixpence. Item, for every churching of women sixpence.

Parish Clerk and Sexton. There is also due to the Parish Clerk (who is Sexton also) one pound per annum paid from the Assessment of the Hamlet, and a small collection from the Inhabitants at Easter. For every funeral one shilling and sixpence and for every churching of Women three pence.

Church. Belonging to the said Hamlet are first the Chapel an ancient Building containing in length (with the Chancel) Sixty six feet, in breadth thirty five feet within the walls, and the Chancel fifteen feet in breadth. The Steeple is eleven feet by twelve feet three inches within the Walls.

Furniture and ornaments. Within and belonging to the said Chapel are one communion table, one linen cloth, and one napkin, one pewter flaggon, one silver chalice with the following inscription (Daniel Ellingham bought me, Churchwarden 83 – supposed to be in the year 1683),[10] one oak chest,[28] one pulpit[7] and reading desk, one pulpit cushion covered with crimson velvet, one green baise desk cloth, one quarto bible of the last translation printed one thousand seven hundred and sixty two, two common prayers printed 1790 and 1809. One surplice. The Lord's Prayer and belief written on the walls. Five Bells with their frames.[9] The first or least Bell is two feet five inches and a quarter in diameter with the following inscription (Richard Chandler made me 1709). The second two feet eight inches in diameter with the following inscription (F. Ellingham C.W. John Bryant Hertford Fecit 1807). The Third is two feet ten inches and three quarters in diameter (1637). The Fourth is three feet one inch and a quarter in diameter with the following inscription (Be it well known to all that do me see, that William Emerton of Wootton made me 1775, Thomas Eames John Cooper Churchwardens). The Fifth and largest is three feet two inches and a half in diameter with the following inscription (George Chandler made me 1725).

Parish Registers. One Register (part parchment and part paper) of Baptisms and Burials commencing one thousand five hundred and sixty one to one thousand seven hundred and nine. One register of Parchment commencing one thousand seven hundred and nine ending one thousand seven hundred and thirty seven. One parchment Register commencing one thousand seven hundred and thirty nine and ending one thousand seven hundred and ninety three. One Parchment register commencing one thousand seven hundred and ninety three ending one thousand eight hundred and thirteen, and Registers agreeably to act of Parliament from one thousand eight hundred and thirteen to the present time.

15. Stanbridge: View of the church from the west, showing the original south aisle and porch which were rebuilt in 1892–3　　　　　　　　*(Watercolour: George Shepherd c.1820)*

16. Stanbridge: A view of the nave before restoration in 1892–3 showing the open seats in the nave and enclosed pews in the north aisle, the pulpit and sounding board, west gallery and one of the iron tie bars between the clerestory walls. The tablet commemorates Daniel Ellingham who gave the communion cup in 1683.　　　　　　　*(Photograph: Theo. J. Pigott, c.1890)*

Charities. There are Six acres two roods of Open Field arable Land dispersed in the Hamlet of Standbridge, the net rent whereof amounting to Three pounds twelve shillings and fourpence is paid to the Curate which Land was bequeathed by some person now unknown. One acre and half of Arable Land situate in the said Hamlet of Standbridge was given by [blank – traditionally said to have been given by Henry Honner who died in 1627] the Rent of which was to buy Bell Ropes for the said Chapel for ever.[8]

Parish Officers. The Chapelwardens and Overseers are appointed annually at Lady Day by the inhabitants.

5. Sir Stephen Glynne's Church notes, 14 May 1870 (Vol.2, pp.40–41)

STANBRIDGE, St. John the Baptist. The church has Clerestoried nave aisles, chancel, S. porch & West Tower. All the exterior rough cast. The prevailing features are Perpendicular. The windows both of aisles & Clerestory are square headed, of 2 lights & labeled, & there are none at the W end of the aisles. The arcades of the nave have each 4 pointed arches with octagonal pillars having moulded capitals. (The north arcade is loftier than the Southern[i]). The roofs are of flat pitch. The Chancel arch is like those of the Arcades. The Chancel is long has on the NW a single lychnoscopic light with trefoil head. The other windows are Perpendicular of 2 & 3 lights, with depressed arches – a common form in this neighbourhood. There is a piscina at the S.E. with trefoiled arch – There is a debased wood screen across the entrance to the chancel & on the S of it a Perpendicular Priest's door. There are no parapets externally. The Font is Early English – has a plain circular bowl on a clustered stem of 4 shafts.[6] The south doorway has good continued arch mouldings – The outer door of the porch is labeled. The tower is of 3 stages – divided by 2 strings & wholly Perpendicular, has embattles parapet, large buttresses stopping below the belfry & a 2 light W window: the belfry windows of 2 lights & there is an oblong opening in the second stage.

Notes **1.** Robert Richmond *Leighton Buzzard and its hamlets* (1928) esp. pp.78–83 on "Church History of the Hamlets"; **2.** The accounts of the status of the parish in the *VCH* and in Richmond are incomplete and inaccurate. Youngs (p.10) states that Stanbridge became a separate ecclesiastical parish (perpetual curacy) in 1735 and that it came under the peculiar jurisdiction of Leighton Buzzard until 1852 when the area of the peculiar was brought into the Archdeaconry of Bedford; **3.** The deed of endowment dated 1804 (P 57/2/1/10) regarding the Mursley property, also mentioned in the 1822 terrier, refers to augmentations of the cure by Queen Anne's Bounty in 1737, 1775 and 1799; **4.** Papers concerning the creation of Stanbridge Vicarage under the District Church Tithes Act 1865, including copy of *London Gazette* 30 Nov.1866 (p.6654) containing the order in Council (P 57/2/1/11–12); **5.** Pevsner p.148, *VCH* III pp.412–4, Richmond *op.cit.*, and *A Short Guide to the Parish Church of St. John the Baptist Stanbridge* (1992); **6.** The font is of c.1300 and it is described by Glynne. It has a modern cover of 1928 (P 57/2/2/24); **7.** The pulpit is variously described as Elizabethan or Jacobean. The old sounding board was removed in 1892 and subsequently made into a table, still in the church; **8.** Details of the bellrope charity are given in the 1822 terrier. It is said to have been founded by Henry Honour (or Honner) who died in 1627. North (p.194) noted in 1880 that the income was no longer used for the benefit of the bells or for the purchase of bellropes; **9.** The bells are described by North (pp.193–4) and their inscriptions and dates are given in the 1822 terrier. It seems probable that there were five bells by 1709, the date of the treble. There are papers concerning rehanging in 1951 etc (P 57/2/2/31–3) and details of the bells to 1988 are given in the guide; **10.** The cup is inscribed "Daniel Ellingham Curch Warden of Standbridge Bought me 83" (ABE 5). The plate also includes a paten given by the Rev. Thomas Green in 1893; **11.** Churchwardens' accounts 1733–1825 (P 57/5/1) and 1825–1972 (P 57/5/4); **12.** Visitation return, 1827 (RI 5/1); **13.** Boissier (f.386d); **14.** Vestry minutes regarding the 1833 repairs (P 57/8/1) which are not mentioned in the accounts (P 57/5/4); **15.** The vestry agreed to borrow money (P 57/8/1) and there are mortgage papers and correspondence regarding the loan which was not repaid until 1854 (P 57/2/2/1–2); **16.** Vestry minutes regarding proposed repairs, June–Aug.1860 (P 57/8/1) and letter from the Vicar in the Church Commissioners' file (CERC ref: EC file 23070); **17.** Mortgage papers and plans regarding the new Vicarage, 1874 (CUL ref: EDR/G3/40 MGA/BED/55) and outbuildings, 1875 (*ibid* no.59), papers (P 57/2/4/1–2) and photograph of the new house c.1875 (P 57/28/12/5); **18.** According to Green's notes he had the aim of restoring the church in mind from 1871 and began to raise money shortly after his arrival in the parish (P 57/2/2/4). The Church Commissioners records (CERC ref: EC file 23070) include a report on the chancel with plans of June 1873. Christian's specification for the other works is dated April 1879 (P 57/2/2/3); **19.** Bathurst's notebook (ABE 3); **20.** Report in *LBO* 11 Jan.1881; **21.** Sources for the restoration of 1892–3 include a very full set of parish papers 1871–97 (P 57/2/2/4–20), the Church Commissioners' file (CERC ref: EC file 23070), pre–restoration photographs of the interior and exterior c.1890 (P 57/28/12/1–4), appeal leaflet 1891 (in SPAB archives), ICBS correspondence and papers (with plans) 1891–3 (LPL ref: ICBS 9651), faculty 1892 (P 57/2/2/12), faculty papers (HCRO ref: DSA 2/1/202) and associated plans (CUL ref: EDR/D3/64/49), and reports in *LBO* 16–23 Sept and 9 Dec.1890, *BT* and *BM* 22 July 1893, and *LBO* 18 July and 23 Sept.1893; **22.** Faculty papers for the east window 1913 (HCRO ref: DSA 2/1/202) and associated drawings (CUL ref: EDR/D3/64/12). The window itself was heightened at the time (CERC ref: EC file 23070); **23.** Faculty for the clock and related papers, 1923–4 (P 57/2/2/22–3); **24.** Faculty and papers regarding organ chamber and organ, 1931–2 (P 57/2/2/27–8). Correspondence and plans (CERC ref: file EC 23070); **25.** Faculties for repairs in the 1950s (P 57/2/2/34–6); **26.** Papers concerning the ringing gallery, 1964–5 (P 57/2/2/37–9); **27.** The full text of the terrier is given here and only the preamble and signatures etc. are omitted; **28.** There is a chest in the church marked "IE HL 1716".

STAUGHTON, Little

The list of incumbents begins in 1245 and the present church has developed from an aisleless C13th building consisting of a nave and chancel of equal width. The south aisle and chapel were added in the early C14th, and the present chancel, clerestory and west tower date from the C15th.[1] The nave has a C15th roof rising from carved stone corbels, one of which represents a cross-legged figure playing the bagpipes.[2] There is a documentary reference to making and painting the ceiling of the porch in 1446.[3] The south door dates from the C15th. There are some fragments of mediaeval stained glass.[4]

By 1712 there were five bells including one mediaeval bell, one of 1628 and two of 1654.[5] The bellframe also dates from the mid C17th. One of the bells was recast in 1755.

In the C18th the church received several gifts and underwent a number of alterations. The plate includes a pewter alms dish made by Thomas Spencer in the time of King George I,[6] and a fine cup and paten of 1740 in a contemporary wooden case covered with tooled leather.[7] A new service book was presented by Richard Welby in 1745.[8] Canon Clarke mistakenly noted a reference to the theft of lead during the course of roof repairs in 1787.[9] Eleanor

Gery gave new linen for the communion table in 1795.[10] By the end of the C18th the church had a west gallery, a three-tier pulpit and desk (of which the pulpit survives), and there were several enclosed pews in the body of the church. These arrangements were described by W.A. in 1852 and they remained unchanged when Arthur Ransom visited the church in 1900.[11]

Archdeacon Bonney's order book shows that repairs were carried out between 1823 and 1826, but attempts to put the church into good order suffered from setbacks when the lead was stolen from the roof and the spire was damaged by lightning in the 1830s. The parish records from 1862–3 refer to minor improvements to the stoves and the acquisition of a harmonium in 1867, but very little was done.[12] Archdeacon Bathurst's notebook indicates the poor condition of the church from 1876, although in 1882 he noted that the chancel was under repair.[13] In 1897 W.H. Wade–Gery gave a Bishop's chair for the chancel.[14]

The Rev. A.A. Hancock arrived as Rector in 1899, and in that year a brass cross from St.Saviour's Luton and new lamps and candlesticks were introduced.[15] The parish was forced into undertaking improvements after the spire was struck by lightning on 12 June 1900, causing considerable damage to the west end of the church.[16] A restoration took place under Mallows and Grocock in 1900–1.[17] The truncated spire was capped rather than rebuilt. The roof was repaired with the old materials, the damaged west gallery was removed, the tower arch was opened up, the enclosed pews were cleared away and the nave was re-seated using the old C16th benches. The treble bell, cracked by the fall of the spire, was recast and the bells were rehung.[5] The church was re-opened on 15 October 1901.

Further damage occurred when many of the western windows in the church were broken in the great hailstorm that caused devastation in the parish on 2 August 1906.[18] In 1910 a new spire was built to the designs of W.B. Stonebridge.[19] In 1916 a new font cover was made from oak taken from the old spire.[20] Stonebridge was also responsible for the work undertaken in 1924–5 when an organ chamber was added on the north side of the chancel, a new Conacher organ installed, and the chancel furnished with new stalls.[21] Further general restoration took place between 1928 and 1937,[22] and in 1934 the bells were rehung.[5] Recent work includes the renewal of the rainwater pipes in copper in 1961 and the reconstruction of the tower parapet in 1982.[23]

1. Extract from glebe terrier, 5 July 1822

LITTLE STAUGHTON.

Church yard. The Church yard is Seventeen pole in Length Eight pole in breadth.

Church. Belonging to the said Parish and Containing in Length with the Chancel ninety Six Feet, in breadth forty Eight Feet. The Chancel is Thirty

Feet by Twenty one. The Steeple is Fifteen Feet Square, the height is Sixty Feet.

Furniture and ornaments. There is a Communion Table with a Covering for the Same of Green Cloth. Also one Linen Cloth for the Same with Two napkins.[10] One pewter flaggon,[6] one Cup, one bason for the offertory.[7] One Table of Degrees. One Chest with three Locks.[24] One pulpit and Reading Desk.[11] One pulpit cushion covered with red Cloth. One Large Bible. Two Large common Prayer Books. The King's arms with the Ten Commandments. Five bells with their frames.[5] One bier. One surplice. Three parchment Registers books (the date beginning 1695[i]).[25] Also one Iron Chest.

Seats in the Church. The present time the Seats in the Church (and Chancel[c]) have Been Repaired for Time Immemorial at the Expence of the parish. The Chancel Repaired by the Rector

Parish Clerk. There is Sixpence for Churching of women, for every Wedding by publication of banns one Shilling, by Licence Two Shillings & sixpence, for every Funeral Toling the Bell one Shilling, for Digin the Grave Sixpence.

2. Archdeacon Bonney's historical notices of churches, c.1820–1840

STAUGHTON PARVA, All Saints. This Church consists of a Nave and South Aisle, Chancel, Tower (embattled[i]) on which rises a Spire at the West End, and South Porch, all of the perpendicular character except the Windows in the South Aisle, and a Sepulchral Arch on the North side of the Chancel. Within this Arch is a more modern Inscription on a Brass.[26] The inscription on the Brass is as follows. Gulielmus Lake. S.T.B. Hujus Ecclesiæ Rector annos 34. Moriens reliquit Hoc Distichon Peccati miserere Deus sub mole gementis / vivat et igniculi Christe favilla tui. / Tit: 2.14. / Obiit 12 Apri' Anno Domini 1679 / Ætate suæ 72. [*Sketch of coat of arms*]

The Font is octangular and plain. On a corbel in the Nave is a Figure cross legged & playing on the Bagpipe.[2] South Door oak, and neat studded Perpendicular. On the Chalice with the Garter are the Arms of the See of Winchester impaling a Pelican standing in her Nest & pecking her breast.[7] Inscription "Little Staughton." Probably the Gift of Bishop Handley whose armorial Bearing is upon it.

3. Archdeacon Bonney's visitation notebook, 1823–1839

STAUGHTON (Parva). This Church consists of a Nave and South Aisle, a Tower surmounted by a Spire at the West End of the Nave and Chancel at the East End thereof. A Porch to the South Aisle.

At the Visitation for 1823, the following Order was given, that the earth be moved from the Exterior of the Walls and the Walls be pointed; the Battlements be restored with Stone, also the Bell chamber windows; The Stone work of the other windows and the doors be restored with Parker's

17. Little Staughton: The spire was struck by lightning on 12 June 1900 and its fall caused considerable damage to the west end of the church. Although consolidated and capped in 1901, the spire was not replaced until 1910   *(Photograph: Anonymous c.1900)*

Cement; the south East side of the Steeple be pointed; the parts of the Windows now blocked up be glazed; casements be made in the West and south East Windows of the South Aisle; other Casements be also made in the North Window near the Pulpit – & in the Chancel Windows; the open Seats be neatly repaired cleansed and oiled; the Pulpit Top be repaired; the Middle Chamber floor in the Steeple, and the Bell Wheels be repaired;

the Sunday School not to be taught in the Body of the church, but in the Belfry.

At the Visitation for 1826 the only Order thought necessary was as follows – that the Lime be taken out of the Windows and glass inserted; the cracked Bell be recast;[5] the floors of the Parlour and Barn at the Rectory-House be repaired; before Easter 1828.

At the Visitation of 1833 It was ordered that a proper Font Bason be purchased, the walls be cleansed – four new oak legs be put to the communion Table – a new woollen covering for the same be purchased – the yellow parts of the Pulpit Desk, Rector's Pew & Gallery be oak grained to suit the Sounding Board of the Pulpit[11] – a new Pall, crimson Cushion for the Pulpit & cloth for the desk be purchased.

The glebe House occupied by a Farmer.

At the Visitation 1836 ordered a new Font Bason. The Lead from the roof having been stolen and the Parish put to Great Expense, the recasting of the Bell was postponed.[5]

At the Visitation of 1839. The following Orders were given. A new Surplice. The Rector to repair the ceiling of the Chancel above the Communion Table – a proper Font Bason to be procured. The cracked Bell to be recast when the Parish has recovered from the heavy charges incurred from the damage of the Spire by Lightning – and the Stealing of the Lead from the Church.

4. Article on the Church by W.A. (no.107), NM 11 December 1852

STAUGHTON PARVA, All Saints. In the chancel are two lofty pews, but more decorously placed than usual. The timber roof remains, in very tolerable condition.

The villagers were occupied, when we saw the church in destroying the "nasty" birds, who had taken possession of some of the decayed parts; thus neglect leads to cruelty.

There is an altar monument, on which is placed a brass,[26] which could never have formed part of it originally. The whitewash has been scraped from the canopy, but abounds in other parts.

The nave has an open roof; there is a slight remnant of the screen, but very difficult to be seen, so oppressed is it with some barbarous modern work. Some curious stone brackets, stoves as usual, and a singing loft.[11] A hideous square box, under the said loft, is, however, outdone by an enormous enclosure at the east end of the aisle. The belfry tower is in a most filthy state. Under the clerk's seat is a receptacle for stove brushes and other improprieties.

The Squire's seat, a "huge cantle",[11] flaming with scarlet and gold, elevated and o'ertopping all. If this and the other pews were properly arranged and reduced the necessity for the ugly loft would no longer exist.

A portion of an ancient stone monument has been used to prevent the heat of the stove from setting fire to the pews.

The font is not used; a basin serves the purpose.

The porch has its windows open, but the wicket denies admission; we were told the incumbent lived on the other side of the *Natural* school.[27]

n.d.   W.A.

Notes **1.** Pevsner p.112, and *VCH* III pp.166–7; **2.** The corbel with bagpipes is noted by Bonney, the *VCH* and by Pevsner; **3.** Will, 1446 (PR 181); **4.** There are C19th drawings of the mediaeval glass quarries (BL ref: Add.Ms. 39918 ff.38, 108); **5.** Five bells are listed in the 1712 terrier (ABE 2 Vol.1 p.342). The bell of 1628 was by William Haulsey of St.Ives and those of 1654 by Miles Graye. The third (for which no date is given by North) was recast in 1755. Bonney's orders for 1826–39 refer to a cracked bell. It is not clear which bell was broken (unless the treble said to have been damaged by the fall of the spire had actually been cracked for over 75 years!). The treble was recast by Taylors of Loughborough in 1901 when the bells were rehung by J.R. Gray of Hertford (P 66/0/1 and *BS* 18 Oct.1901). Two bells (the second and tenor) were recast when the bells were restored by Mears & Stainbank in 1934 (faculty P 66/2/2/4); **6.** Thomas Spencer, master pewterer, is identified as the maker of the alms dish in a letter from A.V. Sutherland-Graeme dated 1935 (P 66/2/1/3); **7.** Bonney identified the arms on the 1740 plate as those of the see of Winchester and Bishop Handley, but the *VCH* says that the arms belong to Bishop Fox of Winchester, founder of Corpus Christi College, Oxford. The College acquired the living in 1616; **8.** Welby's service book still exists (P 66/31/1); **9.** Canon Clarke's notes (CCC Library), citing Quarter Sessions papers for 13 April 1787. A Little Staughton carpenter gave evidence, but the lead was stolen from Colmworth church (not from Little Staughton); **10.** Memorandum concerning Eleanor Gery's gift of "one damask table cloth for the communion and two napkins", 1795 (P 66/31/1). There are memorials to the Gery family in the chancel and a C19th hatchment (Summers p.16); **11.** Arthur Ransom's RC article in *BT* 12 Oct.1900 refers to the gallery, three-tier pulpit, the squire's pew and the other enclosed pews noted by W.A. in 1852. They were only done away with in 1900–1 when the church was restored after the fall of the spire. Bonney ordered repairs to the pulpit top in 1823 and in 1833 suggested the "yellow parts" of the ensemble be oak grained to suit the sounding board. The present pulpit is all that survives of these arrangements; **12.** Vestry minutes 1862–1922 (P 66/8/1–2), churchwardens' accounts 1863–1922 (P 66/5/1) and Parochial accounts 1899–1909 (P 66/5/2). The harmonium of 1867 was sold in 1892; **13.** Bathurst's notebook (ABE 3); **14.** Gift of the Bishop's chair reported in *BS* 14 May 1897; **15.** The service register records the acquisition of the new cross etc. in 1899 (P 66/0/1); **16.** The damage to spire reported in *BS* 15 June 1900 and noted by RC (*BT* 12 Oct.1900) and by Bathurst (ABE 3); **17.** Sources for the 1900–1 restoration include the service register (P 66/0/1), minutes (P 66/8/2), accounts (P 66/5/1–2), correspondence with Mallows in the SPAB archives, and reports in *BS* 18 Oct.1901 and *Ely Diocesan Remembrancer* Nov/Dec 1901 p.221; **18.** The hailstorm damage is noted in the service register (P 66/0/1) and in J.R. Newman's printed account of the damage to property and crops in the village (P 66/28/3); **19.** Sources on the new spire include the drawings and notes on the contract 1910–1 (P 66/2/2/1), service register (P 66/0/2), minutes (P 66/8/2), the Archdeacon's notebook (ABE 3), and report in *Ely Diocesan Remembrancer* Jan.1901 p.16; **20.** The service register mentions the new font cover, 1916 (P 66/0/2); **21.** Plans, faculty and papers regarding the organ and organ chamber etc. 1924–5 (P 66/2/2/2–3) and notes in the service register (P 66/0/3); **22.** Repairs to the leaded roof are mentioned in the Report of the Council for the Care of Churches for 1928–9 (p.49), the service register mentions work on the chancel in 1930 (P 66/0/3), and the SPAB archives include a cutting from *The Times* 24 Oct.1935 about roof repairs under Professor Richardson and a file note "repairs ... being carried out" 1937; **23.** Note on renewal of rainwater pipes in 1961 (P 66/0/6) and faculty for tower repairs 1982 (P 66/2/2/8). There are also photographs of the work on the tower (Z 50/110/8–13); **24.** The existing chest has "IF 1770" scratched on the top; **25.** The registers actually commence in 1598 and the one beginning in 1695 is the second volume. 1598 is the date given in the *Parish Register Abstract* (1831); **26.** For the brass see Lack *et.al.* (p.90); **27.** The National school was established by trust deed dated 1846 (P 66/25/3).

STEPPINGLEY

Although the present church at Steppingley was built in 1858–60, it stands on the site of an earlier building.[1] The first mention of an incumbent is in the late C12th, and it is recorded that money was given in 1255 "for making three windows for the chancel, and for purchasing church ornaments".[2]

The old church consisted of a chancel, nave, north and south porches and west tower. The chancel had been rebuilt in brick, probably in the C18th. Parry's reference to the "low tower, not rising above the neighbouring hayricks" gives an impression of the size of the church which he described as "probably the smallest in the county".[3] In 1848 the Rural Dean described it as "small and low and dark".[4] Boissier considered it "very neat inside ... with good oaken benches and pews".[5] W.A., however, criticised the interior and dismissed the building as "but a very indifferent specimen of ecclesiastical architecture". Bonney described it as "an inferior fabrick of the perpendicular character".

The piscina, incorporating a small carving of the Green Man, survives from the old church.[6] Some of the furniture and ornaments also remain in use. These include an Elizabethan chalice of 1569,[7] a parish chest of 1717,[8] the charity board dated 1801,[9] and the bells.[10] There were four bells by 1710.[11] One of the present bells is dated 1660, but the others were recast in 1807 and 1814. Other items have been lost, including the furnishings provided by Robert Abbott of Steppingley Park in 1722,[12] the ancient font,[13] the early volumes of churchwardens' accounts for 1709–1742,[14] and articles of plate listed in the earlier terriers.[7]

Trouble with the old church appeared in 1850 when the east wall of the chancel began to subside. An attempt was made to repair it, but in 1858 it collapsed. The Duke of Bedford agreed to rebuild the church and commissioned Henry Clutton to prepare plans.[15] Work began in December 1858 and the new church was opened on 19 October 1860. The carving in wood and stone was done by Thomas Earp who made the stone pulpit,[16] the chancel tiles were supplied by Maw & Co., and the organ was provided by Holditch in 1861.[17] The weathervane dated 1864 on the tower was placed here in the 1960s and does not belong to the rebuilding.[18]

The warnings of W.A. that new churches were often "poor substitutes for those destroyed" were to prove prophetic at Steppingley where Clutton's church suffered from serious structural problems. Archdeacon Bathurst noted in 1873 that owing to bad foundations the church was cracked on all sides.[19] The tower had been strengthened in 1868–9, and in 1876–7 the Duke of Bedford spent £1000 on underpinning other parts of the building.[20] Further work was undertaken in 1912 to secure the foundations of the chancel under the architects Adams and Holden.[21] During this work a hoard of C13th silver coins was found beneath the chancel floor.[22]

During the incumbency of the Rev. W.S.A. Grainger (Rector 1922–8) a

18. Steppingley: The old church from the east, showing the "modern chancel of brick" and the low west tower barely higher than the neighbouring hayricks as described by Parry in 1849. It was replaced by the present church in 1858–60   *(Watercolour: George Shepherd c.1823)*

wrought iron screen was set up in the chancel arch and the church was adorned with woodwork and statues designed and made by the Rector himself.[23] Most of Grainger's fittings have since been removed. In the 1960s the church was generally restored, many of the ornaments and fittings were moved about and second-hand items were obtained from other churches.[24]

1. Extract from glebe terrier, 16 October 1822

STEPPINGLEY.

Church yard. The Church yard containing by estimation one rood and an half adjoining the Vicarage yard and land of Jane Parker and William Woodward on the north, by a piece of waste ground on the west and by the Town Street on the south and east, the Gates and Pales round about made by the Vicar.

Church. Belonging to the said Parish are first the Parish Church an Ancient Building containing in length (with the Chancel) seventy one feet, the Chancel in breadth fifteen feet and the Church twenty feet. The Steeple twelve feet square within the walls, in height forty eight feet.

Furniture and ornaments. Within and belonging to which are one Communion Table with a purple Cloth covering for the same The Gift of Mr. Abbott 1722.[12] Also one Linen Cloth for the same and two Napkins. One Pewter Flaggon, one pewter plate, and one Silver cup.[7] One Chest with Locks in the Chancel.[8] One pulpit and reading Desk, one pulpit cushion and Cloth of purple the Gift of Mr. Abbott 1722.[12] One large Bible. Common Prayer Book. Book of Canons. An ancient Book of Sermons published in the reign of Edward the sixth. The King's Arms. A font lined with Lead and a wooden Cover.[13] Four Bells with Frames for six Bells.[10] The first or least Bell being two feet two inches in Diameter with this inscription "Christopher Grey 1660". The Second two feet four inches in diameter with this inscription "William Phillips Richard Taylor S[t]. Neots the founder 1807". The third two feet six inches in diameter with this inscription "Thomas Cook William Phillips John Parker Tidcombe 1814". The fourth two feet ten inches in diameter with this inscription "William Phillips Richard Taylor S[t]. Neots 1807". One Bier and one Surplice. Three registers each begining one thousand eight hundred and twelve for Baptisms, Weddings and Burials.

Parish Clerk. Burial, digging the Grave, ringing the Bell and attendance at the Funeral Four Shillings. A yearly payment by the Parish Officers of Five Pounds.

2. Archdeacon Bonney's historical notices of churches, c.1820–1840
STEPINGLEY, St. Laurence. This Church consists of a Nave and chancel, a South Porch and a Tower at the West End, an inferior fabrick of the perpendicular Character.

3. Archdeacon Bonney's visitation notebook, 1823–1839
STEPINGLEY. This Church consists of a Nave, a Tower at the West End and Chancel at the East End thereof, Porches on the North & South sides.

At the Visitation of 1823 it was ordered that the Bell chamber Windows be repaired with Parker's Cement & Stone, and new weather boards be placed in them, a new plated Flagon and Paten be purchased:[7] the Floor of the Chancel be made level. The Communion Table be cleansed and oiled; the open seats be taken to pieces, cleansed and repaired. The other Seats be repaired & coloured to suit the Open seats – the doors be painted oak colour; The Font be cleansed and a proper Font Bason be purchased;[13] the Floors of the Church be made level; the Earth be moved from the exterior – the Stonework of the Windows and Doors be restored, with Parker's Cement: the Communion Cloth & Pulpit Cushion be repaired & cleansed.[12]

At the Visitation of 1826. The Walls and Buttresses, cornices, Stonework of Windows & Doors be restored according to the Ancient Pattern; the Seats, Pews, Pulpit & Desk be repaired; also the Floors of the Church & Chancel; the Earth be moved from the Exterior of the Building & proper drainage made

– and before Easter 1828 a new pulpit Cloth & Cover for the Cushion be made, to suit the Communion Cloth; also a new plated Flagon & Paten – the Doors & Communion Rails be oak grained; the Bible & Clerk's Prayer Book be repaired. A Casement be made in the Church and another in the Chancel.

At the Visitation of 1833 It was ordered that the Ten Commandments be put up at the East End – a New Prayer Book be purchased for the Clerk.

The Glebe house a thatched Cottage in good repair.

At the Visitation of 1836 – ordered that the defective leaves of the Bible be restored – and next year, a new Pall be purchased.

4. Article on the Church by W.A. (no.17), NM 1 November 1845

STEPINGLEY. This Church was, we suspect, but a very indifferent specimen of ecclesiastical architecture even in its best days, and it has suffered so much from neglect, that nothing short of rebuilding ere long, will be of any avail. This is a step never to be recommended but in an extreme case, as the modern erections are for the most part, poor substitutes for those destroyed. It can well be imagined from this description of its present state, that its interior is in a corresponding condition. The roof is ceiled. The seats are for the most part open, and as it would have been rendered so dark by excluding the light from the west window, it has escaped this mutilation. There is a font, but painted over.[13] A stove with its chimney bored through a hole, made in the north wall, is so clumsily contrived as to admit a good current of cold air; which, though not intended, is probably a fortunate circumstance for the congregation.

The chancel – the roof is ceiled, and the arch partly concealed by plastering. The floor was very dirty; the communion table is rather better than usual. Inside the rails were two boxes. The windows are sadly disfigured, and nearly all traces of their ornaments obliterated.

28 October 1845   W.A.

Notes **1.** Pevsner p.148, *VCH* III p.325, and Andrew Underwood *The Parish Church of Saint Lawrence, Steppingley: A History* (1982). Andrew Underwood has kindly read the draft text and suggested various improvements; **2.** The Annals of Dunstable Priory (cited by Underwood p.3); **3.** Article by J.D. Parry in *GM* Vol. 32 (1849) Pt.II pp.479–82. The dimensions of the old church are given in the 1822 terrier; **4.** Rural Dean's notebook, 1848 (AB/RD/A O). This source also states that there were "No windows on the North side"; **5.** Boissier (f.417–d) also describes Steppingley as "a small poor sand stone & brick church"; **6.** The remains of the piscina were placed in the north wall of the vestry in 1858–60, but restored to their present position in 1962 (Underwood p.4). There are papers concerning the removal (P 82/2/2/7 and 11) and a record of the re–dedication on 16 Dec.1962 (P 82/0/5); **7.** The plate is described by Underwood (p.5) and there are details of the plate from terriers c.1725–1869 in the Rector's commonplace book (P 82/28/9 pp.13–35). The present plate includes a modern silver chalice and paten of 1948 in memory of Kenneth Warner (P 82/0/4 and P 82/28/8) and an alms dish presented in 1962 (P 82/28/7); **8.** The chest has the date and the initials of the rector, John Matthews, crudely stamped on the iron hinges (Underwood p.4); **9.** The charity board gives details of John Parker's charity (established 1704). It is signed by William Phillips, churchwarden, 1801; **10.** The inscriptions and dates of the bells are given in the 1822 terrier. Underwood (p.5) notes bequests "to the makyng of the bells of Stepyngleighe" in the late 1550s. A note in the parish register states that a new crown staple was provided for the great bell in 1671 (P 82/1/2). After their transfer to the tower of the new church in 1860, the bells were rehung with new fittings by Mears & Stainbank in 1878 (Whitechapel foundry daybook 29 Nov.1878); **11.** Glebe terrier, 1710 (ABE 2 Vol.II p.554). There are copies of terriers c.1725–1869 with details of furnishings etc in the Rector's commonplace book (P 82/28/9 pp.13–35) and annotated copies of terriers 1664–c.1720 (P 82/2/1/1); **12.** For the Abbott family and the pulpit cloth and furnishings given by Robert Abbott in 1722 <u>see</u> Underwood (pp.4–6) who quotes a contemporary list from a terrier of c.1725 (in P 82/29/9 p.21). The items still in use in 1822 are listed in the terrier; **13.** The font belonging to the old church is illustrated in the BCRO "extra illustrated" Lysons and described by Underwood (p.5). W.A. noted in 1845 that it was "painted over"; **14.** Churchwardens' account books for 1709–1842 and from 1850, although known to have existed until fairly recent times, appear to have been lost (Underwood p.6); **15.** Sources for the rebuilding include the Bedford Estate report for 1858 (R 5/869/2 p.7 and 55), bills and vouchers 1860 (R Box 680), a report of the opening in *BM* 27 Oct.1860, and Underwood's account (pp.6–7); **16.** The stone pulpit was carved by Thomas Earp in 1860. It was replaced by a wooden pulpit (originally from Misterton in Somerset) in 1968 (Underwood p.7 and faculty P 82/2/2/8); **17.** The organ has the date 1861 stamped on the windchest (Underwood p.9) and it is said to be by Holditch (National Pipe Organs Register); **18.** The weathervane came from Goldington Vicarage (Underwood p.9) but was modified after gale damage in 1987; **19.** Bathurst's notebook (ABE 3) includes notes of 1880 and 1905 regarding the cracks in the structure; **20.** Underwood (p.7) refers to the repairs and underpinning in 1869 and 1877, and there are accounts and vouchers for the later work (R 5/921 and R box 674); **21.** Sources for the work in 1912 include the notebook and papers of William Atkinson (clerk of works) 1912 (P 82/2/2/18–9), the Rector's commonplace book (P 82/28/9 p.47), Kelly's *Directory* 1914 p.173, and Underwood's account (p.7); **22.** For the hoard, <u>see</u> Underwood (p.9) and the sources listed in note 21; **23.** Grainger's work is documented in the commonplace book (P 82/28/9 pp.70–3), the service register (P 82/0/2), the faculty for the side chapel etc. 1926 (P 82/2/2/4), and Underwood (p.15). The statues were removed in 1959 and the iron screen in 1970; **24.** The recent work is documented in the faculties and related papers (P 82/2/2/6–14), service register (P 82/0/6), commonplace book (P 82/28/9) and in Underwood (*passim*).

STEVINGTON

Situated near an ancient Holy Well, Stevington church is of considerable antiquity.[1] The oldest parts of the fabric are the lower stages of the west tower, Anglo–Saxon work with long and short quoins.[2] The original church was rebuilt and enlarged in the C14th when the side chapels (now in ruins) alongside the chancel were added. In the C15th the top stage of the tower was rebuilt, and the clerestory and present roof were added to the nave.[3] There is a C14th font,[4] a Perpendicular screen in the tower arch,[5] and C15th carvings on the pews in the nave and aisles.[6]

The plate includes an Elizabethan cup and paten of 1569.[7] A fresco dated 1633 was discovered on the south wall when the church was restored in 1872.[8] A ring of five bells was hung in the tower in 1654.[9] Other early C17th repairs to the church were recorded in connection with a later dispute.[10] The papers show that the Bromhall family repaired the north chancel aisle c.1605 and later had seats in the north aisle repaired and made into one. In c.1630 the aisle roofs were repaired and new joists and wall plates were put up in the south aisle. In 1643–4 the north aisle roof was mended at the expense of the parish, and the churchwardens paid for repairs to the windows of both aisles in 1657–8.

19. Stevington: The church and holy well from the east, showing the chancel aisles which were left to decay from about 1665   (*Engraving: Thomas Fisher 1812*)

By 1665 the two aisles were "much decayed and part broken down".[10] The matter was brought before the Archdeacon's court where the parties tried to establish who was responsible for repairs. The dispute was chiefly about the chancel aisles. In May 1668 it was reported that "The two Iles of the Chancell is out of repair", and in that October the parishioners claimed that "The Chancell is out of repaire in the leads glasseing and allmost downe".[11] In 1674 the churchwardens were able to report that most of the parishioners had either paid the rate or promised to do so, and Mr. Dyve had undertaken "to repair the Isles of the Chancel" when the others have been done.[12] Although the outcome is not recorded, these events clearly resulted in the chancel aisles falling into ruin. Fisher's view shows that both chapels were roofless and derelict by 1812.[13]

There is little information on the church in the C18th, but there is an embroidered pulpit cloth of 1706.[14] The 1822 terrier mentions that five new pews were set up in the south aisle in 1818. In 1826 the old rood screen was cut down to give a better view into the chancel.[15] Bonney found the carpenters at work in the church when he visited in 1839. In about 1848 the parish spent £100 on alterations to the seating and reading desk.[16] There are churchwardens' accounts and vestry minutes from 1849 but only minor repairs and alterations are recorded.[17] In 1854 a "crimson velvet covering and two cushions for the communion table" were given to Stevington church.[18] The Duke of Bedford contributed towards the cost of repairs in 1858 and in 1859 provided a new harmonium.[19]

In 1870 the vestry embarked on a scheme to restore the church.[20] By May

1871 John Usher's plans had been adopted, after architectural advice from Henry Clutton, and the Duke of Bedford had agreed to pay £1200 towards the cost. The work was carried out in 1871–2 when new roofs were made for the aisles and chancel, the nave roof was repaired, the body of the church was re-seated with deal pews, and new chancel stalls and sanctuary fittings provided. Some of the window tracery was altered,[21] and the plain parapets on the north side of the church and east end were replaced with embattled ones and gable crosses. The church was re-opened on 22 May 1872.

After the church had been restored some further improvements were made. In 1890 adjustments were made to the seating.[22] The harmonium was replaced by a reconditioned second-hand organ in 1904.[23] In 1905 the bells were restored.[9] Work on the tower was carried out in 1935,[24] new chancel furnishings were dedicated in 1938,[25] a new mahogany pulpit was dedicated in 1955,[26] and in 1968 the present organ was installed.[23]

1. Extract from glebe terrier, 2 July 1822
STEVENTON.
Church yard. The Churchyard contains three roods and fourteen perches, with Thomas Alston Esquire on the west and north, Holywell lane on the east, and Vicarage house on the south. The walls and gates thereof round about made by the Parish.

Church. Belonging to the said Parish is first the Church an ancient building containing in length (with the Chancel) Sixty five feet three quarters, the Chancel in breadth is thirteen feet, in length twenty six feet. There are also two decayed Chancels,[13] that of the north side is twelve feet in breadth and in length twenty six feet, also of the south side is the same. The steeple twelve feet square within the walls, in height six one feet.

Furniture and ornaments. Within and Belonging to the said church, to which is ... one communion table with a covering of green cloth. Also one linen cloth for the same with one napkin. One pewter flagon. One silver chalice (weighing about eight ounces).[7] One pewter paten.[7] One pulpit and reading desk.[26] One pulpit cushion of green cloth. Also green covering cloth for the same and this inscription worked in gold thread, viz. "Ex dono Theodosiæ Charissima Uxoris Henrici Chester de East Haddon in Comitatu Northamptonia Armigeri 1706".[14] One large Bible of the last translation. Two large Books of common prayer. The King's arms with the ten commandments. There are five Bells[9] with their frames the first or least bell being two feet six inches and half in diameter with this inscription "John Hodson made me 1654 I.H.L.N. Church W.". The second two feet eight inches and half in diameter with this inscription "John Hodson made mee 1654 I.L.H.N. Church W.". The third two feet ten inches three quarters in diameter with this inscription "John Hodson made mee 1654 I.L.H.N. Church W.". The fourth thirty eight inches and half in diameter with this inscription "John Hodson made mee 1654

I.L.H.N. C.W. W.H.". The fifth or largest three feet six and three quarter inches in diameter with this inscription "John Hodson made mee 1654 John Latton Henry Negous W.H. Church Wardens." No Pall at present, the Parish intend immediately Getting one. One bier (much out of repair). Two surplices. Also two chests, one of iron in the chancel for keeping of the Register Books, also a Chest of wood bound with iron[27] with one lock in the west end of the church for keeping the books and other things belonging to the church. Also a Box withinside with two locks for the Parish Officers' accounts.

Parish Registers. Three new register Books from 1813. Also [blank] other register Books, first begining 1654 ending 1701 (imperfect, some leaves wanting and some parts not legible). Second begining 1701 ending 1731 also imperfect. Third begining 1732 ending 1779. The fourth begining 1763 ending 1810. Fifth begining 1779 ending 1812. Sixth begining 1811 ending 1812.

Seats in the Church. The seats in the Church have been repaired for time immorial at the expence of the Parish. Also five new pews erected in 1818 at the expence of the parish in the south isle of the Church.

Parish Clerk. There is also due to the Clerk for a wedding By Banns one shilling and sixpence, by licence two shillings and sixpence, for a funeral two Shillings Besides his yearly Salarary (sic) of three pounds By the Parish.

2. Archdeacon Bonney's historical notices of churches, c.1820–1840

STEVENTON, St. Mary. This interesting Church consists of a Nave and Aisles separated by slender clustered Piers supporting acute angled Arches. On the Timbers of the Roof are roses, stars and figures holding Shields. On one is R.T.[3] The tower is at the West End of the Nave and is flanked on its sides by the North & South Aisles. There are five Bells.[9] There is a Screen under the Tower Arch,[5] on the Moulding of which are represented Two Men kneeling, and stooping down to a Barrel, drinking Church Ale.[6] On the floor of the Nave is the Effigy of a Man in plate Armour in Brass, with the following Inscription and Armorial Bearing.[28] Orate pro anima Thome Salle armigeri qui obiit XXI die mensis Aprilis Anno Domini MCCCCXXII [*Sketches of two coats of arms* Salle. Two Salamanders]

The lower part of the Rood Screen remains adorned with paintings of a White Hart or Hind, and slips of white flowers issuing out of flower pots.[15] The Piers and Arches, and Windows on the West are decorated, the rest perpendicular. The Chancel, with the Chapels North and South of it, now in ruins, are of the Same Character.[13] There is a Piscina in the Chancel. The Chalice & Cover are Elizabethan.[7] There are a plated Plate and Flagon.

In the North Aisle is a Stone to the Memory of Robert Tayler of this Place, Gent. who died 1618. It has the following armorial Bearing [*Sketch of coat of arms* Tayler].

The Church yard is at the edge of a perpendicular Rock at the Foot of which issues a copious Spring of pellucid Water.[1]

3. Archdeacon Bonney's visitation notebook, 1823–1839

STEVENTON. This Church consists of a Nave and aisles – a Tower at the West End of the Nave and Chancel at the East end thereof – Porches to the North & South aisles.

At the Visitation of 1823. The following order was given, that a new plated Flagon be purchased,[7] also a new covering for the Communion Table; the Earth be moved from the South Side; The Munions, Tracery and Cornices of the Windows & Doors be restored with Parker's Cement; the tower and Walls be pointed; the South End of the Aisle be paved; new Window shutters be placed in the Middle Chamber; a new Ladder be made to the Steeple, the Seats be oakgrained; the Communion Table be cleansed & oiled; a proper Font Bason be purchased, and three Casements be placed in three of the Windows.

At the Visitation of 1826. It appears that no order was deemed necessary.

At the Visitation of 1833 The following Order was given that the Communion Table be oiled – the Bible be rebound – the floors of the open Seats be repaired – the Doors be repaired and oak grained – the upper part of the Walls of the Nave (internally) be repaired & cleansed.

A new & sufficient Glebe House.[29]

At the Visitation of 1836 Ordered the Pavement of the Church be repaired and made level – and the Open Seats be neatly repaired – a new covering for the Communion Table be purchased. Also a lintel of a window in the Clerestory be repaired.

At the Visitation 1839 Found the Carpenters at Work, thoroughly repairing the Seats. Ordered the Churchwarden to put the leads of the Roof into substantial repair by degrees.

4. Article on the Church by W.A. (no.66), NM 3 July 1847

STEVENTON, Virgin Mary. This church is in excellent condition. The altar table most appropriate; but the railings do not correspond; chest &c.,[27] within them were better removed. The chancel roof is not ceiled, but the walls are all whitewashed, totally concealing all architectural ornaments. We regretted to find a large square pew, fitted up with fire–place, &c.; a sad contrast to the remains of stalls on the opposite side. High example will be the only hope of our getting rid of these sad eyesores – enclosed sittings; for the pertinacity with which their retention is contended for by those of an inferior grade can only be described by restorers who have ventured to appeal for the removal of these selfish dormitories.

The nave has a timber roof of high pitch, and the columns are not whitewashed. A portion of the chancel screen remains, with some of the original painting.[15] The sittings are all open. The pulpit,[26] a very good one, detached from the reading pew, and the general effect consequently much improved, and is the best answer to remarks on the subject, in which it is difficult to discover whether ignorance or malice most prevails. The light from the west window is not shut out by a feeble organ and gallery, and a view into the belfry is consequently not obstructed. The font has a drain, but no lining and is apparently not made use of.[4] The whole of the church, in cleanliness, exhibits a very agreeable contrast to many which it has been our lot to visit, especially the last described.[30] The roof of the chancel is of lead; a rare instance of preservation. The churchyard is not locked up. The tub against the wall for receiving rainwater has an unpleasant appearance; and where so much care is displayed in the preservation of the building, it would be good to remove it. The remains of the ruined aisle on the south are preserved with care,[13] and the whole exhibits a proper reverence for holy things which it is pleasant to record. The village cross remains, and the portion which time, or probably bigotry destroyed, has been restored.

28 June 1847   W.A.

Notes **1.** Pevsner pp.148–9, Harvey pp.158–65, *VCH* III pp.102–3, and *A Guide to Stevington Church* n.d. [c.1976]. These accounts differ considerably in their dating of the various parts of the church. For the holy well <u>see</u> Patricia Bell *Belief in Bedfordshire* (1986) pp.7–9; **2.** The Anglo–Saxon work at Stevington is discussed by T.P. Smith in "The Anglo–Saxon Churches of Bedfordshire" in *BAJ* Vol.3 (1966) pp.7–14; **3.** The guide states that the C15th nave roof carries the initials N T and R T under the woolsacks, identifying them (though the evidence seems thin) as those of the wool merchants Nicholas and Robert Taylor. There is a C17th memorial in the north aisle to Robert Taylor (d.1618); **4.** The font (illustrated by Harvey p.161) is "for the most part modern" (*VCH*) and it was probably restored in 1872 (guide); **5.** The tower screen dated from the C15th with a C17th arched head inserted (*VCH*). Pevsner (p.149) wrongly implies that this screen was part of the rood screen. Some of the panelling was renewed in 1963–4 (P 71/2/2/27–8); **6.** Fisher's engraving of 1812 (in *GM* July 1812 pl.II p.9) indicates that the two drinkers – now at opposite ends of a bench in the north aisle – were originally mounted together drinking from a shared cup (said to be a barrel of church ale), and that the head of one was missing. Examination shows that one head is a replacement, and new ends have been spliced on to both cups. Bonney seems to imply that this carving was on the tower screen, but Fisher explicitly states that it was on a seat in the nave; **7.** In addition to the cup and paten of 1569, the 1924 schedule (ABE 5) also lists a plated flagon of c.1780; **8.** The discovery of the fresco dated 1633 (mentioned by Harvey p.161) was reported in *BM* 28 May 1872; **9.** The bell inscriptions noted in the 1822 terrier show that John Hodson supplied a complete ring of five in 1654. The treble was recast by Barwell of Birmingham in 1872 (North p.195) at the time of the main church restoration, and the three largest bells were recast in 1905 by Bowell of Ipswich who rehung the bells in a new frame (P 71/2/2/12); **10.** The repairs of c.1605 to c.1658 were summarised in undated papers of c.1665 in the Archdeacon's court records (ABCP 40–42). When the case was brought before the court, the two aisles were said to be "much decayed and part fallen down". These papers deal with the dispute which resulted in the chancel aisles becoming ruinous; **11.** Archdeacon's visitations 1668–9 (ABC 7); **12.** Archidiaconal visitations 1674 (CRT 170/9/1 p.5); **13.** Fisher's 1812 view (in *GM* July 1812 pl.I p.9) clearly indicates that the south chapel was better preserved than that on the north; **14.** The 1706 pulpit cloth, now displayed in the south aisle, is listed in the 1822 terrier and so it cannot have been presented in 1876 as suggested in the guide; **15.** Harvey (p.161) cites the information of Thomas Orlebar Marsh that "In August 1826, the screen which parted the chancel from the church was cut away to about as low as the pews, to give a fine view of the chancel". Bonney describes the decoration on "the lower part of the screen" and W.A. also mentions it. At the restoration in 1872 the remaining parts were placed along the west walls of the aisles (as noted in the *VCH*); **16.** The work in 1848 is referred to in the BAAS report in *GM* Vol.29 (May 1848) p.529, and in a vestry minute of 28 Jan.1870 (in P 71/8/1); **17.** Churchwardens' accounts 1849–1904 (P 71/5/1) and vestry minutes 1849–72 and

1886–1924 (P 71/8/1–2); **18.** These items were given to Turvey church by W.B.Higgins in 1846, and offered to Stevington when Turvey church was restored in 1854 (P 27/1/5); **19.** The Duke of Bedford's contributions are noted in the Bedford Estate reports for 1858–9 (R 5/869/2–3); **20.** Sources for the restoration in 1871–2 include the vestry minutes (P 71/8/1), parish papers (P 71/2/2/1–8), Usher's plans (CDE 1/1–29), the Bedford estate papers (R 4/198 and R box 674), advertisement for tenders in *BT* 6–13 June 1871 and reports etc. of the opening in *BM* 28 May 1872 and *BT* 14 and 28 May 1872; **21.** Clutton advised that Perpendicular tracery should be used instead of the Decorated style as intended by Usher. The guide notes the main alterations to the windows; **22.** Accounts for seating alterations, 1890 (P 71/5/1) and sketch seating plans (in P 71/28/17); **23.** Papers concerning the 1904 organ (P 71/2/2/11–2), and the replacement organ of 1968 (P 71/2/2/31–2); **24.** Faculty and papers concerning tower repairs in 1934–6 (P 71/2/2/15–6); **25.** The new chancel furnishings included altar hangings and mensa, 1938 (P 91/0/5); **26.** At the restoration in 1872 the old pulpit and reading desk were "fitted up for temporary use" (*BM* 28 May 1872). W.A. had described it in 1847 as "a very good one, detached from the reading pew". The new pulpit was erected as a memorial to Canon Sproule. There is a faculty, 1954 (P 71/2/2/20) and note of the dedication on 6 Feb.1955 (P 71/0/6); **27.** There is a massive parish chest, bound with iron straps, said to date from the C15th (guide); **28.** For the brass, now in the south aisle, see Lack *et.al.* (p.90); **29.** The parsonage was improved in 1835 to plans by James Woodroffe of Bedford, builder (LAO ref: MGA 199) and the parish records include a mortgage to finance the work 1835 (P 71/2/4/1); **30.** The comparison is with Clapham (no.65 in W.A.'s series).

STONDON, Upper

Upper Stondon has existed as a separate ecclesiastical parish since the C13th and the list of incumbents can be traced back to 1239.[1] Apart from the south doorway dating from the C13th hardly any trace remains of the mediaeval church.[2] The font is also ancient and some fragments of old stonework and woodwork survive.[3]

There is a communion cup of 1609–10.[4] Presentments of 1616–7 note "the King's Arms not set up in the church".[5] At the visitation in 1668 it was noted that "The church bible wants binding".[6] In 1708 there was a single bell, replaced in 1819 by the present bell.[7] At some time in the late C17th or C18th the mediaeval church was partly remodelled.[8] The upper stage of the tower was rebuilt in brick, the south and west sides of the nave were rebuilt (also in brick) with a hipped roof of tiles over the west end. In the early C19th the south side of the chancel was also rebuilt. Writing in 1827 Boissier said "This is a small rough uncouth building partly of brick. A brick story is added to the stone porch making this a tower belfry".[9]

In 1832 Sir William Long gave a new set of communion plate.[4] Presentments of 1842–4 refer to the condition of the church which had been "repaired lately" but still had some "walls not upright".[10] W.A.'s account indicates that by 1847 the church was both in poor condition and shabbily furnished. In 1848 the churchyard fences were extensively repaired,[11] but still nothing was done to the church.

In 1852 the vestry considered the Archdeacon's order that the body of the church should be re-seated.[12] In August 1855 Richard Ashby reported on the condition of the building and recommended extensive rebuilding.[13] The church was partially rebuilt, enlarged and re-seated under Ashby soon after-

20. Upper Stondon: SW view showing the west end of the church and upper stage of the porch tower as rebuilt in brick in the C18th and the east end of the chancel described in 1842 as "not upright, but firm".   *(Watercolour: Thomas Fisher c.1815)*

wards and re-opened on 19 March 1857.[14] The work included the addition of a north transept at the expense of Trinity College, Cambridge, to provide seating for the inhabitants of Lower Stondon (then in Shillington parish).[15]

The later C19th parish records refer to further work on the church including repairs to the vestry roof in 1867–8 and the redecoration of the interior in 1884–5.[16] The west window was filled with stained glass as a memorial to Robert Long of Manor Farm (d.1868) and in 1886 a new window by Shrigley & Hunt was placed in the north transept in memory of John and Fanny Lines.[17] The plate given in 1832 by Sir William Long was remodelled at the expense of Mrs. Long in 1891–2.[4] Minor repairs to the fabric in the late C19th and early C20th are also recorded.[18]

In 1908 the church was cleaned and the woodwork varnished, new sanctuary hangings were provided and a new stained glass east window was put up in memory of Mrs. Long.[19] In 1909 a new window was made in the south side of the chancel and a new brass lectern was provided in 1910.

The church was extensively restored in 1971, with new tiled floor and modern seating in the nave.[20] The vestry was rebuilt in 1971 and enlarged in 1994. More recently, the seating has been re-orientated to face west to give a clear view of the altar from all parts of the church.

2. Archdeacon Bonney's historical notices of churches, c.1820–1840

STONDON, All Saints. This small Church consists of a Nave and Chancel, with a Turret over the South Porch containing one Bell.[7] The Turret is brick. The Leach Family were incumbents and Patrons for many years. One of them lies in the Chancel, who died in 1697. The last died in 1808.

On the Chalice & plated Patin "Presented by Sir Wm Long to Stondon Communion 1832".[4]

3. Archdeacon Bonney's visitation notebook, 1823–1839

STONDON. This Church consists of a Nave and Chancel. A Turrit rises from the South Porch.

At the Visitation of 1823 It was ordered that the Communion Table be cleansed and oiled, a plated Flagon be purchased.

At the Visitation of 1826 no further order was thought necessary.

At the Visitation of 1833. It was ordered that a proper Font Bason be purchased – The frames of the windows be painted –

At the Visitation of 1836 Ordered that the North Buttress of the Chancel, and the Chancel Door be repaired – and a new Cushion and Cloth for the Pulpit be procured.

4. Article on the Church by W.A. (no.57), NM 1 May 1847

STONDON, All Saints. This is one of the smallest churches, we believe, not only in this county, but with few exceptions in England. The population is very limited, and it is, therefore, probably sufficiently large for their accommodation. But humble as it is, not the slightest attempt appears to have been made to maintain it in its original state. The picturesque belfry-tower alone redeems it from being mistaken for a very poor barn.[8] The windows are sadly mutilated, and greatly disfigure the church. The chancel roof and that of the nave are not separated: both are as smooth as lath and plaster can render them; most probably concealing the original timber roofs. The covering of the altar is in a most discreditable condition; and the place it occupies is of the smallest dimensions – hemmed in on both sides by sittings. This unseemly crowding of the sacred precinct is caused by the great space occupied by two large square boxes. Over a beam which in former days, and when the church was in its purity, was most probably connected with a rood-screen,[3] is suspended the parish bier. Though we have never seen it before in such a situation, and cannot admire it, it is perhaps a better *memento mori* than the pomp of heraldry so frequently attached to this motto. The north door is blocked up, and whatever architectural ornaments the church may have originally contained are entirely obliterated. In this quarter are some square pews, and more hat-pegs (the village carpenter's favourite ornament) than there could be found hats to hang on them. The whole exhibits sad marks of neglect on the part of the guardians of the building.

We avail ourselves of this opportunity of introducing the following impressive words on the office of churchwarden:- 'What a homestead of Christian peace you may make for yourselves, for the aged and poor, the widowed, and the world-worn, in your parish church and the sacred precincts which encompass it about. Who can say how much is in your hand? If you make the house of God beautiful and honourable in the eyes of your brethren, who can measure the help you give to your pastor's work? Yours is no light charge, no merely secular office; it is related to the holiest things; I pray you use it well. Guard the house of God with a dutiful and loving care, and if the Lord blessed the house of Obed–Edom for the Ark's sake, while it tarried with him, believe that he will not forget your love and reverence for his sanctuary.'*

There is no school, and this is the third parish consecutively in which this neglect prevails.[21] Can it be at all matter of wonder at the low position the county holds, when such things are? Surely the time of the clergy would be far more beneficially employed in taking steps to remedy this deplorable state of affairs than at Quarter Sessions discussing the propriety of erecting new prisons to receive those whose early education the Church has so cruelly neglected. It is well observed in the Minutes of the Council of Education, that the time of the minister can no where be so advantageously bestowed as by his presence at and unceasing superintendence of the school of his parish.

The churchyard is not locked, and cattle were not grazing.[11]

26 April 1847   W.A.

* Archdeacon Manning's Charge

Notes **1.** *VCH* II pp.304–5 and clergy lists; **2.** Pevsner p.161; **3.** Boissier (f.430) mentions the "octagonal and plain" font. An account of the 1857 restoration in a later directory (Kelly 1885 p.113) states that "all the materials of the old church are incorporated into the new, and the former chancel screen converted into altar rails. Interior fitted with open benches, and retains the old desks, pulpit and font". Old woodwork can still be seen in the clergy desk and in a bench in the north transept; **4.** According to the 1927 schedule (ABE 5) there is a cup of 1609–10, and a cup and paten marked "Presented by Sr. Will: Long to Upper Stondon Church 1832. Re-modelled 1891". The vestry minutes of 1892 refer to Mrs. Long's gift "for the remodelling of the silver communion service ... now carried out by the London Goldsmith's Company" (P 55/5/1); **5.** Presentments, 1616–7 (ABC 5 pp.5, 15 and 23); **6.** Archdeacon's visitations, 1668 (ABC 7); **7.** The 1708 terrier (ABE 1) mentions one bell. The present bell was cast by John Briant of Hertford in 1819 and it hangs in a frame (dated 1857) installed when the top stage of the tower was rebuilt; **8.** The old church is described in Ashby's report of 1855 (HCRO ref: DSA 1/80/232) and in Addington (1848) no.125. There are several views by Thomas Fisher (slides 872–3 and 1083) whose sketch (Micf 66 FB 346) includes notes on the building materials; **9.** Boissier (f.430); **10.** Presentments 1842 and 1844 (ABCV 128–9); **11.** The work on the churchyard fences in 1848 is noted in the vestry minutes (in P 55/1/0) and in a record of works at Stondon Manor Farm in 1848–9 (CRT 130 STON 3); **12.** The Archdeacon's order is noted in the vestry minutes, 1852 (P 55/0/1); **13.** Ashby's report dated 31 August 1855 (HCRO ref: DSA 1/80/232). Robert Ashby & Sons, builders, are listed at the same London address in the Post Office *Directory* for 1853 (p.638); **14.** Sources on the work in 1857 include the vestry minutes (P 55/1/0), report in *BT* 28 March 1857, and description in Kelly's *Directory* 1877 (p.93); **15.** Lower Stondon did not become part of the ecclesiastical parish until 1912 (P 55/1/0), but the fact that Upper Stondon church was more convenient for the inhabitants than the parish church at Shillington was recognised by Trinity College, Cambridge (the patrons for Shillington) who paid for the addition on the north transept in 1857. The Trinity College archives record payments of £150 in 1855 towards the north aisle and a further £50 in 1858 towards the repair fund, and there is a petition of the inhabitants of Lower Stondon that the hamlet be joined with upper Stondon (*ex.inf.* Jonathan Smith, Trinity College Library); **16.** Churchwardens' accounts 1864–90 (P 55/5/1) and vestry minutes 1877–98 (P 55/8/1); **17.** The new transept window for Stondon was exhibited at the Royal Academy, as reported in *Building News* Vol.50 (1886) p.731 and *British Architect* Vol.25 (1886) p.491. The window is also mentioned in a report of the new window erected at Shillington for the same donor in *BT* 24 April 1886; **18.** Minor repairs of this period are noted by Archdeacon Bathurst (ABE 3) and in the vestry minutes 1891–1941 (in P 55/5/1); **19.** The improvements and new furnishings of 1908–10 are listed in the service register (P 55/0/1); **20.** Details of the 1971 restoration are recorded on a notice in the vestry; **21.** A school was provided by Robert Long in 1861.

STOTFOLD

The present church has grown from a C12th building which consisted of an aisleless nave and chancel. The north aisle began as a C13th north transept or chapel, extended to the west to form an aisle in the C14th. The south aisle was also built in two stages in the C14th. The Perpendicular west tower was added in the C15th, and the south porch, clerestory and much of the window tracery are also of this period.[1] There is a C15th font.[2]

One of the mediaeval bells survives.[3] Another bell dated "1615" was actually cast at Baldock in 1651, the figures being accidentally reversed by the bellfounder.[4] In 1617 the floor of the chancel was said to be out of repair.[5] In 1674 it was reported that the "Leads of church roof want repair" and that one bell was "crackt".[6] The treble bell was recast in 1740.[3] In 1739 a new silver paten was given "For the use of the Communion Table of the Parish Church of Stotfold".[7] In 1775 the chancel was "ceiled, paved and railed"[8] by Trinity College, Cambridge, during the incumbency of the Rev. Samuel Roe.[9]

Archdeacon Bonney ordered extensive repairs in 1823, and in 1825 the parish borrowed £500 to meet the cost.[10] During the course of this work, old painted frescoes were discovered.[11] The walls and roof were repaired at a total cost of £637.[12] and the work may have also involved the rebuilding of the north porch[13] and repairs to the buttresses of the tower.[14] At about this time the pulpit was moved.[15]

In 1839 Bonney noted that the parish had plans to re-pew the church. This was done in 1840–1 under the supervision of Thomas Smith of Hertford.[16] The contractor was William Seymour of Arlesey. Additional work on the roof was also found to be necessary, and this was carried out by Henry and John Stevens who may have been responsible for the plaster bosses put up in place of ancient carvings in the north aisle.

In 1888 Archdeacon Bathurst noted that "measures [were] being taken for restoration".[17] The architect employed was A.W. Soames, and the work done in 1889–90 included rebuilding the chancel, adding an organ chamber, repairs to the nave roof, erection of embattled parapets and general repairs at a total cost of £1270.[18] The north porch was also removed.[13]

In 1910 a clock was placed in the tower as a memorial to the Rev John

21. Stotfold: This north view shows the appearance of the church before the restoration in 1889–90 when the chancel was rebuilt and enlarged, the north porch removed and an embattled parapet added to the nave clerestory   *(Photograph: Anonymous 1876)*

Holding who is also commemorated by the stained glass in the east window.[19] The south aisle and porch underwent a further restoration in 1914–5 under Freeman and Ogilvy.[20] A stained glass window was erected in the south aisle as a War memorial in 1920.[21] In 1927–8 the west tower was restored under Professor Richardson, who was also responsible for repairs to the north aisle completed in 1932.[22] In 1948 the bells were restored and augmented to six, two further bells being added in 1976.[3] Further work on the west window of the tower was carried out in 1959.[23]

1. Extract from glebe terrier, 5 July 1822
STOTFOLD.

Church yard. The Church Yard contains by estimation one Acre, the fences round about belong to the several Persons whose Land lye next it, each one repairing as far as his Ground reacheth. **Repairs.** The Chancel is repaired by the Tenant of Trinity College and the Church is repaired at the charge of the Parishioners.

Furniture and ornaments. The furniture of the Chancel is One Communion Table, one Green baise Cloth to cover it, one White Diaper Cloth to cover it upon Communion Days, one silver Cup for the Communion with a cover of silver it is dated upon the top 1571,[7] and one silver Plate with a foot for the Bread marked IHS at the Top with an Inscription under it and was given by Dr. Adams in 1739. The furniture in the Church is one Pulpit Cloth and Cushion of Green baise, the Cloth is fringed at the bottom with Green silk fringe and the Cushion is tasselled at the Corners with Green silk Tassels. There is likewise one Green baise covering for the outside of the Desk or reading Pew,[15] one large Bible in folio of the last Translation, one Common Prayer Book in Folio and another for the Use of the Clerk (who is Sexton also) and is always chosen by the Minister. There is one Box with three Locks in which the Surplice &c. and Parish Papers are kept, and an Iron Chest in which the Registers are kept viz., the first beginning in 1559 and ending in 1702 imperfect, the second from that time to 1773, the third from 1773 to 1813, the fourth from 1813 and continued to the present time, all of Parchment and complete. There are likewise two Register Books of Paper for Marriages, the first beginning in 1754 and ending in 1812, the second beginning in 1813 and continued to the present time complete. There are three Bells with their frames in the Steeple.[3]

Parish Clerk and Sexton. The Clerk (who is Sexton also) is always chosen by the Minister. The Clerk's Wages are one shilling for each Farm House and four pence for each Cottage, and also a Dole Basket twice in the Year. His fees are For a Marriage by Banns two shillings and six pence, by Licence five shillings, for ringing the Knell, digging the Grave and Burial three shillings and six pence, for a Stranger five shillings.

School. Henricus Octavius Roe of Baldock Gent. purchased a piece of Land in the Church Crofts at Stotfold adjoining the Church Yard containing by Estimation one Rood which was conveyed by Indenture inrolled in Chancery the twelfth day of March one thousand eight hundred and eight in Trust for a School for the Instruction in Reading, Writing and Arithmetic and particularly in the Church Catechism and principles of the Christian Religion the Poor Children belonging to and resident in the Parish.[24]

2. Archdeacon Bonney's historical notices of churches, c.1820–1840

STOTFOLDE ALIAS STOCKFOLD, St. Mary. This Church consists of a Nave and aisles, Chancel, and a Tower at the West End. The piers are clustered with grotesque heads on the mouldings. The Font is octagonal with elegant perpendicular Panels.[2] The windows are of the same Character. There are three Bells in the Tower,[3] which is a plain Embattled Structure. Much Money has recently been expended on this Church.[16] The new Vicarage was erected by D[r]. Brass.[25] There is a South Porch of entrance to the Church.

3. Archdeacon Bonney's visitation notebook, 1823–1839

STOTFOLD. This Church consists of a Nave, North & South Aisles, a Tower at the West End of the Nave & Chancel at the East End thereof; a South Porch.

At the Visitation of 1823 It was ordered that the open Seats be neatly repaired, the Pulpit taken down,[15] set strait, and the Top repaired, the Steps up to it be new, and both the Pulpit and Desk be oak grained. The Pews be repaired by their proprietors. The Walls washed inside – the Earth be moved from the Walls both of the Church and Chancel, and proper drainage be made. Casements be placed in the Windows of the Aisles; the Tower be pointed;[14] the Stonework of the windows be repaired with Parker's Cement; before Easter 1826. And before Easter 1827 the Stairs of the Tower be capped with Wood; the floors of the Tower be repaired; the West door be repaired.

At the Visitation of 1826, the following order was given that the Lessee of the Rectory (M[r]. Tristram) repair that part of the Fabrick which appertains to him – and the Seats in the Chancel be oiled – a proper Font Bason be purchased.

At the Visitation of 1833 The following Order was given, That the end of a Beam in the Nave on the North side and the Whole Roof be surveyed & thoroughly repaired, also the Lead in the North West corner – the floors of the Seats be repaired – a Pew at the East end of the North Aisle be repaired – a new Surplice be purchased. The Pulpit & Desk (moved by D[r]. Brasse) be otherwise placed.[15]

At the Visitation of 1836 Ordered that the Seats, floor, and singing Loft be repaired – the Staircase boarded up, and the foundation of the Church in placed where the Earth has been removed be pointed with Cement.

At the Visitation in 1839. The Parish have the repewing of their Church in contemplation, & are to send me the Plan & Specification.[16] Offers amounting to £130 have been made towards defraying the expense – M[r]. Chatfield, present Incumbent, has enlarged the Glebe House, erected by D[r]. Brasse.[25]

4. Article on the Church by W.A. (no.90), NM 7 August 1852

STOTFOLD, Virgin Mary. The appearance of this Church exhibits a more than usual attention to cleanliness. The wooden roof is painted; the altar –

> "Some call't the altar, some the holy table,
> The name I stick not at,
> Whether't be this or that,
> I care not much, so that I may be able
>   Truly to know
> Both why it is, and may be called so –"

and railing surrounding it, are partly manufactured of some old carved work. Part of the eastern window is concealed by the Creed &c., painted in very bad style. The chancel is sadly blocked up with private sittings.

The nave and aisles have timber roofs; the sittings mostly open.[16] The tower arch is open and the west window seen. A singing gallery, the front of which is prepared ostentatiously to record the donors of loaves and other gifts for the benefit of the parish.[26] These should seek refuge in the comparative obscurity of the aisle, for it is well that they should be so perpetuated, since it is vain to expect the parochial annals, sometimes entrusted to men who cannot sign their names,* should preserve them from oblivion.

The pulpit and reading desk are placed separately.[15] The pipe of the stove mutilates a clerestory window. The end of the north aisle is enclosed to serve the purposes of a vestry, a miserable substitute for the right thing.

The font has its lead and drain, the latter stopped up with a beer barrel cork.[2]

There are two porches, one a vile cement addition.[13]

We are sorry to record these deficiencies in a Church otherwise in tolerably good order; a very small outlay would easily set all right; it would well become the great college, in whose patronage this vicarage is vested, and which of course absorbs the great tithes, to set a good example in this respect.
n.d.   W.A.

* Those who are incredulous on that point, we beg to refer to Mr.Pashley's work, before quoted, "He cannot write his name, but that's his mark"

5. *Sir Stephen Glynne's Church notes, 11 May 1869 (Vol.2, pp.35–36)*

STOTFOLD, St. Mary. This Church has Clerestoried nave with aisles, Chancel, West Tower & South porch – The walls are mostly of clunch with flints – plastered & occasionally patched externally. The arcades of the nave have some peculiarities – Each has 3 bays with pointed arches with face mouldings of Decorated character. On the N the eastern pier is a wide one marking a break with shafts attached. On the S. the break is a similar pier but is the most Westerly of the 2 instead of the most eastern. The other piers are composed of clustered shafts with moulded capitals – but those on the S. have longitudinal ribs & grotesque heads on the caps. The windows of the aisles are mostly Perpendicular of 3 lights, but at the W. end of the South aisle the window is Decorated, of 2 lights. Those of the Clerestory are Perpendicular of 3 lights.

The chancel arch is pointed on shafts. On its N. side is the rood doorway – on its S. side is a cinquefoiled niche in the wall. The chancel is long – has 2 light Perpendicular windows on the N & S – at the East a very good one of 3 lights. The nave was fitted up about 30 years ago with uniform pews but not such as can now be approved.[16] The Font is a good Perpendicular one – the bowl octagonal – & elegantly panneled – as also the stem.[2] The aisles & porch are embattled, but not the Clerestory. There is a N doorway with panneled spandrels of Perpendicular character – The S. porch has lateral Perpendicular windows & an outer doorway with panneled spandrels. The Tower arch is pointed – The Tower Perpendicular, tall & rather well proportioned & very much of a local style – has battlements – two string courses & base mouldings – belfry windows double – each of 2 lights – a West window of 3 lights – & under it a doorway with panneled spandrels.

(Some mural paintings were once discovered in this church, now washed over[j])[11]

Notes **1.** Pevsner p.150, *VCH* II pp.302–3, *The Church of Saint Mary the Virgin, Stotfold* n.d. [c.1950], and G.H.C. Phillips *A History of Stotfold* (1951 – revised and reprinted 1977), esp. pp.12–20; **2.** The font is described by Glynne. W.A. notes that its drain was stopped up with a beer barrel cork!; **3.** It is said (North p.196) that there were once five bells here, but the tradition seems unlikely as the old frame (removed in 1947) only had pits for three bells. The second bell (usually said to date from 1484) is more likely to be a C14th bell by John Rufford of Toddington. The tenor (recast in 1948) was cast by Miles Graye in 1651, and the treble was recast by Thomas Russell of Wootton in 1740. The tenor was recast and three bells were added to make six in 1948, and in 1976 two more bells were added to make eight (Phillips p.22); **4.** Memorandum in parish register, 1651 (P 83/1/1); **5.** Presentment, 1617 (ABC 5 p.216); **6.** Archdeacon's visitations, 1674 (CRT 170/9/1 p.10); **7.** The 1708 and 1822 terriers mention an Elizabethan chalice of 1571 which is not listed in the 1927 schedule (ABE 5). The plate now includes a paten of 1739 and a cup of 1847–8; **8.** Memorandum on chancel improvements, 1775 (P 83/1/3). According to the College archives, the work cost £16 9s 10d (*Ex.inf.* College archivist); **9.** For Roe, <u>see</u> article by Eric Walker in *B.Mag* Vol.4 (1954) pp.192–6; **10.** Mortgage for repairs, 1825 (P 83/28/1); **11.** The frescoes are described and illustrated in an article on the church in *GM* Vol.97 Pt.II (1827) pp.401–3; **12.** The later ICBS papers indicate that the work in 1826 cost £637 (LPL ref: ICBS 2743). Phillips (p.17–9) describes what was done, but his list seems to be based on interpretation rather than documentary evidence; **13.** The original north porch illustrated by Fisher (slide 2276) seems to have been a wooden structure with boarded walls and roof, replaced in about 1826 by what W.A. described as "a vile cement addition" shown in a photograph of 1876 (Z 50/115/1); **14.** Phillips (p.17) suggests that the buttresses were rebuilt with brickwork covered with Roman cement in 1824. Bonney ordered in 1823 that the tower be pointed; **15.** Bonney's notes indicate that the pulpit was moved during the incumbency of the Rev. John Brassey (1825–1834). The present pulpit dates from 1841, and Smith's plan (LPL Ref: ICBS 2743) of the re–pewing shows the separate desk and pulpit to the left and right respectively of the chancel arch as noted by W.A.; **16.** Sources for the re–seating include a painted board in the church dated 1841, and the ICBS correspondence 1840–42 (LPL ref: ICBS 2743). The evidence in the ICBS papers that Stevens worked here in 1841 suggests that the plaster bosses date from this time rather than from the 1820s as suggested by Phillips. Writing 30 years later Glynne described the seating as "not such as can be now approved"; **17.** Bathurst's notebook (ABE 3); **18.** The 1889–90 restoration is described by Phillips (p.17). There are reports concerning fund–raising and progress *BE* 16 June 1888 and 28 Sept.1889, an account of an accident at the church in *BT* 23 Nov.1889 in which the discovery of an old coffin is also mentioned, and a report of the reopening in *HE* 8 Feb.1890; **19.** Faculty for clock (by Potts) and window (by A.L. Moore), 1910 (P 83/2/2/4), faculty papers (HCRO ref: DSA 2/1/203 and 220), press cutting (in P 83/0/2) and report in *BT* 2 Dec.1910; **20.** Papers concerning the work on the south aisle, 1913–15 (P 83/2/2/5–6). Phillips (p.18) states that the work was completed in 1916; **21.** Papers concerning the war memorial window, 1920 (P 83/2/2/7); **22.** Correspondence on the tower repairs 1928–9 (in SPAB archives) and account in Report of the Council for the Care of Churches for 1928–9 (p.48). The rainwater heads on the north aisle are dated 1932; **23.** Papers concerning the west tower window 1953–9, with note that after debates about possible repair the stonework eventually had to be replaced in 1959 (P 83/2/2/14–15); **24.** Roe's deed of 1808 (P 83/25/21) survives among the parish records with other charity deeds (P 83/25/21–35) and an abstract of Roe's endowments (in P 83/1/3); **25.** There are plans for the Vicarage by William Yorke of Cheshunt, surveyor and builder, 1832 (BRO ref: X 392/7/1–9); **26.** For the charities, <u>see</u> Phillips (pp.30–42).

STREATLEY

There was a church at Streatley by the mid C12th, but the present building dates largely from the C14th. The arcades of the north and south aisles are of this date, but the west tower and some of the window tracery date from the

C15th.[1] There is a fine C13th font.[2] The rood screen incorporates some ancient woodwork. There are tracings of wall paintings on the eastern parts of the nave and on the chancel arch. Some of the benches are of C16th date and others have Jacobean panels.[3]

A will of 1533 indicates that an organ had recently been acquired for the church.[4] Documents of 1555 refer to the sale of a "greate belle" to pay for repairs to the leaded roof.[5] In 1558 a parishioner left money "to newe painte the churche of Stretley with textes of scripture in englishe yf it by the lawes of England it may be suffered".[6]

In 1674 it was reported that the chancel was out of repair.[7] A new communion cup was given in 1685,[8] and in 1708 the plate included "a Communion cup of Silver weight about Eight Ounces and one Large Pewter flaggon both carefully kept from one Communion to another".[9] At that date there were "two Bells to be used on Sundays and other times".[10] One of the bells was sold by faculty in 1773. The pulpit and C18th sounding board still remain in use,[11] and Fisher's view of the interior shows that by the early C19th there were several enclosed pews at the front of the nave.[12] The 1822 terrier mentions that the chancel had been shortened "when last repaired", possibly in 1807.[13]

From 1765 repairs to the church are recorded in the churchwardens' accounts, and there are also vestry minutes from 1794.[14] Although names and trades are given, the nature of the work is seldom stated. Work of this period includes repairs to the steeple in 1765, the recasting of a bell by John Briant in 1804,[10] and roof repairs in 1809–10 (£60) and in 1817–9 (£204) after the vestry had agreed that the church should be "gradually repaired in the Leads as in former years". More work was done in response to Archdeacon Bonney's orders, including extensive plastering by Stevens in 1827–8. The bell was again recast in 1832.[10]

In 1846 the livings of Streatley and Sundon were united and a new rectory was built at Sundon.[15] In 1874 Archdeacon Bathurst found Streatley church in bad condition and his notebook chronicles the deterioration of the building into the early C20th.[16] A new paten was obtained in 1879.[8] The chancel was repaired by the patron in about 1888 and in 1898–9 it was taken down and rebuilt in brick.[13] In 1896 the seats in the church were improved, a new tortoise stove was provided in 1897 and in 1899 Bathurst found that the church had a new lectern, reading desk and lamps.[17] In 1907 a new altar was dedicated and other new furnishings were provided for the chancel.[16]

In the early C20th the building fell into disrepair after a High Church incumbent "estranged the parishioners".[16] The church was closed in 1917. In 1930 the Council for the Care of Churches expressed concern that the church might soon become "a wreck beyond saving".[18] Emergency repairs were carried out in 1931, and in 1937–8 the church was restored under Professor Richardson with Diocesan funds as a memorial to Archdeacon Parnell.[19]

22. Streatley: SW view showing the brick south porch, the shortened chancel (reduced in length before 1822) and makeshift woodwork in the belfry windows

(Watercolour: Thomas Fisher c.1815)

Since the Second World War the church has returned to active use. New altar rails were provided in 1954,[20] the porch was rebuilt in 1957–8,[21] and a further restoration took place in 1961–2.[22] In more recent times an organ has been provided (1972),[23] rooms have been created under the tower (1974) and three bells (from Christ Church, Luton) have been hung in the tower (1979).[10]

1. Extract from glebe terrier, 28 June 1822

STREATLY.

Church yard. The Church-yard contains about three roods, is surrounded by the grounds of the Rev. James Hadow who supports the wall and pales on the East and South sides, the Vicar makes the hedges on the West and North, and the Parish maintains the Gates and Stile.

Church. The Church is an ancient Building in length 58 feet, in breadth 40 feet (exclusive of the Chancel which, having been lessened when last repaired, is in length 18 feet, in breadth 17 feet, covered with Tiles),[13] with a square Tower 52½ feet in height. Two Bells, one measuring 24 inches in diameter with inscription "W. Smith & T. Wells, Church Wardens, J. Haddow, Vicar, John Briant, Hertford fecit, 1804", the other 16 inches in diameter without inscription.[10]

Furniture and ornaments. A Pulpit with Cushion,[24] & reading Desk, a large Bible & Prayer Book, a Communion Table with Linen Cloth & two Napkins, a Silver Cup & two Pewter Plates,[8] a wooden Chest, & an iron d°.

23. Streatley: Interior looking west, showing the south door cut into an old window in the chancel (as noted by W.A.), the pulpit and tester and enclosed pews at the front of the nave

(Watercolour: Thomas Fisher c.1815)

for Registers. Three new Register Books & two older, with part of a more ancient one very imperfect commencing A.D.1693. A bier and hearse cloth.

Parish Clerk and Sexton. The Parish Clerk & Sexton receives a Salary of two Guineas, and Fees equal to half of the Vicar's.

Church Estate. There is Land in the open field of Streatly which belongs to the Church Wardens, and at present in the occupation of T. Smyth, C. Wells & T. Deacon, containing about 6 Acres, in three portions, and the rent amounting to £3 is paid to the Church Wardens.

2. Archdeacon Bonney's historical notices of churches, c.1820–1840
STREATLEY OR STRATLEY, St. Margaret. This Church consists of a

Nave and Aisles separated by Octagonal Piers and pointed Arches, a Chancel and a Tower at the West End with a Staircase Turret. The Character of the Fabrick is the Perpendicular. The font is octagonal & Early English with nail head mouldings, & panels.[2] There is a South Porch.

3. *Archdeacon Bonney's visitation notebook, 1823–1839*

STREATLEY. This Church consists of a nave and aisles – a Tower at the West end of the Nave and a Chancel at the East End thereof.

At the Visitation of 1823 It was ordered that a new Pall be purchased, the Bible be rebound,[25] a metal Flagon, dark blue covering for the Communion Table, Pulpit Cushion and Cloth be purchased;[24] the Communion Table be cleansed and oiled; the Pavement of the Church be repaired; the Seats be oiled and the Pews coloured to suit; the Earth be moved from the Walls of the Church and Chancel. The Chancel Walls be washed; the frame of the East Window be painted; the Windows of the Bellchamber be made uniform with the other windows; the font be cleansed; the Floors be made even; the floor of the Bellchamber be repaired; the Creed, Lord's Prayer, and Ten Commandments be renewed; a lock be put to the Middle Chamber door, before Easter 1826.

At the Visitation of 1826 the only order given was that the windows of the church be restored with Parker's Cement and be thoroughly glazed.[26]

At the Visitation of 1833, no order was deemed necessary.

At the Visitation of 1836, a spout having become loose, it was ordered to be secured.

At the Visitation 1839 ordered the Church Wardens to put the Bellchamber Turret into substantial repair – also the Slates on the Porch, and the south East Buttress of the South Aisle. Recommended additional free sittings either at the West End of the Nave or in the Aisles.

4. *Article on the Church by W.A. (no.19), NM 6 December 1845*

STREATLEY. This church is in very good condition; little alteration would render the interior more satisfactory. It has few enclosed pews which might easily be removed,[12] for the open seats are numerous and of a very fair character.[3] The roof is of wood. The western light is not obscured, but the lower part of the window is boarded up, occupying the space appropriated for the font. This is a very good specimen, but it has not escaped the hands of the dauber.[2] Two apparently very good windows at the western end of the aisles have been blocked up. The stone columns are well covered with whitewash.

The chancel has its roof ceiled, but all appearance of its original state has been entirely effaced by the usual application. A door would appear to have been made through what was originally a window, and was very probably put up at the same time as the deplorable eastern window.[13]

The porch is of brick, with the windows closed up; one of the buttresses is repaired with the same material.

The churchyard is in tolerable order; sheep were not trampling down "the narrow cells" of the forefathers of the village, nor is access denied to such of their descendants as may desire to visit them.

29 November 1845   W.A.

Notes **1.** Pevsner p.150, *VCH* II p.383, RC article in *BT* 5–12 June 1903, and "St.Margaret's Church, Streatley" (1993); **2.** The font (illustrated by Fisher – slide 592) is generally taken to be of C13th date, but Pevsner (p.150) questions the date of the bowl. The will of Richard Herryes of St.Albans, 1476, includes a bequest of 6s.8d. to the fabric of the parish church of Streatley and for a baptismal font (*ex.inf.* Sue Flood); **3.** There are old oak benches at the back of the church and others with Jacobean panels at the front of the nave; **4.** The organ mentioned in will, 1533 (ABP/R 3 f.90d); **5.** Eeles and Brown p.24; **6.** Will, 1558 (ABP/R 15 f.52); **7.** Archdeacon's visitations, 1674 (CRT 170/9/1 p.13); **8.** The present plate (listed in ABE 5) includes a cup of 1685 and a paten marked "Streatley Church, Easter 1879"; **9.** Glebe terrier, 1708 (ABE 2 Vol.II p.422); **10.** One bell was sold in 1555, leaving two bells (as listed in 1708). Another bell was sold in 1773 (P 25/5/1). This seems to have left a large bell and a small one. The large bell was recast by John Briant in 1804 and its inscription is given in the 1822 terrier. It was again recast in 1832 (North p.196). In 1979 three old bells (dated 1860 and 1876) from Christ Church, Luton, were hung in the tower to make (with the 1832 Streatley bell as treble) a chime of four; **11.** The pulpit and sounding board are shown in Fisher's view of the interior (slide 11377); **12.** The enclosed pews mentioned by W.A. are also shown in Fisher's view (slide 11377); **13.** The chancel was shortened before 1822, possibly in 1807 (the date recorded by Ransom on a stone taken from the east window). W.A. noted the plaster ceiling, south door (shown in Fisher's view – slide 11377) and a "deplorable eastern window". It was again repaired in about 1888 (ABE 3), and rebuilt in 1898–9 (Kelly's *Directory* 1910 p.171). Ransom's RC article indicates that the chancel of 1899 was only intended as a temporary structure; **14.** Churchwardens' accounts 1765–1913 (P 25/5/1) and vestry minutes 1794–1831 (P 25/8/1) and 1823–25 and 1840–94 (PC Streatley 9/1); **15.** Union of benefices, 1846 (HCRO ref: DSA 1/11/2) and mortgage papers and plans for new rectory, 1847–8 (CUL ref: EDR/G3/40 MGA/BED/12); **16.** Bathurst's notebook (ABE 3) and report of dedication of altar in *CT* 8 Feb.1907; **17.** The work of the 1890s is documented in the accounts (P 25/5/1), in Bathurst's notebook (ABE 3), and in Kelly's *Directory* 1903 p.160; **18.** Report of the Council for the Care of Churches for 1930–1 (pp.58–9); **19.** Richardson's restoration is documented in the parish papers (P 25/2/2/1), in the SPAB archives, and report in *BT* 27 May 1938. The rainwater heads are dated 1937; **20.** Faculty for the altar rails, 1954 (P 25/2/2/2); **21.** Faculty for porch, 1957 (P 25/2/2/3); **22.** Papers concerning the 1960s work (P 25/2/2/1); **23.** Papers concerning the organ, 1972 (P 25/2/2/9–12). It has since been enlarged (guide); **24.** New pulpit cloth bought (£6 10s) from Warwick, draper, 1824 (P 125/5/1); **25.** Payment (£1 6s) to Hill, bookbinder, in 1824 (P 25/5/1) – probably for rebinding the bible as ordered by Bonney; **26.** The work recorded in the accounts for 1825–8 cost over £180, including payments to Stevens for plaster work.

STUDHAM

There is documentary evidence that a church was built at Studham around the time of the Norman Conquest. A fine Norman font survives from the old church which was rebuilt in the early C13th. The present church was consecrated in 1219. The aisles were altered in the C14th, and in the C15th the west tower was added, the chancel rebuilt, and a clerestory added to the nave.[1]

In 1578 it was reported that "The chancell is oute of repayre".[2] By the late C17th there were four bells, one cast in 1599, another of 1627 and two dated 1666.[3] In 1669 the curate stated that "there is neither surplice, Communion

Cup nor Cushion for the pulpitt & the Church out of reparation".[4] A cup was provided in 1674.[5]

From 1750 the churchwardens' accounts record information on repairs.[6] In 1773–4 almost £90 was spent on repairs, including a payment of £29 7s. in 1774 to "To Joseph Clark for roughcasting the church".[7] The accounts also show how the parish complied with Archdeacon Bonney's visitation orders. In 1825 extensive repairs were carried out at a cost of over £500. The work included re-seating and repairs to the roof, font, windows and tower. It was partly financed by a loan which was eventually repaid in 1837. In 1839 Bonney ordered repairs to the tower which was restored in 1840 under the direction of John Adsetts, the clerk of works on the Ashridge estate. This may have been when the parapet was lowered and the pyramid roof and "spike" removed.[8] By the time of W.A.'s visit in 1847 the church had a west gallery with an organ, enclosed pews and stoves in the nave and chancel.

The roof of the south aisle was renewed in 1876. By 1886 the building was in poor condition, and Archdeacon Bathurst noted the "tower out of repair, trees on roof of nave wall, bad cracks on south chancel wall, and part of the plaster fallen down from the ceiling".[9] At the instigation of Lord Brownlow, the patron, estimates for restoration were prepared in 1890 by J. Sutherland of the Ashridge Estate office. Work began in 1892 with the restoration of the chancel and addition of a vestry, and in 1893 the body of the church was thoroughly restored under the Sutherland's supervision.[10] The pulpit and lectern of Cornish Serpentine by Doney & Evans of St.Austell date from the time of the restoration. The whole scheme cost £1200 and when the work was completed the church was reopened on 23 Aug.1893.

The stained glass in the east window was installed in memory of the Rev. Arthur Anderson who died in 1902, and in 1903 a window by Kempe was placed in the south wall of the chancel as a memorial to Philip Brown who was killed in the Boer War.[11] In 1904 the Rev. J.E. Brown gave additional plate.[5] A new organ by Norman and Beard was installed in 1906.[12] In 1909 the bells were restored and rehung in a new iron frame.[3] The chancel screen commemorates the Rev. J.E. Brown (Vicar 1902–13). It was designed by Noel Rew of Berkhamstead and completed in 1916.[13]

In 1970 the church was restored under George G. Pace of York, and the distinctive leaded glazing and light fittings date from this time. In 1971 the chancel ceiling was also redecorated under Pace.[14] A small kitchen extension was added on the north side of the church in 1987. The organ was rebuilt in 1992,[12] and in 1993 three more bells were hung in the tower.[3]

1. Extract from glebe terrier, 24 June 1822
STUDHAM.
Church yard. The Church Yard containing by estimation one acre and one Rood (more or less) abutting on lands of the said Thomas and Ann Nicoll on

24. Studham: SE view showing the appearance of the church before the work on the tower in 1840 and the general restoration of 1892–3   *(Pencil sketch: J. Buckler 1839)*

the East, West and North parts, and on Land of the Earl of Bridgewater, the Church Road and Land of the said Thomas and Ann Nicholls on the South part, the Fences of which are repaired by the Vicar, the Gates excepted, which are repaired at the Common Charge of the Parish.

Church. The Church is an Ancient Building containing in length [blank] including the Chancel, and in breadth [blank], and the Chancel in breadth [blank].

Furniture and ornaments. The church has four Bells,[3] One Prayer Book, One Bible,[15] two Surplices, a Pulpit Cloth and Cushion covered with Crimson Velvet and Gold, One Silver Cup,[5] two Pewter Plates for the Use of the Communion, and a Communion Table which is Railed in.

Parish Registers. There are [blank] Register Books containing Entries of Baptizms, Marriages and Burials the Earliest commencing in the Year [blank]

Repairs. The Church and Furniture are repaired at the common Charge of the Parish and the Chancel is repaired at the joint Charge of the four Impropriators.

Parish Clerk and Sexton. The Office of Parish Clerk and Sexton is held by one person who is appointed by the Vicar, Who hath for his Salary four pounds four shillings Yearly paid him by the Churchwardens Besides the accustomed Dues, Viz[t]. For every Burial including the Charge for Tolling the Bell and digging the Grave [blank], For every Marriage five shillings by

Licence, 2/6 by Banns, For Publication of Banns [blank], For ever Christening six pence.

Churchwardens. The Churchwardens are chosen yearly in Easter Week, One by the Vicar and the other by the Parishioners in Vestry Assembled.

2. Archdeacon Bonney's historical notices of churches, c.1820–1840

STUDHAM, St. Mary. This church consists of a Nave & Aisles separated by octagonal piers with figured mouldings & supporting low pointed Arches. Chancel. The Font is circular with grotesque ornaments &c. on the Mouldings. The Character of the Church generally, excepting the tower at the West End, Porch & Windows which are perpendicular, are Early English.

Early English ornament on the Moulding of one of the Piers [*Sketch*]

3. Archdeacon Bonney's visitation notebook, 1823–1839

STUDHAM. This Church consists of a Nave and Aisles, a Tower at the West end of the Nave and Chancel at the East End thereof. The Parish is partly in Beds & partly in Herts.[16]

At the Visitation of 1823, the following Order was given that the Floor near the Communion Table be made even; The Ceiling and Windows of the Chancel be repaired; the wood work of the Nave & Aisles be cleaned but neither washed nor painted; the Bible and Two Prayer Books be repaired;[17] the Reading desk be renewed; the Pulpit painted to imitate oak. The Earth be moved from the Fabrick;[18] and the Walls be repaired; a Path be made; the Steeple be repaired; a new Door be made to the Belfry.

At the Visitation of 1826 the whole of this Church was in all respects in perfect order.[19]

At the Visitation of 1833 It was ordered that the stucco on the exterior of the Tower & Church be repaired,[7] and the Walls be cleansed from Green Moss by dry brushing.

At the Visitation of 1836. Ordered that the decayed Panels of the North & South Seats of the Church, and the plaster of the exterior of the church,[7] be repaired – the interior surface of the Chancel Walls be cleansed – and the Spouts on the NE & SE Angles thereof be so arranged as to prevent the Water going upon & injuring the Walls. And that the NE angle of the North Aisle be repaired.

At the Visitation 1839 Ordered that the Tower, Bells (particularly the second bell), Bell Ropes, the Plaster Externally, the Chancel (particularly the South East Buttress) be all put into Substantial repair.[20]

4. Article on the Church by W.A. (no.73), NM 18 September 1847

STUDHAM, St. Mary. The chancel roof is ceiled; the perishable nature of this miserable substitute for oak is plainly exhibited in its decaying state. The rest of this part of the church is, as usual, whitewashed. There is a large square box, with some deal benches; the floor was strewed with faded flowers, most probably brought by children who occupy these benches on Sunday.[21] The period for doing away with the stove having arrived, the hole in the chancel wall for its chimney is plastered up until the return of winter requires it to be re-opened; one among many of the bad results arising from the use of these ugly contrivances. We saw lately a ludicrous effect produced by this removal in another church in this county. The portion of the chimney which has been pushed through the clerestory window is left, and has very much the appearance of a piece of ordnance; it is pointed directly at the head of the preacher, and is perhaps intended by the churchwardens as a symbol of the church militant.

The nave has a timber roof, but the aisles are ceiled. The nave has a timber roof, but the aisles are ceiled. The western window is shut out by a wretched little organ and gallery. Not content with a stove in the chancel, there is one here also, 'another new thing which we are told we cannot do without. Yet our forefathers did not want such comforts, though they had not warm cushioned pews, and green-baized doors as we have. Do away with stoves by all means. The cumbrous pipes or heated flues have destroyed many churches by fire.'*

The pillars, very interesting examples of Early English architecture, are robbed of all their beauty by repeated coats of whitewash, which have been so tastelessly showered upon them. The curious font has also experienced the same indignity. The drain remains, but not the leaden lining. A common pewter basin is used instead of the font itself; not even the Wedgwood manufacture, the delight of a clerk in another church, who concluded its merits by saying it had just cost a guinea!

Pews prevail, occupying the best portion of the nave; humbler open sittings are placed behind them. A corner in the north aisle is appropriated to some benches, the occupants of which must suffer from the damp surrounding them, greatly increased by the unsparing use of whitewash under which the church suffers. The rotting wood-work in the aisles preventing the free circulation of air, adds its testimony to the bad effects of this dirty application. A piscina in the south aisle is boarded up; we wondered it was not left open, as it forms a convenient receptacle for prayer books or hats, a purpose to which it is very generally destined in other churches. The pulpit and reading-desk are placed together, the latter of unnecessary size. the roof of the chancel is tiled. Cattle were grazing in the church-yard. There is no school.

13 September 1847   W.A.

* Hints to Churchwardens

5. Sir Stephen Glynne's Church notes, before 1840. (Vol.1, pp.7–8)

STUDHAM. This neat Church has an Early English nave with side aisles, & a chancel & West Tower of Rectilinear character. The date of its foundation is said to be 1220. The exterior is plastered, & there is no battlement to the body. The nave has 4 pointed arches, with octagonal piers which have the capitals enriched with magnificent foliage of varied character. The Clerestory windows are square headed & of 2 lights. Those of the side aisles are also square headed, some having Curvilinear, some Rectilinear tracery.

The Chancel arch is Early English, the imposts having foliage & on each side of the arch is a square aperture.

The Chancel is Rectilinear & plain, the East window of 3 lights, & there is a small doorway on the South side. The Interior is particularly neat – the arches, pillars & Font all cleaned from whitewash, & the pews new & uniform.[22] The Tower is plain Rectilinear & embattled. The Font is one of the finest specimens that can be found of early work, & its beauty seems to be appreciated from the neat state in which it is kept – it is clearly Norman – the basin circular, the upper part sculptured with figures of dragons & grotesque animals biting pieces of foliage – The shaft is cylindrical upon a circular base ornamented with pieces of foliage.

Notes **1.** Pevsner p.151, *VCH* III pp.430–31, J.E.Brown *Studham: The story of a secluded parish* (1905), John and Norah Robson *Studham: The Village, Church and People* (1981), and church guide by Barry Harris (1996); **2.** Archidiaconal visitations (ABC 3 p.207) 1578 in BHRS Vol.69 (1990) p.180; **3.** North (p.197) gives particulars of the old bells. The 1599 bell was recast when the bells were restored in 1909. There are now six bells and a tolling bell, as described in Harris's guide; **4.** Archdeacon's visitations, 1669 (ABC 7); **5.** The plate (schedule ABE 5) includes the cup of 1674 inscribed with the name of Nathaniel Fisher, Churchwarden, and a cup and paten given by the Rev. J.E. Brown in 1904; **6.** Churchwardens' accounts or vestry book 1750–1922 (P 86/5/1). This volume, extensively quoted by Brown and Robson who give dates and other information for the main repairs and alterations to the church and its furnishings, is the source for most of the material in this account unless other material is cited; **7.** It is generally accepted that the church was first roughcast with cement in 1774. Bonney refers to the stucco or plaster on the exterior in 1833 and 1836. The rendering was renewed in 1892 (Brown p.47); **8.** Buckler's view of the tower dated 1839 shows a high parapet, a pyramid roof with a spike and weathercock (BL ref: Add.Ms. 36356 f.56). The appearance of the tower may have been altered in 1840 or in 1893 when the roof was again renewed; **9.** Bathurst's notebook (ABE 3); **10.** Sources for the restoration in 1892–3 include the accounts book (P 86/5/1), related papers (P 86/5/2), faculty papers 1892 (HCRO ref: DSA 2/1/204), correspondence in the SPAB archives, invitation to tender in *Building News* 23 Dec.1892, and the descriptions of the work by Brown (p.47) and Robson (pp.20–24); **11.** For the windows see Robson (p.18) and Harris's guide; **12.** There are accounts of the organ fund (in P 86/5/1). It was dedicated on 17 Sept.1906. Harris states that the organ was rebuilt and improved by Saxon Aldred in 1992; **13.** The account book (P 86/5/1) includes notes on the screen which is described in detail. The cross was removed in 1970 and now rests in the tower; **14.** The work by Pace at Studham is listed in Peter G. Pace *The Architecture of George Pace 1915–75* (1990) p.246; **15.** The accounts mention the purchase of a new bible and two prayer books (£2 6s 6d) in 1765 (P 86/5/1); **16.** Since 1897 when the parish and county boundaries were altered, the whole parish has been in Bedfordshire (*VCH* III p.426 and Youngs p.10); **17.** Payments in accounts for carriage of books to London (1s) and "Binding the Bible" (£1 5s), April 1824 (P 86/5/1); **18.** Payments for moving the earth recorded in 1823 (P 86/5/1); **19.** By 1826, the extensive repairs (costing over £500) had been completed; **20.** The tower was repaired under John Adsetts in 1840 (P 86/5/1); **21.** Bathurst noted in 1873 "Chancel not used except as Sunday School" (ABE 3); **22.** The pews referred to by Glynne were evidently installed when the church was repaired in 1825.

SUNDON

There was a church at Sundon by the early C13th and the list of vicars goes back to 1226. The present building was begun in the late C13th and completed in the second quarter of the C14th. The style of architecture is chiefly Decorated, but the arcades and the east window of the north aisle are of an earlier period. The tracery in the south transept is especially fine. The top stage of the tower dates from the C15th and the chancel was also rebuilt in the C15th.[1] The church retains a C13th font of Purbeck marble from the previous church.[2] There is a Perpendicular rood screen.[3] The C14th oak chest is carved with flowing tracery.[4]

In 1518 the chancel was said to be in an extreme state of deterioration, but by 1530 it had apparently been repaired.[5] There is a communion cup of 1628.[6] The font has a C17th wooden cover. The church is now seated with chairs, but in the early years of the C20th there were some C17th benches and C18th pews in the nave.[7] Round the walls of the aisles there are stone seats.

Terriers of 1710 and 1730 indicate that there were once three bells at Sundon.[8] In 1763 a faculty was obtained for the sale of two bells "which have for upwards of forty years been broke to pieces".[9] The money was to be used to "new pew" the church and to erect a clock.[10] The churchwardens' accounts from 1767 provide information on church music and on repairs to the fabric of the building.[11] Roof repairs were undertaken in 1783–4, 1793 and 1801 and the Vicar's pew was repaired in 1790.

Archdeacon Bonney ordered repairs in 1823 and work costing over £54 is recorded in the accounts for that year. This may have involved the rebuilding of the south porch.[12] In 1833 Bonney ordered that the commandments be placed on the east wall and the Lord's Prayer and Creed over the north and south doors.[13] When he visited in 1839 the windows were being repaired.[14] W.A. described the church in 1845 as recently whitewashed.

In 1846 the benefices of Sundon and Streatley were united and a new parsonage was built at Sundon in 1848.[15] The accounts mention minor repairs to the church in 1850 and to the tower in 1858. In 1874 Archdeacon Bathurst noted that the church was in poor condition.[16] The roof of the nave was badly damaged in the great storm in October 1880, and after an appeal to raise money a new roof was provided in 1883.[17] At the same time, a new vestry was constructed inside the church and some work was done on the interior.

More needed to be done, and a restoration committee was formed in June 1887.[18] Some work was done at a cost of £38. The Vicar of Luton, the Rev. James O'Neill, was invited to report on the state of the church and in July he recommended "that a first rate Church Architect should be consulted". Nothing more seems to have been done until 1897 when work on the interior and exterior costing £53 was carried out by Foster and Hill.[19] In 1901 the west

25. Sundon: S view showing the fine decorated tracery in the south transept, the quatrefoiled clerestory windows and the chequer work (exaggerated in this view) on the tower

(Watercolour: Thomas Fisher c.1815)

window was repaired after the glass had been smashed in a hailstorm.[20] Additional plate was provided in 1904 and 1907,[6] and in 1907 a new pulpit was given in memory of William Anstee.[21]

In 1906–7 the upper part of the tower was restored at a cost of £400 under Mallows and Grocock of Bedford.[22] The same architects also prepared plans for a general restoration of the church, but the scheme was abandoned. Soon after the arrival of the Rev. C.T. Mundy as Vicar in 1908 the churches at both Sundon and Streatley fell into disuse and decay. The Archdeacon considered that the Vicar had estranged the parishioners by trying to introduce High Church practices.[16] Mundy applied for a faculty to restore the church in 1913.[23] Nothing could be done, and the church was closed soon afterwards. For the next twenty five years services were held in a room at the Vicarage.

In 1922 the Society for the Protection of Ancient Buildings became concerned about the state of the building.[24] Through the Society's intervention the church was eventually restored. The tower was found to be in danger of collapse in 1930, and it was secured by the construction of additional buttresses under W.A. Forsyth in 1931.[25] Further work followed and the church was reopened in 1938.

Recent additions include a new lectern obtained in 1953, a second-hand organ obtained in 1965 from a church in Bedford, and the stained glass of 1966 in the east window.[26]

1. Extract from glebe terrier, 28 June 1822

SUNDON.

Church yard. The Church yard containing about one Acre, bounded on the East by a Close and Hedge belonging to the Farm occupied by Charles Tomson, on the South by the Vicarage Pightle before mentioned, on the West by Land of Sir G.O.P. Turner Bart., and on the North by the road to Dunstable. The Fence on the North side is maintained by the Vicar, the other Fences by the occupiers of the Lands contiguous, the Gate by the Church Wardens.

Church. The Church is an ancient Building, in length 58 feet, in breadth 33 feet; a South Transept 9½ feet by 12½ feet, with a Tower in height 52 feet, & 19 feet square, and a Chancel 26 feet long & 16½ feet wide.

Furniture and ornaments. It contains a Pulpit & Cushion, & Reading desk, a large Bible & Prayer Book,[27] a wooden Chest,[4] & iron do. for Registers,[28] three new Register Books, & two old & imperfect, the oldest commencing A.D.1696, a Communion Table, one Silver Cup, & two Pewter Plates, one Linen Cloth and two Napkins, two Surplices, one Bell measuring 36 Inches in diam[r]., with Inscription "Ave Maria",[8] one Bier, and Hearse Cloth.[29]

Parish Clerk and Sexton. Fees to the Parish Clerk and Sexton are half of the amount payable to the Vicar [i.e. for marriage by banns two shillings and sixpence, by licence five shillings, for churching sixpence, for burial one shilling and threepence].

Church land. Extract of particulars of the Estate of Sundon when offered for Sale A.D. 1802 – "The whole of Stocking Close contains 28 Acres 1 Rood 18 Perches, but 1a. 2r. 28p. belong to the Church Wardens, and 1a. 0r. 27p. to the Poor of the said Parish, for which is paid a yearly rent of 17s. to the Church Wardens and 13s. to the Poor."

2. Archdeacon Bonney's historical notices of churches, c.1820–1840

SUNDON ALIAS STONDON, St. Mary. This interesting Church consists of a Nave and Aisles, a South Transept, Chancel. The Tower rises from the West End of the Nave supported on three sides upon lofty Piers and Arches. There are two richly decorated Niches in the South Transept and at the East End of the Chancel, on either side the Window, and a Piscina. There is a South Porch. The whole Character of this Church is the Decorated, and lofty in its proportions. The Church Chest and the lock on the South Door are both of this Character & very interesting specimens.[4]

The Cheyne and Denham Families lie in the Chancel.

In a North Window is this Armorial Bearing. [*Sketch of two coats of arms* also Faldo. Denham].

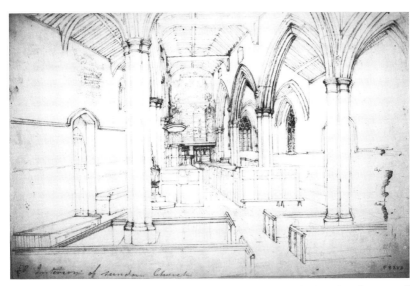

26. Sundon: Interior view showing the font and cover, pulpit and sounding board, rood screen and the commandments etc. painted on a screen in the chancel arch

(Pencil sketch: Thomas Fisher c.1815)

3. Archdeacon Bonney's visitation notebook, 1823–1839

SUNDON. This Church consists of a Nave, North & South Aisles a South Transept & a Chancel at the East End of the Nave & Tower at the West end thereof.

At the Visitation of 1823 The following order was given that a new plated Flagon be purchased, that the Seats within the Communion Rails be removed, and the Communion Table be placed against the Wall; the Bible be repaired, there be a new Door to the Chancel. Casements be placed North and South in the Body of the Church; the south Porch be rebuilt; there be a new North Door; the floor under the Steeple be repaired; the Plumbers' fire be removed; and the Earth taken from the Walls on all sides.[12]

At the Visitation of 1826. The new Communion Table and covering for the same was ordered.

At the Visitation of 1833 the following order was given. that the weather boards of the Bellchamber be repaired – the tracery of the Windows be repaired with Parker's Cement. The Prayer Books & Bible be repaired; the Arch leading into the Chancel be laid open; the Commandments be placed below the East window & the Lord's Prayer and Belief over the North & South Doors.[13]

At the Visitation of 1836. Ordered that the Munions and Tracery of the Windows of the Aisles and Tower be restored with Cement, and also the Buttresses of the Aisles. The lead of the Roof over the Desk repaired; a spout be put up on the East side of the Transept to prevent the water falling upon the wall. The Clerk to be punctual in opening the Casements, for the airing and drying of the Church.

At the Visitation 1839. Found the Work man restoring the windows[14] – ordered the Churchwardens to repair the Buttresses – and the impropriator to repair the Entrance to the Chancel on the South & South Wall thereof.

4. Article on the Church by W.A. (no.18), NM 22 November 1845

SUNDON. This church is in a very good state, and requires but little to render it what churches should be. The wooden ceiling remains; the light from the west is not shut out, but admission through the western door has been for some years apparently prevented. The tricks which have been played with the font are much to be lamented.[2] It is buried in a square pew, but only half is visible there; this portion is well whitewashed, the corresponding half, which is nearly boarded up, has escaped this indignity. There are several open seats remaining, and a smaller proportion than usual of enclosed boxes.[7] The Church had recently suffered an additional coat of whitewash, rendering the opportunity of tracing the outlines of two apparently fine niches impracticable. A stove contributes its share in the disfigurement of the building; an erection very like an oven, intended it is presumed to support the belfry tower, is a very awkward contrivance for that purpose.

The chancel is small, and the space rendered smaller by two square pews,[30] the passage between which is so narrow as to render access to the communion table on the days of celebration unpleasant. The chancel is ceiled, and the walls whitewashed. The roof is tiled, but the lead remains on the nave. The porch is rendered as ugly as repeated coats of whitewash can make it, and brick has been apparently substituted for stone where external repair has been necessary.[12]

10 November 1845   W.A.

Notes **1.** Pevsner pp.151–2, *VCH* II pp.385–7, Ransom's RC article in *BT* 12 June and 10 July 1903, and *St.Mary's Church Sundon 1226–1976* by Margaret Truran n.d. [1976]. I am grateful to John Ledster for kindly showing me round the church and pointing out a number of interesting features I might otherwise have missed; **2.** The C13th font is of Purbeck marble. Fisher's sketch (Micf 66) suggests that the shafts between the bowl and base may have been added or replaced since the early C19th. Boissier (f.390) describes the font as "octagonal, panelled on each face with 2 equilateral arches" and notes "the neck is circular & the base again octagonal". W.A. found the font "buried in a square pew" and only half visible; **3.** The screen is shown *in situ* in Fisher's sketch of the interior; **4.** The chest is illustrated in the *VCH* (facing p.384); **5.** Visitations of 1518 and 30 (quoted by Truran p.5); **6.** The plate (schedule in ABE 5) includes a cup of 1628 bearing the name of John King, Churchwarden, a cup given by Henry Norris in 1906 and a silver paten hallmarked 1904; **7.** The old pews and seats are described in the *VCH* and illustrated in Fisher's interior view of c.1815 and in Thurston's photograph of 1887 (reproduced in S.Bunker *North Chilterns Camera 1863–1954* (Book Castle, 1989) p.67). Some of the pews may have been erected in 1763 from the proceeds of the sale of two bells; **8.** Terriers of 1710 (ABE 2 Vol.II p.33) and 1730 (FAC 35/12). North (p.197) records a tradition that there were once five bells here, but this seems unlikely both on the evidence of the terriers and from the fact that the mediaeval bellframe clearly had pits for only three bells. The remaining bell was cast by one of the Ruffords of Toddington in the late C14th; **9.** Faculty papers regarding the sale of bells, 1763 (ABF 2 p.13 and ABF 3/198–9); **10.** The churchwardens' accounts from 1767 (P 24/5/1) record expenditure on maintaining the clock which was eventually sold in 1814. It seems to have been disused from about 1795; **11.** Churchwardens' accounts 1767–1869 (P 24/5/1). The accounts refer to a pitch pipe for the singers 1783, and books and teaching to sing psalms (£3 15s 7d) 1804; **12.** The accounts for 1823 record payments to Bass (£23 0s 7d), the carpenter (£14 3s 11d), and Travell, the glazier (£17 6s 5¹/₂d). The south porch is not mentioned in the accounts, but if these payments refer to the implementation of Bonney's orders then they probably cover the rebuilding of the porch in its present form; **13.** Fisher's sketch of c.1815 shows that the Royal arms, commandments and creed were painted on a plaster partition above the screen in the chancel arch. This was evidently removed in 1833 when the arch was "laid open", the commandments placed on the east wall, and the creed and Lord's prayer over the north and south doors; **14.** The accounts for 1839 record payments to Bass the bricklayer and Baker the glazier totalling £15; **15.** Union of benefices 1846 (HCRO ref: DSA 1/11/2) and mortgage papers and plans by E.F. Law, architect, Northampton, for the new vicarage 1847–8 (CUL ref: EDR/G3/40 MGA/BED/12); **16.** Bathurst's notebook (ABE 3); **17.** The damage in 1880 was noted in the Toddington parish magazine for October 1880, and the repairs were reported in *LBO* 29 May 1883 and *BM* 2 June 1883; **18.** Minutes of committee and work of 1887 recorded in vestry minutes (P 24/8/1), and payment of £38 10s to Mr.Heady for work carried out noted in accounts (P 24/5/2); **19.** Work in 1897 by Foster and Hill noted in minutes (P 24/8/1) and accounts (P 24/5/2); **20.** New west window after hailstorm (W.Carrington £18 10s 4d) 1901 (P 24/5/2); **21.** Vestry minute regarding the pulpit 1907 (P 24/8/1) and faculty papers (HCRO ref: DSA 2/1/205). The pulpit was made by William Wade of St.Neots; **22.** A letter from the Rev.C.T. Mundy in the SPAB archives gives details of the Mallows and Grocock scheme of 1906–7 and the repair of the tower was reported in *CT* 8 Feb.1907; **23.** Vestry minutes refer to 1913 faculty application (P 24/8/1) and in the letter in the SPAB archives Mundy claimed that his attempts to get further work done had failed because the Bishop suspected him of popish practices; **24.** Papers of 1922–30 in the SPAB archives; **25.** Tower repairs noted in the Report of the Council for the Care of Churches for 1930–1 (p.58); **26.** Truran (p.9) lists the later improvements to the church. The organ came from Christ Church, Bedford. It was made by Trustam in 1884, and its history is recorded in a pencil note on the underside of the organ stool; **27.** A prayer book was bound in 1777 (P 24/5/1); **28.** An iron chest for the registers was bought in 1812 for £4 6s (P 24/5/1); **29.** The churchwardens "Paid Mr. Harrison for a Paul" (£2 17s 6d) in 1813 (P 24/5/1); **30.** A report in *BM* 2 June 1883 mentions "Two large old–fashioned family pews behind the chancel screen, one for the Vicar's family and the other for the Lord of the Manor".

SUTTON

The nave is the oldest part of the present church. It dates from the late C12th or early C13th. A south aisle was added in the C13th. The chancel was rebuilt in the C14th when the north aisle, south porch and former vestry (on the north side of the chancel) were also added. The west tower was added in the C15th.[1] There is a C15th chancel screen.[2] The north aisle has an enclosure containing some fine monuments to the Burgoynes of Sutton Park.[3]

There is Elizabethan plate of 1569.[4] One of the bells (since recast) was dated 1602, and three more were cast in 1655.[5] The pulpit is dated 1628 and carries the initials of Oliver Bowles (Rector 1606–1645).[6] There is a C17th communion rail, and some of the seats in the nave and aisles are of C17th and later date. The west tower was partially rebuilt in 1686, probably after the collapse of the south-west corner.[7] The chancel was ceiled with plaster in 1764.[8] A beam in the tower dated 1806 probably relates to further repairs, and in about 1807 a clock (made by Charles Butcher of Bedford c.1730) was put up in the tower.[9]

In 1808 the living fell into the hands of the notorious Rev. Dr. Edward Drax Free whose incumbency ended with his ejection in 1830 after protracted legal proceedings.[10] Free's misdemeanours included keeping pigeons in the belfry, turning out his pigs in the churchyard, and using the porch as a stable. In the court proceedings against him, it was proved that in 1820 he had unnecessarily removed the lead from the chancel roof and replaced it with Welsh slate, converting the proceeds to his own use.[11] The workmen claimed that the lead was only about fifty years old (i.e. contemporary with the plaster ceiling of 1764)[8] and that it was "good to all appearance". One consequence of Free's neglect is that there is no 1822 terrier for Sutton.

Once steps had been taken to bring Free to justice, the parish began to put the church in order. Archdeacon Bonney played an influential part in the proceedings and encouraged the parishioners in their actions. In 1824–5 repairs to the interior and alterations to the seats were carried out under the direction of Mr. Swepson of Bedford.[12] In 1825 the old vestry was taken down, and new decalogue boards etc. were placed on the east wall of the chancel. Further repairs were undertaken after Free was finally ejected in 1830, and in 1831 the Royal Arms were re–painted,[13] new mural tablets were put up in memory of members of the Burgoyne family[14] and the barrel organ on the west gallery was introduced.[15] In 1836 Montague Burgoyne left funds to provide for the upkeep of the organ.

In 1840–1 the church was partially re-pewed and redecorated by Thomas Stevens at a cost of £225.[16] The work was financed by a loan, repaid in 1847. In 1841 a sounding board from Everton was placed above the pulpit, and in the following year new brass candlesticks were provided for the pulpit.[6] In 1842 the churchwardens proudly stated that "the Church has undergorn a thurrer Repair to the Amount of upwards of three Hundred Pounds".[17]

The churchwardens' accounts record other minor repairs in the later C19th, including redecoration and roof repairs by J.H. Miller in 1860 and alterations to the pews in 1869.[18] Dates scratched on glass quarries refer to window repairs in 1848 and 1867. Two of the bells were recast in 1856.[5] A very fine stained glass east window by Lavers and Barraud was put up in 1864, and further stained glass windows (all unsigned and undated) were erected in the chancel and north aisle in the 1870s.[19]

From 1876 Archdeacon Bathurst made frequent observations on the unsatisfactory state of the church, and in 1894 he found "the frame of the bells is rotting owing to neglect in replacing the broken & decayed wooden windows and trellis shutters. The snow and rain have free course".[20] In 1898 E.Borrisow, the Ely Diocesan Surveyor, reported on the condition of the tower and bells.[21] Nothing was done immediately, but in 1905 the exterior of the

27. Sutton: West view, showing the tower (partially rebuilt in 1686) with the clock dial (dated 1807).   *(Pencil sketch: Thomas Fisher c.1815)*

church was partially restored at a cost of £500.[22] More recently, the barrel organ was restored in 1967.[15] Since 1970 extensive repairs have been carried out to the fabric of the church.[23]

2. Archdeacon Bonney's historical notices of churches, c.1820–1840

SUTTON. This Church consists of a Nave and Aisles, South Transept, South Porch, Chancel and Tower embattled at the West End. All of the Perpendicular Character. The Burgoyne Family have several Monuments to their Memory in the North Aisle,[3] and amongst them the following in Brass on the Floor.[24] [*Sketch of cross*].

3. Archdeacon Bonney's Visitation notebook, 1823–1839

SUTTON. This Church consists of a Nave, North and South Aisles, a Tower at the West End of the Nave and a chancel at the East End thereof. A south porch.

At the Visitation of 1823 the following Order was given that the Vestry be thoroughly repaired; the screen between the Tower and the Body of the Church be new and painted oak colour; the open seats be thoroughly repaired, set even, be cleansed and oiled; the Font be cleansed, & the Top oiled, and a proper Font Bason be purchased; proper drainage be made round the Church, particularly on the North side; the Porch be repaired; the Church Yard Walls be repaired; the Stone work of the Windows be restored with Parker's Cement, before Easter 1825.[12]

At the Visitation of 1826, no further orders were deemed necessary

At the Visitation of 1833 The following order was given, that the surplices be repaired, the walls dry brushed, the stonework of the Windows be repaired according to the ancient Pattern, with Parker's cement; the four windows on the north side of the Clerestory be glazed down to the sill;[25] the Minister's Prayer Book be renewed and the present Prayer Book be used by the Clerk; the doors of the Church & Chancel, and the Screen be cleaned and oak grained; the Mouldings of the Stonework be restored with Parker's Cement;[26] the Pewter Flagon & Plate be disposed of and a new Plated Flagon be purchased.[4]

At the Visitation of 1836 ordered the Stonework of the Windows in the Church & Tower to be restored, the arches & columns cleaned, the north door repaired and oak grained. The Rector promises the Churchwarden he will give a new covering to the Communion Table.

At the Visitation 1839 The following order was given, the interior of the Church to be washed light drab stone colour.[16] The Timbers of the Roof to be cleansed & refreshed with oil & umber; The Bell Chamber Windows to be restored with Parker's Cement; the Old Vestry door to be stopped up on the exterior. The Crack in the South side of the Nave to be filled up. The East Window of the South Aisle now in a wooden frame, either to be reduced in size and restored with stone, or to be built up, it being unnecessary for lighting the Church. The Pulpit to be placed at the South East angle of the Nave.[6]

4. Article on the Church by W.A. (no.83), NM 19 June 1852

SUTTON, All Saints. The chancel is ceiled,[8] and whitewash so profusely used as sadly to mar the ornaments of the sedilia and piscina. The priest's door blocked up, and this preventing circulation of air, increases the ravages damp is making so disagreeably palpable. The altar cushions are in a miserable state; there was neither chair or faldstool to be seen. Two huge pews contribute to the unseemly appearance of this part of the fabric.

The rood screen though it has escaped the plasterer's, has not escaped the painter's daubing.[2]

The nave has its timber roof, as well as the aisles. the walls are whitewashed. Open seats are, however, the rule here, and rejoicing in the additions that have been made in the same manner, we will not quarrel with the task.[16]

The western arch is open, but a complete view is prevented, by an organ[15] and some wooden work to conceal the ringers.

The stove pipe mutilates one of the clerestory windows.

In the north aisle, the space for the seat of the principal family, with the monuments of their ancestors,[3] in all the pride of heraldry and pomp of power, comprise about one sixth of the church. The remainder of the sittings in this aisle are square pews. The monument of the time of James I is a curious specimen of the pastry cook style of the period. The other monuments of a later date rejoice in pagan decorations.

The font has its lead and drain, but Wedgwood's basin is used instead.

There is a piscina in the south aisle which, marvellous to relate, is not quite boarded up – a small gap is made, sufficiently large to obtain a view.[27]

One of the entrance porches is gone. We regretted to see sheep trampling over the humble graves of the departed. The recent charge of the amiable Archdeacon, points out the remedy for such desecration, and we close our remarks with an extract from one* whose labours in promoting a better feeling in all matters relating to church restoration have, we believe, been most useful. "Nor should a spirit of paltry economy lead to the admission of cattle into churchyards for pasturage, or to save the labour of those, who ought, by their own exertions, to preserve them in a proper state of decency. Why should we ever be driven by our own negligence and carelessness to the necessity of *protecting* a grave from injury and insult in consecrated precincts?

"With wicker rods we fenc'd her tomb around,
To ward from men and beast the hallow'd ground."

This living is in the gift of a wealthy college,[28] who possess others in this county – and it is with regret we record, that their churches, are for the most part in a more deplorable condition than those, in other patronage – confirming the observation, that if it were not for "lay patronage, the church would be ruined."

5 June 1852   W.A.

* Markland, on the reverence due to holy places.

5. Sir Stephen Glynne's Church notes, before 1840 (Vol.1, pp.46–47)

SUTTON. This Church has a Western Tower, a nave with side aisles, & a Chancel & exhibits good specimens of both the later styles. The Tower has long belfry windows of 2 lights & a battlement. The whole of the Clerestory & side aisles has a battlement, as has the South porch, but not the Chancel. The aisle windows are mostly Rectilinear of 3 lights, those of the Clerestory square headed of 2 lights, excepting the last towards the East which are of 3 lights. The South Porch has side windows with good Rectilinear tracery & square heads. The doorway is of Tudor form & over it is a niche of plain workmanship. The North door has good tracery on the woodwork. The nave is divided from each side aisle by 4 pointed arches with Curvilinear piers composed each of 4 shafts set in lozenge form with moulded capitals. The North aisle is of considerable width. At the East end of the South aisle is a niche with piscina, having a fine crocketed ogee canopy.[27] There are some gorgeous monuments to the Burgoynes of the age of Elizabeth or James.[3] Between the nave & chancel is pointed arch in which is a wood screen.[2] The Chancel is principally Curvilinear, & its windows of 2 lights. The East window is of 3 lights, & rather an early character. On the South side of the altar are 3 very fine stone stalls with very rich ogee canopies having crockets with finials, & feathering – to the eastward of them is a double piscina beneath a similar canopy. The South doorway of the Chancel is small & Rectilinear & on the South wall is a curious ancient painting. The Font is of cylindrical form upon a base of lozenge form. The Church is principally fitted up with ancient open seats.

Notes **1.** Pevsner p.152, *VCH* II pp.248–50, and "All Saints, Sutton" by James Dyer, in *Bedfordshire Magazine* Vol.12 no.89 (Summer 1969) pp.35–9; **2.** According to the *VCH* the screen is said to have come from another church in the County; **3.** The Burgoyne monuments are listed by Pevsner (p.152) and include one by Grinling Gibbons to Sir Roger Burgoyne (d.1679) and one by Edward Stanton to John Burgoyne (d.1709); **4.** The plate consists of an Elizabethan cup and paten of 1569 and pewter flagon and dishes made by H.Little of London (*VCH* II p.250); **5.** The inscriptions of the two bells recast in 1856 are recorded in J.R.D. Tyssen's notes at the Society of Antiquaries Library. Described as "Two bells from Biggleswade", the bells were inscribed "John Dyer made this bell 1602" and "Christopher Graye made me 1655". The other two bells at Sutton were also cast by Graye in 1655 (North p.197) and the accounts (P 123/5/1) show that the recasting of the bells in 1856 was handled by Morton and McMinnies of Biggleswade; **6.** The full history of the pulpit and sounding board (made in about 1729 for Everton and given to Sutton in 1841) is recounted in "Berridge's Pulpit Sounding Board" by Chris Pickford in *Beds.Mag.* Vol.20 no.157 (Summer 1986) pp.187–192. This article also provides a detailed account of the C19th repairs and alterations to Sutton church; **7.** The date 1686 on the west face of the tower evidently relates to a rebuilding of the south-west corner after a major collapse. Inside, this part is the tower is constructed of brick. A beam in the middle chamber of the tower marked "WW / 1806" clearly relates to later repairs; **8.** The plaster above the chancel arch is dated 1764, and the evidence of workmen at the time of Dr. Free's trial suggests that the lead on the chancel roof was also renewed at this time; **9.** The clock is signed by Charles Butcher of Bedford and it must date from c.1730 (see BHRS Vol.70 p.94). There is no mention of a clock at Sutton in the 1708 terrier (ABE 2 Vol.I p.161) but payments for maintenance occur in the accounts from 1825 (P 123/5/1). It may have been put up in 1807 – the date on the clock dial shown in Fisher's pencil sketch of c.1815; **10.** The extraordinary case of Dr.Free and his misdemeanours as Rector of Sutton (1808–30) has recently been recounted in detail by R.B. Outhwaite in *Scandal in the Church: Dr. Edward Drax Free, 1764–1843* (Hambleden Press) 1997; **11.** Outhwaite (pp.52–3) cites the Court of Arches papers (LPL ref: H.427/55–6) as a source of information on Free's misappropriation of the lead from the chancel roof. Local sources on Free and the fabric of Sutton church include letters of 1825 (ABA 6/23 and 26), papers concerning the case 1823–30 (ABCP 391/1–22), and a copy of the *Letter from Montagu Burgoyne Esq, Churchwarden of Sutton, to his Brother Churchwardens, in the Diocese of Lincoln* (1830) issued by Burgoyne concerning the ejection of Drax Free, April 1830 (P 123/28/2); **12.** The churchwardens' accounts etc. 1824–61 (P 123/5/1) contain information on the work done by Swepson, the removal of the vestry, and the new commandments etc in 1825. The old vestry is shown in Rugeley's crude sketch of the church published in *GM* Vol.87 (1817) p.395 (copy at Z 49/196); **13.** The Royal arms are those of 1714–1801, but the names of the churchwardens and "W IV R / 1831" were added when they were repainted (Pardoe p.6). The accounts record a payment to "Mr. Fisher for painting court (*sic*) of arms" (£2 17s), April 1832 (P 123/5/1); **14.** Burgoyne's dispute with Dr. Free was fuelled by difficulties over the family vault, and the erection of three new memorial tablets in 1831 to members of the family who died between 1788 and 1818 was a final act of triumph. All the tablets were made by M.W. Johnson of New Road, London, who later erected a further tablet in memory of Montague Burgoyne; **15.** The barrel organ was made by T.C. Bates in 1820. It is described and illustrated in Boston and Langwill *Church and Chamber Barrel–Organs* (Edinburgh 1967) pp.49, 73, and 98. In his will (proved in 1836) Burgoyne left and endowment for the upkeep of the organ and this is recorded on a painted board in the church. The barrel organ was restored in 1966–7 (P 123/2/2/8); **16.** The work by Stevens is documented in the accounts for 1840–1 (P 123/5/1); **17.** Churchwardens' presentment, 1842 (ABCV 128); **18.** Churchwardens' accounts 1861–1923 (P 123/5/2); **19.** The stained glass is not well documented. The east window of commemorates Annie Susan Crommelin (d.1864) and it is a striking and important early work of Lavers and Barraud, designed by N.H.J. Westlake. Another window in the chancel commemorates the Rev. Charles Dethick Blythe (d.1876). Windows in the north aisle commemorate Elizabeth Burgoyne (d.1850) and Sir John Montague Burgoyne (d.1858), but both appear to date from the late 1870s and may be by Heaton Butler and Bayne; **20.** Bathurst's notebook (ABE 3); **21.** Report on bells and tower, 1898 (P 123/2/2/1); **22.** The restoration in 1905 is only alluded to in the parish records (P 123/5/2) and in Bathurst's notebook (ABE 3) but according to Kelly's *Directory* 1914 (p.177) the church was "partly restored in 1905 at a cost of about £500"; **23.** Recent work is documented in the church log book 1957–83 (P 123/2/2/21) and papers concerning repairs 1969–78 (P 123/2/2/12–19); **24.** For the Burgoyne brass, see Lack *et.al.* (p.91); **25.** The lower parts of the clerestory windows are still blocked; **26.** Payment in accounts to "Mr. Wade for rep. of Church windows & doors as per contract" (£12 10s), April 1834 (P 123/5/1); **27.** W.A. and Glynne both refer to the piscina in the south aisle. The gap in the boarding, mentioned by W.A., must have been made when the pews were altered by Stevens in 1840–1 (i.e after Glynne's visit); **28.** The living belonged to St.John's College, Oxford, and the relationships between the College and parish at this time are described and discussed in Outhwaite *op.cit.*

SWINESHEAD

Swineshead was in Huntingdonshire until 1896 when the county boundary was adjusted.[1] It was outside the Archdeaconry of Bedford until 1914, and consequently the parish is not covered in the main sources for this volume. There is, however, a glebe terrier of 1822.[2]

The church is largely in the Decorated style and it was built between about 1330 and 1360. It has a pretty frieze below the parapet all round the south side of the church. The original intention seems to have been to build the tower at the west end of the north aisle, but this idea was abandoned and the lower stages of the existing west tower were built with the rest of the church in the C14th. The belfry stage and spire were completed in the C15th.[3] The east end of the north aisle was extended in the C15th to form a vestry from which a passage leads to an opening in the north side of the chancel. The passage opens into the chancel through a doorway cut into a tomb recess or Easter Sepulchre.[4] The screen is Perpendicular,[5] some of the benches are of C15th date, and there are fragments of mediaeval glass.[6]

The valuables and ornaments are listed in the 1552 inventory.[7] These included three bells, one of which was recast by John Dier in about 1590. In 1629 the number of bells was increased to five.[8] The old clock, now displayed in the church, also dates from the early C17th.[9] There is an inventory of church goods dated 1634.[10] A new alms dish and flagon were obtained in 1679–80, and in 1700 the Elizabethan cup of 1569 was remodelled in its present form with the inscription "The Town of Swineshead".[11]

A beam in the roof of the nave has the carved inscription "IH WD 1706" which may relate to repairs. In 1748 the Archdeacon ordered the "plough & rubbish to be remov'd, walls to be clean'd, Roof of Mid Isle to be examined & repair'd, Belfry to be pav'd" and chancel roof to be repaired.[12] In 1771 a new inventory was compiled in compliance with the Archdeacon's instructions.[13]

28. Swineshead: This SE view shows the chancel as restored (c.1852) and the decorative frieze running right round the south side of the church can be seen below the parapets

(Photograph: Anonymous c.1900)

The notebook of James Banks Hollingworth (Archdeacon of Huntingdon 1825–55) gives some information on the state of the church in the mid C19th.[14] In 1838 he found the "Lead of the Church roof about to be repaired". The date 1841 on the eastern beam of the nave roof refers to repairs at this time. In 1847 Hollingworth noted the "Church under repair". By 1852 the work on the church was still unfinished, but the chancel had been "well repaired". In 1853 he noted that the steeple had been pointed and that the seats in the body of the church were about to be repaired.

The main Victorian restoration of the church and chancel is not document-ed, but Hollingworth's notes indicate that the work was undertaken early in the incumbency of the Rev. William Airy (Rector 1845–74). An article enti-tled "Rubble or Rubbish" written by Airy in 1851 refers to the removal of plaster from the chancel walls and the discovery of the passage[4] leading to the vestry and Hollingworth's notes imply that the restoration of the chancel was completed by 1852.[15] The repairs to the rest of the church seem to have been undertaken gradually between 1847 and 1855 when the churchwardens paid £76 to Mr. Farmer, probably for repairs to the nave seating.[16]

In 1872 glass quarries by Powell of Whitefriars were placed in the east window. This window was rearranged in 1880 when a new centre light of the Crucifixion was inserted as a memorial to the Rev. William Airy (d.1874).[17] There is an inventory of 1888–91.[18] The tower and spire were repaired in 1907–10 under S.Inskip Ladds of Huntingdon.[19] The roofs were extensively repaired in 1935.[20] Further repairs were carried out to the church between 1957 and 1974.[21] The bells, stolen from the church at the time of repairs to the spire in 1969, were replaced by a new light ring of five in 1989.[22]

1. Extract from glebe terrier, 3 July 1822

SWINESHEAD.

Church yard. The Church Yard, containing one rood and twenty five perches, adjoining the street on the South and West, Hitchcock's Estate on the North, and Packwood's Estate on the East. The walls and Gates thereof made by the Parish, except on the North and East, which are made by Hitchcock and Packwood

Church. Belonging to the said parish are first the parish church, and ancient building, containing in length thirty nine feet, in breadth thirty six feet. The Chancel twenty five feet in length, and fourteen feet in breadth. The porch seven and half feet long and six feet broad. The steeple eleven feet by eight, within the walls, in height one hundred and twelve feet.

Furniture and ornaments of the Church within and belonging to the church are one Communion table, with a covering for the same of green cloth, also one linen cloth for the same, with one napkin, one pewter flagon, with two pewter plates, one silver cup,[11] one iron chest, two Oaken chests, One pulpit and reading desk, One pulpit cushion, and covering, both of green cloth, One large Bible, One large prayer book, An old book of the Homilies and sermons. The Kings Arms with the ten commandments, the Lord's prayer and the creed. One church clock.[9]

The Bells Five bells with their frames,[8] the first, or least bell, one foot seven and half inches in diameter, with this inscription (1629), the second, one foot eight and half inches in diameter with the same (1629), the third, one foot nine and half inches in diameter, with the same (1629), the fourth with this inscription "Johannes Dier Campanani fecit 1629" and is two feet in diameter, the fifth or largest bell, two feet three and half inches in diameter, with this inscription (1629). One bier, One hearse cloth, one surplice.

The Registers There are two Parchment Register Books (containing Baptisms, Marriages and Burials), the one beginning in 1550 and ending in 1712, the other beginning in 1713 and ending in 1753. Two others (containing baptisms and Burials), the one beginning in 1754 and ending in 1795, the other beginning in 1797 and ending in 1812. One other Register Book of Marriages only, beginning in 1756 and ending in 1812. Three others also beginning in 1813 and continued to the present time

Seats in the Church The seats in the Church, as well as the Church itself, have been repaired for time immemorial at the public expence of the parish, except when the Rental of the Land above specified [the Church Land – details not extracted here – producing income of £2 10s for the repairs of the church] has been sufficient to defray the same. The Chancel is repaired by the Rector.

Parish Clerk. There is also due to the parish Clerk for every poor family sixpence, [for most of the – crossed out] From each farmer one shilling and sixpence, for every wedding by Banns two shillings and sixpence, by Licence five shillings, for the Bell and Grave at funerals, one shilling and sixpence. Also a piece of Land belonging to the Clerk called the Clerk's Land [which makes at present – crossed out] let at present for the yearly sum of one Pound, the fence on the South made by the Clerk, the rest by Howarth & the Parish.

Notes **1.** For information on the boundary changes <u>see</u> *VCH* III p.168 and Youngs p.10; **2.** The records of the Archdeaconry of Huntingdon include terriers of c.1610, 1709, 1727 and 1822 for Swineshead (copies at BCRO ref: FAC 35/1–4); **3.** Pevsner pp.153–4, *VCH* III p.169–70, RC article in *BT* 26 Oct.1900, and article on Swineshead by Geoff Brandwood in *Blue Guide: Churches and Chapels, Southern England* by Stephen C. Humphrey (1990) p.73–4. Boissier (f.342) gives an interesting account of the church as it was in 1827; **4.** The recess may have been an Easter sepulchre or a canopy for a tomb. In his paper "Rubble or Rubbish" (in AASRP Vol.1 (1851) pp.372–81) the Rev. William Airy illustrated the recess before and after the removal of the plaster when the opening into the passage was uncovered. He considered the original structure to have belonged to the tomb of Richard Aytrop whose memorial slab (now displaced) still exists in the church; **5.** Boissier (f.342) mentions that in 1827 the screen still had some of its original gilding; **6.** There are C19th drawings of some of the mediaeval glass (BL ref: Add.Ms. 39918 f.29; 39915 f.126) and in Airy's scrapbook (P 100/28/19) which also includes other illustrations of features in Swineshead church; **7.** Inventory of 1552 in S.C. Lomas *Edwardian Inventories for Huntingdonshire* (Alcuin Club) 1906 pp.16–7; **8.** Details of the bells are given in T.M.N. Owen *Church Bells of Huntingdonshire* (1899) p.136; **9.** The clock is not mentioned in the 1634 inventory but there was a clock in the tower by 1709; **10.** Inventory, 1634 (in P 96/1/1); **11.** Details of existing plate from schedule dated 1916 (ABE 5); **12.** Archdeacon's notebook, 1748 (Hunts.R.O. ref: Archdeaconry 305); **13.** Inventory, 1771 (P 96/2/1/1); **14.** Archdeacon's notebook of James Banks Hollingworth, 1838–55 (Hunts.R.O. ref: Archdeaconry 306) ; **15.** Visitation returns for 1854 describe the chancel windows as in bad repair and the date of restoration may be later than indicated by the other sources (*ex.inf.* Peter Meadows); **16.** Churchwardens' accounts 1845–1928 (P 96/5/1); **17.** Information from the Powell archives, 1872 and 1880 (V&A ref: AAD 1/56 p.32 and 1/58 p.9); **18.** Inventory of church goods 1888–91 (P 96/2/2/1); **19.** Papers concerning tower and spire repairs, 1907–10 (P 96/2/2/2); **20.** Papers concerning roof repairs by Marriott of Rushden under Professor Richardson, 1935–6 (P 96/2/2/4); **21.** Papers concerning repairs, 1957–74 (P 96/2/2/7–13); **22.** The theft of the bells in 1969 was reported in *BT* 4 July 1969 and in the parish magazines (P 65/30/19). The new bells were dedicated on 21 Dec.1989 and there is an account of the bells in *The Ringing World* 26 Jan.1990 pp.89–90.

T

TEMPSFORD

Tempsford was the scene of confrontation between the Anglo-Saxons and the Danes in 921 and 1010, and there is every likelihood that there was a church here in pre-Conquest times. A church is mentioned in 1129. The earliest parts of the present building date from the mid C14th and include the Decorated work in the west tower and aisles.[1] There is a C14th font, part of the C15th screen survives,[2] and there is a good C15th Perpendicular wooden pulpit.[3]

In 1617 it was reported that the vestry was "not covered",[4] and extensive repairs to the church followed in 1621. The work of 1621 amounted to a virtual rebuild of the south aisle and clerestory, part of the north aisle and clerestory, and the west tower. The distinctive coloured stone banding is of this period. The date 1621 occurs on the south clerestory, and there are two separate inscriptions regarding the work on other parts of the building.[5]

Also of the C17th are the bells dated 1614 and 1656.[6] Another bell was recast in 1703 by Richard Chandler of Drayton Parslow who was buried at Tempsford on 5 Oct. 1705. By 1706 there were five bells.[7] The communion plate is dated 1660.[8] The tenor bell was recast by Thomas Mears of London in 1829, and in the same year a new clock was placed in the tower. The clock was made by "Paine, High Street, Bloomsbury, London, Inventor of the Illuminating dial, 1829".[9] Boissier visited Tempsford in 1827 and his notes supplement the information on the church provided by Bonney, W.A. and Glynne.[10] These accounts together provide most of what is known about the church in the mid C19th.

The body of the church was restored and re-seated by Edward Browning of Stamford in 1873–4.[11] The work was paid for by William Stuart of Aldenham Abbey, whose family also owned Tempsford Hall, and the church was reopened on 26 May 1874. A new lectern was provided and the floors were laid with tiles. Four tall pinnacles were added to the tower, but these were removed in 1882.[12] The chancel was restored and re-furnished in 1882 at the joint expense of the Rector and Col. Stuart. It was reopened on 18 November 1882.[13]

After the church had been restored further improvements were made. In 1894 a new reredos, altar and altar rails by Jones and Willis were introduced and a clergy vestry was formed in the west end of the south aisle.[14] An organ by Norman and Beard was installed in 1898.[15] In 1903 the first of several stained glass windows by Percy Bacon was placed in the church.[16] This was the centre light of the east window, and in 1908 the rest of the window was filled with stained glass. Another window was erected as a War Memorial in 1920 with an oak memorial board carved by J.P. White of the Pyghtle Works, Bedford.[17] Further windows by Bacon were placed in the chancel between 1921 and 1928.

29. Tempsford: SW view showing date 1621 on the clerestory and inscription on the SE buttress of the tower, the open belfry windows (in which Bonney ordered shutters to be placed) and the old wooden porch   *(Watercolour: Thomas Fisher c.1815)*

Other C20th work included the restoration of the bells in 1924,[6] the erection of a lych gate in 1931,[18] the introduction of Lucy Turner's sculpture of the Good Virgin in 1951 and the renewal of the roofs with aluminium in 1952.

1. Extract from glebe terrier, 17 August 1825
TEMPSFORD.
Church yard.[19] Item the Church yard adjoining to a Highway on the North, the Turnpike Road on the East, to the House and grounds of Mrs. Caton on the South, and to the House and Barns belonging to the Rector on the West. The Gates and Fence on the North and East made and repaired by the Parish. The House and Fence belonging to Mrs. Caton is the Fence on the South.

Furniture and ornaments. There are four Pews in the Chancel belonging to the Rector. Within the Church are one Communion Table with a covering for the same of purple Cloth. Also one Linen Cloth for the same with one napkin. One Silver Chalice and lid. One Paten.[8] An Iron chest to contain the Registers and an old Chest. There are 5 Bells.[6] One Surplice. A Book of common Prayer and a Bible, & two Books of offices.

Parish Clerk. There is also due to the Parish Clerk for every person keeping a seperate House four pence yearly. For every Wedding by Banns two shillings and six pence, by License five shillings. For every Funeral for tolling the Bell and digging the Grave three shillings and six pence. At each Sacrament one shilling.

2. *Archdeacon Bonney's historical notices of churches, c.1820–1840*

TEMPSFORD, St. Peter. This Church consists of a Nave, Aisles, separated by octagonal Piers with plain Mouldings, and obtuse angled Arches; a Tower at the West End, and a Chancel. The Greater part of the Character of this Edifice is the decorated, the remainder Perpendicular. The Pulpit is handsome Perpendicular.[3] There are north & south Porches.[20] The Rood Screen remains in good preservation.[2] There is a Piscina in the Chancel under a trefoil Arch, a decorated Monumental Arch, a Canopy and a Niche, a plain piscina & cupboard in the South Aisle. At the End of the North Aisle is the Vault of the Chetwaes [?Chetwood] & Paynes, and Monuments to the Memory of Sir Gilies Payne, Bart. 1801 and to Elizabeth wife of John Payne Esqre. eldest Son of Sir Gilies, 1780.

A Window at the West End of the North Aisle [*Sketch*].

The Pulpit at Tempsford [*Sketch*].[3]

3. *Archdeacon Bonney's visitation notebook, 1823–1839*

TEMPSFORD. This Church consists of a Nave, North and South Aisles – a Tower at the west End of the Nave and Chancel at the East End thereof. Porches to the North and South Aisles.[20]

At the Visitation of 1823 It was ordered that a plated Flagon be purchased,[8] the Earth be moved from the Walls; Shutters be placed inside the Bellchamber Windows; the Door be repaired; the Long Seats be repaired, cleansed and oiled; The Pulpit,[3] Desk and Screen be oakgrained;[2] The font be cleansed; and the Cover of the Font oak grained; a proper Font Bason be purchased – the Communion Rails be oak grained; the Table be cleansed and oiled; The Lord's Prayer and Ten Commandments be placed over the Table; the Stonework of the Windows and Doors be restored with cement, before Easter 1826.

At the Visitation of 1826. That part of the above order concerning the Flagon & Font Bason was renewed.

At the Visitation of 1833 It was ordered, that the Bible be rebound – the Prayer Book be repaired – the Walls cleansed by brushing – a proper Font Bason & Flagon be purchased – the Open Seats in the North Aisle be repaired, & the windows cleansed.

At the Visitation of 1836. Ordered that a casement be made in one of the Chancel Windows on the South side – the Clerk's prayer Book be repaired – a proper Font Bason – and the King's Arms be procured – the Rector to repair his Pew – the Communion Cloth be repaired – a plated Paten and deep Plate for the Alms be procured.[8]

At the Visitation 1839. the following Order was given the Foundations of the Church & Chancel to be attended to – the weeds removed therefrom, and the Walls repaired. The Drains on the East to be opened, and free passage given for the water to flow off – The lead work of the windows to be examined and repaired – The flashing of the Leads against the Tower to be repaired – some means (say wire work) adopted to prevent Birds entering the Bellchamber, a proper Font Bason to be procured.

A new "Common Prayer Book" already ordered.

The Glebe House under thorough repair and nearly finished.

4. Article on the Church by W.A. (no.81), NM 5 June 1852

TEMPSFORD, St. Peter. We may mention that the distance from the church, where the clerk, who keeps the key resides, is in many instances very inconvenient. In the present case, we had to walk nearly two miles to obtain admittance.

The chancel is whitewashed, wooden rood and all.[2] A new eastern window, we were told, was in preparation, not before it was absolutely necessary. Seats, but no pews. The timber roof of the nave remains. The sittings are for the most part open, but a few pews present the usual ugly aspect. A stove, with long pipe gracefully making its exit through a hole in the roof. Some blunderer has imagined that we quarrelled with the stove, and not its unfitness, but we believe that the talented manufacturer of the one that drew forth these remarks, has too much good sense to be deceived by such a perversion of our meaning; and we make no doubt that he, as well as many others, would, if employed, soon find a more scientific, as well as elegant way of warming churches.

In what was a chantry chapel,[21] a hideous cubical mass of stone, covering a family vault, occupies, as well as disfigures, this part of the church.

At the east end of the south aisle, a piscina and other appurtenances of a chantry chapel, including a fine Early tomb, are obscured by the wooden work of pews. Fine specimens of hat pegs ruthlessly plugged into the columns, prevail in this part of the fabric.

Belfry arch stopped up by the singing gallery, &c. In the belfry, amid rubbish, is deposited the ancient church chest, the use of which has been superseded by a mercantile one of iron, preserved in the chancel. The font has no lead lining, but a drain; of course not used, since the usual broth basin is inside.

Several of the windows have been blocked up, and broken glass is the ornament of several others.

Two wooden porches remain as yet unmutilated.[20]

27 May 1852   W.A.

5. Sir Stephen Glynne's Church notes, 31 January 1863 (Vol.2, pp.21-22)

TEMPSFORD, St. Peter. This church is of the usual form – the nave having N & S aisles & Clerestory – with Chancel, Western tower, N & S porches. The features are principally Perpendicular. The parapets are moulded. There is a curious diamond shaped window at the W. end of the N. aisle, containing a quatrefoil & apparently Decorated. At the E. of the same aisle is a Decorated window of 2 lights, & a Flamboyant one of 3 lights at the E of the S. aisle – the other windows are Perpendicular – mostly of 3 lights, of plain character without tracery. The nave has 4 pointed arches in the north arcade, & 3 in the Southern – the piers being octagonal. The Tower arch & Chancel arch are similar. The Clerestory has plain 2 light windows & one of 3.

The Chancel is Perpendicular, the E window of 5 lights, the others of 3. There is a trefoiled & arched piscina & a sedile in the SE window all divided by an elbow – also a Priests door & oblong recess to the E of it. The rood screen is good Perpendicular.[2] There is a piscina also in the S aisle. The Font is a plain octagon. The Chancel is externally embattled. The North & South porches are of plain wood frame work.[20] The tower is of 3 stages, embattled & buttressed chiefly Perpendicular but with a Lancet on its S side about the middle; belfry windows of 2 lights. There is no gallery & the seats are mostly open. There are variegated courses of stone in the Chancel.

Notes **1.** Pevsner p.154 and *VCH* II pp.253–4; **2.** The screen seems to have been "in good preservation" in Bonney's time but now only the lower half remains. W.A. implies that it had been whitewashed; **3.** The pulpit (illustrated in *VCH* II facing p.254) was restored in 1874 (*BT* 30 May 1874) and its present stone steps and iron rail were provided (*BT* 11 Nov.1882); **4.** Presentment, 1617 (ABC 5 p.107); **5.** There is an inscription on the west face of the masonry between the tower and clerestory "Thomas Barit / gave to the re / pare of this c / two sed 1621" and a tablet in the base of the tower inscribed "William Saunderson Gent and Thomas Staplo Yeoman Overseers of this new work and patentees of [his] Majesties letters patent granted for the same May 12 1621". Enquiries at the Public Record Office have failed to trace the letters patent regarding this work; **5.** Details of the bells are given by North (p.197) and on a framed notice in the tower erected at the time of the restoration in 1924 when three bells were recast and a sixth added. The parish records include a faculty for the restoration (P 20/2) and accounts of the bell fund (P 20/5); **6.** Terrier, 1706 (ABE 2 Vol.I p.175); **7.** The plate includes a cup and cover of 1660 and a modern plated flagon and alms dish (*VCH* II p.254); **8.** The 1706 terrier explicitly states that there was "no clock". John Paine, the maker of the present clock, received a silver medal from the Society of Arts for his method of illuminating clock dials by gas – hence the inscription on the setting dial; **9.** Boissier (f.433–d) describes the east window as "Perpendicular yet very crooked" and mentions the "wooden S porch"; **10.** Sources for the restoration in 1873–4 include the faculty 1873 (CUL ref: EDR/D3/4 pp.240–2) and reports in *BT* 11 April and 30 May 1874; **11.** The pinnacles added in 1874 (shown in contemporary photograph, Z 48/145) proved to be troublesome, and one fell in 1881 causing damage to the nave roof and pews. The vestry agreed to their removal (P 20/8/1) and this was reported in *BT* 11 Nov.1882; **12.** Chancel restoration reported in *BT* 11 Nov.1882; **13.** The work of 1894 is documented in the vestry minutes and accounts (P 20/8/1), the faculty 1894 (P 20/2) and faculty papers (HCRO ref: DSA 2/1/207); **14.** The organ is documented in the vestry minutes (P 20/8/1), reports in *BS* 24 Dec.1897 and 1 July 1898, and in Kelly's *Directory* 1914 (p.178); **15.** The stained glass is all by Percy Bacon, 1903 to 1938. The sources include *Building News* Vol.84 (1903) p.533, *The Builder* Vol.94 (1908) p.754, vestry minutes 1909 (P 20/8/1), report in *BT* 14 May 1920, papers re War Memorial window 1920 and faculties 1921, 1924 and 1928 (all in P 20/2); **16.** War memorial papers 1920 (P 20/2) and report in *BT* 14 May 1920; **17.** Faculty for lych gate (designed by Professor Richardson), 1931, and bills for construction etc (in P 20/2); **18.** The churchyard was enlarged in 1875 (*BT* 24 April 1875); **19.** Both porches were rebuilt in 1874. Boissier notes that the old south porch was a timber one, as illustrated by Fisher (slide 2281). It is not shown in a photograph of c.1870 (X 67/934/64–5) and so it may have been taken down before the restoration of 1873–4. W.A. and Glynne indicate that the north porch was also a wooden one; **20.** For the chantry, see pamphlet by Henry E. Chapman *Tempsford Chantry: The story of a fifteenth century foundation* (P 20/28/4).

THURLEIGH

This is an early church of undoubted pre-Conquest origin but no part of the original building remains. Archaeological investigation in 1970 revealed the structural history of the church. The tower, said by Pevsner to be Anglo-Danish, has now been shown to have been built in c.1150.[1] It has a fine Norman tympanum with Adam and Eve, the serpent and the tree of knowledge.[2] The Norman church had been enlarged by the addition of north and south aisles by the C13th, and in the C14th the chancel was rebuilt. The nave and aisles were again rebuilt and a clerestory added in the C15th. There is a Perpendicular font.[3] At the back of the church there are timbers from the nave roof bearing texts and traces of coloured decoration.[4]

The plate includes an Elizabethan cup of 1577.[5] In 1578 the churchwardens reported "one wyndowe broken of late" but promised to speedily repair it.[6] One of the bells is mediaeval and two of the others were dated 1593 and 1595.[7] A beam in the nave had the date 1619 in iron numerals nailed to the timber, indicating repairs in that year. Some work on the church is recorded in extracts from an old book of churchwardens' accounts, now lost, from 1624 to 1716.[8] When the lead on the roof was carefully examined in 1970 it was found to have dated graffiti and workmen's names from 1724 to 1880.[9] The treble bell was recast in 1743, and in the church there is a painted board with late C18th or early C19th ringers' rules.[7] The Royal Arms of George III bear the names of E.Peacock and I.Austin as churchwardens and the date 1775.[10]

There are churchwardens' accounts[11] from 1822 but they give little indication that the parish acted swiftly to obey the orders for repairs given by Bonney at his visitations in 1823 and 1826. A stonemason, Mr.Thorpe, was paid £15 in 1828, presumably for doing some of the work required by the Archdeacon. By 1829 the exterior of the church had been colour washed.[12] In 1832 the churchwardens paid the draper for "painting and lining Dr. Moore's pew". W.A.'s description shows that by 1852 there were two or three enclosed pews in the nave.[13]

Bonney's final orders of 1836 and 1839 refer to throwing open the chancel to the nave. This seems to have been done in 1840 when, among other work, the churchwardens provided new doors for the belfry.[11] In 1841 the new Vicar, the Rev. Benjamin Trapp, borrowed money to pay for alterations to the church and extra seating.[14] The work was done by John Wildman. Further improvements are recorded in the accounts, including repainting the walls and roof in 1854, the purchase of a stove in 1856, and new chairs and hassocks in 1873.[11] In about 1860 an organ, by Nicholson of Worcester, was installed at the west end of the church.[15] A cracked bell was recast in 1864.[7]

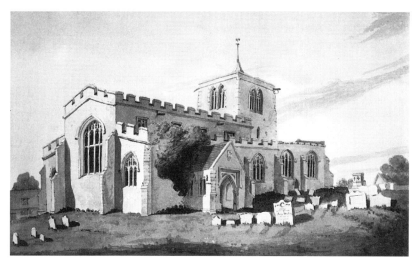

30. Thurleigh: SW view showing the C15th nave, aisles and porch. The clerestory was removed in 1970 and the nave and aisles now have a modern stainless steel roof

(Watercolour: Thomas Fisher c.1815)

In 1874 Archdeacon Bathurst considered the church as "needing restoration".[16] By 1880 plans for restoration had been prepared by Thomas Jobson Jackson.[17] Work began on the body of the church (excluding the tower and chancel) in 1882 when the roof was repaired, the plaster removed from the walls, the floors renewed, the nave and aisles re-seated, and a new pulpit and tower screen were provided at a total cost of £572.[18] The restoration of the chancel followed in 1887, a new oak reredos being given by the patron.[19] A stained glass east window by Hardman was also set up in 1887.[20]

Further improvements were made after the church had been restored. The bells were rehung in 1889.[7] A lych gate was erected in 1894.[21] In 1897 a new clock[22] was put up and a sixth bell was added for the Diamond Jubilee of Queen Victoria and the 60th year of the incumbency of the Rev. Benjamin Trapp to whose memory a stained glass window was placed in the south aisle in 1902.[23]

The further work on the church exterior was necessary in 1908.[16] Between the wars the church began to fall into a poor state of repair, worsened by the explosion of wartime bombs in the vicinity of the nearby airfield. After the arrival of a new vicar in 1948 the parishioners took up the challenge of restoring the church. The chancel was brought back into use for services, and after much fund-raising the church was gradually repaired between 1956 and 1971.[24] The clerestory was removed when the nave and aisles were restored in 1970–1. After restoration the church was rededicated on 5 July 1971. The temporary covering of the roof has since been renewed in stainless steel.

1. Extract from glebe terrier, 1 July 1822

THURLEIGH.

Church. Belonging to the said Parish are first the Parish Church and antient building containing in length 103 feet with chancel & belfry lying between them; the chancel in length is 28 feet, in breadth 17; belfry in length 20 feet, in breadth 15; steeple 220 square feet, 54 high.

Furniture and ornaments. Within & belonging to which are one communion table & green cloth, also one linen cloth & two napkins for the same, one pewter flaggon, one silver chalice weighing about six ounces & two pewter pattens,[5] one table of degrees, one chest with 3 locks in the church,[25] one pulpit & reading desk besides clerk's desk, one cushion in pulpit covered with red cloth, one large bible of the last translation, two large common prayer books, the King's arms & the ten commandments,[10] an iron chest containing registers, five bells with their frames,[7] one dated 1525 2 feet 7 inches in diameter, another 1593 two feet 10 inches, a third 1743 2 feet 4 inches with this inscription "Russell of Wootton maker", & 2 with no dates, one 2 feet 4 inches, the other 3 feet.

Seats in the Church. The seats have always been repaired at the public expense of the Parish.

Church Estate. There is also belonging to the Parish Church, the rents whereof are received & expended by the Church wardens about the repairs of the church, a blacksmith's shop with a dwelling house & part of 6 or 7 acres of land opposite, the whole at the yearly rent of £11 occupied by J. Payne; also two Cottages at Scald End let at 35/- each per annum.

Parish Clerk. There is due to the Parish Clerk £2 per annum for clerkship besides voluntary offerings at Easter, for every wedding by banns 2s., by licence 2/6, for every funeral with making a grave 1/6.

School. There is also a free school founded by George Franklin Esq[r]. in the year 1618 of forty shillings a year for a school master with a part of the land occupied by J. Payne at £3 per annum left out of the £11 for six poor boys to be taught gratis; there is also a dwelling house in the churchyard & the forty shillings are given out of the close called Scots close situated in the Parish of Goldington near Bedford; if no school be given to charitable uses & in default of payment a power is given to seize on the said close. [John Hervey's gift to the poor 1713 – details given].

2. Archdeacon Bonney's historical notices of churches, c.1820–1840

THURLEIGH, St. Peter. This Church consists of Nave and Aisles separated by octagonal Piers with plain Mouldings, a Tower between the Nave and Chancel, but no Transepts. The lower part of the Tower is Norman and has a South Entrance with a semicircular Top filled up with a panel of stone on which is rudely sculptured Adam and Eve standing on each side the Tree forbidden with the Serpent twisted round the Trunk.[2] The Tower has a raised

31. Thurleigh: An interior view from the chancel through the crossing tower into the nave showing the enclosed pews, seating and organ as they were before the church was restored in 1882
(Lithograph: Anonymous c.1878)

leaden roof covering the walls without a parapet. The upper part of the Tower and general Character of the Windows of the Fabrick is Perpendicular.

In the Nave in Brass is ingraved the Effigy of a Man in Armour with his resting on a Dog [*sic*].[26] This armorial Bearing is at the Upper part of the Stone. [*Sketch of coat of arms*, Bermingham].

In Brass against the Wall in the South Aisle. [Sketch of coat of arms]. Here lyeth Edmond Day 1590.

The Font is octagonal with Perpendicular Tracery on the Panels & shields on the Pier.[3] The Chalice is Elizabethan, the Patin, Plate & Flagon are plated.[5]

There is a south Porch, perpendicular. There is an Early English Piscina and Niche in the Chancel & the East window is decorated.

In the Chancel is an Altar Tomb in the middle of the Floor, to the Memory of John Harvey who died 1728.

There are five Bells.[7]

3. Archdeacon Bonney's visitation notebook, 1823–1839

THURLEIGH. This Church consists of a Nave and South Aisles, a Tower between the Nave and Chancel, which extends Eastward of it, a Porch to the South Aisle.

At the Visitation of 1823 It was ordered that the Earth be moved from the Walls of the Church; the Stonework of the Windows and doors be restored with Cement; The Munions of the Bellchamber Windows restored with stone, and weather boards placed in them; the Partitions under the Tower be moved, and the Chancel laid open to the Church; these Partitions be lowered to the height of the Pews, and an open worked gate placed in the middle of each; the Floor be made level; the small windows of the Belfry be glazed; A Casement be placed in a South, North & Chancel Windows, a new Linen Cloth & napkin for the Communion be purchased; the open Seats be neatly repaired & oiled; the other Pews be repaired and cleansed; the floor of the Chancel be repaired; the exterior of the Walls be repaired & pointed.

At the Visitation of 1826 the above order had been only partially fulfilled – It was then ordered that the Seats & Pulpit be newly arranged. The Tower pointed – & a new font Bason be purchased.

At the Visitation of 1833 It was ordered that the Walls of the Chancel be cleansed – the windows thereof be mended and a Casement placed in two of the South windows of the Same – the Communion Rails be repaired and oak grained. The Walls of the Church internally be cleansed from green Moss – the pewter Flagons & Plates be disposed of for a new plated Flagon and Plate[5] – the Pulpit and Desk be moved to a more eligible situation, then pointed out – a proper Font Bason be purchased.

The Glebe House in repair.

At the Visitation of 1836 Ordered that a proper Font Bason be procured. Authorised the throwing open of the Chancel to the Nave – the belfry being drawn with good plaster & a proper open Partition set across the Entrance to the Chancel.

At the Visitation 1839 Ordered the Churchwarden to Cleanse the Walls of the Church. Authorizing the removal of the Pews in the Nave to the North Aisle and arranging the Open Seats as they were originally. Also sanctioned the lowering of the Partitions between the Tower, Nave, & Chancel, to the height of the Pews – a gate bring placed in each, to communicate with either Nave or Chancel. The Belfry to be drawn with plaster – The Belfry door oak grained. The Walls of the Chancel to be cleaned.

4. *Article on the Church by W.A. (no.97), NM 25 September 1852*

THURLEIGH, St. Peter. The chancel has a timber roof, but the sides of the building in this quarter too plainly indicate the ravages of damp.

The priests' door is blocked up. The altar and its covering are miserable affairs.

The nave and aisles have the wooden roof preserved. The seats are for the most part open, but two or three enclosed ones are here obtruded,[13] to the detriment of the poorer members of the congregation. These bits of selection should, if they are permitted at all, be confined to the aisles. In a parish, of which we have some knowledge, an invasion has been made on the free seats, by the appropriation of two open ones, to which doors have been attached; one is fitted up with cushions, &c., and appropriated to the use of the churchwarden. This plea cannot avail in this instance, for it is so situated that he cannot exercise any supervision over the congregation, his back being turned on the whole. We mention this instance as showing how these miserable boxes are eventually established. A generation will hardly pass away, ere the future occupant will claim the seat as a right, and finding his somnolency too patent to the rest of the congregation, he will surround himself with high boards, an example which will soon be followed by his neighbour behind him; "thus bad begins, but worse remains behind." And these invasions are quietly permitted by Archdeacons, Rural Deans and Incumbents, and no one raises his voice to protect those whose accommodation should be specially cared for.

To return to this Church. The rood screen is gone, but some of its remains have been made use of as a door to the clerk's seat.

The font has its lead and drain,[3] but its use is supplied by a common hand basin. The corner of the north aisle is a receptacle for rubbish. The paving in deplorable condition.

The stump of the cross remains in the churchyard, which is full of weeds.

The porch windows are blocked up, and the porch itself greatly out of order.

When we see God's Holy Temple so sadly neglected we are not surprised to find the Poor Law Commissioners thus describing the dwellings of the poorer part of the congregation, "In many instances cottages have only one sleeping apartment, in which the whole family herd together!"

n.d.   W.A.

Notes **1.** The church is described in Pevsner p.154, Harvey pp.526-33, *VCH* III pp.107–8, and *A brief history of St.Peter's Church Thurleigh* (1992). The Anglo-Danish dating of the tower was challenged in "Anglo-Saxon work at Carlton and other Bedfordshire churches" by Michael Hare in *BAJ* Vol.6 (1971) p.38 and the account of "Thurleigh church excavations" by David Hall and John Hutchings in *BAJ* Vol.14 (1980) pp.59–75 offers a full re-interpretation of the history of the fabric; **2.** The Norman tympanum of Adam and Eve was illustrated in 1813 by Thomas Fisher (*Collections* p.95) and sketched in 1843 by Henry Dryden (MIC 117 – from the Hartshorne collection at Northampton Library). For a recent account <u>see</u> "The tympana of Covington and Thurleigh" by Richard Marks in *Beds. Archaeological Journal* Vol.8 (1973) pp.134–5; **3.** The font is illustrated by Fisher (slide 1650) and, with its cover, by Harvey (p.527); **4.** The timbers (described and illustrated in Hall and Hutchings pp.70–71) came from the easternmost truss of the nave roof, by the tower; **5.** The plate now consists of a chalice dated 1577, three silver-plated patens of c.1880, and two pewter flagons dated 1634 (guide p.9); **6.** Archidiaconal Visitations for 1578 (ABC 3 p.5) in BHRS Vol.69 (1990) p.176; **7.** The 1822 terrier (in which the date of the 1595 bell is wrongly given as 1525) lists the bells in date order and not by size. Further details are given in Harvey (p.527) and by North (pp.198–9) who gives the text of the ringers' rules. The bells were rehung in an iron frame in 1889 (*BM* and *BS* 30 March 1889 p.8) and in 1897 a sixth bell was added (*Bell News* 17 July 1897 p.136); **8.** Extracts from churchwardens' accounts 1624–1716 (BL ref: Add.Ms. 34383 ff.32–35d); **9.** Details of the repair dates and graffiti are given in Hall and Hutchings (p.70) and two of the inscriptions on the lead are illustrated (p.72);

10. The third figure of the date is barely legible but close examination from a ladder confirms Pardoe's (p.6) suggestion that the Royal Arms date from 1775; **11.** Churchwardens' accounts 1822–1900 (P 97/5/1); **12.** Thurleigh is mentioned in a letter in the *Hertford etc. Mercury* 17 Jan.1829 as one of the churches where an ochre colour wash had recently been applied; **13.** Some of the enclosed pews mentioned by W.A. can be seen in Harvey's interior view of the church of c.1870; **14.** There are accounts for the work of 1841 (P 97/5/1) and the ICBS papers contain a single letter on the subject from Trapp dated 1841 (LPL ref: ICBS 2872); **15.** The Duke of Bedford contributed towards the Thurleigh organ fund in 1858 (R 5/869/2 p.54) and there is an undated subscription list (in P 97/1/7). The organ can be seen in Harvey's view of c.1870. It was moved to the east end of the church in 1882 (*BM* 22 April 1882); **16.** Mentioned in Bathurst's notebook (ABE 3) and reported in the Deanery Magazine for 1908 (P 80/30/1); **17.** Fund-raising bazaar reported in *BT* 25 Sept.1880; **18.** Sources for the work of 1882 include appeal leaflet, subscription list and accounts (in P 97/1/8) and reports in *BM* 15 April 1882 and *BM* and *BT* 22 April 1882; **19.** Chancel restoration and reredos reported in *BM* 30 April and 7 May 1887, and *BT* and *BS* 7 May 1887. There is a handbill for the re-opening service (P 97/2/2/2); **20.** The Hardman east window was installed in February 1887 (*BS* 19 Feb.1887), before the main work on the chancel was completed, and it is documented in the Hardman archives (Birmingham Reference Library ref: Ms.175/36/15). The window was badly damaged in the war and when the church was restored it was replaced with clear glass; **21.** Dedication of the lych gate reported in *BM* 9 June 1894. The supra-structure was removed in about 1950 and only the stone piers now remain; **22.** The proposed clock is mentioned in *BS* 28 May and 25 June 1897 and a plate on the movement records that it was installed in June 1897; **23.** The Trapp memorial window is by S.Evans of West Smethwick (*BM* 27 Feb.1903); **24.** There is a good account of the post-war restoration in the guide. The work is also documented in the PCC minutes and correspondence (P 97/32/2 and P 97/34/1–4), papers (P 97/2/2/4–16), correspondence in the SPAB archives, and article in *B.Mag* Vol.6 no.46 (Autumn 1958) pp.204–5; **25.** There is an drawing of the chest (slide 580) made in 1840; **26.** For the brasses, <u>see</u> Lack *et.al.* (p.92).

TILBROOK

Tilbrook, now in Cambridgeshire, was in Bedfordshire until 1896 when it was transferred to Huntingdonshire.[1] Historically it belongs with the other parishes in this series and it is covered by all the main sources.

The earliest parts of the present church date from the C12th. The western bays of the north arcade were built in about 1190 and the eastern piers are of the C13th. The church was rebuilt and enlarged in the Decorated style in the C14th when the west tower and south porch were added. Some of the window tracery was renewed in the C15th.[2] There is an unusual squint and angle piscina in the chancel.[3] The Perpendicular rood screen is especially fine.[4] There are some fragments of mediaeval glass.[5]

A will of 1527 mentions a bequest for mending a broken bell.[6] All the present bells are of later date, the tenor of 1628, the treble of 1682 and the second recast in 1763.[7] The tower and spire may have been partially rebuilt or extensively repaired in the early C17th.[8] In 1674 it was reported that the porch was out of repair.[9] The communion plate includes a paten dated 1702.[10]

The churchwardens' accounts survive from 1724.[11] They record the erection of a new wooden screen between the belfry and the nave and other work in 1724. In 1727-8 the roof was repaired. A new bellframe was put up in 1747.[7] A new pulpit was provided in 1752 by a Mr. Wyman, probably John Wyman who also made a pulpit for Melchbourne in the same year.[12] A singers' pew is mentioned in 1754,[13] and in 1756 Wyman was paid for work

32. Tilbrook: General view from the SW, showing the original appearance of the south wall. When the church was restored in 1866–7 the three–light windows were heightened and given Decorated tracery.

(Engraving: Thomas Fisher 1813)

on the pews in the church. In 1763 the Archdeacon advised the parish to repair the roof over the "burying place" of the St.John family in the church.[14] Extensive work was carried out in 1779 when the north aisle was paved and pewed, the steeple was pointed and James Quick supplied a new font.[15] There is also a payment for "Puling ye elder off the Battlements". The church was whitewashed in 1805.

In 1818 the churchwardens spent £55 on repairs to the tower "which was in a dangerous state" and to the lower part of the steeple. The work was financed by a loan from William Hollis.[16] Expenditure on Bonney's visitation orders is recorded in the accounts, including the purchase of a new bible in 1823,[17] new plate in 1826,[10] and a crimson cloth for the pulpit in 1834. In 1843 repairs to the church exterior were undertaken at a cost of £60.[18] A new font (replacing that of 1779) was provided in 1848.[15] In 1858 the spire was repaired by Mr. Eaton for £30.[19]

The main Victorian restoration came in 1866–7.[20] The architect was William White. The south side of the church was largely rebuilt. The nave has bands of pebbles to give colour contrast and the two large Decorated windows represent Victorian enlargements of simple three-light windows depicted by Fisher. The roofs of the nave and chancel were renewed, the church was re-pewed, and new fittings of 1867 include the pulpit of Caen stone, the lectern, the altar rails and encaustic tiles in the sanctuary, and the stained glass windows. The rood screen was restored by the Bedfordshire Archaeological Society.[4]

The spire was damaged by lightning in 1887,[21] and in 1892 Archdeacon Bathurst noted that the porch had been restored.[22] Tilbrook remained in the Archdeaconry of Bedford until 1914 and Bathurst recorded that the aged Rector died three days after his last visitation in 1905. The Rev. N.B. Young, aged 96 when he died, was Rector when the church was restored in 1866–7.

1. Extract from glebe terrier, 4 July 1822
TILBROOK.

Church yard. Item the Church-yard containing three quarters of an acre adjoining to the ground of Mr. Bigrove on the North, the West and the South, and on the East to the Rectory pasture Church Close, the hedges and gates thereof round about made by the Parish except a few yards of dead hedge on the eastern side coming close up to the church-yard Gate that leads to the Rectory garden.

Church. Belonging to the said Parish are first the Parish Church, an antient building containing in length (within the Walls) viz. the Body of the Church (without the Chancel) sixteen Yards, in breadth nearly ten yards. The Chancel nine yards & a half in length, & five yards & a foot in breadth. The Belfrey four yards by two & three quarters. The Steeple is about 56 yards high with the Tower. Item one Vestry about three yards square.

Furniture and ornaments. Within & belonging to which are one Communion table with a covering of green Cloth, one table Cloth & napkin, one Silver cup, one pewter Tankard & one pewter bason.[10] One Chest with three locks in the Vestry. One Pulpit & reading-desk.[12] One pulpit cushion of cloth. One large Bible of last Translation.[17] One large Common Prayer Book. The King's arms on Wood, & also on Glass.[23] The ten Commandments (painted on Wall). Three Bells,[7] the first or least being twenty eight inches in Diameter, the second twenty nine inches & a half, the third thirty three Inches. One Bier. One hearse Cloth. One Surplice.

Parish Registers. Two Parchment Register Books, one beginning in 1573 & ending in 1719. The other beginning in 1720 & ending in 1812. Item one Marriage Register Book beginning in 1754 & ending in 1811 (N.B. There were no marriages in 1812). Item three Registers of Paper, bound in Parchment all begin in 1813. Item one iron chest to contain the Registers.

Church Estate. An Estate with small Cottage & barn for Repairs of Church (by which estate the Pews have been repair'd) has land lying in one allotment rented in 1822 at 26 pounds per annum by William Hollis,[16] Church-warden, at the Northern extremity of the Parish of Tilbrook adjoining to Little Catworth on North, to Stow on East, to Lord St.John's land on South, & to Green lane leading to Spaldwick on the West, containing thirty one acres one rood & twenty seven Perches. Also one Cottage & small Pasture touching the Northern Church Yard Gate, & bounded by Mr. Bigrove's lands on West, by Lands of Lord St.John on East, by road & brook on North, & by Rectory land on South, rented by Rector, at three Pounds eight shillings & a penny (including three shillings and two Pence paid to the Church estate out of the arable field lying within the Parish of Kimbolton as was afore mention'd under the same land.

Seats in the Church. The Pews are repaired by the Church estate.

Parish Clerk. To the Parish Clerk for Weddings one shilling, for digging grave two shillings.

2. Archdeacon Bonney's historical notices of churches, c.1820–1840

TILBROOK, All Saints. This Church consists of a Nave and North Aisle separated by cylindrical Piers and having pointed Arches, on the Mouldings of one of the piers are rude heads, on another small semicircles. At the West end is an Embattled Tower with a Spire rising from it. A Chancel or north Chapel in which are two Effigies well executed in brass,[24] remarkable for having the Female on the Dexter & the Male on the sinister side. A Dog is at the feet of the Male & another Dog lying at the feet of the female. She is veiled in a loose Robe with large Sleeves. He is in a Gown with a Girdle, to which is appended a Sword hanging Strait down the Middle from the Waist, his Beard peaked. This is in the North Chapel which belongs to the Manor. There is a Piscina in it, with a Niche & Slit behind it, affording formerly a view of the high Altar.[3] Near the Chancel Door is holy Water Font. The Rood loft remains,[4] a beautiful Specimen of perpendicular, retaining its ancient Colouring, blue, Vermilion & Gold. The Roof of the Nave & Aisle is supported at the pendants by angels. Moulding of one of the Piers [*Sketch*]. There is a South Porch

[sketch here of the moulding of one of the Piers]

3. Archdeacon Bonney's visitation notebook, 1823–1839

TILLBROOK. This Church consists of a Nave and North Aisle a Tower surmounted by a spire at the West End of the Nave, a Chancel at the East End of the Nave & Chapel on the North Side thereof, a Porch on the south Side.

At the Visitation of 1823 – It was ordered that the Ten Commandments be set up; the Stonework of the Windows be restored with Parker's Cement; the Coping on the North Side be repaired;[25] Casements be made in the South Windows of the Church; & Chancel; also in the North Aisle & Chapel; a new plated Flagon & Paten be purchased;[10] the Screen & loft over it be carefully preserved;[4] & not coloured – a new Bible be purchased.[17]

At the Visitation of 1826 – The following Order was given – that a new Stone Font & Bason be purchased;[15] The Communion Table be repaired; The Doors on the South side be renewed before Easter 1827. The North Door the same before Easter 1828 and the West Door the same before Easter 1829.[26]

At the Visitation of 1833 It was Ordered that the walls be cleansed by dry brushing – and a proper Font Bason be purchased.

At the Visitation of 1836 ordered a New Napkin for ye Communion.

At the Visitation 1836 no order required.

4. Article on the Church by W.A. (no. 105), NM 20 November 1852

TILBROOK, All Saints. The chancel has an open roof; the window is adorned with the Royal arms.[23] The piscina had been purified from the coating that once disfigured it; but the same care has not been bestowed on the rest of the stone work, where it is laid on thickly. A large square pew exhibits here its deformity, notwithstanding the remains of an early open one adjoining it, which, at less cost than that of the ugly box, might have been rendered available for those who occupy the pew.

The screen and part of the rood loft remain,[4] with the original painting; but from the mode in which it is hacked about with nails and matting, there is reason to fear these interesting remains will soon disappear.

The sittings are all enclosed, and preposterous in size. An open timber roof. The columns are of an early period, very interesting, and appear to have been scraped recently from the whitewash which prevails elsewhere. But notwithstanding this degree of respect paid to them, no remorse has been felt in driving nails and wooden pegs to support the perishable rubbish placed to free the garments of the occupants from the dust of neglect; a singing loft has been allowed to destroy the ornaments of one of them.[13]

The font, apparently a new one,[15] with lead and drain.

Remains of the wood-work of a chapel in the north aisle, which has been covered with hat pegs, and as the implements of correction were apparent, it is most probably made use of for a Sunday School. It also furnishes a store closet for sundry rubbish. In its original state it must have been a very inter-esting example; a mutilated brass,[24] most probably of the founder, contributes to the melancholy display of dirt and neglect. So it is; "square stones tell truth scarce forty years. Generations pass away; some trees stand, and old families last not three oaks." A large box also disgraces this chapel – receptacle for coals, straw, and other rubbish.

This church is very interesting to the architectural student; but he must make haste ere it is entirely gone, to be succeeded, perhaps, by one of Mr. Compo's cheap buildings.

The porch is very dilapidated; the windows blocked up with wood-work from some part of the interior.

The church-yard was open, and bore marks of more than usual attention to the decent condition it should always command.

n.d.   W.A.

Notes **1.** For the boundary change, see *VCH* III p.171 and Youngs (p.11); **2.** Pevsner (Beds and Hunts) pp.355–6, *VCH* III pp.173-5, RCHM *Huntingdonshire* (1926) pp.272–5, and references in Carola Hicks (ed.) *Cambridgeshire Churches* (1997); **3.** There are sketches and plans of squint and piscina between the north chapel and chancel, made by F.Woodward in 1897 (MIC 117 – from Dryden collection, Northampton Library); **4.** There are measured drawings of the screen by J.K. Colling, published in 1849 (Z 49/173–4). When the church was restored in 1866–7, the restoration of the screen was undertaken by the Beds. Archaeological Society (*BT* 16 July 1867) and this is mentioned in the AASRP (pp.444 and 497) and in the Rev. W.D. Sweeting's notes of 1877 (BL ref: Add.Ms. 37178 f.23). A letter from Hindley Wilkinson dated 1907 in the SPAB archives refers to the discovery of part of a C14th roodscreen at Tilbrook. Andrew Woodger in Hicks *op.cit.* (p.348) has suggested reasons for the survival of the mediaeval rood screen here; **5.** There are C19th drawings of the mediaeval glass quarries (BL ref: Add.Ms. 39919 ff.31 and 150); **6.** Will, 1527 (BHRS Vol.76 no.71); **7.** The bells are listed by North (p.199). The churchwardens' accounts record the renewal of the bellframe by Mr. Webster in 1747 and the recasting of a bell by Joseph Eayre in 1763 (Hunts. R.O. ref: 2766/5/1); **8.** This is suggested in Woodger's paper on "Huntingdonshire Church Towers" in *Arch. Journal* Vol.141 (1984) p.307 but there seems no reason to accept this view which seems to be based on the fragile evidence that a bell is dated 1625; **9.** Archdeacon's visitations, 1674 (ÇRT 170/9/1 p.7); **10.** The plate is listed in *VCH* III p.175. The accounts record a payment of £9 in 1826 to "Mr.Lyon for the Church Plate" (HRO ref: 2766/5/1); **11.** Churchwardens' accounts 1724–1847 and 1847–1921 (HRO ref: 2766/5/1–2); **12.** There are payments in the accounts to Mr. Wyman (totalling £10) for the new pulpit in 1752–3 (HRO ref: 2766/5/1); **13.** The singers' pew mentioned in the accounts for 1754 was noted in 1852 by W.A.; **14.** The Archdeacon's note of 1763 is pasted inside the cover of the account book (HRO ref: 2766/5/1); **15.** The accounts records payments to "James Quick a bill for Font" (£1 10s 6d) in 1779 and for "New stone font" (£8 4s 0d) on 12 April 1848 (HRO ref: 2766/5/1-2); **16.** William Hollis, who was tenant of the church estate at the time of the 1822 terrier, loaned money for the repairs of the spire in 1818; **17.** "Bought for the Church a new Holy Bible Folio" (£6) 23 Aug. 1823 (HRO ref: 2766/5/1); **18.** The repairs in 1843 were undertaken by Mr.Wimpress, plumber (£49 13s 9d) and Mr.Ellis, bricklayer (£10 11s 7½d) with money (£60) loaned by John Beedham of Kimbolton (HRO ref: 2766/5/1); **19.** The accounts for 1858 record a payment (£29 10s) to "Mr.Eaton for work on the steeple" (HRO ref: 2766/5/2). Andrew Woodger in Hicks *op.cit.* (p.352) suggests that Eaton of Tichmarsh also rehung the bells in 1865; **20.** The sources for the restoration in 1866–7 include the accounts (HRO ref: 2766/5/2), notes in AASRP (pp.417, 444 and 497), and reports in *BT* 16 July 1867, *The Builder* Vol.25 (27 July 1867) p.555; **21.** Memorandum in parish register regarding damage to the spire, 1887 (HRO ref: 2766/1/3); **22.** Bathurst's notebook (ABE 3); **23.** The royal arms in glass, noted in the 1822 and by Bonney, may still be seen in the chancel; **24.** For the brasses, see Lack *et.al.* (p.92); **25.** The accounts (HRO ref: 2766/5/1) record payments in 1826 to Mr.Ellis (£9 3s 10d), Mrs. Wimpress a Bill for the Church (£5 5s), and to John Fisher for work at the church (£6 19s 1d); **26.** There are payments in 1833 to Ashleigh (£18 7s 6d) and Ellis (£3 7s 5d) for work at the church (HRO ref: 2766/5/1).

TILSWORTH

This church is situated on high ground overlooking the mediaeval manor house and gateway and with good views to the south towards the Chiltern scarp. The present church probably stands on the site of an earlier building. The south arcade dates from about 1300 and the north wall was rebuilt in the C14th. The general appearance of the church is of the C15th when the south aisle and other parts of the church were rebuilt in the Perpendicular style. The tower, built within the western bay of the nave, also dates from the C15th. The mediaeval church also had a south chapel (rebuilt as a vestry and organ chamber in 1908) which seems to have been taken down in the early C16th.[1] The south porch is believed to date from around 1500.[2] There is an Early English font.[3] There are some fragments of mediaeval glass. On the north wall there are carved figures and architectural fragments discovered during restoration work in 1905.[4]

The bells, plate, and vestments are listed in the 1552 inventory which states that "the churche body and the chauncell ys tyled ande the Ilye thereof and the stepulle ys leddid".[5] In 1617 the leads were reported to be out of repair.[6] There are some C17th furnishings in the church including the font cover and Jacobean pulpit.[7] In 1674 it was reported that "here the Canonical purgation is wanting".[8] In 1776 the three old bells were taken down and replaced by a new ring of five.[9] The new bells were cast by William Emerton of Wootton. Several enclosed pews were erected in the church during the C18th.[10]

Bonney's orders indicate that by 1823 the church was in a poor state of repair. A new communion cup was provided in 1823,[11] but by 1826 nothing had been done to the church. The Archdeacon renewed his orders with the instruction that the work should be completed before Easter 1828. Some work may have been done at this time. By 1838 the south aisle had been re-roofed and the embattled parapet, shown in earlier illustrations, had been removed.[12] In 1839 Bonney noted "the whole undergoing repair". The brick vestry on the north side of the church was also erected at some time in the mid C19th.[13] W.A. did not visit Tilsworth, but the appearance of the church interior with pulpit and sounding board and enclosed pews in the nave is shown in photographs taken in about 1880.[14] The photographs also show patterned glass in the east window, and one of the windows on the north side of the chancel has stained glass of c.1865 by Done & Davies of Shrewsbury. Glynne mentions an organ in the chancel by 1870.[15]

In 1873 Archdeacon Bathurst noted that the church needed restoration, and when he visited in 1879 he found work in progress.[16] Various improvements were carried out between 1879 and 1883 through the efforts of the

33. Tilsworth: SE view of the church drawn shortly after the embattled parapet had been removed from the south aisle when the roof was renewed. When the church was restored in 1908–9 a new organ chamber and vestry was built between the south aisle and chancel where there had been a mediaeval chapel. *(Watercolour: George Arnald 1838)*

Rev.Thomas Green (Vicar 1879–1923) and F.A. Blaydes.[17] This included repairs to the bells,[9] the removal of the organ to the back of the church,[15] clearing out the old pews and the provision of chairs in the nave.[18] Serious problems with the fabric remained, however, and in 1888 and 1894 Bathurst noted defects in the chancel and in the roof of the nave.[19]

The architect W.D. Caröe was called in to report on the condition of the building in 1902.[20] He commented "this church has escaped restoration, but is in an extremely dilapidated state" and urged sensitive treatment. Green and Blaydes (who took the name Page-Turner in 1903) gradually collected money for a full restoration of the church which was undertaken between 1905 and 1909 at a total cost of £2663.[21] The nave and aisle were restored first and reopened on 3 December 1906. The restoration of the tower and chancel and rebuilding of the south chapel as an organ chamber and vestry was completed in 1909.

The most significant improvement since the Edwardian restoration has been the recasting and rehanging of the bells, done by John Taylor & Co. of Loughborough in 1929.[9]

34. Tilsworth: Interior photographs looking east (left) with patterned glass in the east window and the enclosed pews, pulpit and sounding board in the nave and looking west (right) showing the organ in the tower arch   *(Photographs: F.S. Mills c.1880)*

1. Extract from glebe terrier, 17 June 1822

TILSWORTH.

Church yard. Item the Church Yard containing four roods adjoining the said publick road leading to Stanbridge on the South, adjoining the grounds of the said Sir Gregory Page Turner on the East, West and North. The fence, style and gate thereof made by the Parish but now kept in repair by the tenant.

Church. Belonging to the said Parish are first the Parish Church an ancient building containing in length (with the Chancel) eighty feet, in breadth thirty feet. The Chancel in breadth sixteen feet within the walls. The steeple fourteen feet and a half square within the walls, in height fifty eight feet.

Furniture and ornaments. Within and belonging to which are one Communion table. Also one linen cloth for the same with two napkins. One pewter flaggon. One pewter plate. One silver chalice weighing about twelve ounces.[11] One paten. One chest with one lock in the Chancel of little use. One pulpit and reading desk.[7] One green cloth around the pulpit and a cushion covered with green cloth. One large Bible. One large Common Prayer book. Five bells with their frames the first or least bell being two feet and one inch in diameter, the second two feet and three inches in diameter, the third two feet and six inches in diameter, the fourth two feet and eight inches in diameter, the fifth or largest two feet and ten inches in diameter.[9] One Bier. One Hearse cloth. Two surplices.

Parish Registers. Seven parchment and one other bound Register Books. One book of Marriages intermixed with baptisms and burials beginning in one thousand six hundred and forty nine and ending in one thousand and seventy eight. Another book of Marriages beginning in one thousand seven hundred and fifty four and ending in one thousand eight hundred and four. Another book of Marriages beginning in one thousand eight and seven and ending in one thousand eight hundred and twelve. Another book of Marriages beginning in one thousand eight hundred and thirteen and continued to the present time. Duplicate books of Baptisms; one, containing also burials, beginning in one thousand seven hundred and seventy eight and ending in one thousand eight hundred and twelve. Another book of Baptisms beginning in one thousand eight hundred and thirteen and continued to the present time. Another book of Burials beginning in one thousand eight hundred and thirteen and continued to the present time.

Seats in the Church. The seats in the Church and Chancel have been repaired for time immemorial at the publick expense of the Parish.

Parish Clerk and Sexton. There are also due to the Parish Clerk for every wedding by publication or by license two shillings and sixpence, for every funeral one shilling, and an oblation at every churching of women of six-pence. To the Sexton for making a grave one shilling.

Parish Officers. There is but one Church Warden who is nominated by the Parish and usually continues in office for several years. There are also two Overseers of the Poor who are chosen yearly at Lady day at a Vestry meeting by a majority of votes for the year ensuing.

2. Archdeacon Bonney's historical notices of churches, c.1820–1840

TILSWORTH, All Saints. This Church consists of a Nave, South Aisle, Chancel, and Tower at the West End. Chiefly Perpendicular.

In the Chancel are two Monuments.[22] One to Gabriel Fowler Esqre. who died 16 August 1582.

Here lyeth the Body of Gabriel Fowler Esquire who departed this Life 16th August anno Domini 1582 who took to wife Elizabeth one of the daughters and coheiresses of Roger Moore of Bursiter in the County of Oxford Esqre., by whom he had issue Richard, Mary, Agnes, Elizabeth, and Jane. Mary the Eldest daughter caused this inscription to be set up and has likewise bestowed yearly for ever the Sum of Five Pounds towards the Maintenance of a preaching Minister at Tillsworth, that shall make a sermon the first Sunday of every Month in the Year, and shall begin the 3[d] of October 1621. The first quarter of the Armorial Bearing is as follows [*Sketch of coat of arms*]

The other Monument is to the Memory of Sir Henry Chester K.B. created at the Coronation of K. Charles 2^d. He died 30 July 1666. It represents him kneeling at a Desk, with a Young Man behind him, and a female before him. The armorial Bearing is Chester [*Sketch of coat of arms*].

On the Pavement in the South Aisle is the gravestone with an inscription in Norman to the Memory of Adam de Tillsworth.[23]

3. Archdeacon Bonney's visitation notebook, 1823–1839

TILSWORTH. This Church consists of a Nave, South Aisle, Tower at the West End of the Nave & Chancel at the East End thereof, a Porch on the South Side.

At the visitation of 1823, the following Order was given that the floor of the Chancel be thoroughly repaired & made level; the ceiling thereof & walls whitewashed within & pointed on the Exterior. The Stonework of the windows, particularly at the East End & the Buttresses be thoroughly repaired; The window on the North side of the Chancel be glazed, and Casements be placed in a North & South Window. The frame of the Communion Table & the Rails be oiled; The top of the xxx (*sic*) Table be grained; the Seats in the Chancel be renewed; the wainscot & framework under the Arch leading to the Chancel be removed; except the middle part, which is to be oak grained; The Pulpit Cushion be new covered & a new Cloth for the Pulpit be purchased; the Pulpit & Desk be made firm & painted oak colour;[7] the Walls be cleansed from Moss; the Manor Farm Seats & the rest of the Seats be repaired, & oak grained;[10] the Font be cleansed & a proper Font Bason be purchased; The Belfry be new floored, the Windows be cleaned, the Shaft of the North Window in the Bell Chamber be renewed; M^r. Clarks & Home Pews be repaired;[10] The Stonework of the windows restored with Cement.

At the Visitation of 1826. the above order was renewed and the Whole to be compleated before Easter 1828.

At the Visitation of 1833 The following Order was given that the Bell Wheels be repaired; the Buttresses be capped with Tiles, the Leads of the Tower be recast.

At the Visitation of 1836 – Ordered that the East Wall of the Church be examined and repaired so as to prevent its falling outward; The Walls cleansed; casements be made in the North & South windows of the Chancel & the Casements opened during the week to air the Church – & a Pew on the North side of the Church repaired.

At the Visitation 1839. Ordered the Churchwardens to have the Binding of the Prayer Book & Bible repaired – The Whole undergoing repair.

5. Sir Stephen Glynne's Church notes, 14 May 1870. (Vol.2, pp.39–40)

TILSWORTH, All Saints. This Church has a nave with S aisle – Chancel, South Porch & West Tower; the tower engaged in the W. end of the aisle. The porch is modern & of brick. (The porch though patched with brick has an ancient wooden barge board & some framework[i]).[2] The South doorway has continuous arch mouldings. On the N. of the Nave is a fine flowing Decorated. window of 3 lights & in the N wall a sepulchral arch of the same date with fine mouldings & foliation – crocketed & with flanking pinnacles, under which is a slab commemorating a Priest.[24]

The arcade of the nave is of 3 pointed arches on tight octagonal pillars with capitals. The windows of the S aisle are Perpendicular of 2 & 3 lights. The Tower is very massive & of Perpendicular character – opening to the nave & aisle by pointed arches, that to the nave lofty – each carried on clustered octagonal shafts. The tower has embattled parapet & large buttresses, those at the SE are within the aisle. On the West side is a 3 light window – those of the belfry are of 2 lights & there is no doorway. There is a sculptured corbel at the NE of the nave. The roof of the Nave has tie beams. The Chancel arch is pointed, on octagonal corbels. The Chancel is Perpendicular the E window of 3 lights, with hood on corbels. The other windows are of 2 & 3 lights & rather ordinary in character. There are 2 large & sumptuous Elizabethan tombs in the Chancel incroaching on the windows & on the S. a magnum sedile. A brick vestry has been added on the N.[13] The Organ is in the Chancel[15] – There are candlesticks on the altar. The church is period & unrestored. The Font is EE; the bowl circular & cup shaped swelling out & on 4 short legs with quasi capitals.[3] The roof of the aisle is covered with lead – that of the nave tiled. The walls partially rough cast.

Notes **1.** Pevsner p.155, *VCH* III pp.434–5, Michael Abbott *The Parish Church of All Saints, Tilsworth* (1975 – reissued 1993), and NADFAS inventory 1992–8 (Z 837/4); **2.** Notes on south porch at Tilsworth in "Timber framed porches to Bedfordshire churches" by Terence Paul Smith in *BAJ* Vol.17 (1986) p.92; **3.** The *VCH* says the font bowl is of C17th date, but other sources (including Glynne) date it to the C13th; **4.** Article by W.D. Caröe on the stone figures of knights found in the church at Tilsworth, from the *Proceedings of the Society of Antiquaries* 17 May 1906 (P 130/28/4) and Abbott (p.7); **5.** Eeles and Brown p.8; **6.** Presentment, 1617 (ABC 5 p.91); **7.** Early photographs (P 130/28/5/4–5) show the pulpit, with a sounding board, to the right of the chancel arch. The pulpit was moved to its present position after about 1880 (P 130/28/5/6–7) when the old pews were removed and replaced by chairs; **8.** Archdeacon's visitations, 1674 (CRT 170/9/1 p.13); **9.** There were three bells in 1552 and 1724. Details of the bells of 1776 are given by North (p.200) who mentions the repairs in 1880 also noted in the parish register (P 130/1/4), accounts (P 130/5/1) and reported in *LBO* 26 Oct.1880. The bells were recast and a sixth bell added in 1929; **10.** Bonney's visitation orders mention the Manor Farm seats, Mr. Clark's pew and the Home pews. The old pews can be seen in early photographs of the interior (P 130/2/2/5/3–5); **11.** The plate listed in the 1925 schedule (ABE 5) includes a cup hallmarked 1823 and a paten given by D.T. Willis of Leighton Buzzard in 1909; **12.** The embattled parapet on the south aisle is shown in views of c.1810–20 by George Shepherd (slide 886) and of 1830 by George Arnald (slide 10564), but Arnald's "accurate view" dated 10 August 1838 shows roofline as it is now (Z 693/9); **13.** The vestry is mentioned by Glynne and it is shown (looking very much like a north porch) in a late C19th photograph (P 130/28/5/1); **14.** Photographs c.1880 (P 130/28/5/3–5); **15.** The organ mentioned by Glynne in 1870 was in the chancel, but a photograph of c.1880 shows it in the tower arch (P 130/28/5/3). It may have been moved when it was repaired in 1880 (P 130/1/4 and P 130/5/1). The present organ by Alfred Monk of Holloway Road, London, dates from 1908-9 when the new organ chamber was built on the site of the old south chapel; **16.** Bathurst's notebook (ABE 3); **17.** Green was also Vicar of Stanbridge where he restored the church in 1892–3. F.A. Blaydes was a noted local historian and genealogist, who took the name Page-Turner in 1903 when he inherited the estates of his late uncle Sir Edward Henry Page-Turner (1823–74) on the death of his aunt. Blaydes took a personal interest in Tilsworth church and the accounts for the work of 1879–83 are in his own handwriting; **18.** The work of 1879–83 is noted in the parish register (P 130/1/4), the accounts (P 130/5/1), and in the photographs of c.1880 which seem to show the nave before and after the removal of the old pews (P 130/28/5); **19.** The need for action was increased after storm damage in February 1903 caused a large hole in the roof of the nave. The damage was temporarily repaired with corrugated iron sheeting (LPL ref: ICBS 10531); **20.** This major restoration is not mentioned in Jennifer M. Freeman's biography of *W.D. Caröe RStO FSA: his architectural achievement* (1990). The quotation comes from the architect's report of 1902 (P 130/2/2/3) and accords with Glynne's comment that "the church is period & unrestored"; **21.** Sources on the restoration of 1902–10 include parish papers (P 130/2/2/3–21), Bathurst's notebook (ABE 3), faculty petition 1905 (P 130/2/2/11 – but no faculty papers have been traced in the Diocesan archives), papers (and plans) in the ICBS files (LPL ref: ICBS 10531), correspondence in the SPAB archives, report in *DBG* 20 May 1903, report in *CT* 6 Aug.1909 and an article in *Church Builder* October 1904. The Hulcote parish records include a letter from Page-Turner asking for a donation towards the restoration of Tilsworth church, 1906 (P 113/28/2); **22.** The monuments are described by Abbott (pp.8–9); **23.** The stone of Adam de Tullesworthe is illustrated by Fisher (*Collections* p.98) and Abbott (p.4) mentions that Adam was engaged in law-suits over cattle in 1305; **24.** The tomb recess and effigy are illustrated by Fisher (*Collections* p.99).

TINGRITH

The manor of Tingrith, which belonged to the Willaume family in the late C18th, passed into the hands of the Misses Trevor after the death of their father Robert Trevor in 1834.[1] Although the mansion has been demolished, Tingrith still has the appearance of an estate village of the early Victorian era when the Misses Trevor rebuilt some of the houses (1838 and 1841), built a school (1841) and restored the parish church (1845-8) at their own expense.

The list of incumbents goes back to 1225 but the present church dates from the late C15th. It is a complete building in the Perpendicular style. Like the church at Shillington it has angle turrets at the east end of the chancel.[2] The mediaeval plate and ornaments are listed in the 1552 inventory which also states "the said churche chauncell and steple coveryd with ledde".[3] Apart from the screen under the tower,[4] the bells and their C15th frame few early fittings survive.[5] The plate dates from 1771.[6]

In 1616-7 the church was reported to be out of repair.[7] Repairs to the church and its furnishings from 1736 and recorded in the churchwardens' accounts.[8] There are frequent references to work on the roof, notably in 1751-2 and between 1797 and 1812 when the parish seems to have undertaken a phased programme of repairs. Bonney ordered various minor repairs in 1823.[9] When Boissier visited in 1827 he found the church had been "recently repaired and plastered".[10] The accounts also show that repairs were undertaken to the south aisle at the expense of the parish in 1842 and 1844 when part of the roof was renewed.

By this time, however, a much more thorough restoration of the whole church was needed. Between 1845 and 1848 the church was put in good order at a cost of about £5000 which was borne by the Misses Trevor and the Rector.[11] Unfortunately, the architect has not been identified.[12] Work began

35. Tingrith: A view of the church from the south taken some years after the restoration of 1845–8
(Photograph: W. Daniels c.1865)

with masonry repairs and the renewal of the roofs of the nave and aisles. The carved woodwork from the old roof was incorporated in the new work. When Mary Ann Brooks of Flitwick visited in May 1845 she found the church being restored,[13] and by the time of W.A.'s visit in June 1846 the structural work had been completed but the seating and pulpit had not yet been installed. W.A. was full of praise for what had been done, and he mentioned the "laudable example set by the ladies of Tingrith" in his later article on Haynes. In 1847 the churchyard wall was rebuilt with new cast iron gates at the main entrance. The work was completed in 1848 with the restoration of the chancel and the installation of four new stained glass windows by William Jay Bolton.[14] The decalogue boards etc. also date from 1848.[15]

After the church had been restored further stained glass windows were installed as memorials to the Willaume and Tanqueray families.[16] The bells were rehung in 1883.[17] In 1900 various improvements were undertaken under C.E. Mallows who designed a new oak reredos, created a new baptistery in the west end of the south aisle and removed the childrens' gallery from under the tower.[18] More recently, the church has again been rescued from a dangerously dilapidated state in a programme of restoration work completed in 1997.

1. Extract from glebe terrier, 23 April 1822
TINGRITH.
Church yard. Item the Churchyard containing nearly half an acre surrounded by the Property of Robert Trevor Esquire except on the South, there by a Highway. The Fence and Gates thereof round made by the Parish.[19]

Church. Belonging to the said Parish are first the Parish Church an antient Building.

Furniture and ornaments. Within and Belonging to which are one communion Table with a covering for the same of crimson Cloth.[20] Also one linnen cloth and one Napkin. One silver Chalice.[6] One Paten. One Chest with three locks of little use because of the damp. One Pulpit and reading desk. One pulpit Cushion. One large Bible. Two Large Prayer Books. The King's Arms and Ten Commandments.[15] Three Bells.[5] One Bier.[21] One Surplice. Three Paper Register Books.

Seats in the Church. The Seats in the Church have been repaired from time immemorial at the expense of the Parish.

Parish Clerk. There is due to the Parish Clerk forty shillings yearly paid by the Churchwardens.

Parish Officers. The Churchwardens chosen at Easter, one by the Rector the other by the Inhabitants at a Vestry.

2. Archdeacon Bonney's historical notices of churches, c.1820-1840

TINGRITH, St. Nicholas. This Church consists of a Nave and Aisles separated by clustered piers and pointed Arches, Chancel, and a Tower at the West End, all of the perpendicular Character. The Font is octagonal, on a central and four similar cylindrical Piers. At the upper End of the South Aisle is a decorated Niche.

In the Chancel is a mural Monument to the Memory of Edward Willaume. M.A. Prebendary of Lincoln and Rector of this Church, who died Oct: 13th 1787 aged 51.

On the floor is a Slab to the Memory of William Mole who married a daugh of Sir William Boteler, who died 23[d] Oct[r]. 1606. aged 42. with this Bearing: Mole. Boteler [*Sketch of coat of arms*].

On Brass in the Chancel. "Here lyeth buried the body of Robert Hodgson Esq[re]. some Tyme the Lord of this Mannour, who dyed the 23[d] of May 1611." He is represented kneeling at a Desk. This Armorial Bearing is also on the Plate. [*Sketch of coat of arms*]

3. Archdeacon Bonney's visitation notebook, 1823–1839

TINGRITH. This Church consists of a Nave, North & South Aisles, a Tower at the West End of the Nave, and Chancel at the East End thereof. A Porch on the South side of the South Aisle.

At the Visitation of 1823 The following Order was given that The Seats be repaired cleansed and oiled; the Pews be made oak colour; The Pulpit be painted to suit the Top of it; The Floor in the Nave be made level; the Door of the Tower be renewed; the Stonework of the Chancel Windows be restored with Parker's Cement; a new purple pulpit Cloth & Cover for the Cushion be purchased; also a metal Flagon; the binding of the Bible be repaired;[23] the floor of the Bell chamber be repaired; the Earth be moved from the Walls of the Church, particularly on the North side.

At the Visitation of 1826 no further order was given.

At the Visitation of 1833,[24] the following order was given a casement be made in the window behind the South Door – The End of a Seat in the Nave be repaired. The floors of the open Seats be repaired – a drain be made to make dry the floor of the Nave if practicable.

At the Visitation of 1836. Ordered that an End of a Seat in the Nave, which has been scorched be renewed – The King's Arms & Figures on each side of it be repaired – & the Church Yard Fence be substantially repaired by degrees.[19]

At the Visitation 1839. A crack appearing on the North side of the Church, ordered the foundation to be examined.

4. Article on the Church by W.A. (no.28), NM 20 June 1846

TINGRITH. It is with sincere pleasure that we now record the restoration of a church effected with unsparing liberality by the patronesses of the living.[11] We have reason to believe that the lavish expenditure so ungrudgingly bestowed would almost have rebuilt the whole fabric. All praise to those who have set so good an example; there has been no parsimonious doling out of rates from reluctant contributors, or from trustees of private charities willing enough to divert the whole of the income to this one purpose alone, so that their pockets may be spared, whilst the poor labourer's cottage may crumble to ruin; but a noble dedication of wealth to a noble purpose.

"Possessions vanish and opinions change,
And passions hold a fluctuating seat;
But, by the storms of circumstance unshaken,
And subject neither to eclipse or wane,
Duty exists.

The roof of the nave and aisles is entirely restored with oak, in the most substantial manner, with the ancient bosses and supporters; those which time had destroyed are supplied in perfect character with the original, by a friendly resident, in a manner most creditable to his taste. The seats are all open, of oak, and when varnished and the poppy heads placed upon them they will present a most gratifying appearance. The pew of the authors of this delightful restoration, now towering above the rest, is, we understand, to be replaced by one of similar height with the open sittings. Thus doing away most properly with all distinctions here. The pulpit and reading desk are to be succeeded by others of an improved character, and removed a little further back. It is hardly necessary to state that Churchwarden's whitewash has been most effectually scraped off. When the chancel is restored, and the pews, those "marks of earthly state and distinction," abolished, the whole will exhibit an example of taste, liberality, and piety, which it is hoped will not be without its followers.* The porch is restored, and the plastered up windows thrown open; the paltry wicket that prevents the way-farer availing himself of the benches will, most probably, when the whole work is complete, be destroyed. One or two matters however, we regretted to observe, which cannot be passed over without remark, more especially as they can be remedied on some future occasion. The flooring is laid down with large paving stone, instead of the tiles now so admirably manufactured in imitation of those originally used for this purpose, giving a very chilling appearance. Those who are sceptical on this point will do well to examine the floor of the Temple church, where there are the same apertures for the admission of warm air, so necessary, it appears, in these degenerate days.[25] One more important deviation remains to be noticed. The light from the western window is admitted, but the lower part of the tower and western door are shut out from view, which, beautiful as the screen is that effects this,[4] cannot be justified. The western entrance should always be accessible, for when this is closed and admission prevented, the view of the interior is entirely marred. We earnestly hope the screen will be removed and the door thrown open. Then the font could be restored to its proper position, and the words of the poet who so beautifully describes the approach to the sacred edifice. "Open your gates, ye everlasting piles!" properly appreciated.

In conclusion, we must not omit to render our humble, but earnest praise, in finding the font filled with water, and no miserable pipkin used, as is too generally the case, in the performance of the holy sacrament of baptism.
15 June 1846   W.A.

* The church of Cranfield is undergoing restoration, chiefly as we are informed through the liberality of the incumbent. The pulpit, which ignorance or vanity had placed in the ridiculous manner mentioned in the notice of that church, has been removed to a more appropriate situation.

Notes 1. For Tingrith manor and village see VCH III pp.435–7 and RC article in BT 11 July 1902; 2. Pevsner p.156 and VCH III pp.437–8; 3. Eeles and Brown p.8–9; 4. The screen under the tower was removed from the chancel arch in 1846. In its present position it fronted the children's gallery built under the tower in 1846 and dismantled in 1900; 5. There are three bells, the treble by John Dier c.1590, the second of 1660 by Christopher Graye, and the mediaeval tenor of c.1450. The bellframe is partly of C15th date; 6. The plate consists of a cup, paten and flagon of 1771 and a silver alms dish of 1851 (ABE 5); 7. Presentments, 1616–7 (ABC 5 pp.91 and 94); 8. Churchwardens' accounts 1736–1894 (P 90/5/1); 9. There are no accounts for 1820–27 and so it is unclear what was done in response to Bonney's earlier visitation orders; 10. Boissier (f.417d-8) also gives a good description of the church before the Victorian restoration; 11. Sources on the work of 1845–8 include the Rural Dean's notebook (AB/RD/A O), W.A.'s account of 1846, and brief references in GM Vol.29 (May 1848) p.529 and BT 29 Dec.1849. The Rural Dean's notes and W.A.'s report are especially helpful in indicating the dates of the separate phases of the restoration work; 12. Although Pevsner describes the church as "over restored in 1845–6" the work was competent and, as witnessed by W.A.'s approval, liturgically correct for its date. Of the local architects of the time only J.T. Wing of Bedford would have been up to a job like this, but it seems more likely that a London architect may have been employed; 13. Diary of Mary Ann Brooks, 1 May 1845 (LL 19/2); 14. The Rural Dean's notebook indicates that the original windows of 1848 were three in the chancel and one in the tower, but the Tanqueray memorial window on the south side of the chancel must have been installed very soon afterwards. Michael Kerney has identified these as the work of William Jay Bolton, whose life and work are described in *The Stained Glass Art of William Jay Bolton* by Willene B.Clark (Syracuse University Press, 1992). Until the discovery of the Tingrith windows, a window at West Lynn, Norfolk, was believed to be the only complete window in England by Bolton who is chiefly remembered for his stained glass at Holy Trinity, Brooklyn, in New York; **15.** The decalogue boards etc. date from 1848. Originally on the wall, but they were moved to their present position in the south aisle baptistery in 1900; **16.** The later windows are listed and described in the RC article in *BT* 11 July 1902; **17.** The bells were rehung by E. Franklin of Eversholt (P 90/5/1) and a report in *LBO* 3 April 1883 mentions a concert to raise funds for the repairs; **18.** Faculty papers and plans for work in 1900 (HCRO ref: DSA 2/1/208); **19.** The accounts (P 90/5/1) refer to repairs to the churchyard fences or walls in 1792, 1837 and 1847; **20.** "Pd for a nue Communion Table Cloth & Napkin & making" (13s 6d), 1754 (P 90/5/1); **21.** "Paid for making a new Bear for church" (£1), 1829 (P 90/5/1); **22.** For the brass, see Lack *et.al*. (p.94); **23.** "Paid for repairing Church Bible" (£1 5s), 1833 (P 90/5/1); **24.** "Paid Archdeacon for Inspecting the Church" (10s.6d.), 8 May 1833 (P 90/5/1); **25.** The Rural Dean noted "Pavement stone & ventilated. There are pipes for hot water, which are useless, as they cause a great draught" (AB/RD/A O) and the accounts refer to work on the heating system in 1861 and 1868 (P 90/5/1).

TODDINGTON

Until the early C19th Toddington was a thriving market town. Its existence as a place of some importance goes back to mediaeval times when the market and fair were established.[1] A map of Toddington made in 1581 by Ralph Agas shows the extent of the Tudor town around the broad green and it has miniature sketches of all the buildings including the church.[2]

The church stands on an ancient site. There is a record of the consecration of a new church in 1222. The cruciform plan is of this time, and traces of C13th work remain in the south transept and lower stages of the tower. After extensive rebuilding and remodelling the church was finally completed in the C15th.[3] Its general appearance is that of a Perpendicular church, and its roof is associated by heraldry with Thomas Peyvre who died in 1429.[4] There is a superb carved frieze, recently restored, round the north side of the church.[5] There is a three storey parvise at the north-east end of the church. Inside there are some C14th wall paintings.[6]

Much of the historical interest of the church lies in the transept chapels which contain tombs and monuments of the leading families associated with the parish.[7] The south transept (known as the chapel of St.James or the Cheney chapel) was used from mediaeval times until the late C18th as a burial place for the lords of the manor.[8] It contains tombs of the Peyvre, Cheney and Cooper families.[9] The vault under the north transept (the Wentworth chapel) seems to have been first used in 1632–3 for Lady Maria Wentworth.[10] Later members of the Strafford and Wentworth families are buried there.[11] By the C19th the Lord of the Manor was responsible for the south chapel and the north chapel belonged to the descendants of Lord Wentworth.[12] The lords of the manor were also responsible, as lay rectors, for the upkeep of the chancel.[13]

36. Toddington: The north side of the church with the parvise, Wentworth chapel and the carved frieze running round the northern parapets. The tracery in the transept was renewed in the Perpendicular style in 1880 and the north porch was rebuilt in 1893.

(Pencil sketch: Thomas Fisher c.1815)

The bequest of £10 to buy two silver candlesticks for the high altar is mentioned in a will of 1518.[14] Papers of 1555 refer to a dispute regarding a cross, pyx and chalice, sold in about 1543.[15] Little else is known about the church and its furnishings until the early C18th, but in 1617 the church was reported to be out of repair.[16] The priest's bell was recast in 1665.[17] In 1696 Lady Wentworth had the chancel windows repaired.[18] A terrier of 1708 lists the main ornaments in the church,[19] including the plate,[20] six bells,[21] a clock,[22] and thirteen fire buckets.[23]

From 1707 the churchwardens' accounts record expenditure on church repairs and improvements to the furnishings.[24] In 1713–4 Thomas Ellis, joiner, was paid "for making a pew in the church". In 1714 new fire hooks were obtained.[23] A new communion cup was bought in 1721.[20] In 1734 the wardens spent £20 on "whitewashing, beautifying and painting the church" and on "cleaning the church after it was beautifyed".[25] In 1741 a new set of fire buckets was bought.[23] A second communion cup was acquired in 1760.[20] Roof repairs were undertaken by Joseph Osborn in 1781 and in 1782 a new brass chandelier was bought for the church.[26] In 1792 a new ring of eight bells was hung in the tower in place of the six old bells.[21] Repairs costing over £50 were carried out in 1794 and again in 1806.

The year 1808 saw extensive repairs to the church.[27] The nave was repaired at the expense of the parish, and the transept chapels were put in order by their respective owners. Several early C19th writers commented on the state of the chapels and their monuments before these repairs were undertaken, Lysons observing that the effigies in the south chapel were "much mutilated and lying on the ground mingled with the ornaments of the tombs and the dung of birds and bats" while the Wentworth monuments in the north chapel were "in a condition little better than the Cheneys".[28] The work on the north transept cost £124 and it was done under the supervision of Robert Nixon of Woburn for the descendants of the Wentworths.[29] The south transept was repaired at the same time for John Cooper, the new owner of the manor.[30] Parts of the masonry of both transepts and the parapet and buttresses on the south chapel have been repaired or reconstructed in brick with a coating of rendering. This is almost certainly of 1808–9, although in 1833 Bonney ordered that the battlements on the south side be cemented.

A list of 1816 describes the pews belonging to the Manor and the tenant farmers, including "the large Pews and Footmens Gallery" belonging to the mansion.[31] A later plan shows that the gallery was at the west end of the church.[32] New galleries to provide extra seating were built at parish expense by Thomas Major in 1818–9.[33] In 1825 the vestry agreed to make two pews in a large pew under the gallery.[34] The south and north galleries were enlarged in 1838 and 1840 respectively.[35] Although most of the pews were cleared away when the church was restored in 1879–81 the manor pew to the left of the chancel arch at the front of the nave remained in place until 1921.[36]

The vestry considered further repairs in 1825.[37] When Boissier visited in 1827 he found the church in a much better state than when he first visited it and noted that "considerable repairs were in progress & in contemplation".[38] He attributed the improvement to "the influence of Archdeacon Bonney". The later churchwardens' accounts record further expenditure on the church from 1824 including the alterations to the galleries in 1838 and 1840,[35] work on the battlements at the west end in 1846 (possibly to replace stonework which fell during morning service in 1843),[39] and the recasting of the treble bell in 1850.[21] Other improvements of the mid C19th included the gift of a new set of communion plate in 1846,[20] the reconstruction of the west gallery and installation of an organ in 1856.[40] The Wentworth chapel was repaired at the expense of the Rector in 1845.[41]

The Rev. John Clegg became Rector in 1862 and hoped to restore the church. Tenders were invited for repairs in September 1862 but there is no record of what was done.[42] In 1864 gas lighting was installed.[43] By 1867 J.P. St.Aubyn had prepared plans and specifications for work on the church.[44] Shortly afterwards, probably in 1869–70, the roof of the nave was restored at a cost of £900.[45] In 1875 Clegg had a new chiming clock placed in the tower.[22]

In 1876 the architect Robert W.Edis prepared a detailed report on the church for the Rev. C.E.Haslam (Rector 1876–87) and fund-raising began in

37. Toddington: The interior after the main restoration in 1879–81 showing the manor pew by the chancel arch, the new seating in the nave, the lectern (1884), the organ in the chancel (1881) and the reredos (1885)

(Photograph: Anonymous c.1890)

earnest.[46] Difficulties with the lord of the manor and patron, William Cooper Cooper, regarding pew rights and other matters delayed the work,[36] but eventually a faculty was obtained in 1878. Work began in 1879 with the removal of the north and south galleries, the restoration of the chancel and south aisle and re-seating the nave and aisles. The small window at the west end of the aisle was uncovered and re-opened at the time of these works and filled with stained glass.[47] The Wentworth chapel was restored at the same time and the C17th tracery in the north window was replaced by a new Perpendicular window.[48] The church was reopened on 24 October 1880.

Work did not end there, and in 1881 the north aisle was restored and the west gallery removed.[46] The organ was also rebuilt and enlarged and moved to the chancel in the same year.[49] Further work to the chancel was held up by another dispute between the Rector and Cooper Cooper,[36] but in 1883 new choir stalls were set up. Later improvements included the vestry at the end of the north aisle in 1883, the font cover and lectern in 1884 and the reredos in 1885.[50]

In 1887 it was suggested that the west window be restored for the Queen's Jubilee.[51] This was not done, but in 1888 the west end of the church was re-seated as a memorial to the Rev. C.E. Haslam.[52] In 1892 the south transept was repaired at the expense of the squire and Miss Cooper Cooper gave the stained glass in the south window.[53] Further restoration work under R.W. Edis took place in 1892–3 when the west front was restored, the north porch rebuilt, and improvements made inside the church.[54] The bells were rehung in a new frame in 1906.[21]

Further restoration work under W.A. Forsyth took place in the 1920s.[55] The manor pew was removed in 1921.[36] In 1930 the wall paintings were uncovered and restored.[6] After World War II a new lectern and pulpit with sounding board were provided. In 1946 the west window was filled with stained glass. It was designed by Christopher Webb who was also responsible for the east window installed in 1948 as part of the improvements to the chancel completed under W.H. Randoll Blacking in 1948–9. The reredos was dedicated on 17 Dec.1949.[56]

The church suffered serious gale damage in January 1976 and the repairs involved extensive work on the roofs of the aisles, the loss of the parapets from the upper parts of the nave and west front, and the removal of pews from the aisles.[57] Repairs to the tower followed in 1981–2 and other parts of the church have since been restored.[58] In 1991 a new chapter house was built in the south-east corner of the churchyard.

1a Extract from glebe terrier, 1791 [60]

Furniture in the church. One Bible and Two Common Prayer Books, a Communion Table with Rails, One Scarlet Table Cloth Carpet; One large White Linen Table Cloth and Two Napkins, Two Pewter Flagons, and Two little Pewter Plates; Two Silver Chalices, on One is Inscribed "Toddington in Bedfordshire M[r]: Jonathan Norris, M[r]: William Langford, Church Wardens 1721";[20] On the Other is Inscribed "Williams Watters, Philip Fowler, Church Wardens, Toddington in Bedfordshire, 1760";[20] One Patten of Silver, One

Pulpit Cushion of fine Crimson Velvet on one Side, and on the Other Side fine Crimson Cloth, Six large Bells and a Saints Bell;[17, 21] One Clock and Chimes,[22] Two Surplices, Three Register Books of Parchment. The Oldest Register bears Date in the year 1540. One very small one and Stitched, Two Marriage Register Books of Paper, Two Chests, One with Three Locks and Keys according to the Canon, One Book of Homilies, Two Poor's Boxes, a Book for the Church Wardens,[24] a Stone Font and Pewter Bason,[61] a few Buckets,[23] One Pall, and Cloth, and Bier, a Chandelier,[26] Two Candlesticks, and Burying Cart.[62]

Repairs. No Lands for the Repair of the Church nor any Money in Hand. The Parish Repairs the Church, Lords of the Manor and Rector Repair the Chancel;[13] the Church Furniture, and Church Yard Fence being a Brick Wall are maintained by the Parish, the Soil of the Church Yard belongs to the Rector.

Parish Clerk. The Clerk and Sexton are in one Person, for which he hath a Yearly Salary paid him by the Parish. He hath for every Couple to be ask'd Six pence, and One Shilling when they are Married, with Licence Two Shillings and Six pence. For Burial Bell and Grave Two Shillings, if in the Church Five Shillings. For the Use of the Burying Cart One Shilling,[62] and for every Churching Four pence.

1b Extract from glebe terrier, 1 July 1822
TODDINGTON.
Church yard. Item the Church yard containing three roods and thirty perches.
Church and Furnishings. [not described in this Terrier]
Parish Clerk. There is also due to the Parish Clerk for every Wedding by Banns 2s. 6d., by Licence 5s. 3d., for every Funeral & making the grave [blank]

2. Archdeacon Bonney's historical notices of churches, c.1820–1840
TODDINGTON, St. George. This church consists of a Nave and Aisles separated by octagonal Piers lofty & supporting pointed Arches. Transepts & Chancel with an Embattled Tower rising from their junction. The Piers and Arches are of the decorated Character, but the remainder Perpendicular. There is a stone Altar yet remaining in what is now a Vestry at the North side of the Chancel with a room over it.

Against the South Wall of the Chancel is a Monument with this Inscription:
In memoriam fratris posuit Soror Alicia Bruse amoris ergo.

Gyles Bruse youngest Son of Sir John Bruse of Wenham in Suff. Knight who cominge to Toddington to visyte his sister Alicia Bruse then attending on the Right Hon: the Ladye Cheyne, there dyed the 13th of March 1595 and was by his sayde Syster here intombed ye 14th of March Regno Reginæ

Elizabethæ, 38. Ætatis suæ 33.

In the South Transept under Monumental Canopies inserted in the Wall are two altar Tombs,[9] with quartrefoils in the panels, and escutcheons in the centre: The Effigy of a Man in plate Armour, his head reclining on his Helmet and his Feet on a Lion. A Catherine Wheel for his Crest. Two Angels support his head holding a label, with these words in ancient letters "Miserere me Deus". His sword belt is studded & worn horizontally & his Sword hanging on his right Side. On his breast a Cheveron charged with three fleur de lis.

On the other Tomb is the Effigy of a Female her head resting on a cushion supported by angels & her feet on a Griffin couchant. She is dressed in a Robe, with her hair in a net bound round with a fillet.

[*Sketch of coat of arms*] Peyvre.

There is on another Tomb the mutilated Effigy of a person in Shirt of Mail, who also bears the same Cheveron charged with three fleur de lis. Besides these there are three Altar Tombs to the memory of the Cheneys which are of alabaster admirably carved, & have been splendid specimens.[9]

The North Transept was the burying place of the Wentworth Family and contains three Monuments to their Memories.[11] All of which with their Epitaphs are described in Parry's History of Woburn.[7]

On one of the Chalices is inscribed "Toddington Bedfordshire M[r]. Jonathan Norris, M[r]. W[m]. Langford Church Wardens 1721." On the other "Toddington Bedfordshire. William Waters, Philip Fowler, 1760".[20]

3. Archdeacon Bonney's visitation notebook, 1823–1839

TODDINGTON. This church consists of a Nave, North and South aisles, Transepts, chancel, and a Tower rising from the Junction of the Nave Transepts and Chancel. There are porches to the North & South Aisles.

At the Visitation of 1823 the following Order was given that casements be made in the Windows North & South of the Chancel, a new metal Flagon be purchased;[20] the Pall cleaned – The South Porch and the Steps be repaired. The Earth moved from the Walls and proper drains be made – the Stonework or the Doors and Windows be restored with Cement – the small windows at the West End be altered to a pattern given. The Floor of the Tower be repaired – The Closet under the Tower be removed – the Seat adjoining to remain,[36] and be made to range with the other Pews – The Roof of the South Aisle be repaired – before Easter 1826

At the Visitation of 1826 – no further order was given.

At the Visitation of 1833 The following Order was given, that the Walls, Roof, and Window of the North Transept be repaired; The Battlements on the South Side be cemented – the North Porch be repaired; the cracked Bell be recast;[21] the Corner of the Vestry be secured from taking wet; a Casement be placed in one of the South Windows of the chancel.

At the Visitation of 1836. Gave permission to the Churchwardens to allow

M[r]. Cooper's Tenants to be seated in a vacant Place under the Tower.[36] (the Rector being present)

At the Visitation 1839 Ordered the interior of the Tower which is visible to the Church to be cleaned & restored – and the Earth to be moved from the South Side of the Church – Sanctioned a proposition to change the Position of the Pulpit and Desk to a more suitable situation near the Tower Arch,[63] and an alteration of the Arrangement of Sittings in the Men's Gallery in order to accommodate more Persons.

4. Article on the Church by W.A. (no.23), NM 21 February 1846

TODDINGTON. This noble church exhibits sad evidence of decay; in its perfect state it must have been a very fine specimen of English architecture. The indignities it has suffered from neglect, or what perhaps is worse, from the hands of injudicious restorers, are most disagreeable to contemplate. It betrays marks that the parties employed in such restorations as have been attempted, were utterly ignorant of ecclesiastical architecture.

Under a mistaken notion of economy, it is too much the custom to employ the village mason or carpenter, instead of obtaining the aid of an architect who would prevent the blunders arising from their incapacity. The roof of the nave is a fine specimen of timber framing,[4] in pretty good preservation, the roofs of the aisles are also of wood; this is a redeeming point when it is considered how rarely they are to be found in many of the churches in this county. The pews are very ugly, and for the most part high;[36] even this did not seem to satisfy some of the occupants, who still further to screen themselves from observation have had them fitted up with curtains. On one we observed a brass plate recording the name of its proprietor, placed there, it is presumed, to keep intruders out. Another pew is furnished like a private sitting room. We observed no free seats; how the large population of Toddington is provided for in a church so exclusively fitted up is not easily to be understood. Can any one wonder at the increase of dissent, when the poor are thus shouldered out of their parish church.

The upper part of the western window is filled with coloured glass, its pattern resembling a harlequin's dress;[64] but as we noticed a blind with a shop-front sort of cornice above it, we think it should always be drawn down to hide this deformity from view. Galleries disfigure the building;[33, 35] and the pillars of the nave are painted to imitate black marble.[65]

The font is in a proper position.[61] The chancel is whitewashed; the roof is ceiled, but divided into compartments. There are no pews in this part of the church. The altar cloth is decent.

The northern transept is not quite in so bad a condition as when noticed by Lysons in 1813, it having been partially repaired;[29] but the southern one remains almost in the same state of neglect as when he saw it.[28] The monuments are much decayed, and will soon prove the truth of the poet's description:-

"Wonder not, mortal, at thy quick decay –
See! men of marble piecemeal waste away;
When whose the image we no read,
But monuments themselves memorials need

We know not in whom is vested the duty of preserving this part of the church and its contents, but its appearance evinces gross neglect.[12] Surely the inheritors of the titles and property of those to whom these costly monuments have been erected, might at least deem them worthy of some little attention, and rescue them from further decay. The windows of both transepts are partially blocked up.

17 February 1846   W.A.

Notes **1.** For the history of Toddington generally see *Toddington: Its Annals and People* (1925) by Joseph Hight Blundell, *VCH* III pp.438–447, and Richard Hart *Old Toddington* (1984); **2.** Sections of the Agas map are reproduced in Blundell and BCRO holds a complete photographic copy (X 1/102). The original is in the British Museum; **3.** For the church, see Pevsner pp.156–7, *VCH* III pp.444–6, Blundell especially pp.92-114 (church), pp.135–47 (monuments), and pp.157–77 (parish accounts), and church guide n.d. [c.1990]; **4.** The angels on the roof carrying heraldic shields are illustrated by Fisher (*Collections* pl.102); **5.** The frieze is illustrated by Fisher (*Collections* pl.101) and there is an account of its recent restoration in "The frieze of Toddington church" by Pam Ward and Omer Roucoux in *B.Mag* Vol.25 no.196 (Spring 1996) pp.141–3; **6.** The wall paintings, believed to have been covered with whitewash in 1734, were rediscovered at the time of the main Victorian restoration and conserved by the Rev. F. Conquest Clare in 1930 (P 8/2/5); **7.** The monuments have attracted antiquarian curiosity since the late C16th, and there are several general accounts including a record of the arms and epitaphs in the church, 1594 (BL ref: Add.Ms. 5527; 5832 f.171b), notes on Toddington, 1800 (BL ref: Add.Ms. 34383 f.109), drawings of tombs, C19th (BL ref: Add.Ms. 42013 f.86; 42030 f.81), notes and drawings by the Rev.D.T. Powell c.1810–2 (BL ref: Add.Ms. 17456), Parry's *History of Woburn* (1831), various articles in *GM* (see Conisbee p.210) and the Cooper-Cooper scrapbook (P 8/28/10). Blundell (pp.135–47) also gives details of the monuments; **8.** The south chapel was neglected in the C18th but repairs were carried out by the Cooper family of Toddington manor in 1808–9 and in 1892-3. In the C19th the Lord of the Manor erected an iron fence as a clear sign of his ownership; **9.** Illustrations of Peyvre and Cheney tombs by George Shepherd and Thomas Fisher (slides 610, 894–900, 1551–4); **10.** For the Wentworths see Blundell (pp.51-8). The tombs include that of Henrietta Maria Wentworth (1657-86), the mistress of the Duke of Monmouth; **11.** Blundell (p.75) states that the vault was opened in 1785 when the inscriptions on eleven coffins were recorded by Thomas Gregory, the parish clerk, and again in 1845. There is an undated plan of the coffins in the parish register (P 8/1/5) and another plan of 14 June 1845 (in P 8/28/10 no.5); **12.** In the C19th the owners acknowledged and accepted their liabilities to pay for repairs to the chapels, although both Parry (1831) and W.A. (1846) observed that the south chapel was less well maintained than the northern one. Parry commented that it had merely been "slightly repaired ... to prevent injury by the weather"; **13.** The descent of the advowson is noted by the *VCH* III p.446. It was generally held by the lord of the manor apart from a period in the early C19th. By 1850 William Cooper Cooper again held both the manor and the patronage, but his disagreements with the Rector led to difficulties over the chancel in 1883 and 1906 (X 341/20 and 23). An exchange of letters dated Nov-Dec 1883 concerning the ownership of the chancel, listing minor repairs and alterations etc. and reciting the history of the lay rectorship, was published in the parish magazine in Feb.1884 (P 8/30); **14.** Will, 1518 (BHRS Vol.76 no.101); **15.** Eeles and Brown pp.26–7; **16.** Presentment, 1617 (ABC 5 p.91); **17.** The priest's bell was cast by Chandler of Drayton Parslow in 1665; **18.** Chancel repairs mentioned in Lady Wentworth's accounts, 1696 (CRT 130/36 p.32); **19.** Terrier, 1708 (ABE 2 Vol.II p.424) quoted in Blundell (p.81); **20.** The plate listed in the 1708 terrier consisted of "a pewter Chalice" and a "Silver cup with a lid (12 ounces)". Bonney gives the inscription of the new chalices acquired in 1721 and 1760, also noted in the

1791 terrier. The accounts for 1720 record a payment (£4 4s 6d) "to Mr.Bayley for a new Communion Cupp &c 1721". The present plate dates from 1846 and each piece carries the inscription "The Gift of Elizabeth Cooper Cooper, Lady of the Manor of Toddington, to Toddington church A.D. 1846" (ABE 5). The accounts for 1848 record the sale of old plate for £4 3s 3d; **21.** The terriers of 1708 to 1791 list six bells, replaced in 1792 by the present ring of eight. The churchwardens' accounts for 1792 record the expenditure on the new bells and the contract with Thomas Mears, the bellfounder, is entered in the volume (P 8/5/1). The treble (noted as cracked by Bonney in 1833) was recast in 1850, and in 1906 five bells were recast when the whole ring was restored (Blundell p.88). The bells were rededicated on 18 April 1906 (P 8/1/40); **22.** There was a clock in 1708 and frequent repairs are recorded in the accounts. Chimes (playing tunes) seem to have been first put up in 1712 and the 1791 terrier mentions "one clock and chimes". A new clock with Cambridge quarter chimes was put up in 1875, as reported in *BM* and *BT* 25 Dec.1875. The accounts for the new clock were published in the parish magazine of September 1876. A report in *BT* 14 Dec.1878 refers to repairs and a new dial was put up in 1894 (*BS* 6 July 1894); **23.** The accounts refer to fire hooks in 1714–5 and there are several entries regarding new fire-fighting equipment in 1741 including payment for two dozen fire buckets (£3 18s), carriage from London (2s.6d.), and pins to hang them upon (2s); **24.** Churchwardens' accounts 1707–1824 (P 8/5/1). A later volume for 1824–61 has been lost since the 1920s but Blundell published some extracts and his notes (CRT 130 TOD 1 pp.122–4) provide some additional information from the missing volume; **25.** Blundell (who misread the date as 1737 instead of 1734) suggests that this was when the wall-paintings were first covered up; **26.** The accounts record the purchase of the chandelier from John Horseley and Son of London for £24 3s 6d in 1781–2 (P 8/5/1). Sherlock (p.54) suggests that it was removed in 1876; **27.** Blundell (p.84) states that "in 1808 the main fabric of the church seems to have undergone some renovation, but not the chapels". It is now known from other sources the chapels were restored at this time. The accounts record parish expenditure (about £40) on the church in 1808 and there is an entry "Paid the Arch-Deacon and Expences in viewing the State of the Church"; **28.** Lysons, whose description was published in 1813, must have been referring to the state of the chapels before the repairs of 1808–9. Other writers who mention the state of the chapels and monuments include the Rev.D.T. Powell who visited in 1810 (BL ref: Add.Ms. 17456 ff.20–21) and found that the monuments had been "lately ... yellow washed (or rather plaistered)", Boissier (f.392d–4) who noted that the monuments had been irreparably damaged when the roof of the south transept had fallen in, J.D. Parry in his *History of Woburn* (1831) pp.134–7, and a writer in *GM* Vol.73 (1803) p.86; **29.** Letters and accounts regarding repairs to the north transept, 1808–9 (in P 8/28/10 p.72); **30.** Plan of mausoleum in south transept, 1809 (in P 8/28/10). Parry notes that by 1816 the South Chapel had been repaired at "a very considerable expence" by the Lord of the Manor, Mr.John Cooper, who had recently purchased it; **31.** Thomas Gregory's list of pews, 1816 (X 341/7); **32.** Plan of church showing the manor pew and footmen's gallery, n.d. (X 341/12); **33.** The accounts records payments to Thomas Major for building the gallery (£56) in 1818–9 and a further payment "for timber and labour in the church" (£19 11s 6d) in 1820; **34.** Vestry minute, 5 Aug.1825 (AD 566); **35.** Work on galleries in 1838–40 was noted by Blundell from the account book, now lost; **36.** Gregory's list of 1816 identifies all the pews associated with the Manor (X 341/7) and W.A. gives a description of the pews in 1846. William Cooper Cooper fell out with the Rector in the 1860s and attended church at Harlington instead. He resisted any interference with the private pews at Toddington, as shown by the legal correspondence of 1879–1906 (X 341/8–23) which mentions repairs to the large manor pew in 1834 and the loss of a pew when the pulpit and desk were moved. Bonney's orders refer to the pews of Mr. Cooper's tenants in 1836. Matters were eventually resolved when Canon Hicks acquired both the advowson and the lordship of the manor in 1921. He afterwards assigned his rights to the PCC (P 8/2/21–2); **37.** Vestry resolution, 22 April 1825 (AD 566); **38.** Boissier (f.392d–94); **39.** Report of fall of masonry in *BM* 23 Sept.1843; **40.** A report in *BT* 26 Jan.1856 mentions "a new gallery of chaste design" and "a large and beautifully toned organ" given to the church by W.D.C.Cooper of Toddington Manor. The organ was later said to have come from Harlington (in *LBO* 20 Sept.1898) but the dates of known work to the two organs makes this seem unlikely; **41.** A note dated 19 July 1845 in the later churchwardens' account book (extract in CRT 130 TOD 1) states that the northern transept was repaired by the Rev. E.B.Lewis at his sole cost and never at the expense of the parish. The repairs may have been done some time before 1845, the year of Lewis's death; **42.** Advertisement for tenders in *BT*

1 July 1862; **43.** Gas lighting reported in *BT* 5 April 1864; **44.** Reports in *BT* 19 Feb, 21 May and (advertisement for tenders) 30 July 1867 refer to fund-raising and mention the plans of J.P. St.Aubyn; **45.** Blundell (pp.85–6) mentions that the nave roof was repaired during Clegg's incumbency and the later ICBS papers refer to "last repairs in 1870" costing £900 (LPL ref: ICBS 8222); **46.** Sources for the restoration of 1876-81 include the vestry minutes (P 8/8/1), parish magazines (P 8/30 etc), faculty citation 1878 (P 8/2/14), faculty papers and plans (HCRO ref: DSA 2/1/209 and 220), ICBS correspondence and plans (LPL ref: ICBS 8222), reports in *BT* 7 July 1877, 8 June 13 July and 14 Sept.1878, *LBO* 14 May, 17 Sept. and 24 Dec.1878, 10 June and 30 Sept.1879, 15 March and 14 Oct.1881, and account in Blundell (pp.85–6); **47.** The discovery of the window and addition of stained glass noted in the parish magazine (August 1880) and the glass is mentioned in the Powell archives, 25 Sept.1880 (V&A ref: AAD 1/58 p.47); **48.** Report and estimate concerning Wentworth chapel repairs, 1880 (P 8/2/4), reports in the parish magazine 1880, and Blundell (p.86); **49.** The work on the organ, re-opened on 18 Oct.1881, is covered in some detail in the parish magazines for 1880–1 (P 8/30); **50.** The choir stalls, lectern etc. are noted by Blundell (p.86) and the various gifts were noted in the parish magazine (P 8/30); **51.** The parish magazine for April 1887 refers to the need for repairs to the west window, also in *LBO* 1 Aug.1887; **52.** The re-seating of the west end in memory of Haslam is recorded on a brass plaque in the church, and noted in the parish magazine for May 1888, by Blundell (p.86), and in *BS* 28 April 1888; **53.** Report of south transept repairs and new stained glass window (by Heaton, Butler and Bayne) in *BM* 7 Jan.1893, and sketches of the window design (in P 8/28/10 p.64); **54.** Sources for the restoration under Edis in 1892–3 include the ICBS correspondence 1892–5 (LPL ref: ICBS 9654), papers in the SPAB archives, and reports in *BM* 7 Jan, 7 Oct. and 16 Dec.1893 and 17 Feb.1894 and in *LBO* 3 Jan, 21 Feb, 11 July, 3 Oct. and 5 Dec.1893 and 13 Feb.1894. The SPAB criticised the architect's approach to the work, but Edis retorted that "he was not prepared to be dictated to by the Society in professional matters"; **55.** Canon Hicks launched an appeal for £7000 in 1922 (guide). The SPAB archives include papers of 1925–7 regarding Forsyth's work, which is also mentioned in the Report of the Council for the Care of Churches for 1928-9 (p.48); **56.** A faculty was obtained for the west window in 1941 (P 8/2/20) but owing to the war the work was not finished until 1946. The pulpit and lectern, the sanctuary improvements and reredos, and the east window are documented in the parish papers (P 8/2/23, 26–7) and the order of service has notes on the craftsmen etc (Z 913/10/3). The work on the sanctuary is featured in the Report of Central Council for the Care of Churches 1951 (p.vii); **57.** Papers concerning repairs after gale damage in 1976 (P 8/2/28–30 and Z 889/2/49); **58.** Recent work to 1988 is summarised in the guide (c.1990); **59.** The start of work on the Chapter House is noted in *B.Mag* Vol.22 no.174 (Autumn 1990) p.240; **60.** The text of the 1791 terrier (ABE 1) is given here to compensate for the lack of detail in the 1822 terrier; **61.** The font has an usual base, described by Boissier (f.392d–94) in 1827 as "a spiral Grecian ornament ... in bad taste". The accounts record the purchase of "a Pewter Bason for the Font" in 1770 (P 8/5/1); **62.** The account book (P 8/5/1) includes a minute *re* purchase of burying cart for the parish, 3 Jan.1783, and a payment (£13 12s 6d) to Jeffrey Osborn for making it, 1783; **63.** The plan of the pews (X 341/12) shows both the former position of the pulpit and desk towards the back of the church and the new location to the right of the chancel arch. In a statement of c.1880 (X 341/11) refers to a pew belonging to Major Cooper having been given up for the pulpit and desk when his son (James Lindsay Cooper Cooper) was Rector; **64.** There are drawings of the tinted glass in the west window (P 8/2/3) which can also be seen in a late C19th photograph (Z 913/9/1c); **65.** Parry also mentions that "the pillars of the Church were washed a dark lead colour" (*History of Woburn* (1831) pp.134–7).

TOTTERNHOE

There was a church at Totternhoe by the C12th and the list of incumbents goes back to 1220. The present building is all of later date. The chancel dates from the C14th and the rest of the church is largely of the late C15th and early C16th.[1] It was rebuilt through the munificence of the Ashwell family whose rebus is to be found in the aisle roofs and on a respond of the north arcade.[2] William Ashwell left money in 1545 for building the tower.[3] There is flush-

38. Totternhoe: SE view showing the church before the alterations to the chancel and porch in 1833. Notice the chequer–work masonry of the chancel, the stumps of pinnacles on the nave and aisle and the tiled roof of the south porch.   *(Watercolour: Thomas Fisher c.1815)*

work over the chancel arch and the nave and aisles have embattled parapets with pinnacles.[4] There are some old benches with linenfold panelling. The screen dates from the C15th.[5] There is a Perpendicular font.[6]

In 1617 it was reported that "The North parte of the church is in great decay & like to fall downe".[7] By 1708 there were five bells, probably a complete ring of 1654–5 by Anthony Chandler of Drayton Parslow.[8] There is an oak chest dated 1677 with the initials of the churchwardens.[9] The church is also noted for its C18th windmill graffiti.[10] There is no old plate, but a new paten was obtained in 1819.[11]

Early C19th illustrations show that many of the pinnacles on the nave and aisles were missing or damaged, the south porch had a tiled roof, and the chancel had flushwork masonry, plain coping on the east wall and no battlements on the south side.[4] In 1827 Boissier noted the "Chancel much out of repair".[12] Bonney's order book shows that in 1833 "the whole church was under a thorough restoration ... according to the original architecture, and in excellent style". Bonney authorised the use of slate for the roof of the nave and aisles. The work seems to have included the repair of all the pinnacles, alterations to the south porch, the addition of a vestry, and a complete remodelling of the chancel by raising the walls and adding embattled parapets. The chancel was ceiled with plaster and the exterior was rendered.[13]

W.A. refers in 1847 to "the restoration recently effected", although he disliked the ceiling and benches in the chancel and expressed disapproval of the western gallery. A new weathercock was erected on the tower in 1848.[14] A bell was recast in 1865.[8] The roof of the porch was repaired in 1883.[15] The church was generally kept in order, and Archdeacon Bathurst refers to "several partial restorations" between 1876 and 1888.[16]

A further restoration of the roofs took place in 1890–1, the architect being James Sutherland of Little Gaddesden who was clerk of works on the Ashridge Estate.[17] The work on the nave roof and on the tower cost £190. In 1892 the cracked tenor bell was recast and the bells were rehung.[8] A jewelled altar cross with candlesticks and vesper lights was acquired in 1892.[18] The reredos behind the altar in the south aisle was carved by Lizzie Pratt in 1896.[19] A new organ was obtained in 1901.[20] In 1906 a new stained glass window was installed in the south side of the chancel. In 1912 the chancel was improved with new choir stalls and an opening was made into the organ chamber.[21] A new lectern was given in 1912 and the present pulpit by Jones and Willis was set up in 1914.[22]

Further restoration work was undertaken between 1920 and 1930,[23] including repairs to the tower and bellframe after damage by fire in 1923.[24] A sixth bell was added in 1930 and two more bells were added in 1953 to make a ring of eight.[8] A new ringing gallery was erected in the tower in 1967.[25] The east window now contains modern stained glass of 1971 designed by John Piper and made by Patrick Reyntiens.[26]

1. Extract from glebe terrier, 1 July 1822

TOTTERNHOE.

Church yard. The Church yard contains three Roods (more or less) bounded on the East by Church Green, on the South by Ground of Thomas Hunt and on the West and North by Ground of Thomas Pratt. The Fence next Church Green is repaired by the Parish and on every other part by the Owners of the adjoining Ground respectively.

Church. The Church is an ancient Building containing in length Eighty four Feet including the Chancel and in breadth Thirty four Feet, and the Chancel in breadth Fifteen Feet.

Furniture and ornaments. The Church has five Bells,[8] two Common prayer Books, one Bible, a Pulpit and Reading Desk, a Cushion covered with purple Cloth for the Pulpit and a Cloth of the same for the Pulpit and reading Desk, two Surplices, one Communion Table railed in, One Linen Table Cloth, one Napkin, one Silver Cup and one plate of the same for the use of the Communion.[11] Seven Register Books containing Entries of Christenings, Marriages and Burials the earliest commencing in the year [blank].[27] One Bier and one Black Cloth Pall.

Repairs. The Church and furniture is repaired at the common charge of the parish, the Chancel is repaired by the Earl of Bridgewater as Impropriator.

Parish Clerk and Sexton. The Office of Clerk and Sexton is held by one person who is appointed by the Vicar and who hath for his Salary Four pounds Yearly paid him by the Churchwardens Besides the accustomed dues viz'. For every Burial including charge for Tolling the Bell and digging the Grave four shillings and sixpence, for every Marriage two shillings and sixpence, for publication of Banns one shilling, for every Christening sixpence.

Churchwardens. The Churchwardens are chosen yearly in Easter week, one by the Vicar and the other by the Parishioners in Vestry assembled.

2. Archdeacon Bonney's historical notices of churches, c.1820–1840

TOTTERNHOE, St. Giles. This Church consists of Nave, Aisle, South Porch, Chancel and Tower at the West End. The Piers are octagonal and the whole is perpendicular. The Roof is elegant. There are five Bells.[8] On a boss in the North East of the Nave is an Angel with expanded wings holding an escutcheon on which is a Tree with a Label across it, and a Well with a label also across it; which is a Rebus, as for Ashwell or Beechwell or Oakwell or Elmwell &c.[2] Almost the whole of the Fabrick is embattled.[4]

In the Chancel within the Rails, on a Slab beneath the full length Effigy of a Male, in brass,[28] is this inscription:

Here lyeth buried the bodye of William Michell second son of Thomas Michell of Totternho, Gentleman which William deceased y[e] XVII of December Anno Domini 1621.

Without the Communion Rails, on a Slab, under a male Effigy in brass in Pontificalibus with a Chalice bearing a Wafer in his Hand, is this Inscription – Pray for the Soule of Sir John Warwekhyll sumtyme Vicar of this Church whyche decessed the XX day of October the yere of our Lord MV[c]XXIV. on whose soule Jesu have mercy.

3. Archdeacon Bonney's visitation notebook, 1823-1839

TOTTERNHOE. This Church consists of a Nave, North and South Aisles, a chancel at the East end of the Nave and Tower at the West End thereof, and a South Porch.

At the Visitation of 1823 It was ordered that the communion Table and Rails be cleansed and oiled – a new covering for the Table be purchased; the Seats in the Chancel be removed – the floor of the Chancel be repaired & cleansed – Casements be placed in two of the Windows of the Chancel – a metal Flagon be purchased – The Seats against the wall on the North ile be removed – the rest of the Seats be repaired & oiled. The Font be cleansed – The South Door be repaired – and the Seats, as pointed out – the floor near the South Door be repaired.

At the Visitation of 1826 no further order was given.

At the Visitation of 1833 the Whole church was under a thorough restoration, according to the original Architecture, and in excellent Style.[13] Leave was given to cover the Nave and Aisles with blue Slate instead of Lead. There being £800 in readiness for the purpose of building a Vicarage House; M^r. Wroth agreed to submit the Plan of it to the Bishop without delay.[29]

At the Visitation of 1836 – no order required.

At the Visitation 1839 – Ordered a New Prayer Book for the Minister – the Bible to be repaired & the Prayer Book also, the latter for the Clerk's use. The Plaster in the Chancel is to be repaired by Lady Bridgewater.

4. Article on the Church by W.A. (no.47), NM 20 February 1847

TOTTERNHOE, St. Giles. The condition of this church affords an agreeable contrast to the last one noticed;[30] nothing can be in better order, and the restoration recently effected has been done with care.[13]

The chancel roof is ceiled, which is to be regretted, but the railing and altartable are such as become this part of the building. It has no pews, but open benches against the side of the wall, a great improvement when the necessity for such accommodation is required. It is, however, but a sorry alternative, and we can hardly be induced to believe that means may not be found to avoid placing any portion of the congregation in this part of the church.

The nave and aisles have wooden roofs; the sittings are *all* open; there is not a solitary bit of exclusive appropriation to mar the beautiful effect procured by this arrangement. We are sorry to observe a stove, with its ugly chimney-shaft poking through the roof. The best mode of airing churches will be the restoration of daily service; but it must be the result of sincere conviction of the duty, and with an equally sincere desire to urge the attendance of the many who can have no excuse for neglecting it. It must not be conducted in the spirit which we accidentally witnessed in a sadly desecrated church in a town in this county.[31] It was our lot to find a seat under the clergyman's eye, and beside us were a few of the aged congregation: the benches were miserably high, and we looked for a touch of sorrow when the words 'Let us pray,' fell from the reader's lips; the means for kneeling being not only unprovided, but the benches were so placed that it was impossible to do so even on the floor. The clerk, evidently annoyed at being taken from his secular employment, for, being a festival, there was a sermon, was arrayed in a white driving coat. Although we were under the eye of the preacher, no offer of a book was made to the stranger. Mute was the organ, for in this large church it was admissible, though miserably placed, and when we heard from the pulpit a recommendation of sacred music, we could not avoid casting our eye to the silent instrument, which, for ought we knew, heralds the worshipful corporators on Sunday to their luxurious seats. We felt, on leaving, the full force of the sarcastic remark in a popular work, 'What business has a gentleman in church on any day but Sunday?'

The western window being closed up by boarding and gallery, consequently compelled the adoption of ugly tin candlesticks, for which as the innovation of evening service had not taken root here, there would have been otherwise no necessity. The pulpit and reading-desk occupied a better situation than usual; they are very poor efforts of the joiner. The font,[6] in consequence of the ugly gallery, was removed from its appropriate site. There were no monumental tablets, or as they have been well called, 'marble blisters,' in the chancel, and the church-yard was open.

15 February 1847W.A.

5. Sir Stephen Glynne's Church notes, before 1840. (Vol.1, pp.6–7)

TOTTERNHOE. This is a neat Church,[32] with Tower, nave & aisles all Rectilinear, & Chancel with Curvilinear windows of 2 lights. Most of the aisle windows are of 3 lights, but that East of the South aisle is of 4 & very good. There is a good deal of the Clerestory & of the Chancel worked in flint & stone chequers,[4] but the battlement is of stone & the whole well finished & handsome. The South porch has a good doorway, the buttresses were intended to be surmounted by pinnacles, which are unfinished.[4] The tower is embattled & has a square turret at the S.E. angle. The Chancel has a tiled roof. The Interior is very neat & light – & has the appearance of being well taken care of, the whitewash being carefully rubbed off from the arches & pillars. The nave has on each side 4 pointed arches with octagonal pillars. the Clerestory windows of 3 lights & square headed. The roofs are of wood & very handsome, enriched with panneled compartments, bosses, & figures of angels bearing shields. The seats are ancient & open – the Font a plain octagon.[6] Between the nave & Chancel is a wood screen.[5] South of the Altar is a trefoil niche & piscina, also a brass of John Warthellyet Vicar, 1524.[28] The Chancel has a Rectilinear East window, but some of the side windows are Curvilinear.

Notes **1.** Pevsner p.158, *VCH* III p.450, and leaflet *St.Giles' Church Totternhoe: Visitors' Guide* (1996). I am grateful to Joan Curran for kindly commenting on the draft text; **2.** The rebus is noted by Bonney who, unable to identify the tree as an ash, suggests "Oakwell" and similar variants as the name of the benefactor; **3.** Will of William Asshewell of Totternhoe, 1545 (ABP/R 11 ff.55-6). The bequest of £3 6s 8d in 1545 to building of the steeple" casts doubt on the assertion by the *VCH* that the tower dates from the C15th; **4.** The early illustrations show the stumps of pinnacles (Glynne describes then as unfinished) on the nave and aisles (Z 50/127/113 and slide 901), and the views by Powell (BL ref: Add.Ms.17456 f.15) and Fisher (slide 1555) show flush-work on at least two sides (east and south) of the chancel as noted by Glynne who seems to have visited before 1833; **5.** The chancel screen, mentioned by Glynne, was repaired in 1912. It is now under the tower; **6.** The old font (illustrated in a drawing of 1814, BL ref: Add.Ms. 36357 f.189b) was replaced in the C19th by a new one (shown in *VCH* III facing p.450) and the old one was relegated to the churchyard until restored to the church in 1930; **7.** Presentment, 1617 (ABC 5 p.50); **8.** The 1708 terrier (ABE 2 Vol.II p.430) lists five bells. Four of the bells noted by North (p.202) were by Chandler but the second had been recast by Warner in 1865. The tenor, noted as cracked, was recast by Warner in 1892. The bells were rehung in 1892 and 1924, and augmented to six and eight in 1930 and 1953 (notice in the tower); **9.** The chest bears the initials of Daniel Clithero and Reynold Wells who were churchwardens in 1676–7 (leaflet); **10.** "Windmill Graffiti at Saint Giles' Church, Totternhoe" by Terence Paul Smith in *BAJ* Vol.14 (1980) pp.104-6. Unfortunately the graffiti have suffered from weathering and from erosion due to the softness of the stone; **11.** In 1708 the church possessed "for the Communion a pewter flagon, a silver Chalice with a cover so made as to serve for a Paten it holds about a pint". The *VCH* states that there is a cup dated 1818 but the schedule (ABE 5) only mentions a modern cup and implies that it is the paten which is inscribed "Totternhoe Parish, the Rev. W.B. Wroth, Vicar, 1819"; **12.** Boissier (f.391d); **13.** There is no supporting evidence of what was done at this time, but references to the repayment of loans in 1843-7 and 1856 (in P 58/5/1) may indicate that some of the work listed here was done after 1833; **14.** Churchwardens' account book 1843-1920 with vestry minutes 1844–1925 (P 58/5/1); **15.** "Paid George Twidell for roof of the Porch & making good the walls &c &c as per account" (£4 2s 11d) 1883 (P 58/5/1); **16.** Archdeacon Bathurst's notebook (ABE 3); **17.** The sources for the work of 1890–1 includes minutes etc.(P 58/5/1 and P 58/8/2), accounts (P 58/2/2/2), the faculty papers and plans 1891 (HCRO ref: DSA 2/1/210), and report in *LBO* 13 May 1890; **18.** The cross etc. came from Englefield church "where they were no longer required", 1892 (P 58/5/1); **19.** Carvings mentioned in the minutes (P 58/5/1) and reported in *BM* 17 October 1896; **20.** The organ is by Atterton & Son, 1901 (National Pipe organs register); **21.** The work of 1912 is documented in the minute book (P 58/5/1), faculty and bills etc (P 58/2/2/5), and faculty plans and papers (HCRO ref: DSA 2/1/210); **22.** Faculty for pulpit, 1914 (P 58/2/2/6) and faculty papers (HCRO ref: DSA 2/1/210); **23.** Minutes and papers concerning repairs in the 1920s (P 58/5/1 and P 58/2/2/7-16 *passim*); **24.** Papers concerning repairs to tower and bells 1923-5 (P 58/2/2/9–10, 13–15); **25.** Plans and papers concerning the new ringing gallery, 1967 (P 58/2/2/29-30); **26.** Order of service for dedication of the window, 1971 (in P 58/0/6); **27.** The registers commence in 1559 (BPRS Vol.71). The volume for 1673–1726 has a note that it was "bought at Leighton by Thomas Pratt, Churchwarden of this parish" for 8s, in 1673 (P 58/1/3); **28.** For the brasses, see Lack *et.al.* (pp.94-8); **29.** There is a faculty to pull down the old vicarage at Totternhoe and build a new house for the Rev.W.B. Wroth, 1829 (ABF 2 p.150 and ABF 3/204–6), a plan by John Stevens, Woburn, 1829 and papers re new vicarage 1823–9 and 1835 (BW 884–5); **30.** Eaton Bray was the subject of W.A.'s previous article; **31.** This description does not, as wrongly stated in Part I (BHRS Vol.73 p.15), offer an account of a service at Totternhoe but rather "in a sadly desecrated church in a town in this county"; **32.** Glynne offers few clues as to the date of his visit, although his notes on nearby Eaton Bray are dated 1831 and he may have visited Totternhoe on the same journey. He refers to the chancel having a tiled roof, and this seems to confirm that he describes the church before the major alterations of 1833.

TURVEY

The village of Turvey stands at the western edge of the County where the river Ouse marks the boundary with Buckinghamshire.[1] It is an estate village with historic associations with the Mordaunt family whose Turvey property was sold in 1786 to Charles Higgins. After his death in 1792 the estate was divided between two separate branches of the Higgins family to whose C19th improvements the village owes much of its character and interest. Charles Longuet Higgins of Turvey Abbey,[2] in particular, was responsible for the restoration and enlargement of the church.

The church has Anglo-Saxon origins, the masonry of this period being most clearly visible in the round arches above the south arcade.[3] There is Early English work in the tower. The south aisle and porch were built in the C13th and the north arcade in the early C14th. In the C15th the south porch and the west tower were heightened. The north aisle was extended eastwards to form a mortuary chapel, leaving the east end of the church with north chapel, chancel and Lady Chapel of equal length.[4] Surviving mediaeval fittings include the south door with its C13th ironwork,[5] a font of c.1200,[6] and a C14th painting of the crucifixion in the south wall of the Lady chapel.[7] There are monuments of the Mordaunt family in the south aisle and in the north chapel and brasses in the Lady Chapel.[8]

There are some fragmentary churchwardens' accounts of 1551–2.[9] These

39. Turvey: A view of the church before the restoration of 1852–4 when the chancel (the central section of the east end in this view) was completely rebuilt and extended eastwards and new tracery was placed in the east window of the Lady chapel (or south aisle). This view also shows the appearance of the tower before the present pyramid roof was erected in 1864.

(Watercolour: Anonymous c.1840)

mention the visit of the Edwardian Commissioners but no 1552 inventory has survived. A dated stone indicates that the vestry at the south-west corner of the church was built in 1593. One of the bells was dated 1609 and the existing bellframe indicates that there were probably five bells in the tower by about 1630.[10] The old weathercock from the tower is dated 1630.[11] Two of the bells were recast in 1682, another in 1750 and the tenor in 1815 when the former sanctus bell was added to its metal.[10] The plate was given in 1788 by Margaret Mordaunt, the daughter of the Hon. Henry Mordaunt.[12]

In 1790, shortly after he acquired the Turvey Estate, Charles Higgins had new pews erected in the nave and built a gallery.[13] The churchwardens' accounts from 1797 provide information on later repairs and alterations.[14] They mention the new vestry built on the north side of the church under a faculty in 1804.[15] At this date the old chancel screen was destroyed and a painting or altar piece presented to the church by the Rev. Erasmus Middleton (Rector 1804–5).[16] Middleton and his successor the Rev. Legh Richmond (Rector 1805–27) were both noted evangelicals.[17] During their incumbencies the church was appropriately furnished as a "preaching box" with triple-decker pulpit, enclosed pews, galleries. Its appearance at the time is recorded in several contemporary illustrations.[18] Richmond also had the monument of Sir John Mordaunt and wife Edith moved from its original position in the north chancel in 1810 to give room for additional seats.[8] In 1823 the churchwardens paid Thomas Pinkerd "for writing texts of scriptures in the Church".[14] The Higgins mausoleum was erected in the churchyard in 1825,[19] shortly before Richmond's death in 1827.

Visiting in 1827 Boissier described the church as "sadly disfigured by pews",[20] but soon all was to change. While his father had been an evangelical, Charles Longuet Higgins was to become an advocate of Tractarian principles. Improvements to the church began with the gift of an organ (by Hill and Davison) by Miss Ann Higgins in 1838.[21] In 1844–5 the seating in the church was rearranged and parts of the church were repaired at a cost of over £180 under Richard Sheppard of Newport Pagnell.[22] Chairs, cloth and cushions for the communion table were given in 1846,[23] when Higgins also presented a new organ (by Hill).[24] Further alterations to the pews were carried out in 1849.[25]

However, W.A.'s article written in 1847 shows that he still found plenty to criticise in the new arrangements while in 1848 Glynne noted that although the interior had been recently embellished it was "not quite in a satisfactory style". It must have been clear to Higgins that a more extensive re-ordering would be needed to give the church a liturgically correct setting for worship. In 1852 he sought advice from George Gilbert Scott who suggested the extension of the chancel. Scott's letter indicates that he felt compromised by "so radical a change" because of the views he had recently expressed against destructive alterations.[26] Higgins felt no such qualms, and Scott was commissioned to restore the church and rebuild the east end with a new chancel, vestry and organ chamber.

The church was in the hands of the builders from July 1852 until October 1854 when it was re-consecrated.[27] Scott transformed the interior into what has been described as "the finest mid-Victorian ecclesiastical ensemble in Bedfordshire".[28] Richly furnished with Minton tiles, stained glass and brass ornaments by Hardman, polished marble columns and brightly coloured organ pipes, the chancel is a High Victorian period piece. The woodwork including the carved oak choir stalls, pulpit,[29] lectern and the seating in the nave is also of 1854 as are the quarry glass windows by Powell of Whitefriars.[30] The organ was again enlarged and rebuilt by Hill in 1854.[31] The entire cost of this work was borne by Charles Longuet Higgins.

Further gifts to the church included an alms dish of 1855 by A. Keith of Westminster (designed by Butterfield),[32] the lych gate erected in 1856,[33] and wooden alms dishes and a sanctuary desk presented in 1859.[34] In 1858 the tower was struck by lightning and its roof was damaged by fire, fortunately put out before it could cause any serious damage to the church.[35] Although Scott provided plans for restoring the tower roof,[36] the present pyramid roof and cross on top of the tower were actually put up in 1864 under James Horsford of Bedford.[37] A sixth bell was added to the ring in 1864.[38] In the same year a new heating apparatus was provided.[39]

40. Turvey: Interior looking east, showing the west gallery, enclosed pews in the nave and aisles, with the chandelier and triple–decker pulpit in the nave.   *(Watercolour: Anonymous c.1830)*

As organist, Charles Longuet Higgins took a particular interest in church music and Turvey became noted in the 1860s for its choral services and festivals.[40] After his death in 1885 the organ was again restored in 1886,[41] and in 1887 a monument by H.H. Armstead was erected in his memory.[42] Other improvements at this time included a new credence table by the sedilia in 1886 and a tapestry curtain for the east wall in 1887.[43] A new heating system was installed in 1891.[44] In 1893 George Sargent gave a new church clock in memory of his parents.[45] Work on the bells was undertaken in 1896, 1900 and 1906, including the addition of two trebles in 1900 to make a ring of eight.[38] New oil lamps were provided for the aisles in 1903–4.[46]

In 1899 it became necessary to undertake repairs to the roof of the Lady chapel. It had not needed attention when the church was restored in 1852–4. The work was carried out in 1900 by a local builder at a cost of £335 under Matthew Holding of Northampton.[47] In 1909 repairs to the tower were carried out under George Grocock of Bedford, although his proposal for replacing the pyramid spire with an ordinary roof was not pursued.[48]

Subsequent repairs and improvements have included further work on the organ in 1924,[49] the restoration of the wall painting in 1931,[7] the creation of a new choir vestry under the tower in 1934,[50] and Bernard West's modern work of 1972 on the west screen and altar rails and the light fittings of 1975.[51]

1. Extract from glebe terrier, 24 June 1841 [52]

TURVEY.

Church yard. The Church Yard which is the only Glebe belonging to the Rectory contains One Acre and is fenced round with a stone wall at the charge of the Parish.

Furniture. There are belonging to the said Parish Church 2 Surplices, one linen cloth for the Communion Table and one Napkin, two silver [gilt] flagons weighing 3 lbs. 11 oz. each, Two silver [gilt] chalices weighing 1lb. $2^1/_2$ oz. each, one paten weighing $10^1/_2$ oz., and one plate for the offertory weighing 1 lb.[12] There is also a crimson cloth covering for the reading desk and pulpit and a cushion for the pulpit covered with the same. One folio Bible. Two folio Common Prayer Books and one Quarto Prayer Book for the Communion Table. A folio Book of Homilies. The Queen's Arms with the ten commandments and five bells with their frames,[10] also a clock.[45]

Parish Registers. Four Parchment Register Books and five paper ones, the oldest containing Baptisms, Marriages and Burials begins in the year 1629 and ends in 1655, the second begins 1678 and ends 1751, the third begins 1751 and ends 1804, the fourth containing Baptisms and Burials only begins 1805 and ends 1812, the fifth containing Marriages begins 1754 ends 1812. The remaining modern ones containing Baptisms, Marriages and Burials from 1813.

Repairs. The Church and furniture with the fence of the Church yard being a stone wall are maintained at the common charge of the parishioners, the Middle Chancel by the Rector, and the two side Chancels by Thomas Charles Higgins Esquire.

Charities. Mrs. Ann Mordaunt ... left £100 for the purchase of communion plate.[12]

Sunday School. The Interest of £300 bequeathed by Charles Higgins Esquire for the support of a Sunday School. Land has been added to this latter sum by the present John Higgins Esquire of Turvey Abbey to produce £20 per annum.

School. The Interest of £700 (less by duty) bequeathed by Miss Anna Maria Higgins for the benefit of the Turvey National School.

Parish Clerk. The appointment of the Clerk is by the Rector who is paid by the Churchwardens £8 per annum besides the accustomed dues (viz.) a churching 3d., for putting up Banns 1s., for a Marriage by Banns 2s., by License 5s., for a Burial from 1s. 6d. to 4s. 6d. according to the depth of the Grave, if a Brick Grave or in the Church 10s. 6d., for a head stone in Church yard 1s.

Sexton. The Sexton is appointed by the Rector and is paid by the Churchwardens one shilling for each Sunday and for other days when there is divine service.

2. Archdeacon Bonney's historical notices of churches, c.1820–1840

TURVEY, All Saints. This Church consists of a Nave and Aisles separated by octagonal Piers and low Arches, a Chancel with side Chapels, South Porch, and Tower at the West End. The south Chapel is separated from the Chancel by Piers and Arches similar to those of the Church, but the North Chapel by late Perpendicular. The Character of the other parts of the Fabrick is Early Decorated. There are five Bells.[10] The Font is ancient[6] and as well as the Chancel Arch are Early English. The Communion Plate is silver Gilt, viz. Two Flagons, Two Patins & Two Chalices, given by Margaret daughter of Henry Mordaunt 1788.[12]

The Earl of Peterborough who is so much noticed in the History of the Early part of the Eighteenth Century is buried in a Vault under the North Chapel without any Monument to his Memory. The Plate on his Coffin bears this Inscription "The Right Hon[ble] Charles Earl of Peterborough and Monmouth, General of Marines and Knight of the most noble order of the Garter died at Lisbon October 1755 aged 78."

In the same Vault lie the remains of another notable Branch of the Mordaunts without any Monument to his Memory, but the Inscription on his Coffin Plate is as follows: "The Right Honourable John Earl of Peterborough, Baron of Turvey, Marshal General of the Field for the Parliamentary Forces, Lord Lieutenant of Northamptonshire, deceased the 19th of June 1643 in the 43[d] year of his age."

On brass in the pavement of the South Chapel are the following lines & Bearing.[8]

Quisquis eris qui transieris sta perlege plora

Sum quod eris fueram que quod es pro me precor ora

There were four shield on the Stone – but one remains. [*Sketch of coat of arms* Mordaunt].

It is probable that this is in memory of Sir John Mordaunt. In the same Chapel is a Piscina and there are three sedilia, Early English. Also a Monumental Arch above which is a fixed painting on the Wall and these Bearings. [*Sketches of two coats of arms*].

The oldest Monument in the North Chapel is that of Sir John Mordaunt who founded a Chantry in it. He and his Lady are recumbent on a perpendicular altar Tomb.[8] He was at the Battle of Stoke 16 June 1484 and died in 1504. The next to be mentioned is on the S side of the chancel to the Memory of his Son Sir John Mordaunt created & summoned to Parliament as a Baron 4 May 1532. He married Eliz: d of Sir Henry Vere of Drayton Co. Northampton & died in 1562.

In the North chapel is also a handsome Tomb to the memory of John second Lord Mordaunt.[8] He is recumbent in armour – and by his side his wife Ellen FitzLewes of West Thorndon, Essex. He died 1572. The third Monument in the North Chapel is to the Memory of Lewis third Baron, who died in 1601, and the last to be mentioned is the Tomb of Henry fourth Baron who died in 1608.

The South Porch had formerly a groined stone Roof. The Door has beautiful iron decorated ornaments.[5]

A window in Turvey Church.[53] [*Sketch of window*].

On a small brass placed upon an Altar Tomb outside the S. Chapel is the following Inscription:[54] "I.H.S. Anno Domini 1612. here lyeth John Richardson under this Wall, a faithful true Servant of Turvey Old Hall, Page to the first Lord Mordaunt of fame, servant to Lewis, Lord Henry & John, Payneful & careful & just to them all Till death took his lyfe. God have mercy on his Soule. Amen."

On the Chancel Floor, under the Effigy of a Female in Brass, above which is a Bearing of Ten Quarterings of which a Bear rampant is the First, is the following Inscription: [*Sketch of coat of arms* Bernard].
Here lyeth the Body of Alice Bernard the wife of Richard Bernard Esqre, & daughter of John Chubnoll of Astwood Esq[re]. who departed this life 24th of April 1606, being of the age of 64 years, in remembrance of whose virtues and religious piety her husband Richard Barnard hath laid this Monument.
Specimen of one of the Ornaments on the Font,[6] Turvey [*Sketch*].

3. Archdeacon Bonney's visitation notebook, 1823–1839

TURVEY. This Church consists of a Nave, North and South Aisles extending on each side the Chancel and a Tower at the West End of the Nave. A Porch to the South Aisle.

At the Visitation of 1823 the following Order was given, that the Earth be moved from the North Side of the Church, and proper drainage be made; the north door be new faced with Oak; the Stairs of the Tower be repaired; and a proper Font Bason be purchased.

At the Visitation of 1826 no further Order was given

At the Visitation of 1833 It was ordered that the walls be pointed, and the plaster of the North Chapel be repaired

At the Visitation of 1836 no order required

At the Visitation 1839 Ordered the floor of the first Loft in the Tower to be repaired, and a new Prayer Book next year to be procured.

4. Article on the Church by W.A. (no.70), NM 7 August 1847

TURVEY, All Saints. The whole of this church is in most excellent order. The chancel has a timber roof; a very good communion-table, the railing around it is heavy, and the chairs not very ecclesiastical. The window contains some execrable painted glass;[55] it would be far better removed, and its place supplied by quarries of ground glass, until a time arrives when a really good painted window shall be determined upon, or can be modified. Some monumental tablets – those `marble blisters' – are suspended over the table; in this

40a. Turvey: The interior as restored and embellished for Charles Longuet Higgins by George Gilbert Scott in 1852–4. The chancel has been described as 'the finest mid-Victorian ecclesiastical ensemble in Bedfordshire', *(Lithograph: Anonymous 1878)*

instance the less excusable, as the south aisle affords so admirable an opportunity for placing these memorials by those who desire this notoriety for the departed. The seats placed here are happily open, and designed after the pattern of the original stalls, become less objectionable than those 'dozy cupboards' too often seen in this quarter. We wished them executed in better taste, for truth to say, they are very clumsy. The columns are whitewashed, and there is a chandelier better fitted for the ball-room than a church.[56]

The nave has a timber roof of high pitch. The pulpit and reading-desk are separated, but the sounding-board mars the propriety of the separation.[18] We rejoiced to see the lectern restored; an unusual sight, though a very good one may be seen at Leighton, stowed away among other church furniture, removed to make way for the modern fittings-up in that church. What was at Leighton rejected has been deemed worthy of engraving as a pattern for church restorers in the Instrumenta Ecclesiastica. The pavement is in very good order. The seats are enclosed, but low; the more unsightly and ostentatious pews are in the aisles.[18] A very large organ, with its gallery for the performers (causing, we fear, a regular wheeling round of the congregation when they begin) blocking out the western light, is a sad drawback from the generally good appearance of the interior. The organ would appear to be of most anniversary (*sic – recte* unnecessary) size in so small a building.[24] 'If some little attention to the chants and services were but given by our higher orders as a duty, and they would bring their books into church, with voices as well as minds ready to sing God's praise, what a service would ours be! There would be nothing like it in dignity and devotion under Heaven; far superior to the Church of Rome, with all its boast, for there the music is for *display*, with the character of the opera or theatre. In ours it is meant to be solely for *religion*'*

The beautiful stalls in the south aisles are clogged up with whitewash. A font of an early date,[6] and we are glad to say it is used; there is no miserable basin within it for a substitute. The monuments in the north aisle are preserved with care.[8] There are three services – one of course in the evening. If there is a necessity for the latter, there is not a word to be said, otherwise for those who have so little opportunity of home enjoyment in the winter, or an evening stroll in the summer eve, we cannot think this innovation on the Church of England practice an improvement. There is a school, which we rejoice is well attended during the week, and that the Sunday-school is very prosperous. The churchyard is kept locked.

2 August 1847   W.A.

*Rev. W.J. Bennett, Sermon on the Choral Service.

5. Sir Stephen Glynne's Church notes, November 1830 and 1848. (Vol.1, pp.25–27)

TURVEY, All Saints. This church has portions of very good work & deserves careful examination. The nave is lofty with a Clerestory & has side aisles, the Southern being of great width. The Chancel has also an aisle on each side extending quite to the end. There are portions of all three of the later styles – the Clerestory has 4 Rectilinear windows of 2 lights & an embattled parapet, which last the aisles & South Chancel also have. The Tower at the West end is of the same style, having a battlement, octagon corner turret, double belfry windows, & a 3 light window on the west side. (The Tower is large, having a poor coarse battlement. On the W. only a single belfry window – the others double[i]). The South porch is of 2 stages but open to the roof, the stone groining never having been finished. The inner doorway has deep Middle-Pointed mouldings, and very rich iron work on the door itself ramifying into foliage & 2 rings.[5] The windows of the South aisle are of the plainest & earliest Curvilinear work, some of 3 lights – those on the North are of 2 lights, & of finer & rather later tracery. The nave has on each side 3 pointed arches with octagonal pillars, the Northern arches having very fine deep mouldings apparently Middle-Pointed. The beams of the roof are supported on wooden figures & have spandrels. (The Chancel & N. Chancel have roofs flatter than that of the nave[i]).

The Chancel arch is set in the midst of much dead wall & is Early English, on half octagonal shafts having foliated capitals. On the South side is a small doorway placed high up that formerly opened into the rood loft. The Chancel has a Curvilinear East window of 3 lights. The North aisle opens to the Chancel by 2 wide Tudor arches with an octagonal pier & is of late Rectilinear work. To the South Aisle there were once 3 arches, but 2 have been thrown into one in order to admit a large Statue Monument.[8] In this South chancel are some windows of a transition from Early English to Curvilinear & one Rectilinear, also 3 fine ascending Early English sedilia trefoiled, with shafts, having moulded caps & bases – Eastward of which is a similar piscina. Westward of the sedilia is a pointed arch recess. There is in this part a curious painting on the wall.[7] (The painting on the wall in the S. Chancel is difficult to make out – but has figures of the Blessed Virgin – of Kings & several confused figures[i]). (The E. window of this aisle has 3 lancets under a containing arch [*sketch of window here*][i]). There are several large & handsome tombs of the Mordaunts, but of late period.[8] One South of the Altar to John Lord Mordaunt (1550) is very rich – of alabaster & Italian work. The canopy is very lofty & gorgeous & the effigy work preserved.

In the North Chancel is a late Rectilinear tomb of grey marble with pannelled sides – to Sir John Mordaunt & his Lady 1504 – the figures in alabaster – also one of later date to Henry Lord Mordaunt & two wives – the tomb very rich, the effigies & canopy wholly of alabaster. The Font is a magnificent Norman one & has been judiciously cleansed from whitewash – the character is curious & difficult to describe, or convey any notion of without a drawing.[6] (The font has a bowl of cup shape. & 4 large shafts at the angles terminating in fleur de lys which run into the bowl itself[i]).

(The W window of the N. aisle is single & rather elegant – of this form [*sketch of window here*][i])[53]

(In 1848, on revisiting this church I found the interior in decent order & embellished in some measure,[22] since 1830, yet not quite in a satisfactory style. In the Chancel some seats arranged stall-wise, apparently formed out of old materials – the nave crowded with new pews – & in a West gallery an Organ of vast size[i])[24]

Notes 1. For Turvey generally, see Harvey pp.169-238 and *VCH* III pp.109–17; 2. For Charles Longuet Higgins see the *DNB*, a chapter in J.W. Burgon's *Lives of twelve good men* (1888) Vol.2 pp.342–422, and article by C.D.Linnell in *B.Mag* Vol.5 no.37 (Summer 1956) pp.21–7. The Turvey Abbey scrapbook (MIC 84) contains a lot of information on the family and on Turvey people and buildings; 3. The Anglo-Saxon work is described and discussed in H.M. and Joan Taylor *Anglo Saxon architecture* (1965) Vol.II pp.626–7 and in "The Anglo-Saxon Churches of Bedfordshire" by Terence Paul Smith in *BAJ* Vol.3 (1966) pp.7–14; 4. Pevsner pp.158–60, Harvey pp.201–14, *VCH* III pp.115–6, "Turvey church and its monuments" by Charles Longuet Higgins in *AASRP* Vol.6 (1862) pp.279–84, leaflet on *All Saints: Turvey's Parish Church* n.d. [c.1986], and article on Turvey by Geoff Brandwood in *Blue Guide: Churches and Chapels, Southern England* edited by Stephen C. Humphrey (1990) pp.74–5. The contents were recorded by NADFAS in 1995 (Z 837/2); 5. The south door has fine C13th ironwork tentatively attributed to Thomas of Leighton (fl.1294); 6. The font, as noted by Glynne, is a curious and unusual piece. It was sketched by Fisher (Micf 66 FB 398) and in a drawing of c.1840 (slide 2136). Boissier's notes of 1827 (f.373-d) state that the font was "placed in the chancel" and Burgon's sketch of 1734 shows it in this position (Z 50/128/57); 7. The wall paintings are mentioned by Glynne. Some of the paintings were destroyed when the church was restored in 1852-4, but they are briefly described in early C19th notes by John Manson in the Turvey Abbey scrapbook (pp.384–5). The surviving painting in a recess in the south aisle depicts the Crucifixion. Its restoration in 1931 is noted in the register (P 27/1/5) and descriptions appeared in *The Times* 3 Aug.1933 and in the *Burlington Magazine* Vol.58 (1936) p.96; **8.** The Mordaunt tombs are described in Higgins (1862), by Harvey and in the NADFAS survey (Z 837/2). Their present locations are marked on the plan in the current guide or leaflet. For the brasses see Lack *et.al.* (p.98). The notes of the Rev. D.T. Powell, c.1810–2 include details of the memorials (BL ref: Add.Ms. 17456 ff.89-90). The Turvey Abbey scrapbook records the removal of the tombs to new positions in 1810 (pp.117 and pp.385–98) and this is also mentioned by Harvey (p.208). The monuments were restored to their original positions in 1852–4 (account of restoration in HG uncat 9); **9.** Churchwardens' accounts, 1551–2 (Northants.R.O. ref: SS 1808) published in BHRS Vol.69 pp.170–4; **10.** Details of the bells of 1682, 1750, 1815 and 1839 are given by North (p.202–3) who mentions that the metal of the disused sanctus bell was added to the tenor when it was recast in 1815. The saints bell is mentioned in a terrier of 1709 (quoted by Harvey p.196). Writing in about 1790 Oliver St.John Cooper implies that one of the bells in his time was dated 1609 (BL ref: Add.Ms. 34366). A recent survey of the bellframe suggests that it was constructed for five bells in about 1630 (X 586/20/1); **11.** The weathercock dated 1630 was salvaged when the tower was struck by lighting in 1858 and it is now displayed at the back of the church; **12.** The plate was provided under a bequest of Margaret Mordaunt in 1788 (not Ann Mordaunt as stated in the 1841 terrier), but it is actually hallmarked 1791 and signed by the makers Andrew Fogelburg and Steven Gilbert (NADFAS inventory Z 837/2); **13.** The repewing in 1790 is mentioned in Linnell's article in *B.Mag* Vol.5 p.213; **14.** Churchwardens' accounts 1797–1860 (P 27/5/1); **15.** Faculty for a vestry on the north side of the church, with battlements and gothic windows, 1804 (ABF 2 p.93 and ABF 3/207–8); **16.** Harvey (p.203) refers to the destruction of the screen and erection of the altar piece in 1804–5. The altar piece represented the question addressed to our Lord by St.Peter (St.John 21 v.21). It hung over the altar until 1852 when it was removed to the belfry where North (p.203) saw it in 1883; **17.** For a recent biographical account of Richmond see the introduction of "Some unpublished letters of the Revd. Legh Richmond" by Simon Houfe in BHRS Vol.72 (1993) pp.95–115; **18.** The illustrations of the interior with pews and west gallery include watercolours of c.1830 from four different viewpoints (Z 50/128/53–6) and a sketch by J.W. Burgon dated 1834 (Z 50/128/57); **19.** The Mausoleum was erected by faculty in 1825 (ABF 2 p.143 and ABF 3/209–10), and the Higgins family papers include related correspondence (HG 1/13–20) and a sketch in the Turvey Abbey scrapbook (pp.13 and 146); **20.** Boissier (f.373–d); **21.** A letter of 1837 refers to the proposed new organ (HG 12/6/5) and the installation of the organ in 1838 was reported in *BM* 17 March and 29 Dec.1838 and noted in the Turvey Abbey scrapbook (p.381) and in the list of gifts (in P 27/1/5). The organ on the west gallery can be seen in an interior view of the church of c.1840 (Z 50/128/58); **22.** The work of 1844–6 is documented in the accounts (P 27/5/1), vestry minutes (P 27/8/1), advertisement for tenders in *BM* 20 April 1844, Harvey (p.206), and in the accounts by W.A. and Glynne; **23.** The chairs and communion cloth etc. 1846 are mentioned in the list of gifts (in P 27/1/5). The cushions and cloth were given to Stevington church in 1854; **24.** The new organ of 1846 is documented in the list of gifts (in P 27/5/1), Harvey (p.206), and report in *BT* 15 Aug.1846. The family papers include a programme (with specification of the organ) for recitals on the instrument while it was still at the organ builder's works in 1846 (in HG uncat 9). Like the 1838 organ, this instrument was on the west gallery; **25.** Mentioned in the vestry minutes, 1849 (P 27/8/1); **26.** Scott's letter is undated but postmarked 30 March 1852 (HG 12/6/46). It includes a sketch plan of the proposed alterations; **27.** Sources for the church restoration and new fittings of 1852–4 include the detailed accounts by Charles Longuet Higgins (HG uncat 9), a similar account in the parish register (P 27/1/5), and descriptions by Harvey (p.201–8) and by Julian Litten in "Faith or Fantasy: Gothic Revived in Bedfordshire" in *B.Mag* Vol.15 no.113 (Summer 1975) pp.3–7. There are a few sketch plans in the family archives (HG uncat 51). The reopening of the church was reported in *BT* 30 Sept. and 14 Oct.1854 and the work is noted in the BAAS report for 1855 (p.167); **28.** George McHardy, quoted by Pevsner (p.159); **29.** The pulpit and lectern were designed by Scott and given by the Rev. W.B. Russell and by Miss Gorst of Preston, probably in 1854 although Harvey's statement that Russell gave the pulpit when he was Rector may indicate that they were not installed until slightly later. Russell, who read the prayers at the reopening in 1854 (*BT* 14 Oct.1854) did not become Rector until 1856; **30.** The quarry glass is recorded in the NADFAS survey (Z 837/2) and documented in the Powell daybooks for 1853–4 (V&A ref: AAD 1/49 pp.115–7 and 212); **31.** There is a specification of the rebuilt and enlarged organ in *BT* 23 Sept.1854 and the rebuilding is noted in the main accounts of the church restoration (HG uncat 9 and P 27/1/5). Pipework from the 1846 organ was retained and incorporated in the new instrument in 1854; **32.** The alms dish is noted by Higgins (HG uncat 9) and in Harvey. It is not mentioned in Paul Thompson's biography of *William Butterfield* (1971); **33.** The lych gate was designed by Scott and built in 1856 (note in P 27/1/5). An inscription records that it was restored in 1925; **34.** Russell's gift of wooden alms dishes and desk noted in the list of gifts (P 27/1/5); **35.** The lightning strike in 1858 is mentioned by Harvey (p.202) and it was reported in *BM* 26 July 1858; **36.** Scott's plans for the tower are mentioned in the vestry minutes of 1861 (P 27/8/1) but his scheme seems to have been abandoned; **37.** Horsford's work on the tower in 1864 is documented in the vestry minutes (P 27//8/1), accounts (P 27/5/2) and in a report in *BT* 21 June 1864; **38.** A sixth bell was added in 1864 (North p.202 and *BT* 21 June 1864). In 1895–6 one of the bells was rehung. Two trebles were added in 1900 (*BS* 3 Aug and 12 Oct.1900) but the hanging was unsatisfactory and the bells were again rehung (and the tenor recast) in 1906 (P 27/8/2 and notes in P 27/1/5); **39.** Heating system mentioned in vestry minutes, 1864 (P 27/8/1); **40.** Reports of the music festivals can be traced through the BCRO card index to the local news columns of the *Beds. Mercury*. An undated cutting (in ABE 3) refers to Higgins's involvement in the festival, last held in 1877; **41.** The work on the organ in 1886 is mentioned in the list of gifts (P 27/1/5) and reported in *BT* 8 May 1886; **42.** Faculty papers regarding the Longuet Higgins memorial by Armstead, 1887 (HCRO ref: DSA 2/1/211) and report in *BS* 23 July 1887; **43.** Gifts of the table and tapestry noted in the list of gifts (P 27/1/5); **44.** The new heating system was installed in 1891 and there is a copy of the appeal leaflet (in P 27/1/5). Archdeacon Bathurst commented "stove put in without a faculty yet under the advice of the Diocesan Surveyor, Mr.Highton, runs up the tower and cuts into the framework of the bells!!!" (ABE 3); **45.** There was a clock in 1552, but although a clock is listed in terriers from 1709 to 1865 there is virtually no other evidence of its existence. The present clock was put up in 1893 (*BM* 10 June and 12 Aug.1893); **46.** New lamps mentioned in list of gifts to church (P 27/1/5); **47.** Work on the Lady chapel roof noted in the register and in the vestry minutes (P 27/1/5 and P 27/8/2) and reported in *BS* 27 July and 26 Oct.1900. The Rector also corresponded with the SPAB about the repairs (SPAB archives); **48.** Grocock's proposals noted in vestry minutes (P 27/8/2) and the Archdeacon noted in 1910 that the tower had been lately repaired (ABE 3). The work was reported in the Deanery Magazine for July to Oct.1909 (P 80/30/1); **49.** The organ was restored in about 1903 (cutting in ABE 3) and further work was undertaken by Hill in 1924 (notes in P 27/1/5). The organ is mentioned in Clutton and Niland *The British Organ* (Batsford 1963) p.280), and in an article in *The Organ* 1934; **50.** The work was carried out by L.M. Savage, a local builder, under Usher and Anthony in 1934 (*ex.inf.* Mr.Savage, Churchwarden); **51.** Bernard West's work is noted in the leaflet and in the NADFAS inventory (Z 837/2); **52.** Although the accounts of 1822–3 record a payment "for a Terrier" no terrier of 1822 has survived, and so the later terrier of 1841 is published here instead; **53.** Bonney's sketch shows the west window of the north aisle, also sketched by Glynne; **54.** The Richardson inscription was recorded by Thomas Fisher (Micf 66 f.1208); **55.** The glass in the east window mentioned by W.A. was also noted by Harvey (p.202) who states "in 1842 the east window, of three lights, contained some poor modern pieces of stained glass, the only coloured glass in the church"; **56.** The chandelier can be seen in the pre-restoration interior views of the church (Z 50/128/55 and 58). The vestry minutes indicate that it was made secure in 1851 (P 27/8/2).

U

UPPER GRAVENHURST – *see* **Gravenhurst, Upper**

UPPER STONDON – *see* **Stondon**

W

WARDEN, OLD

The parish church was associated with Warden Abbey and the advowson is mentioned in a charter of 1135.[1] There is Norman work in the lower stages of the west tower and possibly in the north wall of the nave. The chancel was rebuilt in the C13th and the arcade of the south aisle dates from the C14th, but the mediaeval fabric has been obscured by later alterations and repairs.[2] The font is of C14th date, and there is some mediaeval glass in one of the north windows of the nave.[3] One of the bells dates from the C14th, another is a late C16th alphabet bell, and others were cast in 1623 and 1653.[4]

In 1617 the chancel was said to be out of repair.[5] In 1669 it was reported that a pulpit cloth was wanting.[6] In 1674 the parish lacked "a Booke of Homileyes and common prayer booke".[7] In 1728 a faculty was granted for a monument to be erected in place of a pew at the west end of the church.[8] This refers to the monument to Sir Samuel Ongley (d.1726) at the back of the church, carved by Scheemakers and Delvaux.[9] In 1787 a faculty was granted for the Ongley vault and mausoleum in the churchyard.[10] The benefice of Old Warden was united with Southill in 1797.[11] The 1822 terrier records that the ancient plate was stolen in March 1821, and the present plate includes a paten dated 1822.[12] When Boissier visited in 1827 he found that the church possessed a small organ.[13] Bonney's order book shows that the chancel was repaired in 1836 by William Henry Whitbread, the patron.

In the early C19th the village of Old Warden was improved in the picturesque style by Robert Henley, Lord Ongley.[14] In 1841–2 he turned his attention to the church. The fabric was repaired, re-roofed, and the whole church was fitted out inside with an amazing display of old woodwork which Ongley had assembled for the purpose.[15] The work included a new gallery on the south side of the church and a tall pulpit and reading desk against the north wall. The floor was paved with encaustic tiles, including those round the old font carrying inscriptions in gothic letters.[16] A new barrel organ was erected in a gallery under the tower in 1842.[17] These alterations are commemorated by a brass plate in the chancel erected by the parishioners in 1844.[18]

The woodwork quickly attracted numerous visitors to the church.[19] A description published in the *Bedford Times* in January 1846 was followed later in that year by W.A.'s account of the building.[20] The original appearance of the woodwork is captured in two detailed views of the interior drawn and published by John Sunman Austin in 1854.[21]

Minor repairs and alterations to the church are recorded in the vestry minutes and accounts.[22] A new stove was obtained in 1866, the woodwork was varnished in 1867, and in 1876 a harmonium was bought by subscription. In 1871 the Old Warden estate was sold to Joseph Shuttleworth whose family afterwards took a great interest in the church. In the 1880s Frank Shuttleworth

41. Old Warden: SE view showing the church before the alterations of 1841–2 and chancel before the east end was rebuilt in 1888–9. *(Watercolour: Thomas Fisher c.1815)*

presented an old pulpit to replace the one put in at the time of Ongley's alterations to the church.[23] In 1887 he gave a new organ and bore the cost of the new organ chamber erected on the north side of the chancel.[24]

In 1888–9 the chancel was restored at the expense of Samuel Whitbread of Southill.[25] The east end was rebuilt and Caroline Shuttleworth paid for the stained glass in the new east window as a memorial to Joseph Shuttleworth (d.1883).[26] Between 1889 and 1913 most of the windows in the church were gradually filled with stained glass as memorials to members of the Shuttleworth family.[27] Caroline Shuttleworth (d.1899) is commemorated in a window on the south side of the chancel and by a lavish memorial designed by C.H. Mabey in the south-east corner of the nave.[28] In 1899 the bells were restored and augmented to six as a permanent memorial of Queen Victoria's Diamond Jubilee.[4] A vestry was built on the north side of the church in 1901 to the designs of Charles Hodgson Fowler of Durham.[29]

Later work included repairs to the tower and south aisle in 1935,[30] restoration of the mediaeval glass in 1935,[3] the erection of a new south porch in memory of Richard Ormonde Shuttleworth in 1952,[31] and extensive repairs to the fabric under Richardson and Houfe from 1955–6.[32] A new oak eagle lectern was presented by Dorothy Shuttleworth in 1958.[33] Sadly, much of the carved woodwork was stolen in March 1997.

42. Old Warden: Interior view looking west, showing the church as fitted out with carved wood-work by Lord Ongley in 1841–2. When the chancel was restored in 1888–9 the brattishing on top of the panelling, the finials from the altar rails and the traceried panels in the windows were removed. Notice the organ gallery and Ongley monument at the west end of the nave

(Lithograph: John Sunman Austin 1854)

1. Extract from glebe terrier, 5th July 1822 [Southill cum Warden] [11]

WARDEN.

Church yard. Item the Church Yard containing One Acre and thirty seven poles bounded on the North, East and West by Land belonging to Lord Ongley and on the South by a Road leading to Warden Wood, the fences on all the sides belonging thereto are maintained by the Parish.

Church. Belonging to the said parish are first the Parish Church, an ancient building containing in Length with the Chancel Seventy five feet, in breadth forty feet, the Chancel in Length thirty feet, in breadth twenty three feet Six inches within the walls, the Steeple twenty feet square within the walls, in height Sixty two feet.

Furniture and ornaments. Within and belonging thereto are one Communion Table with a Covering for the same of Green Cloth. Also one linen Cloth for the same with two Napkins. Also two pewter Flaggons.[12] In the Month of March 1821 a Silver Sacramental Cup and Salver which belonged to this Parish were stolen and have not yet been replaced.[12] One pulpit and Reading desk, one Bible of the last translation and two large Common Prayer Books. Four Bells with their frames,[4] the first or least Bell being two feet five Inches diameter with this inscription "Miles Gray made me 1653". The second two feet Eight Inches with the Alphabet in large character thereon. The third three feet with H.V.D.R.O.S.H.P.G. thereon. The fourth three feet two Inches and an half with this inscription "God save our King 1623". One Bier, one hearse Cloth, one surplice.

Parish Registers. There are three Parchment Registers belonging to the Parish of Warden one beginning in 1576 and ending 1719 complete, the second beginning in 1720 and ending in 1813 complete, the third continued from that period to the present time according to the Act of Parliament of that year.

Seats in the Church. The Seats in the Church have been repaired for time immemorial at the Public expence of the Parish.

Parish Clerk & Sexton. There is also due to the Parish Clerk and Sexton for every funeral and making a Grave two shillings, for publication of Banns two shillings, Marriages three shillings and sixpence, by Licence five shillings, Churching of Women Sixpence. He receive an Annual Stipend from the Church Wardens in lieu of Parish dues exclusive of those enumerated.

Poor House and School. There has also been built on this Estate a Poor House to which is attached a Garden, and also a new School Stud Clay and tile with a yard belonging.

2. Archdeacon Bonney's historical notices of churches, c.1820–1840

WARDEN, St. Leonard. This Church consists of a Nave and South Aisle separated by octagonal Piers and obtuse angled Arches a Chancel and Tower at the West End & South Porch. Character of the Fabrick is perpendicular [*written over* decorated]. In a North window of the Nave are two Effigies in glass – one of them an Abbot in the dress of his Order, kneeling, in the attitude of prayer, a crosier over his Shoulder, & his garment White.[3] A W crowned with a ducal Coronet is in the Window, and from his Mouth proceed this Legend "Cliftone Walter; rogo Martha ... ... voco." There is another mutilated effigy represented in glass under a rich Canopy, it is dressed in green Garments.

This occurs in a South East Window [*Sketch of crowned M motif*].

This Church has recently been fitted up with rich old Carved Oak at the Expence of Lord Ongley.[15]

3. Archdeacon Bonney's visitation notebook, 1823–1839

WARDEN. This Church consists of a Nave and South Aisle – a Tower at the West End of the Nave and Chancel at the East End thereof.

At the Visitation of 1823. It was ordered that a new Cloth Covering for the Communion Table be purchased. The Communion Table & Rails be cleansed and oiled; The Creed, Lords Prayer, and Ten Commandments be set up; The Earth moved from the Walls of the Church and Chancel; the Open Seats to be made even; the Walls of the Church and Chancel be pointed & the Buttresses be repaired; The Stonework of the Windows and doors be restored with Parker's Cement; the West window of the South Aisle be restored with Stone; the Woodwork under the Arch between the Church and Chancel be removed; the Old Flagon be disposed of and a new plated Flagon purchased; and also a deep Plate for the Alms.[12]

At the Visitation of 1826. No further order was given.

At the Visitation of 1833. It was ordered that the Stone Work of the Chancel Windows & North East Buttress thereof be restored.

At the Visitation of 1836 – no order required – Mr Whitbread having thoroughly repaired the Chancel on the Exterior, & given orders for the restoration of the interior.

At the Visitation 1839 Ordered the Church Wardens to repair the flashing on the South Aisle – and when the Walls are cleaned to adopt a light drab stone colour to cleanse the heads & woodwork of the Roof from all wash and leave them their natural Colour – to repair the tiling on the Tower – and attend to the state of the Bells.[4]

4. Article on the Church by W.A. (no.39), NM 26 December 1846

WARDEN, St. Leonard. The rich man's duty to contribute liberally to the building, repairing, beautifying, and adorning of churches*, has in the instance of this church been most effectually performed.[14] The solemn air, and the grateful impression which the mind of the spectator receives on his entrance form a striking contrast to the chilling effect produced by masses of whitewash, and the appearance of neglect and decay. The rich decorations, the costly specimens of carving,[15] and the delightful order which prevail throughout this elaborately ornamented building, render it one of the bright spots among the miserably neglected churches of the county. We hope that the example will have ere long many followers, "in an age wherein many of our churches, if by no other causes, yet by bare length of time, are become so far decayed as to stand in need, either of being wholly rebuilt, or else very much repaired." Where the noble desire to render this House of Prayer worthy of the purpose for which it is intended has been so unbegrudgingly carried out, it is not without reluctance that we touch upon any blemished, but as honest chroniclers we must be permitted a few remarks which occurred on our inspection. We were sorry to see, beautifully decorated as they are, enclosed pews. Their selfish appearance detracts considerably both from the effect of the interior, and the pleasure derived from the general aspect. The singing gallery with the organ,[17] as well as shutting out the western window, protrude most unpleasantly. In so small a building, surely the well-trained choir of this parish could easily spare the instrument. Relieved from this and the gallery, the effect would be greatly improved. The pulpit and reading desk occupy sorry positions.[15] By the abolition of the latter puritanical introduction, and placing the pulpit in its right quarter, space would be gained possibly sufficient to obviate the necessity for the enclosed pews in the chancel, always objectionable; but if sittings must be in that portion of the church, stalls would be far less offensive, and in a great degree remove the indecorum of the back of the occupant being turned to the Altar. And we would most earnestly wish that the monument in a Roman dress could be removed to the sculpture gallery;[9] here it is sadly out of keeping. The following passage from a writer+ who has paid much attention to monumental sculpture, is far more impressive on this subject than any we could use in speaking of the monuments of bygone days. "There were no such things as statues; no figures, sedentary or upright; no action, no representation of active life, of motion; repose was the thing to be expressed; death or sleep as symbolical of death; the figures were always recumbent, and this general rule is without exception. To represent a man as a prostrate, dependent being in the hands of his Maker was the sculptor's aim, not man in the pride of life, in the hour of his grandest action, in the stir and success of religious life, in the moving accidents of field and flood. No English orators with Roman togas, flourishing their stony hands in mockery of oratorical triumphs once won in the Commons House of Parliament, "bishops, soldiers, and civilians, stretched out in that long sleep which comes alike to all, and which all monuments should remind us of; all are represented as bowing to the common sentence of death, forcible reminding the living not of fights, intrigues, speeches, political debates, but of the end of the pride of life."

Deeply shall we regret that any remarks which we have been induced to make, shall appear, in the slightest degree, to detract from the tribute of respect, however humble, we most earnestly desire to offer to the noble author of the beautiful and costly improvement which this church has received at his hands, and who has left a memorial of his deeds, in the spirit of that "high philosophy, which tells him he has not given in vain."

December 19th, 1846.   W.A.

* Edward Wells, D.D.   + Rev. J. Armstrong

Notes **1.** Account of Warden Abbey in *VCH* I pp.361–6; **2.** Pevsner pp.130–1, *VCH* III pp.254–5, and Don Hills *The Parish Church of St.Leonard, Old Warden* n.d. (reprinted c.1991); **3.** The mediaeval glass is said to have come from the Abbey. It is described by Bonney and it is illustrated in a drawing dated 1839 (X 254/88/259). It was restored in 1935 (P 105/2/2/5 and Hills p.6); **4.** The bells are listed in the 1822 terrier and details are given by North (p.203). The tenor was recast in 1840 in compliance with Bonney's orders, and in 1899 the bells were restored and augmented to six (P 105/2/2/2); **5.** Presentment, 1617 (ABC 5 p.214); **6.** Archdeacon's visitations, 1669 (ABC 7); **7.** Archdeacon's visitations, 1674 (CRT 170/9/1 p.11); **8.** Faculty citation for the Ongley monument, 1728 (ABF 3/211); **9.** The monument of Sir Samuel Ongley (d.1728) is signed by "P. Chiemaker en L.Delvaux" and it is by Laurent Delvaux and Peter Scheemakers (Gunnis p.126). W.A. considered such a monument "sadly out of keeping" and suggested that it should be removed to a sculpture gallery; **10.** Faculty for the burial vault for Robert Henley Ongley, 1787 (ABF 2 p.45 and ABF 3/212–3); **11.** Union of benefices of Southill and Warden, 1797 (P 105/2/1/1). Both livings belonged to the Whitbread family of Southill and they remained united until separate incumbents were appointed in the 1880s; **12.** The plate listed in the 1927 schedule (ABE 5) consists of a paten hallmarked 1822–3 (replacing the one stolen in 1821) and a cup of 1903–4; **13.** Boissier (f.434d); **14.** For the Ongleys see "The Ongleys of Warden Park" by Joyce Godber in *B.Mag* Vol.6 no.48 (Spring 1959) pp.291–4 and "Old Warden and the Ongleys" by Sylvia Woods (unpublished BCRO exhibition handout). There is no documentation on Ongley's village improvements or on the work at the church in the surviving family papers; **15.** The woodwork (before the loss of many of the carved pieces in 1997) and its origins are described by Hills (*passim*) and by Pevsner (pp.130–1), and in "Woodcarvings in two Bedfordshire churches" [Old Warden and Cockayne Hatley] by John Lea, in *Beds.Mag*. Vol.2 no.14 (Autumn 1950) pp.225–8. On liturgical grounds W.A. objected to the gallery, pulpit and desk, and organ. The pulpit was later replaced; **16.** The tiles can be seen in Austin's 1854 views of the interior (Z 50/129/37–8). Round the font is the inscription "Suffer little children to come unto me and forbid / them not, for of such is the kingdom of God" in gothic lettering in yellow letters on blue tiles; **17.** The barrel organ was supplied by Gray in 1842 to the order of Lord Ongley (Boston and Langwill *Church and Chamber Barrel–Organs* (Edinburgh 1967) p.73). The instrument must have failed, as in 1876 the parish bought a new harmonium for the church (P 105/8/1); **18.** The plate in the south side of the chancel is inscribed "September 1844 – Old Warden. This church was thoroughly repaired and beautified and the galleries and organ were erected in the years 1841 and 1842 under the entire direction and at the sole expense of the Right Honourable Robert Henley Lord Ongley and during the repairs owing to his judicious and thoughtful arrangements divine service was not omitted even for a single day. Not any notice having been recorded of the above facts the parishioners thought it right thus to engrave them together with the name of the noble individual to whom they are so much indebted, and who with such great judgment without the least ostentation expended his substance for the glory of his God and to the benefit of his fellow creatures"; **19.** There are visitors books 1845–85 (P 105/28/1); **20.** Article on the village in *BT* 10 Jan.1846; **21.** Austin's views, 1854 (Z 50/129/37–8); **22.** Vestry minutes 1857–1920 (P 105/8/1) and churchwardens' accounts 1874–1941 (P 105/5/1); **23.** The pulpit was bought in Edinburgh in the 1880s (Hills p.7). Bathurst noted in 1905 that the pulpit had been "moved to north east corner of nave" (ABE 3); **24.** The gift of the new organ is mentioned in the vestry minutes for 1888 (P 105/8/1) and it was reported in *BS* and *BT* 20 Aug.1887; **25.** The vestry minutes refer to the restoration of the chancel in 1888–9 (P 105/8/1) but no other documentary information has been found; **26.** The stained glass commemorates Joseph Shuttleworth who died in 1883 but it was put up after the present tracery was put in the new east window of 1888–9. The gift of the window was reported in *Beds. Express* 27 April 1889; **27.** The stained glass windows are described by Hills. There is a faculty for the stained glass window in the chancel in memory of the Rev. Robert Lang, 1910 (HCRO ref: DSA 2/1/189); **28.** Bathurst in 1905 noted the "Beautiful alabaster monument to Mrs.Shuttleworth" (ABE 3); **29.** Plans and specifications for vestry etc, by Charles Hodgson Fowler of Wood, Fowler and Oakley, architects, Durham, 1901 (X 428/4); **30.** Faculty, 1935 (P 105/2/2/5); **31.** There is a drawing of the proposed porch (SL 5/178), and faculty and related papers 1949–1952 (P 105/2/2/8–9); **31.** Papers concerning repairs, 1955–6 (P 105/2/2/11–7); **33.** Faculty for the lectern, 1958 (P 105/2/2/19).

WESTONING

The chancel, nave and aisles of the present church were built in the Decorated style in the C14th, but some C12th carved stones from the previous building have been built into masonry. The south porch also dates from the C14th. In the C15th the west tower was added, the aisle walls were heightened and the body of the church was re-roofed. There is a C13th font from the earlier church, and the lower parts of a C15th rood screen remain in their original position.[1]

The Edwardian Inventory of 1552 lists the plate and valuables and states that "the churche chauncell steple and porche" were "all covered with leed".[2] In 1629 William Rawlins left money for "a cloth and carpet for the communion table and a long cushion and a faire pulpit cloth",[3] insisting that the pulpit cloth should have his name on it. In 1672 the four mediaeval bells were augmented to five by the addition of a treble.[4] New plate was provided in 1685.[5]

One of the bells was recast in 1722.[4] From 1743 expenditure on the church is recorded in the churchwardens' accounts.[6] The book begins with the recasting of two bells by Thomas Russell of Wootton in 1743.[4] In 1753 the pulpit was painted and a new pulpit cloth and cushion were provided.[7] Repairs to the leadwork on the roof were carried out in 1779–81 at a cost of some £32. The leaded spire was repaired in 1785 and the accounts record a gift of sixpence to "the workmen having a difficult job at the steeple".[8] Further roof repairs were done between 1787 and 1795. In 1799 the ten commandments were set up in the chancel arch.[9] The bells were rehung by John Farmer in 1805 and in 1807–9 repairs costing £35 were carried out by Messrs. Drew and Carte.[10] In 1810 the church clock was repaired or replaced.[11] In 1812 a new paten dated 1777 was added to the plate.[5] In about 1815 "a rough temporary gallery" was built with the name of the churchwarden, William Woodward, painted on the front.[12] The accounts also mention a robbery at the church in 1822.

Here at Westoning the evidence in the contemporary sources fits together especially well in showing how Archdeacon Bonney's orders were implemented. The accounts refer to getting the church ready for his visitation,[13] and the volume contains a note on the laws regarding pews and the duties of churchwardens entered "by order of the Archdeacon" in 1825. Several of the furnishings listed in the 1825 terrier had been replaced or repaired in response to Bonney's orders, and in 1824–5 repairs to the church were carried out at a cost of £87.[14] This included the enlargement of the west gallery. The later accounts refer to the purchase of new hassocks in 1828–9,[15] the recasting of the third bell in 1829,[4] repairs by William Hindes in 1837–8 and minor work in 1850.[16]

In 1857 the church was completely restored under William Slater at a cost of £1757. The work involved repairs to the stonework and roofs, a new roof on the chancel, the addition of a vestry and a new stair turret on the tower. The

43. Westoning: SE view. The roofline on the tower indicates the appearance of the church before the present roof was erected in the C15th. The chancel roof was raised to a steeper pitch when the church was restored in 1857.   *(Watercolour: Thomas Fisher c.1815)*

west gallery and the decalogue boards in the chancel arch were also taken down at the time of the restoration.[17]

Further work on the church took place in 1893 after an appeal was launched to meet the cost of repairs and improvements.[18] Lamps were provided "to make evening service possible", the stonework was repaired in 1893 by Samuel Foster of Kempston, and in 1894 the bells were rehung in a new frame.[19] At the same time chancel improvements were undertaken by J.G. Coventry Campion who in 1895 placed stained glass in the east window in memory of his parents.[20] In 1903 a further stained glass window was placed in the south aisle. One of the bells was recast in 1903 and in 1923 a sixth bell was added.[4] The oak eagle lectern was presented by Mrs. Newland in 1908.[20] More recently, a major programme of restoration to the fabric was completed in 1996.[21]

1. Extract from glebe terrier, 24 June 1825
WESTONING.
Church yard. Item the churchyard containing three roods by estimation, bounded by the land of John Everitt Everitt Esquire on the North and West, by the Public Road on the East, and by the Vicarage premises on the South, railed and paled on the North and East at the expence of the Parish, the West fence is a quick set hedge belonging to John Everitt Everitt Esquire, the South fence is maintained at the expence of the Vicar, the gates thereof made by the

Parish. There is a public foot path through the church yard.

Church. Belonging to the said parish are first the parish church an ancient building containing in length within the walls 92 feet in length, the body of the church 46 feet in length, 38 feet in breadth, the length of the chancel is 33 feet, the breadth 17 feet, the steeple is 63 feet high, 13 feet long and 11 feet broad.

Furniture and ornaments. Within and belonging to which one communion table and a covering for the same of blue cloth,[3] likewise another of linen and two napkins. Two surplices, a flaggon plated,[5] a silver cup, & paten, a pewter bason for the offertory, an iron chest for the registers & other parish documents,[22] 3 wooden chests, one pulpit and reading desk, one pulpit cushion covered with blue cloth,[7] one large bible of the last translation,[23] two large common prayer books.[24] The book of homilies. The ten commandments.[9] One church clock.[11] Five bells with their frames,[4] the diam[r]. of the first bell is two feet five inches & a half, of the second is two feet eight inches, of the third bell is two feet ten inches & a half, of the fourth bell is three feet one inch & a half, of the fifth bell is three feet five inches & a half. A bier. A hearse cloth.[25]

Parish Registers. A parchment register book beginning 1563 ending 1723,[26] another beginning 1724 ending 1793, another beginning 1793 ending 1812, another of marriages beginning 1754 ending 1802, another register of marriages beginning 1802 ending 1812, likewise 3 register books for baptisms, marriages, & funerals respectively, according to the statute, beginning 1813, and also a register for banns beginning 1824.

Seats in the Church. The seats in the body of the church repaired by the parish, those in the chancel by the Rector. There is also a gallery erected by William Woodward Churchwarden for the use of the singers enlarged last year for the use of the Sunday School.[12]

Parish Clerk. There is also due to the Parish Clerk from the Parish two guineas per annum. For every funeral two shillings, for every marriage by banns two shillings and sixpence, banns one shilling, for every marriage by licence five shillings, for a woman's churching sixpence.

2. Archdeacon Bonney's historical notices of churches, c.1820–1840

WESTONING, St. Mary Magdalen. This church consists of a Nave, aisles separated by large octagonal Piers and lofty pointed Arches with plain Mouldings, Chancel, & Tower at the West End, on which is a short leaden Spire.[8] The Font is circular on a circular Base. The general Character of the Church is early decorated.

On the Chalice is this Inscription "George Whittimore John Dix Churchwardens of Westoning in Bedfordshire 1685".[5]

3. Archdeacon Bonney's visitation notebook, 1823–1839

WESTONING. This Church consists of a Nave, North and South Aisles, a Tower at the West End of the Nave and Chancel at the East End thereof.

At the Visitation of 1823,[13] The following Order was given that – the third Bell be recast in the Course of three years;[4] a blue Cloth Covering for the Communion Table be purchased,[3] and also a plated Flagon;[5] the Seats be made Oak colour – The long Seats be taken up, made even, repaired, & set down again & oiled; the same be done to the Pulpit and Reading desk; The Earth be moved from the Walls of the Church & proper drainage be made.[14]

At the Visitation of 1826. It was ordered that the Stonework of the Cornices, Doors, and Windows of the Tower be restored with Parker's Cement – & new Weather boards be placed in the Windows.

At the Visitation of 1833 The following Order was given, that, a new Font Bason be purchased – the Windows of the Bellchamber be restored with Cement – the Fence of the Church Yard be repaired.

At the Visitation of 1836 Ordered that the Windows of Bell Chamber, Church Yard Fence, and timbers of the North Aisle be repaired[16] – also that the Pulpit Cloth & Covering of the cushion be turned and cleansed.

At the Visitation 1839. Ordered, the Communion Table to be oiled, the Gallery to be painted to suit the Seats – The Clerk's Prayer Book to be repaired.[24] The Tower to be put into Substantial repair, particularly the Bellchamber Windows and Roof. The steps before the Communion Table to be set even – & the Parish Chest to be set on Feet to secure the things kept in it from damp.

4. Article on the Church by W.A. (no.8), NM 2 August 1845

WESTON ING. This church was in a very neglected state;[27] the dirty condition which it exhibited, and for which there can be no excuse, must disgust every one, even those who are indifferent to Church architecture. It seemed in character with the dirty chancel, and stagnant water, which you pass in your way from the high road to the Church. White washing, however, had not been neglected, and it had been so perseveringly applied that the mouldings were nearly obliterated. In the porch especially this was the case, where the windows, apparently very good specimens, had been bricked up. Why this was done we are at a loss to conjecture, more especially as there is a miserable wooden gate to prevent the

> "Offering a sunny place to them
> Who deck the house of worship."

The wooden roof remained, but a gallery of the most unsightly description ran along the whole of the western entrance The arch was boarded up, the western light, of course, excluded. The originator of this disfigurement had thought so well of his work as to record his name.[12] There were none of the original sittings left, but the "lidless boxes" prevailed over them, one of which almost entirely excluded an apparently very good niche. The font was

painted. The chancel was in as dirty condition as the rest of the building. The wooden roof remained, the crown of the arch had been boarded up, for the purpose it is presumed of placing in the wrong situation, the ten command-ments, &c., badly executed.[9] Over the centre of the miserable communion table, some former incumbent had had the bad taste to erect a tablet in mem-ory of himself and wife.[28] We hope the Venerable Archdeacon, on his next vis-itation, will order it to be removed. There were two large pews in the chancel not much better, and equally offensive as the other boxes for which this por-tion of the sacred edifice appeared to be the receptacle. The lead on the roof had not been removed. The Church–yard was in a neglected state.
July 29th 1845

Notes **1.** Pevsner pp.161–2, *VCH* III pp.453–4, and Bernard Anderson *Parish Church of St.Mary Magdalene, Westoning* (1997); **2.** Eeles and Brown pp.9–10; **3.** Memorandum in parish register, 1629 (P 16/1/2). The 1629 pulpit cushion was replaced in 1753 (note 7) and in 1824 the parish bought a new "blue cloth for communion table" from Mr.Mellor (£2 15s), as ordered by the Archdeacon; **4.** Details of the bells are given by North (p.204). There were four bells in 1552 and so the treble dated 1672 was probably an addition. The bell of 1722 was recast in 1903. The recasting of the second and tenor bells in 1743 is fully documented in the accounts (P 16/5/1), as are the rehanging of the bells by John Farmer (£23 5s) in 1805 and the recasting of the third (as ordered by Bonney in 1823) by Mears in 1829; **5.** According to the *VCH* and the modern sched-ule (ABE 5), the plate includes a cup (hallmarked 1655 but inscribed and dated 1685 as noted by Bonney), flagon and alms dish of 1685, a paten (hallmarked 1777) acquired in 1812, and a paten of 1876. The accounts (P 16/5/1) record the purchase of a new plated flagon (Rev.Mr. Pearse £1 15s 6d) in 1824 in compliance with Bonney's visitation orders; **6.** Churchwardens' accounts 1743–1841 and 1841–94 (P 16/5/1–2); **7.** The new pulpit cloth and cushion of 1753 probably replaced those of 1629. The accounts for 1753 record payments for the new pulpit cloth (£4 3s), and "A Piller and Feathers for the Coshen and Making" (7s) (P 16/5/1); **8.** The accounts record payments of about £18 to John Carte (plumber), Thomas Stanbridge (carpenter), and William Wildman (bricklayer) for work on the steeple in 1785 (P 16/5/1); **9.** The churchwardens paid "John Carte's bill for Erecting the Ten Commandments & other repairs for the church" (£20 13s 4½d) in 1799 (P 16/5/1). As noted by W.A. and in the appeal leaflet for the 1857 restoration (BS 601) the commandments were painted on a partition in the chancel arch; **10.** Payments to Mr.Drew (£13 3s 10d) and Mr.Carte (£22 3s) 1807–8 (P 16/5/1); **11.** A clock is listed in the 1708 terrier but there is no mention in the churchwardens' accounts until 1809. It seems that the clock was restored or renewed in 1810 by Thomas Hardwick of Ridgmont. It is mentioned in the accounts for 1842, but it was probably removed when the tower was restored in 1857; **12.** The ICBS papers (LPL ref: ICBS 5056) mention "a rough temporary gallery put up without a faculty about 35 years ago" and the descriptions in the terrier and by W.A. suggest that it bore the name of William Woodward as churchwarden. He held office from 1810 to 1835. The gallery was enlarged in 1824 as indicated by the terrier; **13.** Payment for cleaning "when the Archdeacon came to inspect the church" 1823 (P 16/5/1); **14.** The accounts (P 16/5/1) record payments in 1824–5 to Mr. Stanbridge, Mr. Taylor, and to Mrs. Rees for work in the church and the total cost of the work was later given as £87 (LPL ref: ICBS 5056). Mrs Rees was paid "for painting the pews seats & the two Ends of the gallery and Repairing the Church windows" but the other pay-ments in the accounts give no detailed information on what was done; **15.** Payments to George Rich for 18 Hassocks (£1 3s) in 1828, and for a long hassock in the chancel before the altar (15s.) in 1829 (P 16/5/1); **16.** Bill of William Hindes for repairs to church and churchyard (£16 1s 4d) in 1837–8 (P 16/5/3), and payments in accounts to W.Hinde (£9 16s 8d) and Mr.Sheard (£12 10s 3d) 1850 (P 16/5/2); **17.** Sources for the restoration in 1857 include memoranda and minutes in the account book (P 16/5/2), appeal leaflet with print showing Slater's impressions of the restored interior Jan.1857 (BS 601 and X 254/88/262), a ground plan by Slater (at the church), the ICBS papers (including a plan) 1826–8 (LPL ref: ICBS 5056), and reports in *BT* 31 Oct. and 7

Nov.1857, *The Builder* 7 Nov.1857 p.645, and AASRP p.244; **18.** Appeal leaflet and accounts regarding the work of 1892–4 (P 16/2/2/1–2 and P 16/5/2). Archdeacon Bathurst (ABE 3) also refers to the repairs done in 1893; **19.** Papers concerning the rehanging of the bells, 1894 (P 16/2/2/1), including plans of the new bellframe; **20.** The stained glass of 1895 and 1905 and the new lectern of 1908 are mentioned in Kelly's *Directory* 1914 (p.184); **21.** The recent repairs are described in detail by Anderson pp.18–9; **22.** The iron chest was purchased (£2) in 1823 (P 16/5/1); **23.** The Church bible was bought (£1 10s) in 1765 and the accounts record a payment to "Mr.Franklin new binding bible" (£1 7s 6d) in 1831–2 (P 16/5/1); **24.** The churchwardens bought a "New Common Prayer book" (£1 1s) in 1777 and another one (£2 3s) in 1812 (P 16/5/1). In 1846 Mr.Dodd of Woburn received 6s.6d. for repairing a prayer book (P 16/5/2); **25.** A "Black cloth for town burials" was bought (1s) in 1754–5, and a Mr.May of Ampthill supplied a "new paull" (£3 6s) in 1808–9 (P 16/5/1); **26.** This volume is incomplete. The section for 1595–1653 must have been missing for some time as a gap is noted in the *Parish Register Abstract* (1831); **27.** The remark is surprising considering the level of upkeep and care evident from the other sources; **28.** In a letter in *NM* 30 August 1845 J.D. Parry took exception of W.A's comment about the memorial tablet. Parry assumed that the Rev. R.H. Whitehurst was the subject of the tablet concerned and wrote in defence of the latter's character, describing his good works. In a post-script to the Ridgmont article in *NM* 6 Sept.1845 W.A. admitted his error in implying that the tablet had been erected during the incumbent's lifetime but stated that Parry was in error of having assumed he was referring to Whitehurst's memorial. He maintained his view that "nothing can justify the position the tablet occupies".

WHIPSNADE

This list of incumbents at Whipsnade goes back to 1220, but the original church has been entirely rebuilt. The tower, built in brick in the late C16th, incorporates a re-used west door of c.1480.[1] The old bellframe was probably contemporary with the tower and one of the bells was dated 1630.[2] In 1674 the steeple was reported to be "out of repair" and there was no church bible.[3]

The body of the church was rebuilt in the classical style in 1719 at the expense of Thomas Vaux.[4] It had no chancel. The new church consisted of a simple brick nave with north and south doors and round-headed windows. The north door has a rusticated surround. Some of the surviving fittings came from the old church in 1719. These included the Jacobean pulpit and sounding board,[5] the C17th altar rails and the painted royal arms which are of Stuart origin.[6] The arms were later altered to show the Hanoverian arms, probably when the church was rebuilt, and the painted decalogues may also date from about 1719.[7] There is now a small panel of C18th Flemish glass in a window in the chancel. Two of the bells were recast in 1740.[2] A Book of Homilies was purchased or re-bound in 1780.[8]

Bonney's order book refers to the need for minor repairs in the 1820s and 1830s. There are several references to the font.[9] Its position must have been resolved by 1847 when W.A. noted that a font of "poor modern manufacture" had been provided. W.A. also describes the use of the east end of the church as a chancel and mentions the pulpit and desk which were on the north side of the church.[10]

In 1859 the Rev. J.C. Orlebar called in the architect E.C. Hakewill to report on the state of the church and prepare plans for restoration and enlargement.[11] The result was that in 1860 a new brick chancel and apse were added and the

44. Whipsnade: NW view showing the C16th west tower with its original belfry windows and the body of the church as rebuilt in 1719   *(Watercolour: Thomas Fisher c.1815)*

church was re-seated and repaired. New plate was provided.[12] At some time in the second half of the C19th the original belfry windows on three sides of the tower were replaced with round-headed brick openings.[13]

Between 1873 and 1894 Archdeacon Bathurst noted the need for further restoration work,[14] eventually completed in 1898–9 when the parish spent £118 on unspecified repairs.[15] In 1904 Bathurst noted that the church was "in substantial repair".[14] Further repairs were undertaken in 1913 when the paint was removed from the pulpit, altar rails and table, and part of the tower which had "fallen due to weather" was repaired.[16]

The tower was restored in 1949–50 under Professor Richardson.[17] A major programme of repairs was completed between 1974 and 1979,[18] and in 1980 the three old bells were taken down and replaced by a new ring of six.[2]

1. Extract from glebe terrier, 28 June 1822
WHIPSNADE.

Church yard. The Church Yard contains One Acre and ten Poles adjoining to the Lands of David Batchelar on the South and West, to Whipsnade Green on the North, and to the Rectory Garden and Home Close on the East. The Fences are made by the Rector and the Gate and Stile by the Parish.

Church and Furniture. The church contains in length fifty one feet and in breadth twenty two feet. There are three Bells,[2] one large Bible, two Prayer Books, one Surplice, Six Register Books containing Entries of Baptizms,

Marriages and Burials, the earliest commencing 1682. The Church is repaired at the common charge of the parish.

Parish Clerk. The Parish Clerk is appointed by the Rector who hath for his [salary] the sum of Four pounds Yearly paid him by the Churchwarden Besides his accustomed Fees (viz[t].) for every Funeral Four Shillings, for every Christening Six Pence, for every Marriage by Licence Five Shillings, by Banns Two Shillings and six, and for every Publication of Banns Six Pence.

Churchwarden. There is one Churchwarden who is chosen by the Rector.

2. Archdeacon Bonney's historical notices of churches, c.1820–1840

WHIPSNADE, St. Mary Magdalen. This is a brick Church, consisting of Nave & Chancel under one roof & a Tower at the West End. The latter may lay claim to the perpendicular Character, the former to that of a Style prevailing at the Early part of the 18th Century. It was rebuilt in 1736.[4]

3. Archdeacon Bonney's visitation notebook, 1823–1839

WHIPSNADE. This Church consists of a nave, with a Chancel at the East End, & Tower at the West End thereof.

At the Visitation of 1823 The following Order was given that the Font[9] be placed at the Corner of a Seat on the North side near the Door, made of Totternhoe Stone, according to the pattern given; The floor near the Communion Table be repaired – The Brasses of the Bells be renewed – the floor of the Bellchamber and the Steeple be repaired.

At the Visitation of 1826. It was ordered that the font be placed near the Clerk's Desk.[9]

At the Visitation of 1833 It was ordered that a new woollen Cloth be purchased for the Communion Table – a small stone Font be placed on the South Side of the Communion Rails, the Bellropes be repaired.

At the Visitation of 1836. Ordered that the South Door be repaired; the Surplice be renewed, if it cannot be put in order. The Minister's Prayer Book be repaired if it be possible, and the leaves made smooth, if not a new PB be procured, of the same size.

At the Visitation 1839 ordered the Churchwardens to set up a proper Font[9] – and accommodation for kneeling in the Free sittings to be furnished – The Floor of the Second Loft of Tower & the Tiling upon a Buttress of the Tower, a ridge Tile at the East End, a Bracket on the Pulpit & the Doors of the Tower & North side the Church to be repaired – The South Door (being quite useless) may be stopped up and the Font set near it.[10]

4. Article on the Church by W.A. (no.72), NM 4 September 1847

WHIPSNADE, St. Mary Magdelen. In this church, a very humble building, there is now no separation of chancel and nave; most probably it was not so originally. The chancel part has a plastered ceiling, and all around it has the same coating. A very small altar table is hemmed in by two large enclosed boxes, which must totally prevent the occupants of the humble sittings obtaining a view of the clergyman when he is performing the service.[10]

The flooring is of common tiles, rather better arranged than usual. The porch doors are quite closed; entrance is obtained by a door in the tower, which is in a dirty condition.

Pulpit,[5] reading desk, and clerk's pew packed one over the other,[10] but if we recollect right, a horrid sounding-board, the invention of a barbarous period, was not added to complete the ugly picture.

The western window is closed by a common lath and plaster preparation. The entrance for the congregation is through a mean door, hardly high enough for a tall man to pass through without stooping.

The font is a poor modern manufacture;[9] bad as it is, no use is made of it. The roof is tiled. The churchyard is accessible.

There is no school; it is melancholy to reflect on the neglect in this respect, which prevails too generally in this county. We are well aware of the opposition to the promotion of education by those whose means and situation ought to render them happy and willing assistants in so good a cause – but we fear in this county, whatever may be the cause in others, there is a class above the labouring, who sadly stand in need of the schoolmaster. Until this generation of ignorance has passed away or become wiser, the epithet applied at educational meetings of 'Poor Bedfordshire,' will still be deserved.

The church is surrounded by a beautiful village green; it was with deep regret we heard there was reason to fear it would not exist long, but fall into an enclosure. The words of the poet will soon cease to have any reality:–

> 'Twilight's soft dews steal o'er the village green
> With magic tints to harmonise the scene.'
> While the following will thus become too true –
> 'All, all are fled, nor mirth nor music flows,
> To chase the dreams of innocent repose.'

30 August 1847   W.A.

5. Sir Stephen Glynne's Church notes, before 1840 (Vol.1, pp.8–9)

WHIPSNADE. This small Church though in a very pleasing situation is a most uninteresting structure. There is only one aisle & a Western Tower, all of brick work – the body very plain & without any pretensions to architecture.[4] The Tower appears to be of about the age of Elizabeth, much resembling of Acton, & Chelsea old Church. The parapet is plain, the belfry windows square,[13] the West door pointed, & there is an octagonal cornice turret. The brick work of the Tower is not bad, & it being overgrown with lichens its effect is rendered somewhat picturesque. The Pulpit has some carving of the 17th century.[5]

Notes **1.** Pevsner p.162, *VCH* III pp.456–7, typescript "notes" on the history of the church (July 1980); **2.** Details of the bells are given by North (p.204) and in a report of 1961 which also describes the bellframe and fittings (P 87/2/2/5). Terriers of 1710 and 1724 indicate that there were three bells before the two smaller ones were recast by Edward Hall in 1740. In 1980, the old bells were replaced by a new ring of six hung in a new frame; **3.** Archdeacon's visitations, 1674 (CRT 170/9/1 p.13); **4.** The date of 1719 for the rebuilding is given in a terrier of 1724 (BW 183) and confirmed in a return made by the Rector who described the church as "lately rebuilt" at the Bishop's Visitation in July 1720 (MIC 119). The date of 1736 given by Bonney must be incorrect. It has been suggested that the new church was designed by Nicholas Hawksmoor, but this seems unlikely; **5.** The pulpit and sounding board are Jacobean and were apparently painted until 1913; **6.** Pardoe (p.6) states that the original Stuart arms were updated between 1714 and 1801. The arms were re-painted in 1913 (P 87/8/1) and again restored in 1927 ("notes") and 1980; **7.** The decalogues are painted on canvas. They were restored in 1979; **8.** The book of homilies (1563 edition) is marked "Whipsnade Church 1780. David Jenks Rector" (P 87/28/1); **9.** Bonney's orders suggest much prevarication regarding the font, and in 1842 the churchwardens stated that there was no font! (ABCV 128). The present font must date from 1842–7; **10.** The arrangement of the chancel, enclosed pews and pulpit described by W.A. is shown in a plan of 1860 (P 87/2/4). This plan also shows the font by the south door; **11.** Hakewill had previously worked with Orlebar at Heath and Reach where he enlarged the parsonage in 1852. Sources for the work of 1860 include the vestry minutes (P 87/8/1), ICBS papers 1859–60 (LPL ref: ICBS 5478), plan of church before and after alteration in 1860 (P 87/2/4), advertisement for tenders in *Dunstable Chronicle* 10 March 1860 and a tablet in the chancel; **12.** "The plate is modern" (*VCH*) and includes a cup of c.1860 (ABE 5); **13.** The belfry openings were in their original form (like the remaining one on the east side of the tower) in Fisher's time (slide 1085) and when Glynne visited in about 1840, so the round–headed brickwork cannot be C18th as stated in the *VCH*. This alteration probably took place in 1866 or (more likely) in 1898–9; **14.** Bathurst's notebook (ABE 3); **15.** Accounts for repairs, 1898–9 (in P 87/4/1); **16.** Minutes concerning the work of 1913 (P 87/8/1); **17.** Richardson's work, 1949–50 (P 87/2/8 and P 87/8/1); **18.** The recent work of 1974–9 is summarised in the "notes".

WILDEN

This is a Perpendicular building of the C15th, but the re-set C13th piscina in chancel and a Decorated window in the south wall of the nave survive from an earlier church. It consists of an aisleless nave with chancel, south porch and west tower.[1] Over the west door there is a carving of an owl. There is a Perpendicular font.[2] The south door carries some C15th ironwork. There are fragments of early glass in the tracery lights of the east window, mixed with C19th coloured quarries, above the stained glass of 1911 in the main lights.[3] Acoustic jars are visible in the chancel walls.[4]

There are a number of C17th fittings including the communion table, a for-mer chalice dated 1628,[5] and chests of 1623 and 1637.[6] A purple pulpit cloth with "The gifte of RS 1625" survived until the late C19th.[7] There were five bells by 1708,[8] including the existing bells of c.1610, 1637 and 1649.[9] The bellframe is dated 1650 and bears the initials of the churchwardens A.Smith and W.Grove whose names are on the treble bell dated 1649. By 1708 there was a church clock.[10] In 1715 Robert Paradine gave a new paten.[5] One of the bells was recast in 1717.[9]

From 1781 expenditure on the church is recorded in the churchwardens' accounts.[11] A new pulpit cushion was made in 1786.[12] Roof repairs costing £27 were carried out in 1797. In 1808–9 the wardens bought a new bier, a pall,

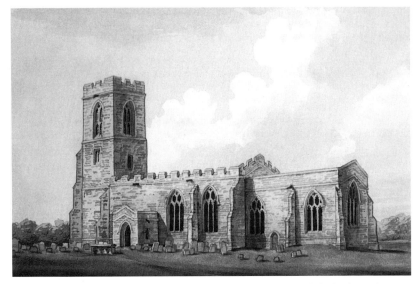

45. Wilden: SE view. Apart from the addition of gable crosses the church looks almost the same today. This view does not show the turret on the tower, perhaps added in 1825, which was removed in 1964   *(Watercolour: Thomas Fisher c.1815)*

and "2 Yards of Green Baiz to Lay over the Communion Table". Further roof repairs were undertaken by Mr.Love in 1817. Bonney's visitation orders were swiftly acted on not only with regard to furnishings and books etc,[13] but also for repairs. The tower was repaired by Mr. Berrill in 1825 at a cost of £60, the church roof was mended for £110 in 1826–8, and in 1830 the floors were paved with brick and tiles.[14] In 1836 the Archdeacon noted "much has been done at this church".

Further improvements were to follow under the influence of the Rev. W.S. Chalk who became Rector in 1835. In 1836 the parsonage was rebuilt by John Green of Bedford to the designs of William Railton.[15] The same architect and builder were employed on the church in 1837. Their work, which cost £260, is recorded on an inscription below the Royal Arms of 1837.[16] Railton was responsible for installing high painted deal pews, a triple–decker pulpit and desk, and for restoring the east window and the font for which he provided a cover made up of woodwork from the old pulpit.[17] A report in the local paper in 1838 says that the church had been "restored and very neatly fitted up for the accommodation of an increasing congregation".[18] W.A.'s comments show how unfashionable the liturgical arrangements had already become by 1852.

A report of 1863 refers to the recent restoration of the east window and mentions that the chancel had been re-pointed.[19] In about 1885 a lean-to vestry was added on the north side of the chancel.[20] The later churchwardens' accounts mention the purchase of new crimson hassocks for the altar in 1885 and record that a new tortoise stove was placed in the church in 1895.[21] At about this time a harmonium or American organ was installed with the choir seats at the back of the church.[22]

In 1894 Archdeacon Bathurst found that the roof was in a very bad state, noting "the lead is in holes and one sheet has slipped so that half an inch of daylight [comes in]. The inside walls & seats and floor bad".[23] In 1900 he noted "walls lean and are cracked & windows bad. The stove too near font and woodwork". A further restoration under Mallows and Grocock took place in 1902,[24] when the roof was repaired, the nave re-seated with open deal pews and a new pulpit and lectern provided.

Later work includes additions to the stained glass in the east window in 1911,[3] the restoration of the bells in 1922,[9] the acquisition of an organ in 1930,[25] further roof repairs in 1960–2 and repairs to the top of the tower in 1964 when the south-west corner turret was removed.[26]

1a. Extract from glebe terrier, 20 April 1822 [27]

WILDEN.

Church and Furnishings. The Church Built of Stone and Covered with Lead has a Porch on the South side, a Square Tower with 5 Bells,[9] a Stone Font Lined with Lead,[2] Communion Plate Silver Cup and Salver,[5] a Clock without Face.[10]

1b. Extract from glebe terrier, 28 August 1828 [28]

WILDEN.

Church yard. Church yard Fenced with hedge the north east side from Gate to gate belonging to the Parish, south west side belonging to the Rector.

Church. The Church is a stone Building 90 feet by 20 d°. and covered with Lead, has a Porch on the south side covered with lead. The Tower a square stone one about 56 feet covered with lead, has 5 bells and Furniture complete.[9] A Clock with no face.[10]

Furniture and ornaments. A Stone Font.[2] Cushion & hangings for Pulpit.[7, 12] A Large Bible & Three Common Prayer Books new.[13] A Parish Chest.[6] Communion Plate, Cup & Salver (silver ones).[5] An Iron Chest containing Six Register Books, Three old & three new.[29]

Parish Clerk and Sexton. The Election of Clerk by the Rector, the Sexton by the Parish. Clerk's Fees Marriages two shillings & sixpence, Baptisms & Burials none, Banns one shilling, Churching sixpence. Sexton's Fees two shillings for Bell & Grave.

Church Estate. A Charity for the repairs of the Church let at twelve Pounds a year.[30]

School. A third charity to endow a school about twenty six Pounds a year.[31]

2. Archdeacon Bonney's historical notices of churches, c.1820–1840

WILDEN, St. Nicholas. This Church which is a handsome freestone Fabrick consists of a Nave & Chancel, with a Tower at the West End, all embattled. One window on the South Side is decorated, the rest of the Church is perpendicular. The Font is octagonal & Perpendicular with panels & escutcheons bearing St. George's Cross & a Cross Patonce alternately.[2] There are five Bells.[9] The chalice & Patin are Silver on the latter is inscribed "Ex dono Rob[t] Parridine A.M. Rectoris de Wilden".[5] There is a South Porch.

Armorial Bearing Wilden [*Sketch of coat of arms*].

3. Archdeacon Bonney's Visitation notebook, 1823–1839

WILDEN. This Church consists of a Nave and chancel and Tower at the West end of the Nave.

At the Visitation of 1823 the following Order was given that the Stone work of the Windows and Doors be restored with Parker's Cement; the Tower–Stairs be capped with wood; the Bell Chamber windows be restored with Stone according to the ancient architecture;[14] the West Door be thoroughly and neatly repaired & painted oak colour; the white wash be brushed off from the staircase door and the Door oak grained; the open Seats be neatly repaired, set strait and oiled; the Chancel Pews, Door & Ceiling be repaired; the Font be cleansed and a proper Font Bason purchased;[2] the old Flagon be sold and a new plated Flagon & Deep Plate for the Alms & new Surplice be purchased;[5] the Walls of the Church be pointed.

At the Visitation of 1826 It was ordered that a new Prayer Book & Bible be purchased for the Minister and the Leads be repaired, before Easter next;[14] The Font be cleansed and a proper Font Bason by purchased; The Floor and open seats be renewed before Easter 1828; the steps up the Steeple be repaired before Easter 1829; the Rector restore the Stonework of the Chancel and renew the Door thereof.

At the Visitation of 1833 The following order was given, that the floors of the Seats be repaired, a new napkin for the communion & proper Font Bason be purchased, and a new door be made for the Chancel

At the Visitation of 1836 Ordered that the floors of the Seats be repaired. Much has been done at this Church.

At the Visitation of 1839 found this Church entirely renewed and in beautiful order.[17] Cost of this including Chancel ab[t] £260. Ordered the binding of the Bible to be repaired and a new 8[vo] Prayer Book for the Clerk

4. Article on the Church by W.A. (no.94), NM 4 September 1852

WILDEN, St. Nicholas. The timber roof of the chancel remains. There are a few pews of better design and more appropriate than those generally observed in this quarter of the church, where it is to be wished none of any kind, unless in case of absolute necessity should be placed. But we viewed with equal sorrow and astonishment, a space behind the altar separated by a screen, concealing half the window, used, as we were told, for vestry meetings.[20]

Those who know well how much jarring in general takes place on these occasions, especially if a proposal is made to extract some trifle from the farmer's pocket for Church purposes, will condemn unhesitatingly the appropriation for such objects this the most sacred part of God's temple.

"Lo! discord at the altar dares to stand."

The roof of the nave is in good order; the belfry arch and west window plastered up and hidden from view – an act which the then incumbent joins with his churchwardens in recording. In general this union does not occur; but if those fresh from the architectural magnificence of our Universities sanction these proceedings, they most deservedly merit castigation. Over this record are flauntingly displayed the Royal arms.[16]

We hope we shall not be accused of disloyalty, or dislike to ornament, in protesting against the unpleasant obtrusion of this device, in general so miserably executed, and always misplaced. We have a true Gwillim love and for the "display of heraldry" in its appropriate place; but "the function of ornament is to make you happy; not in thinking what you have done yourself; not in your own pride; not your own birth; not in your own being, or your own will, but in looking at God; watching what He does, what He is, and obeying His law, and yielding yourselves to His will. You are to be made happy by ornaments; therefore they must be the expression of all this; not copies of your own handiwork; not boastings of your own grandeur; not heraldries; not king's arms, nor any creatures arms, but God's arm, seen in his work; not manifestation of your delight in your own laws, or your own liberties, or your own inventions; but in divine laws, constant, daily, common laws; not Composite laws, not Doric laws, nor laws of the five orders, but of the Ten Commandments."*

There is no singing gallery, but an inclosed box, we believe, enshrines a performer.

The sittings are for the most part open, but of a villainous hue; a few private pews for the chiefs of the parish.[17]

An ingenious but despicable abuse has been perpetrated on the font.[2] The bowl has been filled up with cement, leaving room for a little marble basin in the centre – a sham, to give the appearance of the font itself, being made use of at the baptismal ceremony.

We mention with grateful recollection, that the church-yard being accessible, we were enabled to rest in the porch, which is in good order, with its windows not blocked up.

n.d.   W.A.

* Ruskin: Stones of Venice, p.214.

Notes **1.** Pevsner pp.162–3, *VCH* III pp.225–6, *Wilden* by Michael Rider (1995) and Ransom's RC article in *BT* 15 Sept.1899. The furnishings in Wilden church were recorded in detail by NADFAS in 1993 (Z 837/1). I am grateful to Michael Rider and the Rev. Robin Rogers for their comments on the draft text; **2.** The font was illustrated by Fisher (slide 1466) and the 1822 terrier shows that then it had its leaded lining. It was repaired in 1837 (inscription in church) when a new font cover was made from the old pulpit (RC article). Bonney's order that a font basin be provided was first made in 1823 and repeated in 1826 and 1833. By 1852 the basin had been set in cement inside the original font, as noted by W.A. in 1852 and in the BAAS and RC articles of 1863 and 1899; **3.** The glass in the east window is of three different periods, as described in the NADFAS inventory (Z 837/1) and in the 1925 terrier (P 106/2/1/3). In 1827 Boissier (f.404) noted "Some small remains of very ancient stained glass". Ransom records that further old glass was discovered in 1837, and the brightly coloured heraldic glass doubtless dates from 1837 when the east window was restored. The lower lights in memory of members of the Chalk family are of 1911 by A.L. Moore. There are faculty papers and plans of 1911 (HCRO ref: DSA 2/1/212 and 220) for the window which was dedicated in 25 June 1911 (P 106/0/2); **4.** The acoustic jars are mentioned in the RC article; **5.** The plate consisted of a cup dated 1628 (stolen in the 1950s) and a paten given by Robert Paradine in 1715 (*VCH* III p.226); **6.** There are two chests, the old wooden parish chest dated 1637 (or possibly 1657) and a smaller iron–bound chest of 1623 (NADFAS inventory Z 837/1); **7.** The pulpit cloth of 1625 is mentioned in the RC article; **8.** Terrier, 1708 (ABE 2 Vol.I p.362); **9.** There are five bells in a frame dated 1650, the treble by Norris of Stamford 1649, the mediaeval second recast in 1922, an alphabet bell of c.1610 by Watts of Leicester, the fourth of 1717 by Chandler recast in 1922, and the tenor by Hugh Watts of Leicester in 1637. The bells were restored in 1922 (note in P 106/5/3); **10.** A clock is mentioned in the 1708 terrier and payments for repairs and maintenance occur in the accounts from 1781 to 1837 when it was repaired by Thomas Clare (P 106/5/1–2). The 1822 terrier states that it was "a Clock without a face". It disappeared some time ago, but there is still a disused clock weight is the base of the tower; **11.** Churchwardens' accounts 1781–1963 (P 106/5/1–3); **12.** Payments to "Mr.Savill for the Civer of the Cushin" (£1 1s 9d) and "Walker for Macking the Cushin and Silke" (2s) refer to the new pulpit cushion, 1786 (P 106/5/1); **13.** "Paid Mr.Webb as proper Receipts for Prayer Book & Bible for the Minester" (£7 12s 6d), April 1828 (P 106/5/1). There is a Bible dated 1821 (Z 837/1); **14.** The repairs of 1825–30 are recorded in the accounts (P 106/5/1) and the later ICBS application mentions that the tower was repaired in 1825 at a cost of £60 and a further was £110 spent on roofs in 1826–8 (LPL ref: ICBS 2165); **15.** Plans by Railton for the new Rectory 1836 (LAO ref: MGA 206) and mortgage papers 1837 (CUL ref: EDR/G3/40 MGA/BED/2); **16.** Pardoe (p.6) compares the Wilden Royal arms with the earlier ones at Oakley and suggests that they were repainted in 1837 with "V R" and an inscription regarding the repairs; **17.** Railton's work of 1837 is documented in the accounts (P 106/5/2), vestry minutes (P 106/8/1), the ICBS papers 1837 (LPL ref: ICBS 2165) and plans before and after the alterations (Society of Antiquaries Library), reports of contributions from the Duke of Bedford in *BM* 12 Aug.1837 and *NM* 26 Aug.1837 and the Bedford estate report for 1840 (MIC 118). The 1837 arrangement of the pews, pulpit and desk and seats for the choir are described in the RC article of 1899; **18.** Article on "embellishment of churches" in *BM* 29 Dec.1838; **19.** Report of BAAS excursion to Wilden in *BT* 18 Aug.1863; **20.** In 1852 W.A. noted that an area at the east end of the church was screened off as a vestry. Writing in 1899 Ransom stated in his RC article that a new vestry had been built "about ten or fifteen years ago"; **21.** Recorded in churchwardens' accounts 1867–1963 (P 106/5/3); **22.** An American Organ is mentioned in an insurance policy of 1894 (P 106/2/2/2a) and in 1896 Lord Alwyne Compton gave two guineas to the harmonium fund (*BS* 14 Aug.1896). Its position is mentioned in the RC article of 1899; **23.** Bathurst's notebook (ABE 3); **24.** Sources for the 1902 restoration include the vestry minutes (P 106/8/1), appeal leaflet and restoration papers (P 106/2/2/1–3), service register (P 106/0/1), and reports in *BS* 27 June and 24 Oct.1902 and *BT* 31 Oct.1902; **25.** The organ was dedicated on 22 Dec.1930 (P 106/0/2). It is by Scudamore, in a case of 1859 designed by G.E.Street, purchased for Wilden in 1929 (possibly from Cambridge) and restored in 1990 (Z 837/1); **26.** Papers concerning repairs to roofs and tower, 1960–64 (P 106/2/2/4) and note of re–hallowing of chancel after roof repairs in 1961 (P 106/0/4). The turret removed in 1964 may have been added in the C19th. It is not shown in Fisher's view of c.1815 (slide 909); **27.** Payments in the accounts "for a Terrier of the Church And Parish and Rectory & Parchment" (10s), and "Paid the Bishop for Presentment and Returning of the Terrier (18s.6d.) 1822 (P 106/5/1); **28.** The 1828 terrier (in P 106/5/1) is included to supplement the sparse details in the 1822 terrier; **29.** The parish register for 1678–1734 was already missing by the early C19th (*Parish Register Abstract* 1831); **30.** The Church Lands charity was established by Richard Smith in 1511; **31.** The School charity was founded by Thomas Peat in 1624.

WILLINGTON

The advowson of Willington was granted to Newnham Priory in 1166 and there was evidently a church here by the C12th. Little of the original fabric survives, however, as the church was wholly restored if not rebuilt between about 1535 and 1541 by Sir John Gostwick.[1] An inscription at the east end of the church refers to the completion of the work in 1541.[2] The Gostwick chapel on the north side of the chancel contains the family monuments including that of its builder, Sir John, who died in 1545.[3]

Documents of 1555–6 refer to a dispute concerning plate and vestments used at Willington church.[4] There seem to have been five bells at Willington by 1600.[5] One of them was dated 1591 and another dated 1600 bore the name of William Gostwick of Willington. A sermon of 1614 by Thomas Adams (Vicar 1611–4) included the phrase "some ring the changes of opinion" and this has been noted as a very early literary reference to the art of change-ringing.[6] One of the bells was recast in 1671 by Thomas Tompion[7] and another by an unidentified founder in 1710.[5]

The Gostwick family also gave a fine set of church plate in the late C17th. This includes a cup and cover of 1686, a paten of 1691, and a flagon of 1691.[8] Details of the plate and other church goods are given in a terrier of 1708 which included a "red damask tablecloth with red silk and gold fringe for the Communion Table".[9]

The pulpit and desk were altered by James Usher of Cople in 1808 and again altered and painted by Mr. Elger in 1820.[10] A new font described by Boissier as "an Apothecary's marble mortar enclosed in a wooden case" seems to have been acquired in the early C19th.[11] From 1818 expenditure on the church is recorded in the churchwardens' accounts.[12] Work was carried out in response to Bonney's visitation orders, including repairs by Mr. Woodroffe of Bedford (£58) in 1824 and further work (£80) in 1826.[13] A partition was erected in the tower arch in 1835.[14] Writing in 1847 W.A. noted that the chancel had been recently repaired. It was apparently at this time that the remains of the old rood screen were removed and subsequently lost.[15] Minor repairs are recorded in 1856, fifty new hymn books were bought in 1857, and in 1860 the churchwardens paid for a new cushion and lining for the pulpit.[12]

The year 1858 saw the start of the long incumbency of the Rev. Augustus Orlebar who was to remain Vicar until his death in 1912.[16] A harmonium is mentioned in 1860.[12] In 1867 improvements to the church were carried out by the Duke of Bedford at a cost of £182.[17] The pulpit, desk and pews were altered.[10] A new stone font was provided.[11] Five of the windows were filled

46. Willington: SE view showing the church as restored or rebuilt by Sir John Gostwick in 1535–41   *(Engraving: Thomas Fisher 1812)*

with quarry glass in 1867 by Powell of Whitefriars who later supplied two more windows of this type in 1885–6.[18] In 1875 the organ built for Cople church by the Rev. H.E. Havergal in 1857 was reconditioned and installed at Willington.[19]

The main restoration came when the church was attended to by Henry Clutton for the Duke of Bedford in 1877.[20] The work cost over £2500. The contractor was William Cubitt, and it was at the time of the restoration that the altar rails by Jones and Willis were set up along with the encaustic tiles in the sanctuary.[21] Clutton placed heavy louvres in the belfry windows.[22] In 1885 the east window was filled with stained glass of the Ascension by Heaton Butler and Bayne.[23] The organ was repaired in 1890.[19] The embroidered panels on the reredos were completed by Mrs. Orlebar in 1893.[24] The bells were recast and rehung in 1898, a sixth bell being added.[5]

Later improvements have included the provision of new oak choir stalls in 1914,[25] repairs to the Gostwick chapel in 1928,[26] the new altar and screen erected in the Lady Chapel in 1959 as a memorial to Isaac and Bessie Godber,[27] and the new organ of 1969 by E.J. Johnson of Cambridge.[19]

1. Extract from glebe terrier, 25 June 1822

WILLINGTON

Church yard. Item the Churchyard containing Three Roods and Thirty Perches surrounded by Grounds of His Grace the Duke of Bedford, the Walls and Gates thereof round about made by the parish except the South Fence and part of the Western Boundary which are kept up by his Grace the Duke of Bedford as owner of the adjoining Lands.

Church. Belonging to the said Parish are first the Parish Church an ancient well preserved Building containing in length within the Walls Forty Six Feet, and in breadth Thirty Feet, the Chancel thereof is Thirty three feet long, annexed to which is a Second Chancel or rather Mausoleum. The breadth of the Two Chancels is Thirty Six Feet. In the latter lie interred many Individuals of the Family of Gostwick, a Baronet, who was a Benefactor to the Church, Lord of the Manor, and Proprietor of nearly the whole Lands of the Parish.[3] The Windows in the Chancel are beautiful in their Form and Tracery. The Tower of the Church is thirteen feet by Twelve within the Walls. In the Tower are five Bells with their Frames.[5]

Furniture and ornaments. Belonging to the Church are a Communion Table with a Covering of Scarlet Cloth.[9] One Damask Napkin and Table Cover. One Silver Flaggon weighing Fifty Ounces,[8] engraved thus "The Gift of Charles Gostwick Esquire 1691". A Silver Cup and Cover gilt, weighing Twenty Ounces and a half, engraved thus "The Gift of Sir William Gostwick Bart. 1686". A Silver Paten or Salver weighing Fourteen Ounces, engraved thus "The Gift of Sir William Gostwick Kt. and Bart. 1685". A Box for the Offertory. An Iron Chest containing the Parish Registers from One thousand Six hundred and Seventy six to One Thousand Eight Hundred and Twenty two. A Pulpit and Reading Desk.[10] An old Pulpit Cushion covered with Scarlet Cloth. A large Bible. Two Folio Prayer Books, and a Surplice.

Seats in the Church. The Pews and Seats in the Church are repaired at the common Expence of the Parishioners.

Parish Clerk and Sexton. There is also due to the Parish Clerk who is also Sexton four pence yearly from every Family, for publication of Banns One Shilling, for every Wedding by Banns Two Shillings, for every Wedding by Licence five Shillings, for digging Grave Knell and attending Funeral Two Shillings and six pence, for every Churching six pence, for every Funeral in the Church Yard from another Parish Five Shillings.

Churchwardens. The Church Wardens are chosen in Easter Week, One by the Minister and One by the Parishioners.

2. Archdeacon Bonney's historical notices of churches, c.1820–1840

WILLINGTON, St. Laurence. This Church consists of a Nave and Aisles separated by lofty Piers & Arches, Chancel, & Tower at the West End & South Porch, all of the Perpendicular Character. Five Bells.[5] The fabrick is of Ashlar & fitted up with old oak open Seats with perpendicular tracery at the Ends.

On the Floor of the Nave is this Inscription,[28] "Here lyeth the body of Joanna Gostwyk, who departed this life in A° MCCC°XXVI". "Here lyeth the body of Richard Gostwyk Esq who depart[d] this life in A° MCCC°XV".

There is a Chapel North of the Chancel which is the burial place of the Gostwicks.[3] Here on a Altar Tomb of Alabaster lies the Effigy of Sir William Gostwick, Bart. and this Bearing [*Sketch of coat of arms*].

Against a Pillar at the end of a Tomb, on which are the same Arms with the Exception of the Chief, which is tenne charged with three Nag's heads bridled, are these words. Armiger ill' Johannes Gostwyck. Hoc opus fieri fecit si ergo quid valiant piae vota largire pater ut eterna fruatur portentate 1541.[2]

There is a handsome Monument against the North Wall of this chapel to the Memory of Sir Edward Gostwick.

3. Archdeacon Bonney's visitation notebook, 1823–1839

WILLINGTON. This Church consists of a Nave and North Aisle – a Chancel at the East End of the Nave and Chapel on the North Side thereof, a Tower at the West End of the nave, a Porch on the South Side.

At the Visitation of 1823. The following order was given that the Open Seats be neatly repaired set even, cleansed and oiled; The Earth be moved from the Walls and proper drainage be made;[29] the Stone work of the Doors and Windows of the Tower, Church and Chancel be restored according to the Ancient Architecture with Stone & cement;[13] before Easter 1826. The Doors be repaired & painted Oak Colour, according to the Ancient pattern; The Font be cleansed and a proper bason for it purchased.[11]

At the Visitation of 1833 It was ordered that The weeds be removed from the Walls of the Tower and a new Prayer Book be purchased for the Minister.

At the Visitation 1836 ordered the Font to be cleaned and the covering to the Pulpit cushion turned.

At the Visitation 1839 no order required.

4. Article on the Church by W.A. (no.43), NM 23 January 1847

WILLINGTON, St. Lawrence. The delay in gaining access to the interior of this church was considerable, and without climbing over the gate we could not occupy our time in examining the exterior of the church-yard. All was securely locked fast as a prison. The occupants of the burying ground, which was in sad disorder, were a cow and calf. On inquiring why the church-yard was rendered inaccessible, and cattle allowed to defile it, we were informed that it was let to a farmer, who so willed it. There was no resident clergyman, and non-residence invariably produces many bad results.

The chancel has been recently repaired; it was said that on cleaning the walls some mural decorations had been discovered, but they were again concealed by a new plaster coating. The roof at some time had been lowered so materially as to interfere with the window. Two large pews, resembling cages, were in the chancel; the monuments with their details, so overlaid with whitewash as greatly to detract from their beauty.[3]

The nave is almost entirely fitted up with open seats; the pulpit and reading desk very poor.[10] The west window is blocked up, but as it has escaped the infliction of an organ,[14] there seems to be no necessity for this. There is a miserable substitute for the original font,[11] which perhaps might be discovered on diligent search. The pillars are thoroughly whitewashed; this part of the church is in a mournful condition. A corner near the chancel was appropriated to a mop, scrubbing brush, dirty mats, &c. For the existence of this nuisance in churches there can be no apology. The incumbent and churchwardens would not permit it in their own dwellings.

This church is a beautiful specimen, and might be restored at a little cost as it is of very moderate size.

18 January 1847   W.A.

Notes **1.** Pevsner pp.163–4, *VCH* III pp.264–6, and Jennifer Huitson *The Parish Church of St. Lawrence, Willington* n.d. [c.1985]; **2.** The inscription is illustrated by Fisher (*Collections* pl.107); **3.** For the Gostwick family <u>see</u> H.P.R. Finberg "The Gostwicks of Willington" in BHRS Vol.36 (1956) pp.46–146; **4.** Eeles and Brown pp.25, 30–9; **5.** The bells were all recast in 1898, but North (pp.205–6) gives details of the old bells and there are rubbings of the inscriptions both at the British Library (BL ref: Add.Ms.36819 A71) and in the Society of Antiquaries Library where they are confusingly numbered in date order. There is an account of the old and new bells in *BS* 3 June 1898 (and as a press cutting in AD 987 p.17); **6.** For Thomas Adams <u>see</u> the *DNB*. In his article on "The Development of Change Ringing in the Seventeenth Century" Jean Sanderson (ed) *Change Ringing* Vol.I (1987) p.40 John Eisel notes that this phrase from Adams's sermon on "The Devil's Banquet" (1614) implies that change ringing was probably established in Bedfordshire – and perhaps at Willington – by this time; **7.** The founder of this bell seems to have been Thomas Tompion, the great clockmaker, although as no other bells by him are known it seems likely that he procured it for the parish from an established bellfoundry; **8.** The plate is listed, with details of the inscriptions, in the terriers of 1708 and 1822. According to the 1927 schedule (ABE 5) there are original leather cases for the paten and flagon; **9.** Terrier, 1708 (ABE 2 Vol.I p.43, quoted in Huitson p.3). The covering for the communion table is also mentioned in the 1822 terrier; **10.** The pulpit and desk were altered in 1808 (vestry minute in (P 26/12/3) and again in 1820 (P 26/5/1) and 1867 (P 26/7/1); **11.** The font as described by Boissier (f.359d–60d) was replaced by the present one which was made by S.Jarvis of Bedford (P 26/7/1). As required by the Archdeacon, a new font basin was supplied for 12s. by Mr.Green of Bedford in 1824 (P 26/5/1); **12.** Churchwardens' accounts 1818–1900 (P 26/5/1); **13.** The payments in the accounts relating to the work of 1824–6 are as follows: "Mr.Woodroffe of Bedford repairs at the Church as per Bill" (£58 10s 10d), April 1824, Joseph Berrill for work at the church (£8 16s 6d), March 1826; repairs to church (Robert Smith of Cople £31 3s, Wm.Brown "masoner" £40 18s 6d, and Joseph Barker [glazier] £11 12s – total £80), Oct.1826 (P 26/5/1); **14.** The west window was blocked up in 1835 when the churchwardens paid Joseph Norman five guineas "for Inclosing the belfry" (P 26/5/1); **15.** The screen had already been damaged by 1827 when Boissier (f.359d–360d) noted "a good rood loft Screen but the tracery cut away to admit the ugly canopies of 2 pews". It was noted in *BT* 2 Sept.1854 that the screen "was removed about 8 years ago for reparation, but has not been returned"; **16.** For the Rev. Augustus Orlebar and his associations with Rugby School and Tom Brown's School Days <u>see</u> Huitson (p.4), Conisbee (p.279) and Orlebar's own press–cutting (AD 984–7); **17.** The work of 1867 is documented in the Bedford Estate report for 1867 (R 5/869/4 p.59) and in the parish records (P 26/2/2/1 and P 26/7/1); **18.** The Powell glass is mentioned in the parish records (P 26/2/2/1 and P 26/7/1). Full details of the five windows supplied to the Rev. A. Orlebar for Willington in 1867 are recorded in the Powell archives (V&A ref: AAD 1/54 pp.304, 316 and 327) and the later windows of 1885 (which came from Southover church near Lewes) and 1886 are also recorded (V&A ref: AAD 1/59 p.239 and 329). The Powell window in memory of the Rev. John Scobell is also mentioned in *BT* 16 May 1885; **19.** Report of the transfer of the organ from Cople to Willington in *BT* 11 Sept 1875 (and a copy in AD 984 pp.2–3). The Cople parish records give details of the original organ (P 4/8/1). The later repairs were reported in *BT* 21 June 1890. There are papers about organ repairs, 1922–5 (P 26/2/2/3) and a faculty and other papers concerning new organ, 1968–70 (P 26/2/2/13–4); **20.** There are vouchers for the restoration of 1877 (R box 674) but not other original sources have been traced; **21.** The new tiles, believed to be by Minton, are said to be copies of the original

C14th tiles found in the church and re–laid at the time of the restoration (Huitson p.5); **22.** Wide belfry louvres are a feature of some of Clutton's other churches, e.g. Woburn and Steppingley. Those at Willington (shown in *VCH* III pp.264–5) have since been removed; **23.** The new east window reported in *BT* 2 May 1885; **24.** The reredos and altar panels were wrought and presented by Mrs. Orlebar in 1893 (Kelly's *Directory* 1914 p.186); **25.** Choir stalls mentioned in report in *BT* 19 June 1914; **26.** The work on the Gostwick chapel is mentioned in the report of the Council for the Care of Churches for 1928–9 pp.47–8; **27.** Papers concerning the Lady chapel altar and screen 1958–9 (P 26/2/2/7–8) and Huitson (p.5). They were dedicated on 7 March 1959 (P 26/0/6); **28.** For the brasses, <u>see</u> Lack *et.al.* (p.100); **29.** Payments in the accounts (P 26/5/1) relate to these orders, i.e. "cleaning off the Ivy from the church windows and lowering the earth from round the walls" in 1823, purchase of matting basses and matting for seats, from Mr.Wells, Bedford, in 1824, and colouring and staining seats and pews (Joseph Barker £2 18s 9d) in 1825.

WILSHAMSTEAD (or Wilstead)

There has been a church at Wilshamstead – also known as Wilstead – since at least the C13th. The list of incumbents goes back to 1235. The oldest parts of the church are the C14th south arcade and the south door of c.1340. The north arcade dates from the C15th.[1] The nave roof is of the same period, and when Boissier visited in 1827 he noted that the roofs were then "in part painted".[2] There is a brass of c.1430 to William Carbrok, priest.[3]

In 1518 a parishioner left money for a new bell for the church.[4] In 1611 the churchwardens reported that the church lacked "a pewter stoope".[5] The plate includes a cup and cover paten of 1626, and a further paten obtained in 1723.[6] By 1706 there were four bells and a saints bell in the tower, but one of the bells was cracked.[7] The goods and utensils belonging to the church are listed in a terrier of 1706 and in an inventory dated 1707 which was updated in 1710.[8] From 1722 details of expenditure on the church are recorded in the churchwardens' accounts.[9] Money was spent on repairs to the porch in 1734 and on a new cushion with tassels for the church in 1738.

The west tower collapsed on 11 April 1742. Alternative estimates were obtained for rebuilding the tower (£474) and for merely making good the damage (£40).[10] The Bishop of Lincoln recognised "the Inability of the Parishioners to repair the Steeple according to its ancient Dimensions" and in September 1742 he gave permission for less extensive repairs to be carried out instead. He also authorised the sale of three bells. The accounts show that the sale of old materials raised £71 and the repairs cost £78. Instead of the old tower the parish erected what Bonney later described as "a cupola for a bell". Boissier referred in 1827 to "the west end sadly dilapidated".[11]

After the church had been repaired the churchwardens bore the cost of new communion rails in 1747, painting the royal arms in 1761 and setting up the ten commandments etc in 1765.[9] The bell was recast in 1783 by William Emerton of Wootton.[7] In response to the Archdeacon's articles of enquiry in 1821 the parish officers certified the church to be "in tolerable good repair", admitted lacking "a cover to the Cup", and stated that "the pews in general have Hassocks or other provisions for kneeling".[12] The small bell was recast in 1826.[7] The accounts show that repairs to the church costing £33 were

47. Wilstead: S view showing the south porch and wooden belfry of c.1742 before the erection of the new tower in 1851 and the rebuilding of the porch in 1872–3

(Pen and ink drawing: Anonymous c.1820)

undertaken in 1846–7 and when W.A. visited in 1847 he found part of the aisle "converted into a builder's yard".[13]

In 1850 the church was surveyed by Mr. Woodroffe of Bedford whose proposals were considered by the Vestry in December. By now, the idea of rebuilding the tower and restoring the church had gained ground and instead of accepting Woodroffe's scheme the vestry appointed a committee to manage the business and raise money. After several architects had been invited to submit schemes the plans of Thomas Smith of London and Hertford were adopted in April 1851. In May the committee accepted the tender of Walter Parker of Thrapston for carrying out the work at a total cost of £730. The church was re-opened on 2 November 1851.[14] The Vicarage was also enlarged and rebuilt by Smith and Parker in 1851.[15]

Further work was carried out in 1872–3 when the chancel and porch were rebuilt, an organ chamber and vestry added and the church re-seated and generally restored.[16] The architect for this work was A.W. Blomfield. The chancel was restored at the joint expense of Lord John Thynne of Haynes Park and William Layton Lowndes, the owner of Church Farm.[17] Lord John Thynne also gave the stained glass by Clayton and Bell in the east window and the elaborate reredos.[18] A new organ was also obtained in 1873.[19]

A new heating system was installed in 1887,[20] and later gifts and improvements included new wooden kneelers in 1891,[21] new lamps in 1895,[22] a funeral car for the parish in 1896,[23] and the clock placed in the tower in 1898 for Queen Victoria's Diamond Jubilee.[24] By this time structural problems had arisen in the chancel, and in 1899 the east end of the church was underpinned and the east wall rebuilt.[25] Further repairs to the chancel and south aisle became necessary in 1907–8, and in 1928 the chancel roof had to be restored.[26]

A War Memorial window in the south aisle was completed in 1920.[27] It was designed by John Hall and Sons who provided three further stained glass windows for the church as memorials to members of the Coley and Craig families between 1926 and 1930.[28] In 1953 oak panels were added to the pulpit and new oak communion rails were provided.[29] Extensive repairs to the nave roof were carried out in 1965,[30] and in 1975 new kitchen facilities and meeting rooms known as the Chapter House were added on the north side of the church.[31] Two further stained glass windows were installed in 1984–5.[32] Recent gifts include new vestments, altar frontals, and a new chalice given by the Vicar in 1994.[33]

1. Extract from glebe terrier, 15 April 1822
WILSHAMSTEAD.
Church yard. Church Yard 2 Roods 15 Poles.
[No description of church or furniture, nor information on Parish Clerk.]

2. Archdeacon Bonney's historical notices of churches, c.1820–1840
WILSHAMSTEAD, All Saints. This church consists of Nave and Aisles, Chancel & south Porch. The Tower fell down in 1749.[10] A Cupola at the West end contains one Bell.[7] The Character of the Church is Chiefly Perpendicular, but some are decorated. On the floor in the south Aisle is the demi Effigy of an Ecclesiastic in the Attitude of Prayer with this inscription, all in brass.[3]

Orate pro anima Willelmi Carbrok Capellani cujus anime propicietur deus. Et pro animabus parentum Fratrum, Sororum omnium benefactorum suorum et omnium fidelium defunctorum.

There is also a Monument to the Memory of William Thompson of Wilshamstead who was buried 15th day of Novr 1596, & who gave five Pounds per annum payable out of certain Estates mentioned in the Inscription to the Poor of the parish for ever.

3. Archdeacon Bonney's visitation notebook, 1823–1839
WILSHAMPSTED. This Church consists of a Nave, North and South Aisles, Chancel at the East End of the Nave and Cupola for a Bell over the West End thereof, a Porch to the South Aisle.

At the Visitation of 1823 The following Order was given, that a new cloth for the Communion be purchased; and the Earth be moved three feet from the Sides of the Church.

At the Visitation of 1826. It was ordered that the woodwork over the pulpit Stairs be put back to its proper place over the Corbel – A new font bason be purchased,[34] the Bible be repaired – the lower part of the Walls be pointed.

At the Visitation of 1833 the following Order was given that the Leads be surveyed, and means taken to prevent the Water entering through the Roof – lead flashing be placed at the bottom of the Windows to prevent the entrains (*sic*) of Rain – that the blank Window at the East End of the South Aisle be coloured & marked to resemble glass. The Pulpit Cushion be new covered – the Walls be cleansed in the interior.

A good Glebe House.[35]

At the Visitation 1836 ordered that the flashing of the lead work of the Roof on the North Side be examined & repaired, interior of the Walls of Church & Chancel be cleansed & a proper Font Bason procured.[34]

At the Visitation of 1839 – Ordered the blank part of the East Windows of S. Aisle to be coloured & marked out in imitation of glazing.

4. Article on the Church by W.A. (no.45), NM 6 February 1847

WILSHAMSTED, All Saints. This is but an indifferent specimen of architecture. What has been done has not contributed to render it more attractive. The whole of the interior is covered with a good coat of yellow ochre, and it was thought what did for the inside would be very good for the outside. The same yellow application to tower, body, and all.[36] It is impossible to refrain from laughing at the ridiculous appearance it presents. The chancel is very poor; the pews, not being sufficiently high to screen the occupants from observation, railings with curtains have been added. Damp appears to be making rapid progress. A portion of the aisle is converted into a builder's yard, and contains scaffold poles, ladders, &c.[13] The font of course has not escaped the usual disfigurement, the lead remains, but a trumpery basin is evidently used when the baptismal service is required.[34] The church yard was not locked up.

The daubing of yellow ochre which has been inflicted internally and externally on this church gives us an opportunity of speaking on a subject, to the importance of which our best architects are only just beginning to be awake, and the public in general exhibit an unusual degree of bigotry and ignorance. We allude to the introduction of colour into our ecclesiastical buildings. The chief opposition we have received on mooting this subject has been from ladies. What! they say, colour in churches! it would destroy all the solemnity – so gaudy – distracting – theatrical – what can be more beautiful than the grey stone? &c., &c., &c. ; till we bow our heads meekly under the storm, confessing our error. But now we will venture to say – if, gentle ladies, you really believe that gay tints are unbecoming the church, that they destroy solemnity and distract attention, ought you not to give evidence of the sincerity of this belief by your actions as well as by words? Would it not be well that on the Sunday instead of arraying yourselves in richly coloured attire, you put on pale straw bonnets and drab gowns? If your objections be really true, it matters nothing for the practical effect whether the hues proceed from the walls of the building or the clothes of the congregation, but you must remember that a heavy responsibility rests on you if you continue to introduce what you believe to be dangerous.

We will now come to the reason of the thing; observing as a undeniable fact that all are attracted by colour sooner than by form, the latter almost always requiring a certain degree of education of the eye before it can be at all appreciated. We know that form can tantalise with the fantastic shapes of Moorish Alhambras; delight us with its exquisite grace in Lincoln; and overwhelm us with awful grandeur at York. Analogy would lead us to expect the same powers in colour, and practically we find every one granted but the last and most important one. It will be readily granted (though we suppose no one was ever so rash as to make the experiment) that the most cheerful family could not reside many days in a room glaring with whitewash, without losing their control over their minds; accordingly in our private houses we hang our walls with coloured papers, and our floors are covered with coloured carpets, and the principal room in the new palace of Westminster is resplendent with every tint that can be devised. So far we acknowledge the power of colour; for an instance of it, used for the purpose we are contending for, we are afraid we should search in vain in this country. But as the artist owes all his ideas, his power, and his knowledge both of form and colour, to the works of nature, into whose deep things having reverently lived and taken the little mite that his or any other mortal mind can expect to acquire, expands and interprets it to the world; so to nature we must turn, and try if from her we can get any assistance.

He who on a bright summer's day walks round a garden filled with flowers, will enjoy the delicate and brilliant tints, and his heart will rejoice within him; but let him, on some autumnal evening, gaze from an eminence over a large expanse of beech forest rich with the brown decaying leaves, let his eye pass on to the glorious golden streaks lingering behind the setting sun, and the noble purple of the rapidly accumulating clouds, and we think he will for the future heartily acknowledge that colour can bestow the utmost of solemn grandeur.

1 February 1847   W.A.

Notes **1.** Pevsner p.164, *VCH* III pp.327–8, and "The Parish Church of All Saints, Wilshamstead: a brief History" n.d. [1994]. I am grateful to the Rev. Roderick Palmer and to John Corfield for providing information and ideas on this church; **2.** The nave roof, illustrated by Pevsner (pl.54), has good carved bosses but the traces of painting mentioned by Boissier (f.360–d) are no longer visible; **3.** For the brass, <u>see</u> Lack *et.al.* (p.100). It was known to Pugin, probably through Fisher's engraving (*Collections* pl.105), as noted by David Meara in *A.W.N. Pugin and the Revival of Memorial Brasses* (1991) pp.23–4; **4.** Will of Simon Cawnell, 1518 (ABP/R 2 f.45d); **5.** Presentments, 1611 (ABC 4 p.54 and 64); **6.** In addition to the plate of 1626 and 1723 listed in the *VCH* p.328 the 1924 schedule (ABE 5) lists a paten hallmarked 1803 and a flagon of 1872; **7.** Details of the bells, including information on the fall of the tower in 1742, are given by North (pp.206–7). In 1707 the third bell was cracked (P 22/1/3); **8.** Glebe terrier, 1706 (ABE 2 Vol.I p.47) and inventory of utensils 1707 and 1710 (in P 22/1/3 – published in BPRS Vol.49

pp.120–1); **9.** Churchwardens' accounts 1722–79 and 1831–1935 (P 22/5/1–2); **10.** The events of 1742 are documented in a memorandum in the register (in P 22/1/3 – published in BPRS Vol.49 p.121) and in the accounts (P 22/5/1). Bonney's date of 1749 is incorrect; **11.** Boissier (f.360–d); **12.** Articles of enquiry, 1821 (ABCV 130); **13.** Payments in accounts (P 22/5/2) to S.Middleton "for repairing the Church" 1846 and "Mr.Barkers Bill for Repairs and Painting the Church" 1847; **14.** Sources for the work of 1850–1 include the vestry minutes (P 22/8/1), accounts (P 22/5/2), mortgage 1851 (P 22/2/1/2), copy of the restoration accounts (CRT 130 WIL 4), advertisement for tenders in *BT* 12 April 1851 and notice of reopening in *BT* 1 Nov. 1851; **15.** Plans and mortgage papers for the Vicarage, 1851 (CUL ref: EDR/G3/40 MGA/BED/19) and Parker's accounts, 1851 (P 22/2/3/2). Parker offered a £15 reduction on his price for the church if the same foreman was appointed for both jobs (P 22/5/2); **16.** Sources for the work in 1872–3 include restoration papers and faculty 1872 (P 22/2/1/3), faculty papers (HCRO ref: DSA 2/1/214), accounts (P 22/25/6/3 pp.361–4), notice of consecration service (P 10/28/40), and reports in *BM* and *BT* 3 May 1873 and *The Builder* Vol.31 (1873) p.434; **17.** The estate archives give details of the responsibilities and voluntary contributions of William Layton Lowndes regarding the restoration (Fac 148/2). Lord John Thynne's contributions are listed in the press reports and accounts; **18.** Both the stained glass window and reredos (removed in the 1960s) were by Clayton and Bell (*Builder* 31 May 1873 p.434), but the panels were done for them by Powell of Whitefriars who later cleaned the reredos and, "the finish having gone bad", renewed the enamel free of charge in 1875 (V&A ref: AAD 1/56 pp.60, 115 and 293); **19.** The organ, by Nicholson of Worcester, cost £190 (P 22/25/6/3). It was originally placed in the organ chamber on the north side of the chancel but it has since been moved to the west end under the tower; **20.** Heating apparatus installed in 1887 (*BT* 4 Feb.1887); **21.** New kneelers reported in *BS* 28 Feb.1891; **22.** New lamps noted in *BM* 7 April 1894 and 28 Sept.1895 and *BS* 11 Oct.1895; **23.** The funeral car was supplied by Mr. Wortley "who also made those for Marston Moretaine and Houghton Conquest" (*BS* 11 Sept.1896); **24.** New clock reported in *BS* 2 Dec.1898 and in parish magazine (P 22/30/1); **25.** Papers and accounts concerning repairs to the east end in 1899–1900 (P 22/2/1/17 and P 22/25/6/3 pp.365–6); **26.** The work of 1907 and 1928 is documented in the faculty and accounts (P 22/2/1/10 and P 22/25/6/3 pp.365–6); **27.** The progress on the War Memorial window was reported in parish magazine (P 22/30/3) Feb.1919 to May 1920; **28.** The Coley windows are described in the parish magazine (P 22/30/3), and there are faculties (P 22/2/1/18–19), faculty papers (HCRO ref: DSA 2/1/6/25, 7/25, and 19/9); **29.** Faculty and estimate for communion rails and pulpit panels, 1953 (P 22/2/1/21–2); **30.** Papers concerning roof repairs, 1964–7 (P 22/2/1/9–11); **31.** Plans and papers concerning the Chapter House, 1974–5 (P 22/1/16); **32.** Faculty papers concerning the modern glass, 1985 and 1989 (HCRO ref: DSA 2/1/1051/6 and 18); **33.** Recent gifts noted in the "Brief History"; **34.** The font basin ordered by Bonney in 1826 was eventually obtained in 1839 when the accounts (P 22/5/2) record a payment to "The Rev^d. Mr. Pawsey 1 Baptismal Font" (12s. 6d); **35.** The vicarage had been built or enlarged in 1816 (LAO ref: MGA 86); **36.** A letter deploring the use of colour wash on Bedfordshire churches was published in the *Hertford etc. Mercury* 17 Jan.1829.

WOBURN

The churches of Woburn have an interesting and unusual history closely associated with the Abbey founded in 1145.[1] The original church was not in the present village but at what is now the outlying hamlet of Birchmore. By the time a market was established at Woburn in 1245 there was also a chapel in the High Street which is said to have been rebuilt in the early C16th by Robert Hobbes, the last Abbot of Woburn.[2] After the Dissolution of the Monasteries the Abbey properties passed into the hands of the Russell family (afterwards Earls and Dukes of Bedford). Woburn also became an exempt jurisdiction or peculiar,[3] and this explains why there are no terriers or Archdeacon's visitation orders for this parish. In 1869 the new church of St.Mary was legally substituted for the old one which was retained as a mortuary chapel until eventu-

48. Woburn: The old church from the NE before Blore's alterations of 1829–30 showing the low detached tower with its wooden cupola and the body of the church with the east window of 1750
(Watercolour: Thomas Fisher c.1815)

ally declared redundant in 1981.[4] The old church is now the Woburn Heritage Centre.

The origins of the *old church* in the High Street are uncertain. There are no architectural clues as the original building disappeared long ago. It may have been rebuilt in about 1535.[2] It is said that the tower was built or rebuilt in the early C17th for Sir Francis Staunton using stone and materials from the old church at Birchmore.[5] The church itself was also enlarged and eventually consisted of an aisles nave, chancel and a tower which became detached after the linking structure – described by Dodd as "an apartment supported by an arch, the residence of the parish clerk" – was demolished in the late C18th.[6] The tower also carried an open wooden lantern or cupola with a small bell dated 1637.[7]

There are some fragmentary churchwardens' accounts for 1616–24.[8] The goods and ornaments of the church are listed in an inventory dated 1651.[9] They included plate, chests, communion rails, an hour glass for the pulpit, fire hooks and buckets, a clock "with a bell proper to it", the Saints' Bell and four other bells. Three of the four bells were broken, and when they were recast in 1663–4 a fifth was added.[10] In 1662 the parish paid to have the "Rebel's Arms" erased and the Royal Arms were set up in the church.[11] The chancel was repaired in 1692–3.[12] One of the bells was recast in 1724 and in 1748 a new clock was placed in the church tower.[13]

In 1750 considerable improvements were made to the chancel under Sir William Chambers at the expense of John, 4th Duke of Bedford.[14] Chambers

49. Woburn: The interior of the old church shortly before demolition in 1864. Notice the plastered ceiling of 1750 in the chancel, the east window of 1830, the altar–piece, the seating of 1801, the pulpit as re–located in 1847, the gas lights and the royal arms and armorial roundels on the walls.

(Photograph: W. Daniels c.1864)

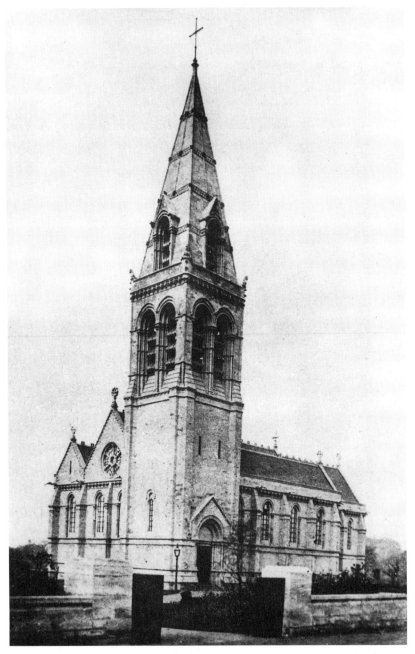

50. Woburn: An early view of the new church designed by Henry Clutton for the 8th Duke of Bedford in 1865–8. It shows the spire which was removed in 1891–2.

(Photograph: Anonymous c.1870)

vaulted the chancel in plaster, paved its floor with free–stone and black marble in squares, altered the side windows of the chancel, and designed a new three–light east window with unusual tracery.[15] From 1753 parish expenditure on the church is recorded in the churchwardens' accounts.[16] A chandelier is first mentioned in 1754. The church was paved in 1755–6. The accounts also refer to church music.[17] Towards the end of the C18th circular panels with armorial shields were put up in the church.[18] In 1796 the Duke of Bedford had special copies of the prayer book printed for Woburn church.[19] There are records of pew rents from 1802.[20]

Further work was carried out in 1800–1 when the floors were levelled, the church re-seated, and new galleries erected.[21] Ten years later, John, 6th Duke of Bedford, again improved the chancel.[22] The work of 1811 included a new altar to accommodate the painting by Carlo Maratti as an altar-piece,[23] an organ,[24] a stove, and a new set of communion plate.[25] In 1813 the churchwardens bought a new barrel for the organ.[24] In 1818 the galleries were enlarged and improved.[26] A silver "christianity bowl" was bought for baptisms in 1820.[27]

By 1818 it was already "in contemplation" to raise the tower and install a new peal of bells.[28] Plans were prepared by Edward Blore and by 1828 preparations were well in hand. In 1829–30 the present tower was built with its fine open lantern and crocketed spirelet.[29] At the same time Blore added the passage between the church and tower, embellished the chancel, and designed a new five–light east window which was filled with stained glass.[15] Six new bells were supplied by Thomas Mears of Whitechapel,[10] and in 1830 a new clock[13] by B.L. Vulliamy was presented by the Duke of Bedford who had met most of the cost of the new tower. The old bells were removed to Park Farm from where they were afterwards stolen.[10]

The original organ was replaced by a new one in 1836.[24] In 1838 Sir Hugh Hoare of Wavendon gave a marble font for the chancel.[30] A new warming apparatus was installed in 1839.[31] In 1840 a new set of pulpit robes was presented to the Vicar.[32] Further alterations to the galleries and seating took place in 1841–2.[33] When W.A. described the church he was critical of many of its arrangements, especially the enclosed pews, the pulpit and desk and the style of architecture. His article prompted an exchange of correspondence with J.D. Parry in the *Bedford Times*.[34] In 1846–7 the Duke of Bedford spent a further £650 on repairs and improvements.[35]

Francis, 7th Duke of Bedford, began an extensive programme of church building on his estates. He died in 1861, but his son William continued the work on succeeding to the Dukedom. At Woburn the 8th Duke wished to fulfil his father's intention to "erect at his own cost a new church in place of the present one" and provide increased accommodation "particularly for the poorer classes".[36] When the old church was demolished in 1864 it became clear that the new church could not be satisfactorily built on the old site.[37] Henry

Clutton was accordingly invited to prepare plans both for the new church and for rebuilding the old church on a smaller scale to serve as a chapel for the old churchyard which was to continue in use for burials.

The present building in Clutton's interpretation of the Perpendicular style was completed in 1865–6 alongside the old tower.[38] The bells also remained, and although the chapel was no longer used for services the belfry became the home of the Woburn Company of Change Ringers established in 1867.[39] Two more bells were added to make eight in 1877.[10] In the later C19th the bells of the old church were rung for services at St.Mary's. The tower fell silent in 1910 when the bells were recast and transferred to the new church. Since the chapel became redundant in 1981 the Woburn Heritage Trust has undertaken extensive repairs.

From 1864 until the completion of the Duke's *new church* in 1868 services were held in a temporary church.[40] Built on a new site in Park Street in 1865–8 Clutton's new St.Mary's is a large church in a style based on French gothic architecture of the late C12th. With stone vaulting and chunky details it is an impressive building, with a raised chancel and a lavishly furnished baptistery and font.[41] It has a crypt originally intended as the burial place for the Dukes of Bedford.[42] One of the windows on the north side is filled with grisaille glass.[43] The tower originally carried a tall pyramid spire and it contained a large bell weighing 55 cwt – the heaviest in the County.[44] The eventual cost of the church and its fittings amounted to £25,000. It was consecrated on 23 September 1868 and in 1869 the new church was legally confirmed as the parish church.[4]

In 1890 the spire was found to be in a dangerous condition. It was taken down in 1891–2 by Dove Brothers under the supervision of Arthur J. Pilkington.[45] In 1894 the east windows were filled with stained glass by C.E. Kempe in memory of Francis, 10th Duke of Bedford.[46] Additional plate was presented by the 11th Duke in 1901.[25] In the early C20th the chancel was completely refurbished with new woodwork including the collegiate choir stalls (1902) and the elaborate carved reredos (1903) by Kempe.[47] The pulpit and tester were also provided in 1902, and in 1904 a new organ was installed at the east end of the north aisle.[48] The case was designed and made by Kempe and the organ by Norman and Beard. The Maratti altar–piece from the old church was placed in the new church in 1906–7.[23] In 1910 the metal of the bells from the two churches was recast to form a new ring of eight, dedicated on 22 December 1910.[10]

Later alterations and improvements include the "Flying Duchess" memorial window of 1938 in the south aisle,[49] the Lady chapel altar set up in the nave in 1946 and improved for the centenary of the church in 1968,[50] and the erection of the armorial panels from the old church in 1977.[18]

The accounts by W.A. and Glynne are the only original texts for Woburn from the standard sources.

4. Article on the Church by W.A. (no.22), NM 7 February 1846

WOBURN. The exterior of this church deserves every commendation; the same praise cannot be bestowed upon the interior, where Christian and Pagan architecture are strangely jumbled together. This chiefly prevails in the roofs of the chancel and nave.[34] The ceiling of the aisles is of the ordinary sort. It is lamentable to see space sacrificed to the system of pews;[20] there are only a few seats in the nave. The position of the reading desk and pulpit is most absurd, and compels the chief part of the congregation to be seated with their backs to the altar.[35] "It is scarcely possible to create a more palpable blemish than that which is occasioned by placing the pulpit in the centre of the nave. In a dissenting meeting house, it may be proper to assign this station to the preacher, but it is quite inconsistent with the intent of our liturgy, and should never be tolerated.[34] The situation of the reading-desk below the pulpit, like the desk of an auctioneer's clerk, is equally inappropriate."

A number of common-looking lamps disfigure as well as blacken with their smoke the walls of the building; this is one result of abandoning the custom of the English Church by changing the afternoon into an evening service; when lighted up, the church presents a very theatrical appearance.[34] The organ excludes the light from the west window of the nave,[24] and a miserable gallery stretches across four other windows in this part of the church;[26] if open seats were substituted for the pews, this gallery might be removed. The floor of the latter was strewed, when we visited it, with a quantity of nutshells.[34]

The font is as much out of character as out of place.[30]

31 January 1846   W.A.

5. Sir Stephen Glynne's Church notes, June 1840 (Vol.1, pp.75–76)

WOBURN. This Church is chiefly of poor Perpendicular work, but has been a great deal renewed of late, & on the whole in good taste. It consists of a nave & Chancel each with side aisles & a tower detached situated on the South (*sic*) side of the East front. This tower has been rebuilt on the site of the former low and mean one & is crowned by an octagonal lanthorn with ogee head.[29]

The nave & aisles are embattled. Over the East gable is a niche. The windows of the aisles poor Perpendicular of 3 lights – of the Clerestory square headed. In the Chancel the windows are large – the lateral ones of 3 lights, the others of 5. The nave is divided from each aisle by 4 pointed arched, upon octagonal columns. The ceiling is panneled. The Chancel pavement is of marble.[14] Some modern stained glass adorns the windows.[15] The pulpit & desk are at the West end.[35] There is a fair organ.[24] The pews regular & at the East end is a painting by Carlo Maratti.[23]

There is in this church a fine brass of John Morton who died on the Feast of the Conversion of St. Paul, 1394 – The figure is gone but there is a very elegant canopy.[51]

Notes **1.** Pevsner p.164–5, *VCH* III pp.461–2, S. Dodd *An historical and topographical account of the town of Woburn* (1818), J.D.Parry *History and description of Woburn and its Abbey* (1831) and revised editions (1845 and 1890), Kenneth G.Spavins and Anne Applin *The Book of Woburn* (1983) esp. pp.30–45 (old church) and pp.71–96 (new church), *Woburn Church Guide* by Anne Applin (1988); **2.** The arms of Abbot Hobbes occurred on the tower and church "whence he is supposed to have rebuilt the whole" (Parry 1845 p.109); **3.** For Woburn as a peculiar, see Dorothy Owen "The exempt jurisdiction of Woburn" in BHRS vol.49 (1970) pp.122–34; **4.** Instrument substituting the new church for the old one, 7 January 1869 (P 118/2/5) and order of redundancy, 1981 (ABV 42/22); **5.** The rebuilding is attributed to Staunton (d.1630) by Dodd (p.23). Staunton's monument remains in the old church; **6.** Description of clerk's apartment from Dodd (p.23). The outline of the building can be seen on the south face of the tower in an engraving published in 1818 (X 254/88/265); **7.** The date of the 1637 bell is recorded in a note concerning the new bells of 1829 (P 118/5/4 p.123); **8.** Churchwardens' accounts 1616, 1618, 1624 (P 118/5/1–3); **9.** Inventory, 1651 (Dodd pp.130–1); **10.** One of the bells may have been cast in 1547 when Bishop Longland left money for a new second bell (*B.Mag* Vol.II p.117). Three of the four bells were broken by 1651, one apparently damaged by young men of the parish in 1641 (BHRS Vol.49 p.131). An account shows that money was given by the Earl of Bedford towards five new bells in 1662 (R 5/79/1). Dodd (p.23) states that the bells were dated 1663 or (p.132) 1664 and one was recast in 1724. The date is given as 1664 in a report of the theft of the old bells from Park Farm (*NM* 3 Jan.1831). North (pp.208–9) gives details of the new bells of 1829 (also documented in P 118/5/4 p.123, R 3/3299 and *NM* 21 Nov.1829) and 1877 (papers at X 586/4/5–6). The dedication of the new bells was reported in *BT* 23 Dec.1910. For a general account see Spavins and Applin (pp.75–8); **11.** Rebel's arms, 1662 (Dodd p.132); **12.** Chancel repairs, 1692–3 (R 5/79/4); **13.** There was a clock in 1651. There is a parish register memorandum regarding the new clock of 1748 (in P 118/1/4 – transcribed in BPRS Vol.3 p.227). For the 1830 clock see Spavins and Applin (pp.35 and 41); **14.** The chancel alterations of 1750 are attributed to Sir William Chambers by Dodd (p.24) who describes the ceiling, east window and marble and stone pavement. The work is mentioned in Basil F.L. Clarke *The building of the eighteenth century church* (1963) p.51; **15.** Parry (1845 p.110) described the tracery of Chambers's east window as "grand but incongruous" with a circular periphery, and three fine arches, with clustered columns, and a plain circle above". It can be seen in the Dodd's frontispiece and in a Buckler sketch dated 1820 (BL ref: Add.Ms. 36356 f.63). Dodd mentions (p.25) that the east window was formerly emblazoned with arms, implying that these were removed when Chambers renewed the tracery in 1750. The present five–light east window dates from Blore's improvements of 1830 and the new stained glass is illustrated as the frontispiece by Parry (1831); **16.** Churchwardens' accounts 1753–1834 (P 118/5/4); **17.** As well as references to music in the accounts, there is a letter of 1816 concerning the opposition of the musicians and singers when the first organ was installed (R 4/608/35, mentioned in Spavins and Applin p.33); **18.** The armorial roundels carry dates from 1086 to 1781 (Parry 1845 p.111) and are believed to have been painted for the old church in the late C18th. They were moved to the new church in 1977 (Spavins and Applin p.37); **19.** Woburn Prayer Book, 1796 (P 118/31/1). The then Duke could not bear the *Benedicite* and so he had special copies of the prayer book printed without it; **20.** Pew rents are recorded in the estate papers (R 4/830–32, R 5/612–751 and R 5/591) and new numbers are given in the parish assessment book 1802–33 (P 118/28/2). There were concerns about the system of pews in 1845 (Parry 1845 p.115) and the abolition of pew rights was discussed by the vestry in May 1859 (P 118/8/1); **21.** The work of 1800–1 is documented in the estate papers (R 4/608/34 and R 5/916), in *NM* 7 May 1801 (illustrated in Spavins and Applin p.41), in Lysons *Magna Britannia* (1806), and in the C19th published accounts of Woburn; **22.** The account of this work in Spavins and Applin (p.34) wrongly indicates that the east window was renewed and filled with stained glass in 1811 (actually done in 1830) and attributes the scheme to Sir William Chambers (who was responsible for the earlier scheme of 1750); **23.** The altar-piece was a painting of the Virgin and Child by Carlo Maratti (1625–1713), which was later placed in the new church in 1906–7 (P 118/8/2 and Spavins and Applin p.73); **24.** A report in *NM* 8 June 1811 refers to the Duke's recent gift of an organ for which the churchwardens bought a new barrel from Flight & Robson in 1813–4 (P 118/5/4). Its installation caused some discontent (see note 17). Writing in 1818 Dodd (p.26) stated "a small, fine–toned organ has been erected by his Grace". The instrument is mentioned in Boston and Langwill *Church and Chamber Barrel–Organs* (Edinburgh

1967) p.73). The new Snetzler organ of 1836 was given to Eversholt church in 1864, and it carried the inscription "The Gift of his Grace / John Duke of Bedford, K.G. &c / 1836"; **25.** The Duke's gift of plate was reported in *NM* 8 June 1811. The modern schedule of plate (ABE 5) indicates that the pieces inscribed "The Gift of John Duke of Bedford to the Parish Church of Woburn A.D. 1811" were all made in London in 1762. Two flagons were given by Herbrand, 11th Duke, in 1901; **26.** Estimate for new gallery 1818, (R 4/608/34). Dodd (pp.23–4) describes the galleries and states "additional ones are in contemplation"; **27.** Paid "for Silver Christianity bowl" (£6 6s), 1820 (P 118/5/4); **28.** Proposals for the tower were mentioned in 1818 by Dodd (p.23); **29.** Sources for the new tower and alterations to the east end include the estate correspondence (R 3/2250–3200 *passim*), Blore drawings (BL ref: Add.Ms. 42029 f.8 and 31), minutes and accounts (P 118/8/1 and P 118/5/4) and report in *NM* 21 Nov.1829; **30.** Parry (1845 p.111) refers to the marble font given by Sir Hugh Hoare of Wavendon in 1838; **31.** Correspondence regarding the warming apparatus, 1839 (R 3/3247–9). Parry (1845 p.114) mentions that memorials were disturbed "to make way for the pipes laid down to *warm* the church"; **32.** New robes reported in *BM* 4 April 1840; **33.** Sources for the work in 1841–2 include correspondence (R 3/4345–4549 *passim*) and papers c.1840 (R box 484); **34.** W.A.'s observations gave rise to a long letter from J.D.Parry in *BT* 14 Feb.1846 followed by further letters in *BT* 28 Feb.1846 (W.A.) and *BT* 7 March 1846 (Parry). W.A. later referred to possible improvements at Woburn in his article on Harrold (*BT* 17 July 1847); **35.** In 1846–7 the pulpit and desk were separated and moved from the west end (as noted by Glynne) to the front of the church, thus undoing the arrangement objected to by W.A. Sources include the estate papers (R 3/5138/2), estate report for 1847 (R 5/869/1 p.31), vestry minutes (P 118/8/1) and report in *BT* 15 May 1847; **36.** Quote from Bedford Estate report for 1864; **37.** Originally a faculty was obtained for rebuilding *in situ* in April 1864 (P 118/2/2) and the difficulties only came to light after the old church had been demolished. There is a full account of events in the Bedford Estate report for 1864 (pp.16–9) and in Spavins and Applin (pp.36–7); **38.** Sources for the rebuilding of the chapel include the revised faculty 10 Dec.1864 (P 118/2/3), faculty papers (HCRO ref: DSA 2/1/215), Bedford estate reports for 1864 (pp.16–9) and 1866 (p.33), correspondence in *BT* 5–26 Jan.1864 and report in *BT* 1 Nov.1864; **39.** The Woburn Company was established in 1867 through the efforts of Charles Herbert, who was also chiefly responsible for the formation of the Bedfordshire Association in 1882 (Spavins and Applin pp.77–8). The papers include the original rules and membership list of the Company (X 586/16/2) and letters regarding difficulties with the Woburn amateur ringers regarding the use of the bells in 1887 (X 586/16/3); **40.** The temporary church was built in April 1864 (Bedford Estate reports 1864 pp.16–9) at a cost of £521 (report 1866 p.33). A writer to the paper complained that it was very uncomfortable (*BT* 1 Nov.1864). It was in use at Woburn from 1864–8 and afterwards taken to Luton where it was used in Brunswick Road as a temporary church from 1873–6 while St.Matthew's church (*q.v.*) was under construction; **41.** Sources on the new church include the Russell Estate reports for 1864 (pp.16–9), 1866 (p.33) and 1867 (pp.58 and 207), accounts and vouchers (R 5/917 and R box 680), vestry minutes (P 118/8/1–2), faculty (P 118/2/2), faculty papers (HCRO ref: DSA 2/1/215), ground plan (P 118/2/4), reports in *BT* 31 March and 29 Sept.1868 and Spavins and Applin; **42.** The Duke obtained a faculty to use the crypt as a burial place in 1868 (HCRO ref: DSA 2/1/215). In *Through Visitors' Eyes: A Bedfordshire Anthology* (1990) p.104 Simon Houfe prints an account of a visit to the church by Augustus J.C. Hare in 1877 when the Duke took a party to see the vaults where he was to be buried; **43.** The grisaille window on the north side was put in as an experiment; **44.** The installation of the big bell was reported in *BT* 25 Feb.1868. Its clapper broke in 1885 (*LBO* 17 Feb.1885) and the estate papers include correspondence about the use of the bell and repairs 1887–1901 (R Pghle H/D). The bell was broken up in the tower in 1910 (*BT* 26 Aug.1910); **45.** Sources on the demolition of the spire include the vestry minutes (P 118/8/2), the Bedford Estate reports for 1890 p.190, 1891 p.210 and 1892 (extracts in CRT 130 WOB 51), drawings in the Dove Brothers archive in the RIBA Drawings Collection, D. Braithwaite *Building in the Blood: the story of Dove Brothers of Islington 1781–1981*, and report in *BT* 28 March 1891; **46.** The Kempe east window reported in *Building News* Vol.66 (1894) p.430; **47.** There is confusion regarding the woodwork, which is documented in the estate papers (R Pghle H/D). The reredos is attributed by Pevsner (p.165) and Spavins and Applin (p.72) to the architect W.D. Caröe. However, the work at Woburn is not mentioned in Jennifer Freeman's biography of Caröe and in *Master of Glass* (1988) Kempe's biographer, Margaret Stavridi, claims the whole scheme for Kempe (p.150). Kempe is also named as the designer of the woodwork in a note signed by the Rural Dean in the vestry minutes (P 118/8/2). Spavins and Applin attribute some of the woodwork to J.E. or J.H.E. Kempe. There is a short article on the new reredos in *DBG* 26 Aug.1903. A report in *BT* 21 Aug.1903 clearly identifies Kempe as the designer and names the principal workmen; **48.** The organ is documented in the vestry minutes (P 118/8/2), estate papers (R Pghle H/D), in Clutton and Niland *The British Organ* (Batsford 1963) p.280 and in an article on "The organ in Woburn parish church" in *The Organ* 1954 pp.180–5; **49.** The "Flying Duchess" window in the south aisle was designed by Albert J.A.Houthuesen in 1938 (Applin) and made by Powell of Whitefriars (V&A ref: AAD 1/72 p.354); **50.** The Lady Chapel is described in Spavins and Applin (pp.73–4). The late Ken Spavins made most of the wooden furnishings; **51.** For the brass, see Lack *et.al.* (pp.100–2).

WOOTTON

Wootton is mentioned in Domesday Book of 1086. There was a church in the village by the mid C12th, and the list of incumbents goes back to 1251. The present building dates from the early C14th and it is in the Decorated style. The south porch was added later in the C14th. The top of the tower dates from the C15th when Perpendicular tracery was placed in the side windows of the aisles.[1] The timber-framed north porch, although much restored, dates from the C14th.[2] There is a C15th rood screen.[3] In the chancel there are memorials and hatchments to the Monoux and Payne families.[4]

A will of 1533 mentions that the arches of the church were in decay, and another of 1536 contains bequests for repairs to the roof and for "mending the organs in Wootton church".[5] In 1578 the chancel was said to be "in decaye at the Queene's defalte".[6] By 1611 a Church Lands charity had been established to provide income for church repairs.[7] Nevertheless, later visitation presentments of 1617 refer to the church and the leads on the roof being out of repair and in 1674 the windows were said to be broken.[8]

Two of the bells were recast in the late C16th, one in 1587 and another in 1595, and the present tenor bell was cast in 1641.[9] A new communion cup was provided in 1640, and in 1685 the plate was augmented by the gift of the new paten and flagon presented by Dame Alice Monoux.[10] The old church clock is said to have been put up in 1662.[11] The church also possessed a "pulpit cushion of cloth dated 1685".[12] In the late C17th or early C18th a brick vestry was added on the north side of the chancel.[13]

In the C18th there was a bell foundry at Wootton, run first by Thomas Russell (fl.1710–1743) and then by William Emmerton (fl.1768–1789).[14] The third bell was recast by Thomas and William Russell in 1736 and the treble by William Emmerton in 1779.[9] The small sermon bell in the niche over the chancel arch was cast in 1748, possibly by William Russell.[15] The names of William Russell and William Emerton also appeared on a piece of lead removed from the spire in 1959.[16] The Royal arms of George III over the north door date from the late C18th.[17] They were originally on a partition in the tower arch at the back of the west gallery.[18]

From 1823 Archdeacon Bonney's order book indicates that the church was in need of attention, and through the 1830s he pressed in particular for repairs

51. Wootton: NW view of the church with the village stocks and the old parish almshouses. Notice the old brick vestry, the bellcote over the chancel arch for the "sermon bell", the timber–framed north porch and the leaded spire   *(Watercolour: Thomas Fisher c.1815)*

to the chancel which seems to have been in poor condition.[19] It was restored in 1845.[20] W.A.'s account of the church in 1846 contrasts with the account of 1849 by J.D. Parry.[21] While W.A. drew attention to instances of meanness, neglect and "pomp and vanity", Parry pointed out that the boarding in the tower arch had been erected for comfort and defended the gallery as a "pious and generous design of our ancestors".[18]

In 1848 the vestry accepted tenders for repairs to the church under the direction of Wing and Jackson of Bedford.[22] The work of 1848 may have involved extensive work to the main roof. Re-seating was also proposed, but a newspaper report of 1854 indicates that this was delayed owing to opposition to interference with the old pews.[23]

The main restoration, about which there is very little definite information, took place during the incumbency of the Rev. Frederick Neale (Vicar 1852–1872). Neale seems to have taken charge of the work himself and largely at his own expense, apparently between 1857 and 1860.[24] He was assisted by the lay Rector, Coventry Payne, who in 1855 gave a new communion cup.[10] Writing in 1866, Glynne commented that the church had been restored "in an excellent & liberal spirit" but he felt the style might perhaps be criticised.

In particular Glynne disliked the western bays added to the aisles with their plaster ceilings, modern and circular windows. These were added between

1854 and 1858.[25] At the same time, the west gallery was removed and the tower arch opened up, the ceiling under the tower was vaulted and the west window was filled with stained glass by Powell of Whitefriars.[26] Powell also supplied quarry glass for other windows in the church in 1859–62. A new font was made for the church in 1857, complete with a wooden cover "of tabernacle work".[27] Neale's sister gave the organ in 1860.[28] Neale also seems to have rebuilt the vestry,[13] installed elaborate candelabra in the nave and aisles,[29] restored the north porch,[3] and provided the new pulpit. The porch, pulpit and font cover all carry sacred inscriptions – clearly a characteristic of Neale's improvements.

The chancel is said to have been restored in 1861 but a report of 1865 refers to work "still wanting".[30] There is evidence of further improvements in 1872 when the floor was re-laid, the memorials restored to their former positions, and the step to the sanctuary laid with encaustic tiles inlaid with an inscription.[31] The chancel has a Victorian roof.[32]

After Neale's death in 1872, further improvements were carried out by his successors. The nave roof was repaired in 1872–3.[33] The bells were restored in 1874.[9] Repairs to the clock were considered in 1875, and in 1884 a new clock was installed.[11] A funeral bier was obtained in 1888.[34] In 1890 Lady Payne gave the stained glass in the east window as a memorial to her infant son.[35] The ancient chancel screen was restored in 1894 and the present canopy was added in 1896.[3] The organ was restored and improved in 1897–8 for the Diamond Jubilee of Queen Victoria.[28] In 1904 the bells were again restored and a sixth bell added.[9] A further stained glass window was placed in the chancel in 1906 as a memorial to Charles Henry Dillon (d.1901).[36]

Recent work includes the re-leading of the spire in 1959,[16] organ repairs in 1964,[28] chancel improvements in 1970, the enlargement of the vestry in 1975, a new roof covering on the nave and aisles in 1989 and improvements to the west end of the church in 1995.[37]

1. Extract from glebe terrier, 25 June 1822
WOOTTON.
Church yard. The Church yard containing three Roods and Sixteen Poles adjoining the Lands of Colonel Buckworth South, and West a Brick Wall Built and repaired by the family of Monoux predecessors of Colonel Buckworth. Fence adjoining the Road by the Parish. North bounded by Lands of John Key, John Berry and Colonel Buckworth. East by the Alms Houses and a Garden belonging to Colonel Buckworth. Gates and Fences repaired by Churchwardens. Rails and pales also.

Church. Lenght (*sic*) fifty feet. Width forty seven feet & Elevation 28 in the inside. Chancel Length thirty five feet. Width eighteen feet. Ninteen feet height (*sic*) maintained in repair by the Impropriator.[19] Belfry fourteen feet by fourteen. The Tower to the Battlements Sixty three feet.

Furniture and ornaments. A Communion Table railed in, with Two Table Cloths. One silver Flagon weighing Four pounds eight ounces & ten penny Weight whereon are engraven these words "The Guift of Dame Alice Monoux to the Parish Church of Wootton In the County of Bedford", with her Coat of Armes.[10] One Silver Salver weighing ten ounces engraven as the Flagon. One Silver Cup weighing one pound twelve penny Weight & twelve Grains Inscribed "Wootton 1640". Two Surplices. A pulpit Cloth & Cushion Green date 1685.[12] Two Wood Chests with three Locks. One Iron Chest. One Large Bible. Two large Common Prayer Books. The King's Arms & Ten Commandments.[17] A Church Clock.[11] A small Sermon Bell diameter thirteen Inches 1748.[15] Five other Bells,[9] first two feet nine inches & half "William Emerton Wootten fecit 1779",[14] second Bell two feet eleven inches $3/4$ "John Dyer made me 1587", Third three feet one inch $1/4$ "Thomas Russell William Russell fecit 1736,[14] Stephen Hudson, Benjamin Rainbow Church Wardens", Fourth Bell Three feet five Inches "John Dyer made me 1595", Fifth Bell Three feet eight $1/4$ "God Save our King 1641." One Bier.[34] One burial Cloth.

Parish Registers. Parchment Register 1562 contained in four books to 1813 when the Register Books were amended by Act of Parliament 28 July 1812. The present Register Books are of Paper.

Church Land. Land left by Deed to the Parish of Wootton let at the present time ... any Sum ... half to go to the repairs of the Church, the remainder to the Poor of the Parish.[7]

Parish Clerk. One Acre three Roods arable Land in Marston bounded on the East by Wootton Field, on the North & West by Mr. Dimmock, on the South by Great Brook. One Rood in Bell Nook bounded on North & East by Great Brook, on the South by Mr. Tongue & West by Mrs. Emery. The Mansion at Wootton Pays five shillings a year. The Parish four guineas. For the care of the Clock two Guineas. For Burial in Church or Chancel three shillings four pence, in Churchyard one Shilling & sixpence. Marriage Banns one shilling. By Licence two & sixpence.

2. Archdeacon Bonney's historical notices of churches, c.1820–1840

WOOTTON, St. Mary. This Church consists of a Nave, aisles separated by lofty semiclustered Piers & arches, Chancel – Two Porches & Tower at the West End upon which is a low slender leaden Spire. A Sanctus Bell under a small arch hangs over the eastern end of the Nave.[15] The North Porch[2] is of wood & the decorated character of which the chief part of the Fabrick is although the perpendicular has been inserted in some part of it.

On the Patin is this Inscription "The gift of Dame Alice Monoux to the Parish Church of Wootton in the County of Bedford 1685." with this armorial Bearing on the Chalice "Wootton 1640".[10] [*Sketch of coat of arms*]

On the Flagon are the same Arms & Inscription. All these are Silver.[10]

In the Chancel is a Monument to the Memory of Sir Humphrey Monoux

1685. Another to Sir Philip Monoux 1707, & others to Sir Philip 1805 and Sir Philip 1809. Dame Elizabeth wife of Sir Philip 1805 – another 1814 and to Eliz: her daughter 1795, with other gravestones to the Family.[4]

The Rood Screen is rich perpendicular.[3]

There is an Estate for Church and Poor the half rent to the church being about £18 per annum.[7]

3. Archdeacon Bonney's visitation notebook, 1823–1839

WOOTTON This Church consists of a Nave, North and South Aisles, Chancel at the East End thereof with a Vestry on the North side of it,[13] Tower surmounted by a short Spire, at the West End of the Nave, North & South Porches.

At the Visitation of 1823 The following Order was given. That the Chancel walls be drawn & cleaned – The Linen for the Communion and the Surplice be mended – a new Cloth Covering for the Table be purchased – The Stonework of the Door and Windows and font be restored with Parker's Cement – and a proper Font Bason be purchased; Casements be placed in the Chancel Windows, The Open Seats be neatly repaired, set Strait, and cleaned; The floor of the Middle Chamber of the Tower be repaired; The North Porch be repaired according to the Ancient pattern & the Door be repaired.[2]

At the Visitation of 1826. No further Orders were given.

At the Visitation of 1833 Mr. Pearce Agent to Col. Buckworth the Impropriator applied to for the repair of the Chancel and East Window & the South Window which require repair with Cement.[19]

At the Visitation of 1836 Ordered the Seats in the Church to be thoroughly repaired – and recommended the taking of them up and new arrangement of them. The blocked up windows in the Chancel to be glazed.

At the Visitation 1839 Ordered the cracked Bell to be recast & recommended the Churchwardens to save the surplus of the rate with consent of Vestry for that purpose.[9] The Prayer Book and Bible to be repaired – I wrote to Col. Buckworth upon the subject of repairing the Chancel,[19] and the Manor Pew.

4. Article on the Church by W.A. (no.33), NM 24 October 1846

WOOTTON. Nearly all the available space in the chancel of this church is occupied by the pomp and vanity of heraldic memorials.[4] The walls are covered with tablets and hatchments, fortunately fast decaying; the floor is paved with monumental slabs. Two large square pews conceal the sedilia, and the lower part of the roodscreen.[3] Damp is penetrating the walls. The altar-table is much better than usual.

The old roof remains only in the south aisle, into the walls of which a black-and-white tablet is inserted. One of the windows is deprived of its tracery,[38] a uniform surface of the commonest glass substituted, and a green parlour-curtain attached. Hat-pegs are very abundant. The pews materially injure the walls, the lower part of which are painted. Every moulding and ornamental detail is embedded in deep incrustations of whitewash. In a corner, which is used as a coal-hole, we observed a broom, dust-shovel, and other rubbish. The font,[27] we trust, is used, as we found no basin in it, but a common pitcher. The pulpit and reading-pew are in a state of decay, which we notice as an instance of the general neglect visible in this church, and not from any feeling of respect for the things themselves; the sounding-board being so clumsy in form and tasteless in colour as to distinguish it amongst its invariably hideous species. The pillars are painted white, with black streaks to imitate marble; their basements are crumbling away so rapidly as to endanger the stability of the fabric. Some of the old benches remain, far preferable, even in their present dilapidated state, to the more pretending modern ones. In the centre of the church is a large stove, its chimney piercing the roof, and attached to the pillars by iron rods. The western arch is blocked up, with the exception of a portion into which is inserted a glazed apparatus bearing a strong resemblance to a cucumber frame.[18] The gallery was strewed with fragments of hymns, Prayer-books and pocket-handkerchiefs. The coal-hole in the south aisle is balanced by a dust-hole in the north, filled with rotting hassocks, matting, &c.; a portion of the wall of this aisle is hung with the latter, in the vain attempt to conceal the ravages of damp and decay. The exterior of the church has fared as badly as the interior. The very beautiful north porch is disfigured with secular notices;[2] the windows in the south one are nearly ruined.[38] the bold iron hinges remain in part only, but sufficient to enable their restoration.

An entrance is broken into the tower, adorned with a pattern of radiated bricks, so common over street doors.[39] A mullion of the window in the tower has been repaired with wood. The vestry not being large enough, we suppose, for comfort, an excrescence of the meanest discription has been added.[13] The recent external restorations of the chancel are entitled to considerable praise, more particularly the introduction of a cross on the gable, at a time when pagan symbolism is alone tolerated.[19]

We are led to conclude the church-yard is used as the village pound, the gate being most carefully locked, and one or two animals wandering about the sacred enclosure.

n.d.   W.A.

5. *Sir Stephen Glynne's Church notes, 6 February 1866 (Vol.2, pp.29–31)*

WOOTTON, St. Mary. A large Church, lofty & of dignity & restored in an excellent & liberal spirit, the style perhaps some points might be criticised.[24]

It has a lofty nave & aisles of equal height, West Tower, North & S Porches & Chancel. The nave is principally Decorated & Perpendicular but there are some earlier features. The aisles have been extended to the West face of the Tower which is a questionable alteration, plaster groining having been put in the Tower & in the extended portion of the aisles, also modern arches dividing the new portions & circular windows which do not seem to suit.[25]

The aisles are embattled & buttressed. The interior has a fine effect – the arcades of the nave are tall, with 3 pointed arches, upon lofty clustered piers, each of 4 shafts with capitals. There is no Clerestory, the arcades reaching to the roof. The roofs are all new, of rather flat pitch.[22] The aisles, though lofty are rather narrow. The Tower arch is of the same character & open, the organ is placed within the Tower.[28] The South doorway & windows of the aisles are Perpendicular – the latter of 3 lights but not similar. At the E end of the S. aisle is a Decorated window of 3 lights. In the S. aisle is a large piscina with trefoil feathering – & one very similar in the North aisle. The nave is fitted with low open seats.[22-3]

The Chancel arch has somewhat of an E.E. look, upon clustered shafts having the capitals moulded, with nail heads. Across it is a fine rood screen in 5 arched compartments with tracery of rather Flamboyant character – & the lower part panneled.[3]

The Chancel has on the N & S flowing Decorated windows of 2 lights & at the E. one of 3 lights & reticulated tracery. The side windows have some modern stained glass.[26] There is a piscina with trefoil arch & a stone shelf. The Chancel roof is original & has been varnished.[32] The Sacrarium is neat – the rails have elegant open tracery. In the Chancel are some handsome monuments (1707) to the Monoux family.[4] One Perpendicular window on the N. has been absorbed by the vestry – which seems to have been rebuilt & opens to the Chancel by a pointed doorway.[13] There is also a lancet lychnoscopic window, now closed, on the North.

On the S. of the Chancel is a doorway rather Early English in character with plain arch mouldings on imposts. The Font is a new one,[27] octagonal with Decorated panneling, & having a fine cover of tabernacle work rising high. The Tower has an ordinary Decorated West Window of 2 lights – in other respects it looks Perpendicular, has double belfry windows – 2 string courses – a battlement & slender spire of wood. The S. porch is plain – the doorway within it has fine continuous mouldings – the windows of the porch square headed. The north doorway has fine continuous arch mouldings. The porch of open wood screen work,[2] with barge board has been fairly restored.

(There is a bell cot with Sanctus bell on the E. of the nave[i]).[15]

Notes **1.** Pevsner p.172, *VCH* III pp.333–4, and article by J.D. Parry in *GM* Vol.32 Pt.II (1849) pp.479–82. I am grateful to the Rev. Christopher Strong and to Carol Parry for information and observations on this church; **2.** The north porch is mentioned by J.D. Parry and by Boissier (f.361) who described it as "of wood but very handsome & with hanging Tracery". Bonney ordered repairs "according to the ancient pattern". Glynne indicates that it had been restored by 1866 and mentions the barge–board which carries an inscription; **3.** The screen is described by Boissier (f.361) and by J.D. Parry who questioned Bonney's statement that it was "rich perpendicular" and suggested that it was an imitation of "the last century". It was restored by Mr. McCullock of Kennington in 1894 (*BM* 4 Aug.1894 and parish magazine Aug.1894) and the canopy was added soon afterwards in 1896; **4.** There are early C19th watercolours of the Monoux memorials (slides 911–6) and the hatchments are described by Summers (p.19–21); **5.** Wills of 1533 and 1536 (ABP/R 4 f.33 and 83d); **6.** Archidiaconal Visitations for 1578 (ABC 3 p.3) in BHRS Vol.69 (1990) p.175; **7.** For the Church Lands charity see *VCH* III p.335 and Charity Commission reports. The deeds from 1611 (P 3/25/1–2) specify that part of the income was to be used for church repairs; **8.** Visitation presentments 1617 (ABC 5 pp.96, 141 and 225) and 1674 (CRT 170/9/1 p.4); **9.** The bells are described by North (pp.209–10). The inscriptions of the bells of 1587 and 1595 are given in the 1822 terrier and in a handwritten note of c.1820 (X 67/600). Bonney noted in 1839 that a bell was cracked, but it was not recast until 1874 when the bells were restored (vestry minutes P 3/8/3, subscription list P 3/2/44, and report in *BT* 4 July 1874). The work on the bells in 1904 is documented in the parish magazine (March 1904 to March 1905); **10.** The plate of 1640 and 1684–5 noted in the 1822 terrier and by Bonney was supplemented in 1855 by the gift of a new cup (ABE 5); **11.** The old clock is said to have been put up in 1662. Improvements were considered in 1875 (P 3/8/3). The new clock is documented in the parish magazines for 1884, and in reports in *BM* 24 May and 23 Aug. 1884 and *BM* and *BT* 20 Sept.1884; **12.** The pulpit cloth is mentioned in the 1822 terrier and in a note on the bell inscriptions (X 67/600); **13.** The vestry shown in Fisher's watercolour (X 254/88/277) had a hipped roof and late C17th details and J.D. Parry says that it was a "heavy brick vestry". Glynne indicates that it had been rebuilt by 1866. It was enlarged in 1975; **14.** For a recent account of the Wootton bell-founders see BHRS Vol.70 (1991) pp.120–2 (Emmerton) and pp.194–7 (the Russells). The bell of 1736 was probably the joint work of Thomas and his son William who, according to a deed of 1739/40, had "for many years last past worked with the said Thomas Russell at his business of Clockmaking, watchmaking, & running of bells" (AD 2421–2). William Russell (d.1770) took William Emmerton as an apprentice in 1752; **15.** The gable for the little bell of 1748 is shown in Fisher's watercolours of c.1815 (X 254/88/276–7). Writing in 1846 J.D. Parry noted "the little bell is over the gable of the nave, but inclosed in a kind of black wooden cupboard, and rung by a rope within the chancel"; **16.** The lead removed from the spire in 1959 was preserved for a while in the church where the present writer saw it but, unfortunately, did not make a note of its date and inscription; **17.** The Royal Arms (see Pardoe p.7) are mentioned by J.D. Parry who records their original position; **18.** J.D. Parry states that the west gallery extended to the side walls and that it was supported by fluted square pilasters. W.A. likened the glazed opening in the boarding in the tower arch to a cucumber frame; **19.** An early C19th watercolour by Thomas Fisher shows that east wall of the chancel was strapped up with iron bands (X 254/88/276). Boissier (f.361) noted in 1827 that the tracery in the east window was "plastered up"; **20.** The chancel exterior was restored in 1845 (Post Office *Directory* 1847 p.1758); **21.** J.D. Parry's comments clearly represent an attack on the Tractarian ideals espoused by W.A. As elsewhere (e.g. Woburn). Parry defended the earlier interior arrangements; **22.** Vestry minutes, 1848 (P 3/8/1). Although tenders were accepted, there is some doubt as to whether the work was actually done; **23.** A report in *BT* 12 Aug.1854 refers to the "attempt made on the part of the new Rector to remove the ugly pews and replace them with open seats of oak"; **24.** Neale's restoration is referred to in descriptions of the church in directories (*e.g.* Post Office *Directory* 1864 pp.368–9) and a report in *BT* 5 Dec.1865 mentions that "the fine old church has been restored within the last few years by the present Vicar ... with great taste and at considerable labour and expense" and with the help of Mr. Payne, the lay Rector. The dates for stages of the work can be established from what is known of the fittings (e.g. font and windows); **25.** The western bays of the aisles are not shown in John Sunman Austin's view dated 1854 (Z 50/136/15) but must have been completed by 1858 when stained glass was placed in the west windows; **26.** There are several entries regarding stained glass and quarries supplied to Neale by Powell of Whitefriars between 1857 (west window) and 1862 (V&A ref: AAD 1/51–3); **27.** A note in BAAS *Notes* no.7 (Nov.1857) p.112 mentions the new font "intended for the church at Wootton". The writer questions the need to replace the old font which is described by Boissier (f.361) and illustrated by Fisher (BCRO extra–illustrated Lysons). In 1866 Glynne described the font as new, and mentions the wooden cover "of tabernacle work"; **28.** An inscription on the case records the gift of the organ in 1860. According to the National Pipe Organs Register the organ was rebuilt in 1860 from an instrument of 1800. The restoration of 1897–8 was reported in the parish magazine and there are papers (P 3/2/41) regarding the improvements of 1896–7 and 1964 (P 3/2/41–3) ; **29.** The candelabra are shown in a photograph of the interior of c.1870–5 (X 67/934/63) but had been removed by the 1890s (Z 357/23). Their chains are still in place, tucked up out of sight among the roof timbers; **30.** Some sources (e.g. the Directories) state that the chancel was rebuilt in 1861 by Coventry Payne. The further work mentioned in *BT* 5 Dec.1865 may refer to the alterations to the floor which were later carried out in 1872; **31.** Faculty for re-location of monuments and alterations to the floors in the chancel, 1872 (HCRO ref: DSA 2/1/216); **32.** The chancel roof has a distinctly Victorian appearance of c.1860, but Glynne's comment in 1866 that "the chancel roof is original and has been varnished" makes it hard to be certain that it is not of later date. The present roof is shown in an interior photograph of c.1870–75 (X 67/934/63); **33.** Vestry minutes regarding nave roof repairs, 29 Dec.1872 (P 3/8/1); **34.** The new bier reported in parish magazine and in *BS* 22 Sept.1888; **35.** New east window reported in parish magazines and in *BT* 9 Aug.1890. It is by Powell of Whitefriars (V&A ref: AAD 1/61 p.94); **36.** The Dillon window is signed by Lavers and Westlake and dated 1905, but the parish magazines show that it was installed in Easter week 1906; **37.** Most of the recent work is commemorated by appropriately positioned plaques in the church; **38.** J.D. Parry also mentions a window "on the south side, barbarised in the loss of its mullions"; **39.** The stonework of this door described by W.A. can be seen in Fisher's view (X 254/88/277).

WRESTLINGWORTH

There is a small Norman window in the north wall of the chancel and other C12th fragments from an earlier church are built into the walls of the present building. The church was rebuilt in the C14th, chiefly in the Decorated style, and a Perpendicular west tower was added in the mid C15th. The roofs were renewed when a clerestory was added in the late C15th.[1] A charity established by Daniel Dennis (d.1709) provides income towards the upkeep of the church.[2]

There is a chalice of 1633.[3] The old bellframe has pits for three bells.[4] A clock was set up in the tower in 1685.[5] From 1725 information on expenditure on the church is available from the churchwardens' accounts.[6] They mention whitewashing the church in 1749, roof repairs in 1757 and recasting the bell in 1774.[4] George Townshend was paid seven guineas for "Painting and putting up the creed, Lord's Prayer and Ten Commandments in the Parish Church" in 1785.[7] Bonney mentions a paten of 1760, no longer extant.[3] The pulpit is also believed to be of C18th date and some of the former box pews were probably erected at the turn of the C19th.

In 1806 a new gallery was built at the west end of the church.[8] The bell was recast at St. Neots in 1820.[4] Following Bonney's visitation in 1823 various repairs were undertaken. The accounts record repairs to the seats in 1824, when the churchwardens certified that many of the Archdeacon's orders had been "obeyed, & the whole will be executed by Easter 1825".[9] In 1828–9 the churchwardens spent over £60 on the roof. In 1830 new rainwater heads and downpipes were placed on the tower.[10] A sounding board was placed above the pulpit in 1833 when the carpenter also repaired the chancel rails and removed a pew. In 1838 Mr. Wade was paid £16 for window repairs, and Bonney's order book suggests that in the late 1830s the chancel windows were also repaired by the Rev. W.C. Twiss.[11]

In 1843 the church was reported to be "under repare".[12] In 1847 the build-

52. Wrestlingworth: Interior looking east, showing the pulpit, stove and east end with the stained glass window in memory of the Rev.W.C. Twiss (d.1888)   *(Photograph: Anonymous c.1900)*

ing was thoroughly repaired by Wade and Yerrill under Mr. Wing, the architect, at a cost of £215 which was partly met by a loan from the Biggleswade Bank.[13] The work must have included the rebuilding of the south porch.[14] The commandments were re–done and placed on the east wall of the chancel.[7] By 1852 the east window had been filled with painted glass.[15] From the 1850s the parish frequently laid out modest sums of money on repairs, for instance in 1862–3 (£28), 1868–9 (£38 on tower repairs under Joseph Miller of Bedford), and 1875–6 (£55 on windows and buttresses).[6] Despite this, Archdeacon Bathurst described the condition of the building in 1876 as "indifferent" and noted that the walls were cracked.[16]

An organ by J.W. Walker was placed on the west gallery in 1868.[17] In 1870 a new paten was added to the plate.[3] A new clock was placed in the tower in 1874.[5] A lectern cloth was presented in 1880.[18] In 1883–4 new lamps were obtained for the church.[6] In 1888 the old glass in the east window was removed to Eyeworth, and new stained glass by Cox, Sons, Buckley & Co. was installed as a memorial to the Rev. W.C. Twiss.[15] In 1889 a new lectern, candlesticks and oak chair were also provided.[19]

By 1907 the roof was in need of repair, apparently carried out in about 1908 under F.C. Eden.[20] In 1908 the altar was raised by the addition of a moveable top.[21] A new stove was provided in 1917.[22] In 1922 the church was redecorated under the supervision of Thomas Cockrill of Biggleswade.[23] In 1961–2 new tapestry panels were placed in the chancel.[24] The interior was modified in 1970–1 with the removal of the west gallery and the remaining box pews.[25] More recently, the base of the tower has been adapted as a vestry and the east end of the south chapel has been furnished as a chapel.

1. Extract from glebe terrier, 1 July 1822

WRESTLINGWORTH.

Church yard. The Churchyard contains between three and four Roods, and is fenced on three sides at the expence of the Parish, and on the side contiguous to the Rectory at the expence of the Rector.[26]

Furniture and ornaments belonging to the church. One large Bible of the last translation. Two common Prayer Books, large. One Book of Offices. A silver Cup, weighing about six ounces, a pewter Flaggon and pewter plate for the Collection of Alms.[3] One Communion Table with a covering for the same of Cloth. A fine Cloth and Napkin for the same. A Surplice, a Pulpit Cloth and Cushion and Desk Cloth. The Kings Arms and the ten Commandments.[7] In the Steeple is one excellent, new Bell.[4] There are frames for more.[4] The Registers of the Parish begin with the month of October in the year 1578, and extraordinarily complete to the present Day. One excellent iron Chest. One also of Wood.[27] One Bier.

Parish Clerk. The Clerk is chosen by the Minister, Churchwarden and other principal Inhabitants. The customary Dues of the Parish Clerk, are, as follows, Marriage with Banns 2s 6d. with Licence 5s. For every Funeral 2s 6d.

2. Archdeacon Bonney's historical notices of churches, c.1820–1840

WRESTLINGWORTH, St. Peter. This Church consists of a Nave, aisles separated by cylindrical Piers & pointed Arches, & chancel and low Tower at the West End, the Character of the Edifice is Decorated. On the Chalice is "Wrestlingworth Communion Cup in Bedfordshire".[3] This is silver. The Patin is pewter & inscribed "Wrestlingworth Church 1760".[3] There are also a Pewter Flagon & Plate. The font is octagonal & Perpendicular with good quarterfoils & Roses in the Panels. The East Window is new, and of the Perpendicular.[28] There is a South Porch.[14]

3. Archdeacon Bonney's visitation notebook, 1823–1839

WRESTLINGWORTH. This Church consists of a Nave, North and South Aisles, a chancel at the East End of the Nave and Tower at the West End thereof & South Porch.[14]

At the Visitation of 1823 The following Order was given – that the Earth be moved from the Walls; The Porch be thoroughly repaired; the Open Seats be taken to pieces, neatly repaired; cleansed & set down again; the Floor be made level; the Font be moved; cleaned; and a new Font Bason be purchased; a new floor be placed in the Steeple; a Surplice and Napkin be purchased; The

Stonework of the Doors and Windows be restored with Parker's Cement; a New Flagon be purchased; the Pillars & Arches be cleansed; The Windows, now blocked up, be glazed; The Bible be repaired.[9]

At the Visitation of 1826 It was ordered that Stonework similar to that in the Windows of the Chancel be inserted in the East Window.[28] A South Window in the Chancel be glazed before Easter 1828.

At the Visitation of 1833 It was ordered that a new Prayer Book be purchased for the Minister & the old one repaired for the Clerk. The exterior of the Stone work of the Windows be restored with Parker's Cement. The Churchwardens were instructed in placing a Farmer in a Pew on the South side of yᵉ South Aisle[25] – & leave was given to take down the low & rude Porch on the South side.[14]

At the Visitation of 1836 ordered a New Napkin, and that the Church yard fence be repaired or renewed.[26]

At the Visitation of 1839. No order required – A New Glebe House had been built,[29] & restorations made in the Chancel Windows by the present Incumbent (Mʳ. Twiss).[11, 28] The Parishioners were surrounding the Church Yard by a brick wall.[26] Sanctioned the rounding of one corner only a few feet.

4. Article on the Church by W.A. (no.85), NM 3 July 1852

WRESTLINGWORTH. St. Peter "Now, ere thou passest further, sit thee down in the church porch, and think what thou hast seen."

In the present instance, we were enabled to follow the excellent George Herbert's advice, and right glad were we to avail ourselves of the quiet rest after a long walk. That this opportunity should be so generally denied is a matter of sincere regret; we trust that in the better spirit, now arising among our younger clergy, this boon to the wayfarer will be no longer withheld.

The porch of this church is judiciously restored,[14] the windows open, affording an agreeable prospect of the adjacent scenery. the external condition of the church is good; the open windows permitted a free circulation of air.

The chancel has a timber roof, clean; and only two pews, which are, however, low. Under the communion table, an iron chest, a sad mark of irreverence: the ancient oak chest is banished into the usual lumber room, discarded for the utilitarian one in question. Painted glass is our delight, but not of the character placed in the eastern windows of this church.[15]

The nave and aisles have their timber roofs. The pulpit is of an appropriate size, and rightly separated from the reading desk. The sittings are for the most part open, of modern construction, but a few boxes are reserved for the exclusives.[25]

We are glad to have an opportunity of referring to the efforts of a minister of the Church of England against the pew system, which he justly deems the "chief hindrance to the church's work," especially in towns.* A large singing gallery mars the belfry arch.[8] The font has lead and drain, but is not used. The floor is paved with plain tiles. A less utilitarian age, will in all probability replace these, with others in better taste, but it is a great gain to find the floor of a church in so good a condition.

We are glad to observe, late in the day as it is, a national school nearly completed. Knowing the difficulty there is in persuading rural occupiers and labourers of the benefits derived from education, we are not surprised a writer+ from whose valuable work we have already quoted, observes, "When the ignorance of the small farmer is like the `slavery that hugs her chain,' and renders him unwilling to incur any trouble or expense for the purposes of education, we need hardly wonder that there should be at least an equal want on the part of the ignorant agricultural labourer of all perception of the necessary tendency and value of education to those who can obtain it."

24 June 1852   W.A.

* A Sermon, by the Rev. E. Stuart, M.A.

+ Pashly, on Pauperism, p.96

Notes **1.** Pevsner p.175, *VCH* II pp.257–8, and "R.C." article in *BT* 7 April 1899; **2.** For the charities <u>see</u> *VCH* II pp.258–9; **3.** The plate is listed in the 1927 schedule which mentions the cup of 1633–4, a paten of 1869–70 and a plated flagon (ABE 5). The paten of 1760 mentioned by Bonney has apparently been lost; **4.** The bellframe probably dates from the early C17th and the size of the pits indicates that it once held three bells with a tenor of about 10 cwt. The present bell of 1820 (North p.210) was cast by Robert Taylor of St.Neots and the churchwardens' accounts show that it had previously been recast in 1774. It is not known when the other bells were sold; **5.** The clock of 1685 is mentioned in a note in the account book (P 52/5/1). There are accounts for the new clock put up in 1874 (P 52/5/2) which is also listed (under Potton) in a catalogue produced by the makers, J.W. Benson of Ludgate Hill, London, in 1882; **6.** Churchwardens' accounts 1725–1921 (P 52/5/1–2); **7.** The commandments were painted in 1785 and re-done or replaced in 1847 when the churchwardens paid £5 to D. Norman, carpenter, for a new frame for commandments and £10 to J.Fisher for "painting, graining and writing in gold" (P 52/5/1–2). RC notes that they were on the east wall in 1899; **8.** The gallery was taken down in 1970–1 but a board carrying an inscription "This Gallery was / erected by subscription / for the use of the / SUNDAY SCHOOL / CHILDREN / R^d Lewis Rector / T Wenham C Warden / 1806" is still preserved in the vestry; **9.** Articles of Enquiry, 1824 (ABCV 130); **10.** The RC article in *BT* 7 April 1899 mentions the date 1830 on water–spouting on north side of the tower. A payment in the accounts of Miller's bill (£10 8s 6d) in 1831 may refer to this work; **11.** The Rev.W.C. Twiss, who is commemorated in the east window, was curate 1827–37 and then Rector until his death in 1888. His ordination papers survive in the parish records (P 52/0/1); **12.** Presentment bill, 1843 (ABCV 128); **13.** The thorough repairs of 1847 are noted in the RC article. The expenditure is recorded in the accounts (P 52/5/2); **14.** Bonney sanctioned the removal of "the low & rude Porch" in 1833, and the present porch – described by W.A. in 1852 as "judiciously restored" – must have been rebuilt in 1847; **15.** The glass mentioned by W.A. in 1852 apparently remained in place until 1888 when the present east window was installed. According to the report in *BS* 13 Oct.1888 it then was transferred to Eyeworth, but it no longer exists; **16.** Bathurst's notebook (ABE 3); **17.** The new organ is mentioned in the accounts for 1868 (P 52/5/2) and in a report in *BT* 22 Sept.1868; **18.** The lectern cloth reported in *BS* 1 March 1880; **19.** The lectern and other fittings are noted in the accounts for 1888–9 (P 52/5/2) and also mentioned by Bathurst (ABE 3); **20.** Bathurst refers in 1910 to the condition of the roof (ABE 3), and the parish archives include a report on its conditions prepared by J.Leonard Williams for the SPAB in 1908 (P 52/2/2/1). The SPAB archives indicate that F.C. Eden was appointed to take charge of the work in 1908; **21.** Letter from Rattee & Kett about the altar, 1908 (P 52/2/2/2); **22.** Papers concerning the stove and other repairs, 1911–7 (P 52/2/2/3); **23.** Papers concerning the work in 1922 (P 52/2/2/4–5); **24.** Papers concerning the tapestry panels, 1961–2 (P 52/2/2/13); **25.** Faculties for the removal of the pews and gallery, 1970–1 (P

52/2/2/6v and at the church). The gallery and box pews were noted by Pevsner. The gallery was built in 1806. Bonney refers to a pew in 1833 and W.A. mentions "a few boxes ... reserved for the exclusives"; **26.** A new brick wall was built round the churchyard in 1840 (P 52/5/2) in response to Bonney's orders; **27.** The churchwardens bought "three padlocks for the church chest" in 1780 (P 52/5/1); **28.** Bonney's notes must refer to a new window installed for the Rev.W.C. Twiss in the late 1830s, as in 1827 Boissier (f.434d–5) noted "the East Window of wood & round headed". Bonney had been pressing for proper repair since 1826; **29.** The Rectory was rebuilt for Twiss in 1837 (mortgage P 52/2/4/1) and there are plans by John Smith of Cambridge, architect, 1837 (LAO ref: MGA 219); **30.** The school was built in 1851 (*VCH* II p.185).

WYMINGTON

The list of incumbents goes back to 1235 but there was almost certainly a church at Wymington long before the earliest documentary reference. The old church was completely rebuilt in the second half of the C14th by John Curteys (d.1391) whose family bought the living in 1361. The church, completed in about 1377, is a remarkably fine building in the Decorated style.[1] The south porch is rib-vaulted and has a carving of the Green Man on the centre boss. Curteys is commemorated on a fine brass between the chancel and south chapel and there are several other brasses.[2] There are wall-paintings, including a late C14th Trinity in the South aisle and a C15th Doom over the chancel arch.[3] There were five bells here before the Reformation and three of them still survive.[4] The Perpendicular benches in the nave are of C15th date.[5] There is a good C14th font.[6]

Since the C18th the church has attracted the interest of antiquarians and students of church architecture. It is described in Oliver St.John Cooper's history of the parish (1785) which gives information on the monuments and bells. Lysons (1806) depicts the east end before the mid C19th alterations and there is a detailed illustrated account of the church in the Brandons' book on *Parish Churches* (1848).[7] The church is also recorded in manuscript accounts by the Rev.D.T. Powell (1810), the Rev. G.R. Boissier (1827), H.K. Bonney (c.1840) and Sir Stephen Glynne (1840). The Rev. W.D. Sweeting (1871) also gives a good description of the monuments.[8] These accounts compensate in some measure for the lack of primary sources and archival evidence on the building.

There is a reference to repairs to the chancel roof in 1617.[9] The draw-out seats added to the old benches in the nave date from the C17th and there is a Jacobean pulpit and tester. The tenor bell was recast in 1676 by Toby Norris of Stamford.[10] The bellframe was also renewed in the same year, and the base timbers of the top frame carry the names of the churchwardens and the date 1676.[11] The tenor bell was again recast in 1814.[10] There was a clock at Wymington in 1706 but the present C17th movement (disused) is believed to have come from Rushden when a new clock was set up there in 1735.[12]

Bonney's visitation orders for 1823 indicate that the building was neglected and falling into disrepair. He suggested a number of improvements. The

53. Wymington: W view showing the tower and spire, the "bullseye" window at the west end of the north aisle and the turret at the east end. *(Watercolour: Bradford Rudge c.1840)*

Rural Dean reported on the condition of the church in 1832, noting "the worst is the state of the pews near the Desk & Pulpit" and "the Walls are much stained by Rain & dirty".[13] He also found green moss in the south aisle, two bells without clappers and two broken windows in the side chapel. By 1833 Bonney was concerned about the east end of the church, and in 1839 he gave permission for it to be "taken down and rebuilt exactly in the same manner as to its Architecture as it is now".

The east end was rebuilt shortly afterwards, probably in 1843.[14] The east window was reinstated in its original form but lancets were substituted for the two-light windows in the side chapels. The work on the chancel was done by John Stevens of Clophill who was doubtless responsible for the stucco on the exterior.[15] In 1843 the cracked bell was recast and the spire was repaired by George Handscombe Miller of Bedford.[16] It is noted that further work was undertaken in 1844–5.[17]

In 1858 the Duke of Bedford gave £5 towards the cost of repairing the spire. Later the Duke offered £35 towards the restoration of the church but the estate report for 1863 notes that "the project did not proceed".[18] The Rev. William Monk became Rector in 1864. He, too, planned a restoration.[19] In 1869 he wrote an excellent paper on the history of the church but in the 1870s he fell into financial difficulties and plunged the living into debt.[20] In 1874 Archdeacon Bathurst described the church as in "bad condition" and a report in a local paper in the same year commented on "the desirability of restoration".[21] Monk was to remain as Rector until 1885, and until his departure little could be done about the state of the church.

In 1873 Stephen Wollaston gave a sixth bell to the church, but owing to shortage of funds it remained on the church floor. A faculty was obtained to hang it in 1884 but this was never done.[22] In 1888 the Archdeacon noted "the new Rector energetically trying to set things to rights" but the church remained "in great need of restoration". The mortgage debt on the benefice was eventually cleared in 1893, and this cleared the way for improvements.[23] New plate was provided in 1894 and gifts for the altar in 1899–1900 are noted in the service register and inventory.[24]

In 1901 C.J. Blomfield prepared plans for a full restoration of the church.[25] An appeal was launched for £2000 but funds were slow to come in and only a limited amount of work was done. Some underpinning was eventually done in 1908 at a cost of £103 and further urgent repairs were undertaken in 1909–10.[26] This work, carried out by Robert Marriott of Rushden, included repairs to the spire. The organ also was restored in 1910.[27]

Major repairs were carried out between the wars.[28] The aisles were re–roofed in 1923 and in the 1920s and 1930s the church was gradually restored under Talbot Brown and Fox of Wellingborough. In 1925 the reredos was removed from the south chapel to the high altar, and in 1938 it was furnished with five statues designed by J.N. Comper.[29] Further restoration work was carried out on the fabric between 1965 and 1979, and the wall-paintings were conserved by Dr. E. Clive Rouse in 1980.[30]

1. Extract from glebe terrier, 24 June 1822
WYMINGTON
Church yard. Item the churchyard, containing with the ground the Church stands on about one Rood and thirty nine perches, the fence round about the same repaired by the parish where it adjoins the road, but where it adjoins any persons property the owner is chargeable. The gate on the North side is repaired by the Rector, the two on the South side by the parish. The said Churchyard is bounded on the North by the Rector's rick-yard and Garden, on the East by a Garden and two houses belonging to John Mackness, and by the property of ... Hollist Esquire, on the south by the public road, and on the West by the Rectory house and premises belonging thereto.

Church. Belonging to the said Parish are first the Parish Church, a very ancient structure covered with lead, containing in length with the Chancel seventy-five feet, the Church in breadth thirty feet, the chancel thirty three feet within the walls. The Steeple nine feet in length and eight feet in breadth within the walls. A porch on the south side in length eight feet and a half, in breadth seven feet and a half within the walls.

Furniture, utensils etc. Within and belonging to the said Church are, one Communion Table with a covering for the same of green cloth. Also one linen cloth and one napkin for the same. One pewter flaggon.[24] One silver Chalice. One Pewter plate. One pulpit and reading desk. One pulpit cushion, covered with green pluch. One table for the Choir. Several forms. Five bells with their frames.[4] One church clock.[12] One ancient stone font lined with lead.[6] One bier. Two surplices. One wooden Chest. One iron Chest containing the Registers of the parish and other papers as follows (Viz):

Registers. One Register book of Marriages, Baptisms and Burials commencing in the year 1662 and ending in 1792. One Register book of the publication of banns and of the solemnization of marriages commencing in 1753 and ending in 1812. One other register book of baptisms and Burials commencing in 1791 and ending in 1812. Three new separate register books of Marriages, Baptisms, and Burials commencing in 1812.

Repairs. The middle Chancel of the said church is repaired by the Rector, and the pews, seats, and every other part by the parish, towards the expence of which there was a piece of land containing one rood and seven perches allotted to the parish at the time of the inclosure, which said land is situated in the north-east corner of an allotment then made to John Achurch but since purchased by William Goosey, which said Church land is particularly specified and marked out in the award and plan annexed thereto.

Ornaments in the church. On the walls of the said Church are painted the Kings Arms, the Ten Commandments [the Creed, and the Lord's Prayer[c]] and in the Chancel are four compartments containing texts of Scripture

Parish Clerk. The office both of Parish Clerk and Sexton has always been in the same person, and he is chosen by the Minister alone and receives his wages of the Parishioners in the same manner following (viz) The Lodge and Manor houses pay each two shillings and six pence per annum, and every other farm house pays two shillings. Some Cottages pay eight pence, and some seven pence annually; one half of which sums is due at Lady Day and the other half at St. Michael. Also the Church Warden pays him ten shillings every half year for looking after the clock, oiling the bells, and cleaning the leads. He has one shilling for every wedding by banns and two and sixpence for every wedding by licence, four pence for ringing a passing bell, one shilling for digging a grave in the Church Yard, two and sixpence for every grave in the Church or Chancel.

2. Archdeacon Bonney's historical notices of churches, c.1820–1840

WIMINGTON, St. Laurence. This Church consists of Nave & Aisles, Chancel & Side Chapels, South Porch, and Tower embattled with a Crocketted Spire at the West End. The Porch has stone groined Roof, and the Whole Fabrick is of one design, late decorated. In the East window of the South Chapel is this Bearing [*Sketch of coat of arms*]. There are 5 Bells.[4]

The Chalice is silver.[24] A plated Plate & Pewter Flagon and Plate. On an altar Tomb in the North Chapel [*Sketch of coat of arms*]:

Vita decessit Gulielmus Nomine Bletsoe Hac Wymingtoniæ Dominus verusque patronus anno M Sex et C nono ter quoqye deno vicesimoque die quarto mensis Februarii ætatis Sex denos tu numerat is est octo annos tres natas Ter Tres notosque reliquit Cum Christo vivit vitam qui vixit honestam.

In the Chancel is a piscina & two sedilia, also a piscina in South Chapel all decorated, in which is also a rich perpendicular Tomb half sunk in the Wall. There are rich Brasses to Bromflet & his wife, & to Curteis, the Founder of the Church.[2] See Lysons.[7]

3. Archdeacon Bonney's visitation notebook, 1823–1839

WYMINGTON. This Church consists of a Nave, North and South Aisles, Chancel at the East of the Nave between a North and South Chapel. And a Tower surmounted by a Spire at the West End of the Nave – a Porch to the South Aisle.

At the Visitation of 1823 The following Order was given That a New Surplice be purchased – the Coal be moved out of the South Chancel; the East window of the Chancel be cleansed and repaired; but none of the painted glass taken out. The Font be cleansed and repaired with Parker's Cement – a handle be put to the Covering & proper font bason be purchased. The floors be made level; Shutters be placed within the Windows of the Steeple: Two Casements be placed in a North and South window; a New Prayer Book be purchased – the Bible be repaired; the Bell wheel be repaired; the Earth be moved from the Walls; the Church & the Steeple be pointed; the Ten Commandments be renewed; the Earth be moved from the Front of the Rectorial House.

At the Visitation of 1826 – It was ordered that the Font be cleansed & left stone colour; the Top be cleansed & oiled & have a handle put to it; The Seats throughout the Church be set strait, repaired, and oiled; Two casements be made according to ye previous order; a New Prayer Book be purchased for the Minister – part of the Wall near a Spout be pointed; The cracked Bell be recast before April 1828.[16] The Communion Table be cleansed and oiled; The floor of the South Chapel be made level; he Font & Wall opposite be cleansed from wash; The East Window be cleansed (in the same Chapel).

At the Visitation of 1833 It was ordered that the crown of the Arch of the East Window in the Chancel be surveyed, & secured from falling – the Seats near the Font be repaired – the floors be made level, weather boards or shutters be placed in the windows in the Rood over the Porch & the wall thereof be repaired – a representation be made to the Bishop by the Archdeacon of the state of the Rectorial Premises – This was done.

At the Visitation of 1836 Ordered that the framework of the fourth Bell be repaired & secured – and the brasses and gudgeons of all the Bells be examined and substantially repaired – also that the Door and open Seats be repaired.

At the Visitation of 1839 Ordered that the Porch be pointed and the Battlements on the South side; the Coping of Two of the Battlements & basement of a Buttress on the Same Side be repaired. The floor of the Chancel be relaid and East End secured.

At a Second Visitation of 1839 I met a Builder with M^r. Lendon the Incumbent – and consented that the East End should be taken down and rebuilt exactly in the same manner as to its Architecture as it now is, & that the Tracery be carefully taken out of the Windows and replaced; as at present.[14]

4. Article on the Church by W.A. (no.114), BT 24 June 1854

WYMINGTON, St. Lawrence. The exterior of the building is in very good order. The churchyard is not locked.

The chancel is tolerably clean, but coloured with lime-wash. The side aisle contains some interesting brasses.[2] The early decorations in this part serve as a receptacle for rubbish. It is most offensive to see this sad inattention, which would not be permitted in the houses of the incumbent or his churchwarden.

An alms box, apparently recently introduced, is in the church.

In general the old open benches remain; a few ugly enclosed boxes have been erected, interfering, as usual, with the view of the occupants of the original sittings.[5] The roof is open; which, we believe, to be generally the case with the few churches not described. This is at least a triumph over the ceiled roof erected to conceal the neglect of the original. The arches are well covered with white–wash; it is pleasant to observe that this incipient step (the removal of this coating) an improvement now so generally in progress – it will save the worthy churchwarden some expense, and prevent the casing of the walls with perishable matting to preserve the congregation's garments from the plasterer's daubing.

The western window is hidden from view; and, of course, the belfry, whereby the ringers are excluded from observation, and not rendered, as they ought to be, a portion of the congregation. See how well this has been provided for in Tingrith church. The font has its leaden lining, and is apparently used. We omitted to mention that the seats which have been introduced into the chancel are open and of fitting character.

12 June 1854   W.A.

5. *Sir Stephen Glynne's Church notes, 1840 (Vol.1, pp.59–61)*

WYMINGTON. This is a very elegant, though not spacious Church, & particularly valuable as being a uniform & unaltered structure, built in 14th century by one John Curteys, Lord of the Manor, obt 1391, to whom & his wife there is a very well preserved brass in the Chancel.[2] Besides which, [it] affords a curious specimen of transition from Decorated to Perpendicular such as might be expected at the date of its erection.

This Church has a West tower with elegant crocketed Spire, a nave & chancel each with side aisles & a South porch. The Tower has an embattled parapet, the battlements pierced with open elongated quatrefoil, as at Pickering, Yorkshire. Beneath the parapet is a cornice of heads intermixed with foliage & a band of quatrefoils. The belfry windows are double on each side & long – each of 2 lights with transom & the arch mouldings very elegantly filled with a series of 4 leaf flowers. There are small apertures in the tower in shape quatrefoils set in squares. The Spire though not very lofty is elegant & crocketed at the angles. At its base round the whole of it is a range of large canopied windows finely crocketed, & one on each face – their transoms having small battlements. There is another similar range of smaller windows higher up in the Spire. The Church has no Clerestory – but the whole of one height & quite uniform – having a good battlement to every part. The S porch has the parvise, & good stone groining with foliated bosses & lighted by elegant square headed small windows having the transition tracery. The East end of the Church externally is singular – the nave & aisles included under one gable in such a way as to give no indication of the existence of aisles. The centre window is a large elegant Decorated one of 5 lights, but the 2 side ones, terminating the aisles are very small indeed, each of 2 lights, & have a curious effect by the side of the large window without any division between them.[14] In the point of the embattled gable is a niche & the East end is flanked on each side by large octagonal turrets with battlements & openings of the same form as those in the parapets of the steeple.

The windows are mostly of 2 lights, square headed with labels & containing tracery of plain Decorated character. On the North of the Chancel is one of 3 lights with rather depressed arch. There is a string course externally above the windows with some gargoyles. The nave is divided from each aisle by 4 pointed arches rising from light octagonal columns. The Chancel has 2 similar arches on the South, & one on the North – the Eastern arch on the S. side has good mouldings & is of ogee form, with a tomb inserted in it to the founders – with their figures beautifully executed in brass, under rich crocketed canopies.[2] On the S side of the altar are two ascending sedilia with triangular crocketed canopies & tracery in the heads of the arches – & a fine piscina with projecting ogee canopy. In the Chancel are also 2 brasses of considerable beauty to Sir Thomas Bromflete & Margaret his wife, daughter to Sir Edward St.John. He was cup bearer to Henry V & died 1430. She died 1407. In a window S of the Chancel is a niche in the angle & beneath a range of 5 fine canopied niches.[29] The Font is octagonal,[6] having round the upper part a band of wavy panneling with quatrefoils – The seats are mostly open,[5] & the altar is not enclosed with rails.

(Engraved in Lysons's Bedfordshire p.150.[7] – The legend on brass runs thus "Hic jacet Johes' Curteys dns' de Wymington quondam maior staple' Lanaru Calesii et Albrede ux ei' qui istam eccliam de novo construxerunt – obiit ei ide' Johes XIX die mensis April Anno dni millmo CCCIXXXXI aiabi' quor ppicietur deus – Amen"[i]).[2]

Notes **1.** Pevsner pp.175–6, Harvey pp.435–43, *VCH* III pp.120–2, Monk's description of the church in AASRP (1869) pp.537–9, and *Guide and History of the Church of St.Lawrence, Wymington* n.d. [c.1990]; **2.** For the brasses, see Lack *et.al.* (pp.102–6); **3.** The wall-paintings were "discovered" in 1909 (*Ely Diocesan Remembrancer* Oct.1910 p.138) and restored in 1980 (P 61/2/79 and 86); **4.** The three surviving mediaeval bells were all cast by William Chamberlain of London c.1440, and the inscriptions of the others (since recast) are noted by North (pp.210–1) who notes his sources as St.John Cooper's history (1785) and Weever's *Funeral Monuments* (in the original edition of 1631 or that of 1767). There was also a mediaeval sanctus bell; **5.** The seats are of the buttressed Perpendicular type (Pevsner). The enclosed pews noted by W.A. in 1854 have been removed; **6.** The font is illustrated by Harvey (p.446). The Victorian font at Northill is a copy, made in 1858, of the one at Wymington; **7.** Published accounts of the church are to be found in Oliver St.John Cooper *An historical account of the parish of Wimmington* (1785), Lysons *Magna Britannia* (1806), and the Brandons' *Parish Churches* (1848) pp.93–4; **8.** Manuscript accounts include those by the Rev. D.T. Powell, c.1810–2 (BL ref: Add.Ms. 17456 f.64 etc.), the Rev. G.R. Boissier, 1827 (BL ref: Add.Ms. 48977 f.373d–5d), and the Rev. W.D Sweeting, 1871 (BL ref: Add.Ms. 37178 f.24); **9.** Presentments, 1617 (ABC 5 p.65); **10.** There is a bond and receipt for the recasting of the tenor by Tobias Norris in 1676 (P 61/6/1–2). It was again recast in 1814; **11.** The bellframe carries the carved inscription (west) "Stephen Newcome & John Church C W 1676" and (east) "MP William Paxton John Gray TF". It is in two tiers, and the walls have been much hollowed–out to give room for the bells to swing. The bells were last rung in the 1890s (ringing reported in *BM* 4 Oct.1890). A scheme for restoration in 1933 was abandoned; **12.** The 1706 terrier (ABE 2 Vol.I p.274) mentions a clock and it is possible that the present clock has always belonged to Wymington, but L.H. Chambers records a local tradition that it came from Rushden (AD 3869/7 p.84); **13.** Rural Dean's report, 1832 (P 61/2/58); **14.** The main source for the "1839" rebuilding of the east end is Monk's paper (quoted by Harvey p.436) but Monk actually wrote in 1869 that the work had been done <u>about</u> thirty years ago. The alterations had not been made when Glynne visited in 1840. Other evidence indicates that the work was done in 1844–3 (bills in P 61/2/59). Monk regretted the change to the windows and considered that they should be changed back again "in the restoration of the church"; **15.** John Stevens of Clophill was a noted plasterer, and as the church is described as "covered with cement with false masonry joints in 1844" (*VCH* III p.120) it seems quite likely that he was responsible; **16.** Bills for repairs to the bell and spire 1843 (P 61/2/59); **17.** The *VCH* (possibly on structural evidence destroyed in subsequent repairs) notes that the exterior was covered with cement in 1844, the arches to nave were rebuilt in 1844, the north chapel screened off by a wall for use as a vestry in 1845, and a doorway in the south wall was blocked in 1845; **18.** Donations by the Duke of Bedford noted in estate reports for 1858 (p.54) and 1863 (p.16); **19.** Harvey (p.438) refers to plans for restoration in 1864, and the proposals were mentioned in a report in *BT* 20 June 1865; **20.** Monk's paper of 1869 (note 1) shows his real interest in the building, but he lost money on a speculative investment and mortgaged the glebe in an unsuccessful attempt to recover his losses. There is information about this in the deeds to advowson 1698–1900 and mortgages of the glebe etc, 1857–1900 (P 61/2/1–38); **21.** Bathurst's notebook (ABE 3) and report in *BT* 12 Dec.1874; **22.** North (pp.210–1) gives details of the 1873 bell which, although a faculty was obtained in 1884 (HCRO ref: DSA 2/1/217), was never hung. It was eventually sold to Odell in 1958 (P 61/2/77); **23.** Events noted by Bathurst (ABE 3). A deed of 1900 refers to the clearance of the mortgage in 1893 (P 61/2/37); **24.** The present plate is of 1894 (ABE 5) and no old plate survives. Other gifts of this period are noted in the service register (P 61/0/15) and inventory (P 61/0/23 p.43); **25.** The Blomfield report of 1901 and the appeal are in the ICBS papers (LPL ref: 10341) and in the SPAB archives; **26.** The work of 1907–10 is noted in the official register (P 61/0/23 p.31 and p.40) and in the Deanery Magazine 1908–9 (P 80/30/1); **27.** The organ is a C19th instrument by Bryceson, provided in place of an older organ in 1910 (P 61/0/23 p.35 and Deanery Magazine 1910); **28.** There are papers concerning the inter–war repairs, 1923–33 (P 61/2/43–54), also noted in the registers (P 61/0/16 and P 61/0/23 p.40). There are further papers in the ICBS archives (LPL ref: ICBS 11508) and SPAB files; **29.** The 1925 reredos and statues are noted in the guide (p.1) and there is a faculty for the statues, 1938 (P 61/2/75). The reredos is described in its former position by Glynne.

Y

YELDEN

There was a church here by 1162 when the advowson passed into the hands of Thorney Abbey. It later belonged to the Trailly family. No traces of the original church remain, but the main walls of the nave and chancel date from the C13th. The church was remodelled in the C14th and the present tower and south aisle are of this period. The Decorated work of the C14th includes a carved frieze (as at Swineshead) on the parapet and a fine tomb recess or monumental arch in the south aisle. There is a mediaeval vestry on the north side of the chancel.[1] The font probably dates from the C15th.[2] There are wall–paintings, including a figure of St.Christopher on the south wall. The church is memorable for its Perpendicular woodwork, including the pulpit, font cover and the benches in the nave and aisles.[3]

Two of the bells date from the early C17th, one of 1610 and another of 1617.[4] Further bells were recast in 1660 and 1717. The plate includes a cup and paten of 1629.[5] The communion table, also dated 1629,[6] carries the initials "CS" and is believed to have been given by Christopher Strickland

54. Yelden: SE view showing the church with its low broach spire and embattled parapets. Apart from the clock dial on the tower (1876), gable cross on the east end and an additional buttress on the south side of the chancel (1892) the church looks very similar today

(Pen and ink drawing: Sebastian Evans 1851)

(d.1628) whose memorial brass states that he "lived in this parish a long time and was a very good benefactor".[7]

On a piece of lead taken from the chancel roof in 1892 there is a lengthy verse written by Thomas Williamson in 1703.[8] It now hangs in the tower. The creed, Lord's prayer, and ten commandments are painted on the north wall of the nave, with wooden a moulded cornice which has been coloured to look like marble. There is no date, but this was probably painted in the C18th. Later accounts refer to enclosed pews in the nave and aisles, also likely to have been set up in the C18th.[9]

Bonney's order book suggests that the church was in need of attention by 1823, especially the tower. Repairs may have been carried out shortly afterwards. The vestry minutes refer to repairs "to the masonwork and spouting ordered by Archdeacon" in 1843 and in 1847 it was agreed to ask "Mr. Derbyshire to give estimate for the repair of the leads".[10]

A new organ by Trustam of Bedford was provided for the church in 1865.[11] A stained glass window was erected in the chancel in memory of the Rev. John Fernie (d.1870). In 1876 a clock was placed in the tower.[12] By 1874, however, Archdeacon Bathurst found the church in "bad condition, especially tower and chancel".[13] The tower and spire were restored in 1882 by William Streather of Raunds under the supervision of John Day of Bedford.[14] In 1885 the second bell was recast, and in 1886 the bells were rehung in a new frame by W. Henson of Finedon.[15] The weathercock was re-fixed on the spire in March 1896.[16]

Extensive work was carried out in 1892 when a new organ chamber was added on the north side of the church.[17] The chancel was also restored at the expense of the Rector. The architect was W. Lewis Baker of Hargrave. The organ was rebuilt by J. & A. Trustam before being installed in the new organ chamber.

Later work includes repairs to the nave roof under S. Inskip Ladds following gale damage in 1906,[18] repairs to the tower and spire under Professor A.E. Richardson in 1934,[19] and further restoration work in 1985–93.[20]

1. Extract from glebe terrier, 24 June 1822

YELDEN.

Church yard. Item the Churchyard containing two Roods and nine poles, fenced on the East with a Stone Wall, on the West, North and South with pales.[21]

Church. The Church, an ancient building, contains in length (with the Chancel) seventy one feet, in breadth thirty two feet. The chancel in breadth fifteen feet. The Steeple is nine feet ten inches square within the walls.

Furniture and ornaments. Within & belonging to which are one Communion Table[6] with a covering for the same of green cloth. Also one linen cloth for the same with a Napkin. One silver Chalice, one bason for the Offertory, one Paten, all marked IHS and weighing together twenty ounces Troy.[5] One oak chest. One Iron chest. One pulpit cloth & Cushion. One large Bible & Prayer book. Two books of offices. Four bells with their frames,[4] the first or least bell being twenty seven inches & a half in diameter with this inscription (Grata sit arguta resonans campanula voce 1717), the second twenty eight inches in diameter with this inscription, (Bryanus Eldridge 1660), the third thirty two inches in diameter with this inscription (Praise the Lord 1617), the fourth or largest thirty four inches in diameter (1610). One bier. One surplice. One parchment Register book beginning 1653 & ending 1812.

Repairs. The Body of the Church, Steeple & Vestry with the Furniture of all sorts is maintained by the Parish as likewise the wall of the Church yard; the rest of the fence by several private persons, viz: the Pales on the South side & West side by the Lord of the Manor, the Pales on the North side by the Parish. The Chancel is maintained by the Rector.

Parish Clerk and Sexton. The Offices of Clerk & Sexton are in one person appointed by the Rector, who (according to the Terrier of 1709) can demand for his accustomed wages of a Farmer at Easter sixpence, at Whitsuntide sixpence, at Christmas tenpence, of Cottager at Easter two pence, at Christmas sixpence, at Whitsuntide twopence. Of all the other houses one penny at Easter, one penny at Whitsuntide & five pence at Christmas. In lieu of these, the Clerk has of late years been accustomed to receive seven shillings per quarter paid out of the Church Rates. The due to him for every wedding by publication is two shillings & sixpence, by licence five shillings. For Bell and Grave two shillings.

2. Archdeacon Bonney's historical notices of churches, c.1820–1840

YIELDEN OR YEVELDEN, St. Mary. This Church consists of a Nave and South Aisle, Chancel and low Spire at the West End and a South Porch. The Piers are cylindrical supporting pointed Arches. The Character of the Church is the decorated. In the South Aisle is a beautiful decorated Sepulchral Arch,[22] and in the North Wall of the Nave a low sepulchral Arch, under which is the Effigy of a Layman. The Porch and Clerestory are perpendicular. The Chalice & cover & Patin are silver, the Flagon plated.[5] In the Chancel under the Effigy of a Priest in his Vestments is this Inscription,[23] "Hic jacet Dominus Johannes Heyne (or Henne) quondam Rector istius Ecclesie Qui obiit XXV° die Mensis Junii Anno Domini Millo CCCC°XXXIII° cujus anime propicietur Deus. Amen". Also in Brass "Here lyeth the body of Christopher Strickland Gent. who lived in this Parish a long time, and was a very good Benefactor he dyed the 12th of Jan. 1628 being of the age of 80 years." He is represented in a short Cloak.[7]

On a Brass against the North Wall of the Chancel is the Effigy of a Man in a long gown with pendant Sleeves. This is Thos. Barker formerly Rector of this Church and fellow of New College Oxford, who died 11 Nov[r] 1617. [*Sketch of coat of arms* Barker].

3. Archdeacon Bonney's visitation notebook, 1823–1839

YIELDEN. This Church consists of a Nave and South Aisle, a Tower at the West end of the Nave surmounted by a low Spire and a Chancel at the East End of the Nave, & S. Porch.

At the Visitation of 1823 The following Order was given that The Open Seats be neatly repaired, according to the ancient pattern; the munions & tracery wanting in the Bellchamber Windows be replaced; and shutters be made to the Windows of the Spire, the floors of the Tower be substantially repaired; the mouldings at the base of the Spire be thoroughly repaired – A casement be made in one of the Windows of the Church and Chancel and in one of the North Windows; a Casement be also placed in the Vestry; a new Clerk's Prayer Book; the Battlements be restored with Stone; a new plated Flagon be purchased.

At the Visitation of 1826 – It was ordered that The Floors of the Chambers in the Tower be repaired, and a Casement be made in the Vestry.

At the Visitation of 1833. It was ordered that the weeds be taken out of the crevices in the Steeple, & the joints filled with Parker's Cement – the East window be restored with Parker's Cement.

The Glebe House in good repair.

At the Visitation of 1836. Ordered that the Communion Table be painted, the Walls cleansed, the Surplice have a new Collar & the Minister's Prayer Book be repaired.

At the Visitation 1839, no Order required.

4. Article on the Church by W.A. (no.102), NM 30 October 1852

YIELDEN, Virgin Mary. The chancel has an open roof; sedilia and other decorations sadly mutilated. The two old crazy seats which are in this part of the church, old and decayed indeed, are far preferable to the huge boxes generally placed here. The pavement, though much worn, is kept clean. Two brasses are here, one of the early date of 1433.[23]

In the vestry is deposited the old oak chest, forming a remarkable contrast to the modern one.

The nave and aisle preserve their timber roofs. There are some original open benches; but for those who must occupy exclusive and enclosed sittings, a portion of the open seats have been used, by adding timber above, and clapping on doors.[9]

To make room for enclosed sittings, here, as elsewhere, little regard is paid to ancient monuments or decorations if they stand in the way of the ignorant village carpenter employed in their erection.[9] In this instance a recumbent figure has been sadly mutilated by the wooden work surrounding it. We would fain have attributed this demolition to the Puritans, whose wrath was kindled by a sermon of the rector's, in the year 1640, and ordered by Parliament to be publicly burnt;[24] but it bears too evident marks of a later period. "Diuturnity is a dream and folly of expectation."

This is a very small church; but two stoves are employed in warming it.

On a small platform is a musical instrument, in what name it rejoices we are ignorant; whatever its tones may be to the ear, it is not agreeable to the eye. Whitewash, as usual, is copiously used, two brackets, supporting arches, were almost indistinguishable.

In the aisle the canopy of a monument is sadly be plastered; and its lower part,[22] by the wooden work of some pews ruthlessly brought in to hasten its destruction.[9] A piscina is obscured by some planks in a state of decay, despite the two stoves; a cherub, over a beautiful bracket, seemed to deplore the surrounding devastation.

The columns appear to be painted, thus preserving the dresses of the occupants from the visitation of whitewash, most generally used. Yet two appear to have been purified from the plaster or paint to which they had once been subjected – an atonement perhaps for the injuries elsewhere inflicted.

The paving is in a disgraceful condition. The font has been scraped,[2] but, although it has lead lining and drain, it is not used.

A sort of squint is constructed in the wooden work, shutting out the belfry arch, which we believe is used as a mode of communication from the bellringers, to him who presides over the interior music.

n.d.   W.A.

Notes **1.** Pevsner pp.176–7, *VCH* III pp.177–9, *Yelden Past and Present* (1972) esp. pp.11–27, and thesis by Jonathan Edis on "The Church of St.Mary the Virgin, Yelden, Bedfordshire: an illustrated description and analysis of its architectural styles" (1994). The accounts of the church by the Rev. D.T. Powell, c.1810–2 (BL ref: Add.Ms. 17456) and the Rev.W.D. Sweeting, 1877 (BL ref: Add.Ms. 37178 f.27) are also useful; **2.** There is a drawing of the font, 1852 (BL ref: Add.Ms.39920 f.85); **3.** The woodwork is mostly of the C15th, and although much repaired has an attractively unrestored feel about it; **4.** North (p.211) gives details of the bells, but the second (originally by Eldridge, 1660) has since been recast by Taylor of Loughborough, in 1885; **5.** The cup and paten both carry the date letter for 1629, and in 1916 the church also possessed a paten of c.1680 and a plated flagon of c.1790 (ABE 5); **6.** The date of the communion table is given as 1629 by the *VCH* but in *Yelden Past and Present* it appears (possibly in error) as 1679; **7.** Strickland's memorial, noted by Bonney, is illustrated by Fisher (*Collections* pl.112); **8.** The version of Williamson's verse in the *VCH* is slightly inaccurate. The date is "17♦03" (i.e. 1703 and not "1700") and the last line reads "Declaring iust (i.e. just and not "I rest") the ...". It is a doodle rather than a memorial; **9.** The enclosed pews are mentioned by W.A. who noted that some of the benches had been converted into pews by the addition of doors and that pews has been allowed to conceal or damage ancient features in the stonework; **10.** Vestry minutes 1835–1906 (P 119/8/1); **11.** The new organ was reported in *BT* 27 June 1865. It was rebuilt and overhauled by Trustam in 1892 when it was moved to the new organ chamber (*BM* and *BS* 22 Oct.1892); **12.** The clock was given under the will of Peter Bunting and accepted as a gift by the vestry in 1875 (P 119/8/1). It was made by Tucker of London and the movement is dated December 1876. It was converted to automatic electric winding in 1974 (*Yelden Past and Present* p.17); **13.** Bathurst's notebook (ABE 3); **14.** Tower and spire restoration discussed by the vestry (P 119/8/1) noted in the parish register (P 119/1/1 f.37d); **15.** Rehanging of bells noted in the register (P 119/1/1 f.37d); **16.** There is a watercolour in the church showing the re-fixing of the weathercock in March 1896; **17.** Sources for the work of 1892 include the vestry minutes (P 119/8/1), papers (P 119/2/2/1–2), the register (P 119/1/1 f.38d), faculty papers for organ chamber 1892 (HCRO ref: DSA 2/1/*), reports in *BM* and *BS* 22 Oct.1892, and *Yelden Past and Present* p.16; **18.** Repairs to the nave roof noted in the register (P 119/1/1 f.39) and in *Yelden Past and Present* (pp.16–7); **19.** The repairs to the spire under Richardson – completed without the use of scaffolding – are noted in the SPAB archives; **20.** The current information leaflet refers to the recent work. The new rainwater spouts on the porch are dated 1989; **21.** The vestry minutes refer to the erection of a new fence on the west side of the churchyard in 1854 (P 119/8/1 and *Yelden Past and Present* p.17); **22.** The tomb recess in the south aisle is illustrated by Fisher (*Collections* pl.111); **23.** For the brasses, see Lack *et.al.* (p.106); **24.** The Rector alluded to by W.A. was John Pocklington (d.1641) who was deprived of the living in 1641 (see *VCH* III p.179 and *DNB*).